JEREMIAH'S EGYPT

ANCIENT NEAR EAST MONOGRAPHS

Editors
Jeffrey Stackert
Juan Manuel Tebes

Editorial Board
Angelika Berlejung
Jeffrey L. Cooley
Roxana Flammini
Tova Ganzel
Lauren Monroe
Emanuel Pfoh
Stephen C. Russell
Andrea Seri
Daniel Justel Vicente

Number 30

JEREMIAH'S EGYPT

Prophetic Reflections on the Saite Period

by
Aren M. Wilson-Wright

Atlanta

Copyright © 2023 by Aren M. Wilson-Wright

All rights reserved. No part of this work may be reproduced or transmitted in any form or by any means, electronic or mechanical, including photocopying and recording, or by means of any information storage or retrieval system, except as may be expressly permitted by the 1976 Copyright Act or in writing from the publisher. Requests for permission should be addressed in writing to the Rights and Permissions Office, SBL Press, 825 Houston Mill Road, Atlanta, GA 30329 USA.

Library of Congress Control Number: 2023937572

Table of Contents

Illustrations vii

Acknowledgments ix

Abbreviations and Symbols xi

1. Introduction: A Return to Egypt 1
   1.1. Review of Previous Scholarship 2
   1.2. Overview of the Book 5
   1.3. A Note about Text Criticism 7

2. In the Shadow of Empire: The Saite Period in Judah 9
   2.1. Prelude to Empire: 664–620 BCE 9
   2.2. The Advent of Egyptian Control: 620–610 BCE 12
   2.3. Nekau's Northern Campaigns: 610–605 BCE 14
   2.4. Nebuchadnezzar II's First Levantine Campaigns:
       605–601 BCE 19
   2.5. Nekau Strikes Back: 601–598 BCE 23
   2.6. The Twilight of Judah: 598–586 BCE 26
   2.7. Further Clashes between Egypt and Babylon:
       586–568 BCE 29
   2.8. Conclusion 34

3. Winners and Losers: Varieties of Judahite Experience during
   the Saite Period 35
   3.1. Elite Experience 38
   3.2. Non-elite Experience 45
   3.3. The Early History of the Judahite Diaspora in Egypt 50
   3.4. Conclusion 60

4. Fulminating against the Pharaoh: Anti-Saite Oracles in the
   Book of Jeremiah 63
   4.1. Jeremiah 2:14–19: No Blood for Egypt! 64
   4.2. Jeremiah 25:15–29: An Oracle of Liberation 71
   4.3. Jeremiah 46:2–26: Celebrating Egypt's Downfall 90
   4.4. Conclusion 114

5. At Home Abroad: Texts Relating to the Egyptian Diaspora
   in the Book of Jeremiah 115
   5.1. Jeremiah 43:8–13: From the Frontlines to the Frontier 115
   5.2. Jeremiah 44: Strange Gods in a Strange Land 130
   5.3. Conclusion 147
   Excursus 148

6. Lions Gone Wild: Jeremiah 51:38–39, the Egyptian
   Destruction of Humanity Myth, and the Judahite Diaspora
   in Egypt 151
   6.1. The "Lions Gone Wild" Motif 152
   6.2. Potential Obstacles 159
   6.3. Historical Background of the Myth's Adaptation .. 166
   6.4. Conclusion 169

7. Conclusion 171
   7.1. Summary of Previous Chapters 171
   7.2. Opportunities for Further Research 172
   7.3. Concluding Thoughts 175

Bibliography 177

Ancient Sources Index 197

Author Index 202

Subject Index 206

Illustrations

Figure 1 Key sites on the Levantine coast showing Egyptian influence in the seventh century BCE 11

Figure 2 Trade routes linking Egypt with the Arabian Peninsula and the Aegean in the late seventh and sixth centuries BCE 13

Figure 3 Key sites in the Egypto-Babylonian conflict, 610–601 BCE 15

Figure 4 Key sites in the second Babylonian invasion of Egypt in 582 BCE 30

Figure 5 Key sites from the three Babylonian attempts to invade Egypt, 601–568 BCE 33

Figure 6 Geographic distribution of the nations included in the earliest form of Jeremiah 25:15–29 80

Acknowledgments

This book began life in 2016 as a postdoctoral project at the University of Zurich and went through several transformations before reaching its current form. Along the way, I received help and support from many people and several organizations.

I would like to thank Konrad Schmid for all of his support and advice over the years. From his initial invitation to apply for a Swiss postdoctoral fellowship in 2016 to his detailed comments on each chapter, he has been nothing but helpful. My scholarship—and this book—are better for having studied with him. I would also like to thank Thomas Krüger, Jonathan Kaplan, Saralyn McKinnon-Crowley, David Crowley, Jo Ann Hackett, and Chris Hays for their comments on earlier versions of the manuscript. Jonathan Kaplan and Saralyn McKinnon-Crowley, in particular, provided crucial advice on how to frame the book's central argument.

Several other scholars kindly shared their knowledge and work with me. Special thanks are due to Paula Perlman for her expertise on Greek paleography, Chris Rollston and Eran Arie for discussing the Burnt Bullae archive with me, Na'ama Pat-El for her insight on appositional relative clauses, John Huehnergard for his help standardizing the Akkadian transliterations, and Theresa Tiliakos for checking and standardizing the Egyptian transliterations and translations. Guy Bunnens, Heath Dewrell, and Philip Zhakevitch generously shared their work with me, some of which was or is forthcoming. The members of the ANE Research Quarantine "Library" Facebook group supplied several otherwise inaccessible secondary sources during the COVID–19 pandemic.

I presented an earlier version of chapter 6 at the joint Prophetic Texts and Their Ancient Contexts / Egyptology and Ancient Israel session at the 2019 Annual Meeting of the Society of Biblical Literature.

I would like to thank Chris Hays for the invitation to present at this venue and the members of the audience for their feedback.

I am grateful to Jeff Stackert, the series editor for the Ancient Near Eastern Monograph Series, and Nicole Tilford, the production manager at SBL Press, for ensuring an absolutely seamless and stress-free editorial process. My good friend, Samuel Arnet, copyedited, typeset, and indexed the entire manuscript. I would like to thank him for his preternaturally keen editorial eye (and apologize for some of the truly bizarre typos I made). Kris Udd kindly granted me permission to use his Lachish 3 font.

The research for this book was supported by a three-year grant for postdoctoral research from the Swiss National Science Foundation and the University of Zurich.

Ultimately, this book would not have been possible without the emotional and intellectual labor of my wife, Saralyn McKinnon-Crowley. She believed in this project even when I didn't. And despite having her own work, she coached me through numerous bouts of writer's block and endured a significant amount of crankiness on my part. This book is dedicated to her with love and gratitude.

Aren M. Wilson-Wright
Nijmegen
July 2020

Since I submitted the manuscript for this book in July of 2020, many things have changed for me both personally and professionally. I have moved to a different country, temporarily switched career paths, and—most importantly—began living openly as a woman. These changes and their associated sorrows and triumphs left me little time to keep up to date on Jeremiah scholarship. Accordingly, this book represents the state of my thinking and research in 2020.

Aren Maeve Wilson-Wright
Chicago
April 2023

Abbreviations and Symbols

⌜...⌝	encloses material that is partially preserved
{...}	encloses material that is restored or repointed on the basis of linguistic analysis or other textual witnesses
[...]	encloses material that is not preserved
⟦...⟧	encloses material that is omitted from the earliest reconstructible form of a passage on text-critical or redactional grounds
ÄAT	Ägypten und Altes Testament
AB	Anchor Bible
ABRL	Anchor Bible Reference Library
AfOB	Archiv für Orientforschung: Beiheft
Ag. Ap.	Josephus, *Against Apion*
AION	*Annali dell'Istituto Orientale di Napoli*
ANEM	Ancient Near East Monographs/Monografías sobre el Antiguo Cercano Oriente
Ant.	Josephus, *Jewish Antiquities*
AOAT	Alter Orient und Altes Testament
ASAE	*Annales du service des antiquités de l'Egypte*
ATD	Das Alte Testament Deutsch
AThANT	Abhandlungen zur Theologie des Alten und Neuen Testaments
ATSAT	Arbeiten zu Text und Sprache im Alten Testament
BA	*Biblical Archaeologist*
BARIS	British Archaeological Reports International Series
BASOR	*Bulletin of the American Schools of Oriental Research*
BdE	Bibliothèque d'étude
BE	Biblische Enzyklopädie
BETL	Bibliotheca Ephemeridum Theologicarum Lovaniensium

BHH	*Biblisch-historisches Handwörterbuch: Landeskunde, Geschichte, Religion, Kultur, Literatur.* Edited by Bo Reicke and Leonhard Rost. 4 vols. Göttingen: Vandenhoeck & Ruprecht, 1962–1966
Bib. hist.	Diodorus Siculus, *Bibliotheca historica*
BIFAO	*Bulletin de l'Institut français d'archéologie orientale*
BJS	Brown Judaic Studies
BKAT	Biblischer Kommentar, Altes Testament
BN	*Biblische Notizen*
BNJ	Worthington, Ian, and Felix Jacoby, eds. *Brill's New Jacoby.* Online. Leiden: Brill, 2015–
BWANT	Beiträge zur Wissenschaft vom Alten und Neuen Testament
BZAW	Beiträge zur Zeitschrift für die alttestamentliche Wissenschaft
CAD	*The Assyrian Dictionary of the Oriental Institute of the University of Chicago.* Chicago: The Oriental Institute of the University of Chicago, 1956–2010
CAL	Stephen A. Kaufman et al. *The Comprehensive Aramaic Lexicon* (http://cal.huc.edu)
CEJL	Commentaries on Early Jewish Literature
CM	Cuneiform Monographs
CrStHB	Critical Studies in the Hebrew Bible
DTA	*Inscriptiones Graecae*, vol. 3, pt. 3, Appendix: "Defixionum Taballae" (Berlin, 1897)
DJD	Discoveries in the Judaean Desert
EA	*Egyptian Archaeology*
EBR	*Encyclopedia of the Bible and Its Reception.* Edited by Hans-Josef Klauck et al. Berlin: de Gruyter, 2009–
EPRO	Etudes préliminaires aux religions orientales dans l'empire romain
ErIsr	*Eretz-Israel*
FAT	Forschungen zum Alten Testament
FGH	*Die Fragmente der griechischen Historiker.* Edited by Felix Jacoby. Leiden: Brill, 1954–1964
FRLANT	Forschungen zur Religion und Literatur des Alten und Neuen Testaments
GELS	*A Greek-English Lexicon of the Septuagint*, Takamitsu Muraoka. Leuven: Peeters, 2009
Geogr.	Strabo, *Geographica*
GKC	*Gesenius' Hebrew Grammar.* Edited by Emil Kautzsch. Translated by Arthur E. Cowley. 2nd ed. Oxford: Clarendon, 1910
GOF	Göttinger Orientforschungen
GöMisz	*Göttinger Miszellen*
HAT	Handbuch zum Alten Testament

HdO	Handbuch der Orientalistik
HeBAI	*Hebrew Bible and Ancient Israel*
Hist.	Herodotus, *Heroditi Historiae*
HSM	Harvard Semitic Monographs
HSS	Harvard Semitic Studies
HThKAT	Herders Theologischer Kommentar zum Alten Testament
IAA Reports	Israel Antiquities Authority Reports
ICC	International Critical Commentary
IEJ	*Israel Exploration Journal*
JAEI	*Journal of Ancient Egyptian Interconnections*
JAOS	*Journal of the American Oriental Society*
JEA	*Journal of Egyptian Archaeology*
JEH	*Journal of Egyptian History*
JESOT	*Journal for the Evangelical Study of the Old Testament*
JNES	*Journal of Near Eastern Studies*
Joüon	Joüon, Paul, *A Grammar of Biblical Hebrew.* Translated and revised by Takamitsu Muraoka, Rome: Pontifical Biblical Institute, 2nd ed. 2006
JQR	*Jewish Quarterly Review*
JSJSup	Supplements to the Journal for the Study of Judaism
JSOT	*Journal for the Study of the Old Testament*
JSOTSup	Journal for the Study of the Old Testament Supplement Series
JSSEA	*Journal of the Society for the Study of Egyptian Antiquities*
KAI	*Kanaanäische und aramäische Inschriften.* Herbert Donner und Wolfgang Röllig. 2nd ed. Wiesbaden: Harrassowitz, 1966–1969
LÄ	*Lexikon der Ägyptologie.* Edited by Wolfgang Helck and Wolfhart Westendorf. 6 vols. Wiesbaden: Harrassowitz, 1972–1986
LAPO	Littératures anciennes du Proche-Orient
LCL	Loeb Classical Library
Let. Aris.	Letter of Aristeas
LHBOTS	The Library of Hebrew Bible/Old Testament Studies
LSAWS	Linguistic Studies in Ancient West Semitic
LSJ	Liddell, Henry George, Robert Scott, Henry Stuart Jones. *A Greek-English Lexicon.* 9th ed. with revised supplement. Oxford: Clarendon, 1996
LXX	Septuagint
MHR	*Mediterranean Historical Review*
MPIL	Monographs of the Peshitta Institute
MT	Masoretic Text
NBS	Numen Book Series
OBO	Orbis Biblicus et Orientalis
ÖBS	Österreichische biblische Studien

OLA	Orientalia Lovaniensia Analecta
OTE	*Old Testament Essays*
OTL	Old Testament Library
PAe	Probleme der Ägyptologie
PBE	Piccola biblioteca di egittologia
PEQ	*Palestine Exploration Quarterly*
PTA	Papyrologische Texte und Abhandlungen
RB	*Revue biblique*
RBS	Resources for Biblical Study
REg	*Revue d'Égyptologie*
REG	*Revue des études grecques*
RIMA	The Royal Inscriptions of Mesopotamia, Assyrian Periods
RT	*Recueil de travaux*
SAA	State Archives of Assyria
SAK	*Studien zur Altägyptischen Kultur*
SAM	Sheffield Archaeological Monographs
SANER	Studies in Ancient Near Eastern Records
SAOC	Studies in Ancient Oriental Civilizations
SBLDS	Society of Biblical Literature Dissertation Series
SJOT	*Scandinavian Journal of the Old Testament*
SO	Symbolae Osloenses
SSLL	Studies in Semitic Languages and Linguistics
SSN	Studia Semitica Neerlandica
SubBi	Subsidia Biblica
TA	*Tel Aviv*
TAD	Textbook of Aramaic Documents from Ancient Egypt. Newly copied, edited and translated into Hebrew and English by Bezalel Porten, Ada Yardeni, 4 vols., Jerusalem: Hebrew University Press, 1986–1999
TdE	*Trabajos de Egiptología*
UF	Ugarit-Forschungen
VT	*Vetus Testamentum*
WMANT	Wissenschaftliche Monographien zum Alten und Neuen Testament
ZA	*Zeitschrift für Assyriologie*
ZÄS	*Zeitschrift für ägyptische Sprache und Altertumskunde*
ZAW	*Zeitschrift für die alttestamentliche Wissenschaft*
ZDMG	*Zeitschrift der deutschen morgenländischen Gesellschaft*

1.
Introduction: A Return to Egypt

The book of Jeremiah exhibits several symptoms of what might be called "Egyptomania." It contains more references to Egypt than any other book of the Hebrew Bible except Genesis and Exodus and mentions Egypt more often than any other foreign nation except Babylon. Many of these references are highly specific, touching on Egyptian geography (Jer 2:16), religious practices (Jer 46:25), and military and political decisions (Jer 37:5).[1] Jeremiah 42:1–43:7 even preserves a tradition that the prophet Jeremiah relocated to Egypt following the assassination of Gedaliah, the Babylonian appointed governor of Judah. The reason for this "Egyptomania," as I will argue throughout this book, is primarily historical. As recent scholarship on Egyptian-Israelite interaction has shown, the pharaohs of the Twenty-Sixth or Saite Dynasty[2] (664–525 BCE) ruled Judah as a vassal state for much of the late seventh and early sixth centuries BCE—the time period during which the book of Jeremiah first began to take shape. My goal in this book, therefore, is to interpret the book of Jeremiah in light of this historical background. Focusing on the experiences of Judahites living under Egyptian rule, I argue, changes how we read and interpret the book of Jeremiah in three important ways: it helps explain the antipathy toward Egypt evident in several passages of this prophetic work; it provides a historical anchor for redactional approaches to dating the text; and it places the work's repeated calls for submission to Babylon in a different light. These calls do not present a choice between Judahite autonomy and Babylonian domination, but rather a choice between Egyptian and Babylonian control.

---

1. Others, of course, are related to the Exodus. Garret Galvin, *Egypt as a Place of Refuge*, FAT 2/51 (Tübingen: Mohr Siebeck, 2011), 125–26.

2. So named for their capital at Sais in the western Nile Delta.

1.1. REVIEW OF PREVIOUS SCHOLARSHIP

Despite the prominence of Egypt in the book of Jeremiah, previous scholarship on the historical context of this work has focused primarily on interactions between Judah and Babylon.³ When scholars do mention Egypt, it is usually in a specific context and with reference to a limited number of extra-biblical sources. Lester Grabbe, for example, connects Jer 43:8–13, 44:30, and 46:13–26 with the Egyptian civil war of 570 BCE and Nebuchadnezzar II's attempted invasion of Egypt in 568 BCE on the basis of the fragmentary cuneiform tablet BM 33041 and the Amasis Stela from Elephantine.⁴ He does not mention, however, that Nebuchadnezzar attempted to invade Egypt at least two other times during his long reign—once in 601 BCE, and once in 582 BCE—and that these events could furnish the historical background of Jer 43:8–13 and 46:13–26 instead. Similarly, Walter Brueggemann observes that "The capacity of Egypt to evoke such hostile commentary is no doubt rooted in 7th–6th cent. politics, where Egypt is a primary threat to a pro-Babylonian reading of political reality," but he does not develop this idea in conversation with extra-biblical sources.⁵

Other works dealing with Egypt in the book of Jeremiah suffer from some methodological problems. Hans Barstad simply assumes a Saite-period date for many of the Egyptian references in Jeremiah and uses them to supplement the sparse Egyptian data on the reign of Nekau II (called Necho in the Hebrew Bible).⁶ But we cannot simply

---

3. Often to the exclusion of Egypt. Neither David Reimer nor Klaas A. D. Smelik mention Egypt in their work on the historical background of Jeremiah (David Reimer, "Jeremiah before the Exile?," in *In Search of Pre-exilic Israel: Proceedings of the Oxford Old Testament Seminar*, ed. John Day [London: T&T Clark, 2004], 207–24; Klaas A. D. Smelik, "The Function of Jeremiah 50 and 51 in the Book of Jeremiah," in *Reading the Book of Jeremiah: A Search for Coherence*, ed. Martin Kessler [Winona Lake, IN: Eisenbrauns, 2004], 93–94).

4. Lester L. Grabbe, "'The Lying Pen of the Scribes'? Jeremiah and History," in *Essays on Ancient Israel and Its Near Eastern Context: A Tribute to Nadav Na'aman*, ed. Yaira Amit et al. (Winona Lake, IN: Eisenbrauns, 2006), 198–99. For a similar conclusion, see William McKane, *Commentary on Jeremiah 26–52*, vol. 2 of *A Critical and Exegetical Commentary on Jeremiah*, ICC (Edinburgh: T&T Clark International, 1986), 1139; and Beat Huwyler, *Jeremia und die Völker: Untersuchungen zu den Völkersprüchen in Jeremia 46–49*, FAT 20 (Tübingen: Mohr Siebeck, 1997), 125. Chapters 3 and 4 provide additional examples of this restricted approach to the Egyptian references in the book of Jeremiah.

5. Walter Brueggemann, *A Commentary on Jeremiah: Exile and Homecoming* (Grand Rapids, MI: Eerdmans, 1998), 423.

6. Hans M. Barstad, "Jeremiah the Historian: The Book of Jeremiah as a

assume that the references to Egypt in the book of Jeremiah all date to the Saite period since Egypt remained an important force in Judahite life in subsequent eras. Garrett Galvin, by contrast, denies the historical reliability of the references to Egypt in the book of Jeremiah, stating that: "these images of Egypt [in Jer 46] resound with ambiguity because they are confusing and multilayered. They do not necessarily provide detailed information concerning Egypt, but rather may be written for an audience with a limited knowledge of Egypt."[7] At the same time, however, he dismisses much of the detailed information in the oracles against Egypt, such as the appearance of the Apis bull in Jer 26:15 LXX, as later expansions or textual variants.[8] My approach in this book is more measured. I neither uncritically accept the historical reliability of the references to Egypt found in the book of Jeremiah nor do I dismiss all of them as later additions to the text. Rather, I assess each passage on a case-by-case basis to determine its likely historical context.

Despite the relative dearth of historical scholarship on Egypt in the book of Jeremiah, the study of cultural contact between Egypt and Israel has progressed significantly, thanks in part to the pioneering work of Bernd Schipper. In his initial foray into the subject, Schipper used archaeological and extra-biblical evidence to reconstruct the different types of Egyptian-Israelite contact that took place during the Iron Age, ranging from trade contacts in the ninth and tenth centuries BCE to Egyptian control in the Saite period. He then investigated how the biblical text reflects the events and material culture of these different periods.[9] Since then, Schipper has refined his conclusions in a series of articles focusing on Egyptian-Judahite contact during the Saite period.[10]

Source for the History of the Near East in the Time of Nebuchadnezzar," in *Studies on the Text and Versions of the Hebrew Bible in Honour of Robert Gordon*, ed. Geoffrey Khan and Diana Lipton (Leiden: Brill, 2011), 91–94.

7. Galvin, *Egypt as a Place of Refuge*, 154.

8. Galvin, *Egypt as a Place of Refuge*, 152.

9. Bernd U. Schipper, *Israel und Ägypten in der Königszeit: Die kulturellen Kontakte von Salomo bis zum Fall Jerusalems*, OBO 170 (Göttingen: Vandenhoeck & Ruprecht, 1999). In this regard, Schipper turns earlier approaches to Egyptian-Israelite contact on their heads. As Shirly Ben-Dor Evian notes, "traditional methodology isolates a specific 'Egyptian' detail from the biblical text, presents its Egyptian parallels, and suggests a historical background based on these parallels" (Shirly Ben-Dor Evian, "The Past and Future of 'Biblical Egyptology,'" *Journal of Ancient Egyptian Interconnections* 18 [2018]: 2).

10. Bernd U. Schipper, "Egypt and the Kingdom of Judah under Josiah and Jehoiakim," *TA* 37 (2010): 200–226; Bernd U. Schipper, "Egyptian Imperialism after the New Kingdom: The Twenty-Sixth Dynasty and the Southern Levant," in *Egypt, Canaan, and Israel: History, Imperialism and Ideology: Proceed-*

According to Schipper's latest historical reconstruction, Pharaoh Psamtik II annexed Judah in the final decades of the seventh century BCE with the twin goals of controlling the trade routes that passed through the Negev desert and maintaining a buffer state between Babylon and Egypt. To achieve these goals, Psamtik II and his successors constructed or co-opted military fortresses in Judah and fortified them—in part—with Aegean mercenary troops, imposed taxes on the population of Judah, and integrated Judahite scribes and officials into the Egyptian bureaucracy of the Levant.[11] While Schipper does not focus on the book of Jeremiah itself, many of his conclusions are relevant for the study of this prophetic book.

This study also benefits from new archaeological data from Daphnae (modern-day Tell Dafana, Biblical Hebrew תחפנחס, Greek Δάφναι) and Memphis, both of which feature prominently in the book of Jeremiah (Jer 2:16; 43:7, 8, 9; 44:1; 46:14, 19). A recently discovered stela from Tell Dafana, for example, shows that Nebuchadnezzar attempted to invade Egypt in 582 BCE. The Jewish historian Josephus mentions this event in *Ant.* 10.182, but until the discovery of the Tell Dafana Stela most scholars dismissed Josephus's account as ahistorical.[12] I will also draw on new editions of important Saite-period texts, such as the Amasis Stela from Elephantine, which provides important information about the Egyptian civil war and the attempted Babylonian invasion of 567 BCE.[13] These new and newly reedited sources prove especially useful for reconstructing the history of the Saite period, which is the focus of the following two chapters.

---

ings of a Conference at the University of Haifa, 3–7 May 2009, ed. S. Bar, D. Kahn, and J.J. Shirley (Leiden: Brill, 2011), 268–90; Bernd U. Schipper, "Egypt and Israel: The Ways of Cultural Contacts in the Late Bronze Age and Iron Age (Twentieth–Twenty-Sixth Dynasty)," *Journal of Ancient Egyptian Interconnections* 4 (2012): 30–47.

11. Schipper, "Egypt and the Kingdom of Judah," 200, 211, 214; Schipper, "Egyptian Imperialism after the New Kingdom," 269–70, 272, 280.

12. Mohamed Abd el-Maksoud and Dominique Valbelle, "Une stèle de l'an 7 d'Apriès découverte sur le site de Tell Défenneh," *REg* 64 (2013): 1–13.

13. Anke Ilona Blöbaum, *"Denn ich bin ein König, der die Maat liebt": Herrscherlegitimation im spätzeitlichen Ägypten—Eine vergleichende Untersuchung der Phraseologie in den offiziellen Königsinschriften vom Beginn der 25. Dynastie bis zum Ende der makedonischen Herrschaft*, Aegyptiaca Monasteriensia 4 (Aachen: Shaker Verlag, 2006), 13–14; Karl Jansen-Winkeln, "Die Siegesstele des Amasis," *ZÄS* 141 (2014): 132–53.

1.2. OVERVIEW OF THE BOOK

Although scholars like Schipper increasingly acknowledge the role of Egypt in Judahite life during the late seventh and early sixth centuries BCE, this new insight has yet to be applied to the book of Jeremiah. My goal in this book is to bridge the gap between these two areas of inquiry. The experiences of Judahites living under Saite rule, I argue, left their mark on the book of Jeremiah. I develop this argument over the course of five chapters.

In chapter 2, I draw on Hebrew, Babylonian, Egyptian, Classical and archaeological sources to re-tell the history of Judah in the late seventh and early sixth centuries BCE. During this time, Judah was a small kingdom caught between two rival superpowers, Egypt and Babylon. In the last thirty-five years of Judah's existence, its ruling elite switched allegiance between Egypt and Babylon at least six times, and this vacillation ultimately led to the loss of Judah's political autonomy in 586 BCE. Although the Saite pharaohs were happy to use Judah as a pawn in their ongoing struggle against Babylon, they cared little for the Levantine kingdom itself. Instead, their strategic interests lay in the trade routes linking Egypt with the Arabian Peninsula and the Mediterranean and the possibility of preserving a buffer state between the Babylonian Empire and the Egyptian heartland. As a consequence of this strategic orientation, they offered little in the way of military support for their on-again, off-again vassal. They also continued to clash with Babylon even after the fall of Jerusalem in 586 BCE, fending off a Babylonian invasion on two separate occasions.

In chapter 3, I move from macro-history to micro-history. In particular, I examine how the Saite pharaohs' strategic orientation toward the Levant affected the population of Judah. Unsurprisingly, the elite and the non-elite had vastly different experiences of this period. Certain members of the Judahite elite participated in the Saite administration of Judah. Some, such as Pediese son of Opay, served as messengers; others, such as the anonymous scribes of Arad and Kadesh Barnea, received training in Egyptian methods of record keeping and produced administrative texts for the Egyptian bureaucracy. In return, they enjoyed access to Egyptian prestige goods such as Egyptian-inspired funerary monuments. The existence of Judahite collaborators helps explain why Judah alternated between Egyptian and Babylonian control so often: certain members of the Judahite elite owed their power and prestige to the Saite pharaohs and were reluctant to relinquish it. This constant vacillation, however, had a negative effect on the non-elite of Judah—those who served as auxiliary troops in the Egyptian army, produced rations for the mercenaries that the Saite pharaohs stationed in the Levant, and paid the taxes which funded the Egyptian army. Continued hostilities between Egypt and Babylon exposed them to further drudgery and danger. Elites and non-elites also suffered different fates after the fall of Jerusalem. While many elite Judahites were exiled to Babylon, some non-elite Judahites became "trapped" in Egypt following the fall of Jerusalem or sought refuge from the horrors of the Babylonian campaign against Judah. They formed an important component of the Judahite diaspora in Egypt.

Drawing on the historical framework developed in chapters 2 and 3, chapter 4 identifies three passages in the book of Jeremiah that decry the injustices of the Saite period: the historical overview in Jer 2:14–19, the "cup of wrath" episode in Jer 25:15–29, and the oracles against Egypt in Jer 46:2–26. Jeremiah 2:14–19, I argue, serves to critique Judahite collaborators for their short-sighted selfishness. While they reaped the benefits of Egyptian rule, their compatriots were conscripted into the Egyptian army and often died in far-flung locales in defense of the Saite state. The "cup of wrath" episode, on the other hand, provides a map of the Saite empire and its neighbors on the eve of the battle of Carchemish and expresses the hope that Babylon will liberate Judah from Egyptian control. Finally, the oracles against Egypt in Jer 46:2–26 contain a pastiche of prophetic material reflecting on at least three different military encounters between Nebuchadnezzar and the Saite pharaohs: verses 3–12 celebrate the devastating Egyptian defeat at Carchemish in 605 BCE; verses 14–24 applaud the attempted Babylonian invasion of Egypt in 601 BCE; and the oracle fragment preserved in verse 24 commemorates either the second Babylonian invasion of Egypt in 582 BCE or the third Babylonian invasion of 567 BCE. Throughout the chapter, I note how a historical approach to dating the text of Jeremiah can supplement existing redaction-critical proposals regarding this prophetic book.

Not all Judahites escaped Egypt's orbit in 586 BCE. Members of the Judahite diaspora in Egypt continued to live under Saite rule and their experiences also influenced the book of Jeremiah. In chapter 5, I identify two texts that either originated in the Judahite diaspora in Egypt or reflect ongoing contact between this community and the remaining population of Judah: Jer 43:8–13 and 44:16–19, 24–25. I also propose and evaluate several historical scenarios to explain how these texts were incorporated into what became the book of Jeremiah. Jeremiah 43:8–13 was composed in the Egyptian city of Daphnae shortly before the second Babylonian invasion of Egypt in 582 BCE and may reflect a shift in attitude toward Egypt among the Judahite diaspora in Egypt. Although they had once suffered under the policies of the Saite pharaohs they now called Egypt home, and Nebuchadnezzar's repeated invasions threatened their well-being. The references to the Queen of Heaven in

Jer 44:16–19, 24–25, by contrast, reflect ongoing contact between Judah and the Egyptian diaspora around 570 BCE and provide the earliest textual evidence for Judahites living in Upper Egypt.

Chapter 6 identifies another text that may have originated in the Judahite diaspora in Egypt: Jer 51:38–39. This text, I argue, dates to the exilic period and adapts a version of the Egyptian Destruction of Humanity myth in order to condemn the lion-like Babylonians. Although they once acted as Yahweh's agents, freeing Judah from Egyptian control in 604 BCE, they have violated their divine mandate by repeatedly invading Judah and Egypt and must be punished. To do so, Yahweh prepares an alcoholic draft for his leonine subordinates that pacifies and ultimately kills them, just as the Egyptian sun god Re uses beer to subdue the lion goddess Sakhmet in the Destruction of Humanity myth. Compared to the texts analyzed in chapters 4 and 5, Jer 51:38–39 radically reevaluates Egypt and Babylon's ability to harm the everyday Judahite. It is now Babylon that poses the biggest threat to non-elite Judahites due to Nebuchadnezzar's continued campaigns in the Levant and Egypt. Egypt, by contrast, merely furnishes the symbolic language used to criticize Babylonian aggression.

The conclusion summarizes the arguments of the previous chapters and suggests two additional avenues for inquiry: the identification of Saite-period texts outside of the book of Jeremiah, and potential contact between Judahites and various Aegean populations during the Saite period.

1.3. A NOTE ABOUT TEXT CRITICISM

Any historically oriented study of Jeremiah must take into account the complicated textual history of this book. As is widely known, the Septuagint version of Jeremiah differs in both size and arrangement from the text of Jeremiah preserved in the Masoretic Text. The Septuagint version of Jeremiah is approximately one seventh shorter than the Masoretic Text version and locates the oracles against the nations in the middle of the book (following 25:14) rather than at the end (following 45:5). The oracles against the nations also follow a different order in the Septuagint compared to the Masoretic Text. Given the overall fidelity of the Septuagint translators to their Hebrew source text, the most concise explanation of these differences is that the Septuagint and Masoretic Text preserve two different literary editions of the book.[14] This con-

---

14. See, for example, J. Gerald Janzen, *Studies in the Text of Jeremiah* (Cambridge: Harvard University, 1973), 181–84; Emanuel Tov, "The Literary History of the Book of Jeremiah in Light of Its Textual History," in *Empirical Models for*

clusion receives support from the Jeremiah manuscripts from Qumran, some of which match the Septuagint, and some of which match the Masoretic Text.[15]

The unique textual evidence for the book of Jeremiah necessitates caution in assessing the textual variants found in the different witnesses to this work. Although the Septuagint preserves an earlier edition of the text, it does not always preserve the best reading. The Hebrew source text of the Septuagint continued to undergo editing and expansion after the initial divergence of the Septuagintal and the Masoretic Text traditions.[16] In several cases, such as Jer 25:1–14, a later editor sought to clear up inconsistencies in the text by smoothing over redactional seams.[17] For this reason, I take a mediating position to the textual criticism of Jeremiah and seek to evaluate each textual variant on its own merits.

Biblical Criticism, ed. Jeffrey Tigay (Philadelphia: University of Pennsylvania Press, 1985), 211–37.

15. Tov, "Literary History of the Book of Jeremiah," 211.

16. Konrad Schmid, "The Book of Jeremiah," in *T&T Clark Handbook of the Old Testament: An Introduction to the Literature, Religion and History of the Old Testament*, ed. Jan Christian Gertz et al., trans. Jennifer Adams-Maßmann (London: T&T Clark, 2012), 433.

17. Georg Fischer, "Jer 25 und die Fremdvölkersprüche: Unterschiede zwischen hebräischem und griechischem Text," *Bib.* 72 (1991): 474–99; Shimon Gesundheit, "The Question of LXX Jeremiah as a Tool for Literary-Critical Analysis," *VT* 62 (2012): 29–57.

2.
In the Shadow of Empire:
The Saite Period in Judah

The extent of Egyptian control over Judah in the Saite period remains underappreciated in the scholarship on Jeremiah. In this chapter, therefore, I retell the history of the Saite period from a Judahite perspective, focusing on the major events of this period, such as the advent of Egyptian control over Judah, Josiah's fateful meeting with Nekau II, and the Babylonian siege of Jerusalem. In particular, I argue that the kingdom of Judah was caught between Egypt and Babylon for the last thirty-five years of its existence, changing hands six times during this turbulent period. As a result, Egypt remained a viable—if precarious—alternative to Babylon for Judah during much of the late seventh and early sixth centuries BCE. The Saite pharaohs, however, had little interest in Judah itself and frequently abandoned the tiny kingdom when it suited their strategic interests.

2.1. PRELUDE TO EMPIRE: 664–620 BCE

The rise of the Saite pharaohs begins somewhat paradoxically with the Assyrian invasion of Egypt in 667 BCE and the consolidation of the entire ancient Near East into a single, unified empire.[1] During this cam-

---

1. For the history of this period see Alan B. Lloyd, "The Late Period (664–332 BC)," in *The Oxford History of Ancient Egypt*, ed. Ian Shaw (Oxford: Oxford University Press, 2001), 364–66; Gregory D. Mumford, "Egypto-Levantine Relations During the Iron Age to the Early Persian Periods (Dynasties Late 20 to 26)," in *Egyptian Stories: A British Egyptological Tribute to Alan B. Lloyd on the Occasion of His Retirement*, ed. Thomas Schneider and Kasia Maria Szpakowska (Münster: Ugarit-Verlag, 2007), 147–48; Olivier Perdu, "Saites and Persians

paign, the Assyrian king Assurbanipal defeated Pharaoh Taharqo and installed Nekau I, the founder of the Saite Dynasty, as a vassal king. Taharqo's successor, Tanutamani, contested Nekau I's control over Egypt, however. In 664 BCE, Nekau I died in battle against Tanutamani and Assurbanipal was forced to invade Egypt a second time in order to restore Nekau I's son Psamtik I to the throne. In the aftermath of the second Assyrian invasion, Psamtik I gained control over Lower Egypt with the help of Carian and Ionian mercenaries—the "bronze men" (χαλκέων ἀνδρῶν) mentioned by the fifth-century BCE Greek historian Herodotus—sent by Gyges king of Lydia.[2] In the process, he established a precedent for the military conduct of his successors. For much of the Saite period, Carian and Ionian mercenaries were a fixture in the Egyptian army.[3]

In the mid-seventh century BCE, the Assyrian Empire went into decline due to a combination of over-expansion, internal turmoil, and outside pressure. During this period, Psamtik I threw off the Assyrian yoke and gradually assumed control of Assyria's former territorial holdings in the Levant. From approximately 640 BCE onward, the material culture of Ekron, Ashkelon, Tell el-Hesi, Tell el-'Ajjul, Tell er-Ruqeish, Tell Sera', Tell Haror, Tell el-Far'ah South, and Tell Abu Salima exhibits strong Egyptian influence (see fig. 1).[4] According to Herodotus, Psam-

---

(664–332)," in *A Companion to Ancient Egypt*, ed. Alan B. Lloyd, 2 vols. (Malden, MA: Wiley-Blackwell, 2010), 141–43; Schipper, "Egypt and the Kingdom of Judah," 201–3.

2. Herodotus, *Hist.* 2.152. See also Diodorus, *Bib. hist.* 1.66. The Ionians were Greek colonists who settled on the western coast of Anatolia, between the kingdoms of Lydia and Caria.

3. Peter W. Haider, "Epigraphische Quellen zur Integration von Griechen in die ägyptische Gesellschaft der Saïtenzeit," in *Naukratis: Die Beziehungen zu Ostgriechenland, Ägypten und Zypern in archaischer Zeit. Akten der Table Ronde in Mainz, 25.–27. November 1999*, ed. Ursula Höckman and Detlev Kreikenbom (Möhnesee: Bibliopolis, 2001), 197–206; Philip Kaplan, "Cross-Cultural Contacts among Mercenary Communities in Saite and Persian Egypt," *MHR* 18 (2003): 1; Damien Agut-Labordère, "Plus que des mercenaires!: L'intégration des hommes de guerre grecs au service de la monarchie saïte," *PALLAS* 89 (2012): 293–306.

4. Seymour Gitin, "Neo-Assyrian and Egyptian Hegemony over Ekron in the Seventh Century BCE: A Response to Lawrence E. Stager," *ErIsr* 27 (2003): 57*; Frank Moore Cross, "Inscriptions in Phoenician and Other Scripts," in *Ashkelon 1: Introduction and Overview (1985–2006)*, ed. Lawrence E. Stager, J. David Schloen, and Daniel M. Master (Winona Lake, IN: Eisenbrauns, 2008), 348–49; Lanny David Bell, "A Collection of Egyptian Bronzes," in *Ashkelon 3: The Seventh Century B.C.*, ed. Lawrence E. Stager, Daniel M. Master, and J. David Schloen (Winona Lake, IN: Eisenbrauns, 2011), 397–420; Christian Herrmann, "Egyp-

2. In the Shadow of Empire

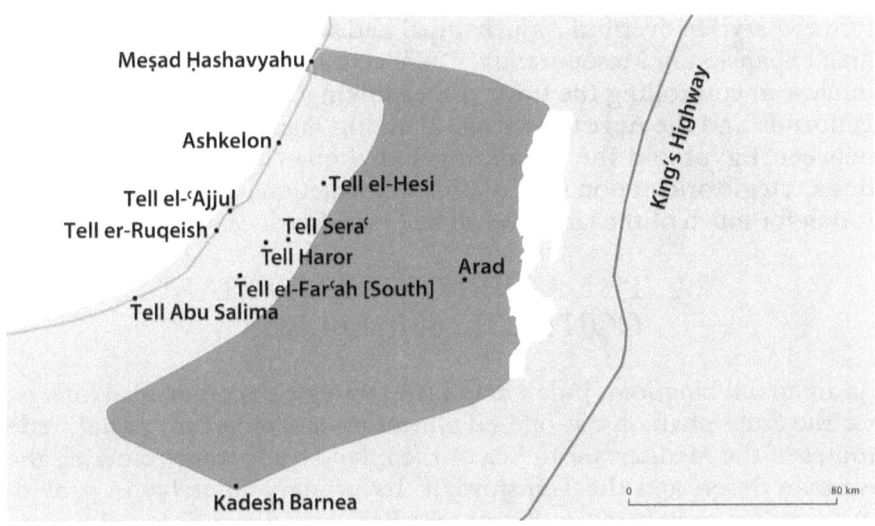

FIGURE 1 Key sites on the Levantine coast showing Egyptian influence in the seventh century BCE

tik I also captured Ashdod at this time.[5] He then allied himself with his

---

tian Amulets," in *Ashkelon 3: The Seventh Century B.C.*, ed. Lawrence E. Stager, Daniel M. Master, and J. David Schloen (Winona Lake, IN: Eisenbrauns, 2011), 359–96; Othmar Keel, "Seals and Seal Impressions," in *Ashkelon 3: The Seventh Century B.C.*, ed. Lawrence E. Stager, Daniel M. Master, and J. David Schloen (Winona Lake, IN: Eisenbrauns, 2011), 341–58; Michael D. Press, "Faience and Alabaster Vessels," in *Ashkelon 3: The Seventh Century B.C.*, ed. Lawrence E. Stager, Daniel M. Master, and J. David Schloen (Winona Lake, IN: Eisenbrauns, 2011), 321–430; Eliezer D. Oren, "Ethnicity and Regional Archaeology: The Western Negev under Assyrian Rule," in *Biblical Archaeology Today (1990): Proceedings of the Second International Conference on Biblical Archaeology*, ed. Avraham Biran and J. Aviram (Jerusalem: Israel Exploration Society, 1993): 103–4; Schipper, "Egypt and the Kingdom of Judah," 207.

5. Herodotus, *Hist.* 2.157 states that Psamtik I besieged Ashdod for twenty-nine years before finally capturing the city. Because this figure seems excessively high, some scholars—such as Dan'el Kahn—have suggested that Herodotus confused the length of the siege with the regnal year in which Psamtik I broke Ashdod's defenses (Dan'el Kahn, "Nebuchadnezzar and Egypt: An Update on the Egyptian Monuments," *HeBAI* 7 [2018]: 67). If this line of reasoning proves correct, then Psamtik I captured Ashdod in 635 BCE. A recently reedited Demotic ostracon may provide corroborating evidence for this interpretation. According to Michel Chaveau, this ostracon refers to an Egyptian campaign to the Levant in Psamtik I's twenty-eighth regnal year, which may have included an initial sortie against Ashdod (Michel Chaveau, "Le saut dans le temps d'un document historique: Des Ptolémées aux Saïtes," in *La XXVIe*

former Assyrian overlord Assurbanipal and sent armies to fight Babylonian expansion in Mesopotamia. These actions reflect a larger strategic interest in controlling the trade routes linking Egypt with the Arabian Peninsula and the Aegean (see fig. 2) and in maintaining a buffer zone between Egypt and the expanding Babylonian Empire.[6] Ultimately, this strategic orientation would inform interactions between Egypt and Judah for much of the late seventh and early sixth centuries BCE.

2.2. THE ADVENT OF EGYPTIAN CONTROL: 620–610 BCE

As an inland kingdom, Judah held little strategic or commercial interest for the Saite pharaohs. It offered almost no access to the coastal trade routes of the Mediterranean Sea or the inland trade routes crossing the Arabian desert and the Transjordan. Its primary value lay in providing a buffer zone between Egypt and Babylon. Accordingly, the Saite pharaohs did not seize control of Judah until approximately 620 BCE, when conflict with Babylon seemed inevitable.[7] This is the earliest date for which we have evidence of Egyptian involvement in Judah. At that

---

dynastie, continuités et ruptures: Actes du colloque international organisé les 26 et 27 novembre 2004 à l'Université Charles-de-Gaulles, Lille 3: Promenade saïte avec Jean Yoyotte, ed. Didier Devauchelle [Paris: Cybele, 2011], 39–45).

6. Nadav Na'aman, "The Kingdom of Judah under Josiah," *TA* 18 (1991): 39; Schipper, *Israel und Ägypten*, 288–90; Alexander Fantalkin, "Meẓad Ḥashavyahu: Its Material Culture and Historical Background," *TA* 28 (2001): 95.

7. Schipper, "Egyptian Imperialism after the New Kingdom," 283–84. Scholars have proposed several other dates for the beginning of Egyptian hegemony in the region, ranging from 640 BCE to 610 BCE. J. Maxwell Miller and John H. Hayes suggest that Judah was under Egyptian control beginning with the reign of Josiah around 640 BCE (J. Maxwell Miller and John H. Hayes, *A History of Ancient Israel and Judah*, 2nd ed. [Louisville: Westminster John Knox, 2006], 450–51). Nadav Na'aman argues that Judah first became an Egyptian vassal in the late 620's BCE after an outbreak of rebellion and civil war in Assyria (Na'aman, "Kingdom of Judah under Josiah," 38–39). And Robert Wenning dates the beginning of Egyptian hegemony between 616 and 610 BCE (Robert Wenning, "Griechische Söldner in Palästina," in *Naukratis: Die Beziehungen zu Ostgriechenland, Ägypten und Zypern in archaischer Zeit. Akten der Table Ronde in Mainz, 25.–27. November 1999*, ed. Ursula Höckman and Detlev Kreikenbom [Möhnesee: Bibliopolis, 2001], 260). 620 BCE, however, is the earliest date for which we have concrete evidence of Egyptian control over Judah.

2. In the Shadow of Empire

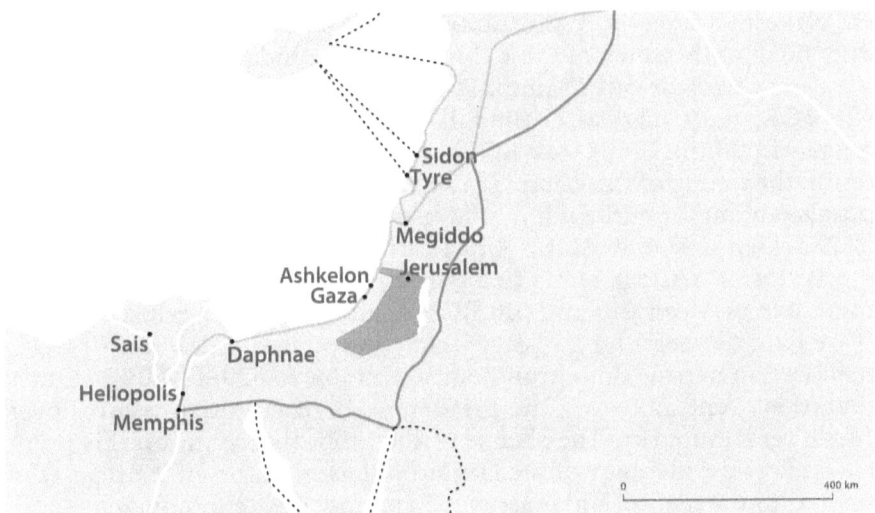

FIGURE 2 Trade routes linking Egypt with the Arabian Peninsula and the Aegean in the late seventh and sixth centuries BCE

time, Psamtik I established an Egyptian fortress at Meṣad Ḥashavyahu (see fig. 1) and fortified it with Ionian mercenaries.[8]

The biblical text, however, does not mention Egyptian involvement in Judah prior to the account of King Josiah's death in 2 Kgs 23:29–30, making it difficult to reconstruct specific events in the history of Egyptian-Judahite interaction between 620 and 610 BCE. Extra-biblical sources offer only a single glimpse into this period. The second century BCE Let. Aris. 1.13 claims that Judahite soldiers assisted a pharaoh named Psamtik against the king of the Ethiopians: "Already a considerable number [of Judahites] had come in with the Persian [king], and before these, other auxiliaries were sent out with Psamtik to fight the king of the Ethiopians" (ἤδη μὲν καὶ πρότερον ἱκανῶν εἰσεληλυθότων σὺν τῷ Πέρσῃ, καὶ πρὸ τούτων ἑτέρων συμμαχιῶν ἐξαπεσταλμένων πρὸς τὸν τῶν Αἰθιόπων βασιλέα μάχεσθαι σὺν Ψαμμιτίχῳ).[9] Unfortunately, however, three differ-

---

8. Alexander Fantalkin argues that Meṣad Ḥashavyahu was founded around 620 BCE based on finds from the nearby port of Yavneh-Yam, which served as a supply station for Meṣad Ḥashavyahu (Fantalkin, "Meẓad Ḥashavyahu," 134). Excavators at Yavneh-Yam uncovered a scarab bearing the name of Psamtik I in stratum IX, which dates to approximately 620 BCE due to its typological similarities with scarabs found in the first phase of Naukratis. For the relationship between Meṣad Ḥashavyahu and Yavneh-Yam in the Saite period see Nadav Na'aman, "An Assyrian Residence at Ramat Raḥel?," *TA* 28 (2001): 272.

9. André Pelletier, *Lettre d'Aristée à Philocrate: Introduction, texte critique,*

ent Saite pharaohs bore the name Psamtik and the Letter of Aristeas does not specify which of these three rulers the Judahite soldiers served. We can safely rule out Psamtik III since he ascended to the throne in 526 BCE, sixty years after the fall of Judah. But this still leaves the reigns of Psamtik I (664–610 BCE) and Psamtik II (595–589 BCE). As a result, the timing of this campaign remains debated—with scholarly proposals ranging from the reign of Manasseh (697–643 BCE) to the reign of Zedekiah (597–586 BCE)—but Dan'el Kahn plausibly suggests that the Letter of Aristeas refers to a contingent of soldiers sent by Josiah sometime between 640 and 610 BCE to aid Psamtik I against Nubia.[10] If we date the beginning of Egyptian control over Judah to 620 BCE, then we can narrow this chronological window to 620–610 BCE. Other than this event, however, the first ten years of Egyptian control over Judah remain murky. The silence of the biblical account on this point may reflect the ideology of the Deuteronomistic editors of 2 Kings, who wanted to portray Josiah as an active and independent monarch.

2.3. NEKAU II'S NORTHERN CAMPAIGNS: 610–605 BCE

The Saite pharaohs first enter biblical history following the death of Psamtik I in 610 BCE and the ascension of Nekau II. Almost immediately, the new pharaoh traveled to Harran in what is now southeastern Turkey (see fig. 3) to confront the Babylonians and support his ailing As-

---

traduction et notes, index complet des mots grecs, Sources Chrétiennes 89 (Paris: Les Éditions du Cerf, 1962), 108–9; Benjamin G. Wright, *The Letter of Aristeas: "Aristeas to Philocrates" or "On the Translation of the Law of the Jews,"* CEJL 9 (Berlin: De Gruyters, 2015), 121. Unless otherwise stated, the translations of all ancient texts are my own.

10. Dan'el Kahn, "Judean Auxiliaries in Egypt's Wars Against Kush," *JAOS* 127 (2007): 513–14. Other interpretations of this passage appear less plausible. Albrecht Alt argues that Judahite troops participated in Psamtik II's Nubian campaign of 593 BCE, but as Kahn points out, Zedekiah was a Babylonian vassal at this time and most likely would not have supplied Nebuchadnezzar's rival with troops (Albrecht Alt, "Psammetich II. in Palästina und in Elephantine," *ZAW* 30 [1910]: 295–96; Kahn, "Judean Auxiliaries," 508–9). S. Sauneron and J. Yoyotte, on the other hand, argue that Manasseh sent troops to Egypt to aid Assurbanipal and his vassal Psamtik I against Tanutamani in 664 BCE (Serge Sauneron and Jean Yoyotte, "Sur la politique palestinienne des rois saïtes," *VT* 2 [1952]: 131–36). Yet the Assyrian Chronicle for 664 BCE does not mention the participation of vassal troops as it does for Assurbanipal's 667 BCE invasion of Egypt—which did include Judahite forces—and there is no evidence that Psamtik I even participated in the 664 BCE campaign.

2. In the Shadow of Empire

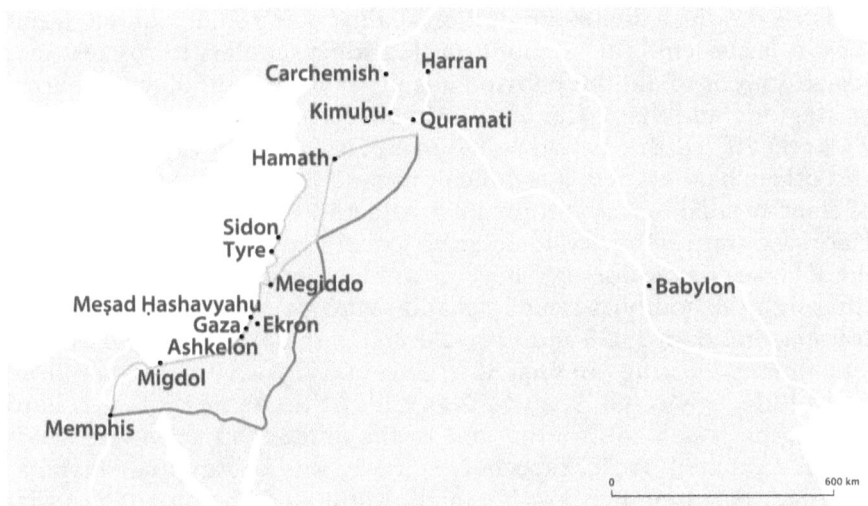

FIGURE 3 Key sites in the Egypto-Babylonian conflict, 610–601 BCE

syrian allies. Egyptian aid, however, proved futile. The Babylonian king Nabopolassar soundly defeated the Egypto-Assyrian alliance and sacked Harran, putting an end to the Assyrian Empire as an independent state.[11] Nekau II suffered few if any ill effects of this defeat; he remained in control of the Levant and was able to resume his campaign against Babylon in 609 BCE.[12] In July or August of that year, he met Josiah at Megiddo as he traveled to Harran.[13] Second Kings 23:29–30 and 2 Chr 35:20–27 present radically different accounts of this event. In 2 Kgs 23:29–30, Josiah goes to meet (וילך לקראתו) Nekau II at Megiddo and is summarily killed. In the Chronicles version, by contrast, Josiah engages Nekau II

---

11. Donald John Wiseman, *Chronicles of Chaldaean Kings (626–556 B.C.)* (London: Trustees of the British Museum, 1956), 62–63; A. Kirk Grayson, *Assyrian and Babylonian Chronicles: Texts from Cuneiform Sources* (Winona Lake, IN: Eisenbrauns, 2000), 95–96. When primary sources are too long, I have summarized their content rather than reproduce them in full.

12. Wiseman, *Chronicles of Chaldaean Kings*, 62–63; Grayson, *Assyrian and Babylonian Chronicles*, 96; Dan'el Kahn, "Why Did Necho II Kill Josiah?," in *There and Back Again—the Crossroads II: Proceedings of an International Conference Held in Prague, September 15–18, 2014*, ed. Jana Mynářová, Pavel Onderka, and Peter Pavúk (Prague: Charles University in Prague, 2015), 513.

13. Wiseman, *Chronicles of Chaldaean Kings*, 62–63; Grayson, *Assyrian and Babylonian Chronicles*, 96. According to the Babylonian Chronicle, the battle of Harran took place over the months of Tammuz (July–August) and Elul (August–September), and so Josiah most likely met Nekau in Tammuz (July–August).

in battle despite a divine prohibition against doing so, is wounded, and dies in Jerusalem. This account has led some scholars to suggest that Josiah sought to aid the Babylonians by waylaying the Egyptian army at Megiddo and that 2 Kgs 23:29–30 reflects an abbreviated version of 2 Chr 35:20–27. But as Nadav Na'aman, Dan'el Kahn, Zippora Talshir, and others have argued, it is difficult to see 2 Kgs 23:29–30 as a variant of the Chronicles account, for linguistic and logistical reasons.[14] The Hebrew phrase employed to describe Josiah's meeting with Nekau II in the Kings account does not have unambiguous military connotations. Although the combination of הלך and לקראת does refer to military encounters in 1 Sam 23:28 and 1 Kgs 20:27, the same expression describes less violent meetings in Gen 32:7, Exod 4:27, Josh 9:11, 2 Sam 19:16, 1 Kgs 18:16, 2 Kgs 8:8, 9, and 2 Kgs 9:18. At the same time, it is hard to imagine Josiah confronting one of the military superpowers of his day in a pitched battle, especially since he was an Egyptian vassal at the time. For these reasons, Na'aman, Kahn, and Talshir suggest that the Chronicles account provides a later theological justification for the otherwise righteous Josiah's sudden and unexpected death at the hands Nekau II: he disobeyed Yahweh by engaging Nekau II in battle.[15]

Because 2 Chr 35:20–27 is a later, ideologically motivated composition, we must rely on 2 Kgs 23:29–30—as cryptic as it is—to provide the most accurate account of Josiah's fateful meeting with Nekau II. Fortunately, comparative biblical evidence provides a clue as to the nature of this meeting. The phrase used to describe Josiah's encounter with Nekau II in 2 Kgs 23 matches the phrase used in 2 Kgs 16:10 to describe King Ahaz's audience with his Assyrian suzerain Tiglath-pileser III 123 years earlier: both Ahaz and Josiah "go to meet" (וילך לקראת) their overlord. Accordingly, Na'aman and Kahn suggest that Nekau II summoned Josiah to Megiddo for an audience, a common practice among ancient Near Eastern emperors.[16] In 2 Kgs 23:33, for example, Josiah's successor Jehoahaz meets Nekau II at Riblah near Hamath, where he is imprisoned and deported for his trouble.

While Na'aman and Kahn agree that Nekau II summoned Josiah to Megiddo for an audience, they disagree on the purpose and tenor

---

14. Na'aman, "Kingdom of Judah under Josiah," 54–55; Kahn, "Why Did Necho II Kill Josiah?," 516–17; Zipora Talshir, "The Three Deaths of Josiah and the Strata of Biblical Historiography (2 Kings XXIII 29–30; 2 Chronicles XXXV 20–5; 1 Esdras I 23–31)," *VT* 46 (1996): 216.

15. Na'aman, "Kingdom of Judah under Josiah," 55; Kahn, "Why Did Necho II Kill Josiah?," 518; Talshir, "Three Deaths of Josiah," 236.

16. Na'aman, "Kingdom of Judah under Josiah," 52; Kahn, "Why Did Necho II Kill Josiah?," 518.

2. In the Shadow of Empire

of this meeting. According to Na'aman, Nekau II summoned Josiah to Megiddo to renew his loyalty oath—a common practice in the world of ancient Near Eastern politics—and executed Josiah in the heat of the moment for suspected treachery. The pharaoh was, after all, campaigning far from Egypt and could not afford trouble in his Levantine territories.[17] He could not risk a Judahite rebellion disrupting the supply lines connecting Egypt and the front.

Kahn, by contrast, envisions a more complex scenario: following the Egypto-Assyrian defeat at Harran in 610 BCE, Josiah stopped paying tribute to Egypt in the hope that Egyptian control over Judah would soon come to an end.[18] Nekau II then summoned Josiah to Megiddo to give an account of his actions and, unsatisfied with Josiah's response, executed him for treachery.[19]

Overall, I find Kahn's reconstruction more plausible. Na'aman's proposed scenario relies on the assumption that vassals needed to renew their loyalty oaths upon the death of the reigning monarch. Such a policy, however, would prove highly impractical since it would turn every succession into an opportunity for rebellion. Furthermore, 2 Kgs 23:33 lends support to Kahn's reconstruction when it states that Nekau II imposed a tribute (ויתן ענש) of one hundred talents of silver and one talent of gold on Judah. This punitive fine can best be explained as a replacement for tribute withheld by Josiah.

Following his meeting with Josiah, Nekau II continued on to Harran, where he suffered another defeat at the hands of the Babylonian army.[20] In his absence, "the people of the land took Jehoahaz son of Josiah and anointed him and made him king in place of his father" (ויקח עם הארץ את יהואחז בן יאשיהו וימשחו אתו וימליכו אתו תחת אביו, 2 Kgs 23:30). Nekau II apparently did not appreciate the people's initiative. On the way back to Egypt, he met and imprisoned Jehoahaz at Riblah and appointed Jehoiakim in his place. He then brought Jehoahaz back to Egypt (2 Kgs 23:33–34). Unfortunately, the laconic account of 2 Kgs 23:30–34 does not explain why Nekau II disapproved of Jehoahaz's succession or why, for that matter, the people of the land chose Jehoahaz to succeed Josiah. Perhaps Nekau II acted to restore the order

---

17. Na'aman, "Kingdom of Judah under Josiah," 52–53.
18. Kahn, "Why Did Necho II Kill Josiah?," 519, notes that vassal states often revolted during the first year of a new sovereign's reign, particularly when they suffered a military setback.
19. Kahn, "Why Did Necho II Kill Josiah?," 519–20.
20. Wiseman, *Chronicles of Chaldaean Kings*, 62–63; Grayson, *Assyrian and Babylonian Chronicles*, 95–96.

of succession and replace Jehoahaz with his older brother, Jehoiakim.²¹ Or perhaps Jehoiakim was simply friendlier to Egyptian interests.

A partially preserved letter from the Judahite fortress of Arad (Arad Ostracon 88), dated between 620 and 597 BCE, may refer to the issue of Judahite succession following Josiah's death. The three preserved lines of this text contain the phrases "I have become king over a[ll] ..." (אני מלכתי בכ[ל] ...), "strengthen (your?) arm!" (אמץ זרע) and "the king of Egypt" (מלך מצרם).²² The phrase "I have become king" allows us to date the ostracon more precisely to 609 BCE, the year of both Jehoahaz's and Jehoiakim's ascensions.²³ It is unclear, however, which king is the implied speaker of the text. Both Yohanan Aharoni and Bernd Schipper identify the sender as Jehoahaz and suggests that the ostracon refers to a military conflict between Jehoahaz and Nekau II.²⁴ According to their interpretation, Jehoahaz wrote the letter to inform the commander of the Arad fortress that he has become king, tells him to be on guard, and identifies the king of Egypt as a possible enemy.

Given the fragmentary state of the letter, however, other interpretations are possible, especially since neither Kings nor Chronicles refers to an armed conflict between Nekau II and Jehoahaz.²⁵ If we identify the speaker as Jehoiakim, then the letter could refer to the king of Egypt as Jehoiakim's overlord in much the same way that the slightly earlier Bar-rākib Inscription (*KAI* 216) identifies the Assyrian monarch Tiglath-pileser III as Bar-rākib's patron: "because of my father's righteousness and because of my righteousness, my lord, Rakibel, and my lord Tiglath-pileser caused me to sit upon the throne of my father" (בצדק . אבי . ובצדקי . הושבני . מראי . רכבאל . ומראי . תגלתפליסר . על . כסא . אבי). Alternatively, the ostracon could report on the circumstances surrounding Jehoiakim's ascension: Jehoiakim became king *because* the king of Egypt deported Jehoahaz to Egypt.²⁶ In light of these different possibil-

---

21. For the relative ages of Jehoahaz and Jehoiakim in 609 BCE, see 2 Kgs 23:31 and 2 Kgs 23:36.

22. Yohanan Aharoni, *The Arad Inscriptions* (Jerusalem: The Israel Exploration Society, 1981), 103.

23. No other ascensions are attested between 620 and 597 BCE.

24. Aharoni, *Arad Inscriptions*, 104; Schipper, *Israel und Ägypten*, 237.

25. Aharoni and Schipper's interpretation gains plausibility from the account of Josiah's battle with Nekau II in 2 Chr 35:20–27. But as mentioned above, the Chronicles account tries to explain away Josiah's sudden and ignominious death and cannot be used as evidence for a military conflict between Josiah and Nekau II. And if it is implausible that Josiah met Nekau II in a pitched battle, then it is equally implausible for Jehoiakim to have done so.

26. Intriguingly, the phrase "the king of Egypt" in the ostracon is followed by a ל, which could form the first letter of the verb לקח found in the description

ities, it may be best to see this letter as simply another piece of evidence for Judahite-Egyptian interaction in the Saite period, rather than to reconstruct historical scenarios on the basis of incomplete data.

Despite the turmoil in Judah and the military setback at Harran, Nekau II succeeded at containing Babylonian expansion in Syria for several years. In 606 BCE, he defeated the Babylonian garrisons at Kimuḫu and Quramati on the upper Euphrates and installed Egyptian troops there.[27]

2.4. NEBUCHADNEZZAR II'S FIRST LEVANTINE CAMPAIGNS: 605–601 BCE

605 BCE marks a turning point in the conflict between Egypt and Babylon. In this year, the Babylonian army under crown prince Nebuchadnezzar II fought the Egyptians at Carchemish, an event that is mentioned in the Babylonian Chronicle, Berossus's *Babyloniaca* (preserved in Josephus, *Ag. Ap.* 1.135–41), and Jer 46:2–12. Each of these sources offers a different perspective on the battle, but they all come to the same conclusion: Nebuchadnezzar emerged as the overwhelming victor. The Babylonian Chronicle emphasizes Nebuchadnezzar's military prowess:

> He [Nebuchadnezzar] went to Carchemish, which is on the banks of the Euphrates. He crossed the river [to meet the Egyptian army] that was encamped at Carchemish ... they fought each other. The Egyptian army fell back before him. He defeated [and] utterly annihilated them.
>
> ana ᵘʳᵘgal-[ga]-meš šá GU₂ pu-rat-tú DU-ma [ana UGU ERIN₂.ME ᵏᵘʳmi-ṣi]r šá ina ᵘʳᵘgal-ga-meš na-du-ú ID₂ i-bir-ma [... a-]ḫa-meš im-ḫa-ṣu-ma ERIN₂.ME ᵏᵘʳmi-ṣir ina IGI-šú BAL-⌈ma⌉ [BAD₅-BAD₅]-šú-nu iš-kun EN ⌈la⌉ ba-še-e i[g-mu]r-šú-nu-tú[28]

Nebuchadnezzar then overtook the remainder of the Egyptian army at Hamath and defeated it a second time.[29] Berossus (*Ag. Ap.* 1.138) includes a detail not found in the Babylonian Chronicle: "and the prisoners of

---

of Jehoahaz's fate in 2 Kgs 23:34: "and Jehoahaz he took and he brought him to Egypt" (מצרים {ויביאהו} לקח יהואחז את). Here I read ויביאהו "and he brought him" with the parallel text in 2 Chr 36:4 and the Lucianic recension of the Septuagint.

27. Wiseman, *Chronicles of Chaldaean Kings*, 46, 66–67; Grayson, *Assyrian and Babylonian Chronicles*, 98. For the locations of these sites, see figure 3.

28. Wiseman, *Chronicles of Chaldaean Kings*, 66–67, and Grayson, *Assyrian and Babylonian Chronicles*, 99.

29. Wiseman, *Chronicles of Chaldaean Kings*, 68–69; Grayson, *Assyrian and Babylonian Chronicles*, 99.

the Jews [= Judahites], Phoenicians, Syrians [= Assyrians?], and those of the nations belonging to Egypt, he [= Nebuchadnezzar] placed under the command of some of the advisors to take back to Babylon along with the heavy infantry and the rest of the booty" (καὶ τοὺς αἰχμαλώτους Ἰουδαίων τε καὶ Φοινίκων καὶ Σύρον καὶ τῶν κατὰ τὴν Αἴγυπτον ἐθνῶν συντάξας τισὶ τῶν φίλων μετὰ τῆς βαρυτάτης δυνάμεως καὶ τῆς λοιπῆς ὠφελείας ἀνακομίζειν εἰς τὴν Βαβυλωνίαν).[30] This passage suggests that Judahite soldiers served in the Egyptian army at the battle of Carchemish.[31] And Jer 46:2–12, which will be treated in detail in chapter 4, celebrates the Egyptian defeat as a prelude to the liberation of Judah.

Archaeological evidence provides additional insight into the battle of Carchemish. In the early twentieth century, C. L. Woolley uncovered a Greek-style bronze greave from the western gate of the inner city as well as a distinctive Gorgon shield from a private residence located in the outer town (called House D in Woolley's excavation report).[32] The Gorgon shield was found alongside several Egyptian objects, including four seal impressions of Nekau II, a bronze ring incised with the name of Psamtik I, fragments of an alabaster bowl bearing an Egyp-

---

30. *BNJ* 680. If Berossus is correct in locating Judahite soldiers at the battle of Carchemish, then Jer 46:2–12 could be based on an eyewitness account.

31. Because *Ag. Ap.* 1.135 only lists Egypt, and the regions of Coelesyria and Phoenicia as Nebuchadnezzar's adversaries, John M. G. Barclay suggests that Josephus may have added Ἰουδαίων to his source text in order to strengthen his arguments about the antiquity of the Jewish people (John M. G. Barclay, ed. *Flavius Josephus: Against Apion*, Flavius Josephus Translation and Commentary 10 [Leiden: Brill, 2007], 85n455). If he is correct, then Berossus does not provide evidence for the participation of Judahite soldiers in the Saite pharaoh's Mesopotamian campaigns. There are several reasons to question this conclusion, however. First, the list of adversaries in 1.135 and the list of prisoners in 1.138 do not coincide even with the omission of the Jews from 1.138: where the former mentions "Egypt" and "Coelesyria," the latter refers to "Syrians" and "those of the nations belonging to Egypt." The two passages are not true parallels and it is unclear, therefore, whether we can correct 1.138 on the basis of 1.135. Second, Berossus employed Seleucid administrative terminology to describe the geography of the ancient Near East, and in the Seleucid system, Judah belonged to the region of Coelesyria (Dagmar Labow, ed. *Flavius Josephus: Contra Apionem*, vol. 1: *Einleitung, Text, Textkritischer Apparat, Übersetzung und Kommentar*, BWANT 167 [Stuttgart: Kohlhammer, 2005], 138n54). There was no reason to list Judea as a separate region in 1.135.

32. C. Leonard Woolley, *The Town Defenses*, vol. 2 of *Carchemish: Report on the Excavations at Djerabis on Behalf of the British Museum* (London: Trustees of the British Museum, 1921), 81, 128, pl. 24, 25a; Wolf-Dietrich Niemeier, "Archaic Greeks in the Orient: Textual and Archaeological Evidence," *BASOR* 322 (2001): 19–20.

tian inscription, a bronze statue of the Egyptian god Osiris, and two seal impressions of a high-ranking Egyptian official named Harkhebi.[33] Woolley suggests that this house "belonged to a wealthy Hittite sufficiently important to be in communication with the Court of Egypt," but I would argue that it served as an Egyptian command post during the battle of Carchemish.[34] Such an interpretation would explain both the Egyptian objects recovered from House D as well as the extensive evidence of military conflict found there, including hundreds of arrowheads and a broken sword.[35] If I am correct, then the Gorgon shield from House D could attest to the presence of Greek mercenaries fighting on behalf of Egypt at the battle of Carchemish.[36]

In the following year, 604 BCE, Nebuchadnezzar's father, Nabopolassar, died and Nebuchadnezzar ascended to the Babylonian throne.[37] In the second half of the year, Nebuchadnezzar advanced down the Levantine coast, attacking Ekron, Ashkelon, and Gaza and securing the cooperation of Judah.[38] According to 2 Kgs 24:1, Jehoiakim voluntarily became a Babylonian vassal and thereby avoided a military confrontation with the Mesopotamian superpower: "in his days, Nebuchadnezzar king of Babylon came up and Jehoiakim became his servant for three years" (בימיו עלה נבכדנאצר מלך בבל ויהי לו יהויקים עבד שלוש שנים). The Philistine city-states were not so lucky. As the Babylonian Chronicle for 604 BCE reports:

---

33. Woolley, *The Town Defenses*, 126–27; Marco Zecchi, "A Note on Two Egyptian Seal Impressions from Karkemish," *Orientalia* 83 (2014): 202–7.

34. Woolley, *The Town Defenses*, 126. In a similar vein, Edward Lipiński identifies House D as the Egyptian chancellery at Carchemish, while Zecchi states that it is possible that the "people of House D were Egyptian officials in charge of the local administration and able to maintain contacts at the royal court" (Edward Lipiński, *On the Skirts of Canaan in the Iron Age: Historical and Topographical Researches* [OLA 153. Leuven: Peeters, 2006], 157; Zecchi, "Note on Two Egyptian Seal Impressions," 205).

35. Woolley, *The Town Defenses*, 125.

36. It is unlikely that this shield belonged to a Greek mercenary fighting on behalf of Babylon. As Alexander Fantalkin and Ephraim Lytle have shown, there is no evidence that the Neo-Babylonian kings employed Aegean mercenaries in their campaigns (Alexander Fantalkin and Ephraim Lytle, "Alcaeus and Antimenidas: Reassessing the Evidence for Greek Mercenaries in the Neo-Babylonian Army," *Klio* 98 [2016]: 90–117).

37. Wiseman, *Chronicles of Chaldaean Kings*, 68–69; Grayson, *Assyrian and Babylonian Chronicles*, 99.

38. At present there is no evidence that Nebuchadnezzar captured or otherwise subdued Tyre and Sidon during this campaign, but strategic considerations suggest that he did do so. It is difficult to imagine Nebuchadnezzar advancing down the Levantine coast with potentially hostile forces at his back.

He [Nebuchadnezzar] went to Ashkelon and in the month of Kislev he captured it. He seized its king. He snatched its plunder and carried off its booty.

a-na ⸢uru⸣iš-qi⸣-il-lu-nu DU-ma ina ⁱᵗⁱGAN iṣ-ṣa-bat-su LUGAL-šú ik-ta-šad ḫu-bu-ut-su iḫ-tab-ta šal-lat-sa [iš-ta-la-(ma)][39]

Curiously, the Babylonian Chronicle actually understates the violence of the Babylonian campaign despite being a work of royal propaganda: archaeological evidence suggests that Nebuchadnezzar and his army burned the city to the ground, perhaps due to the presence of an Egyptian garrison stationed there.[40]

Contemporary destruction layers at Ekron and the neighboring site of Timnah attest to Nebuchadnezzar's assault on the other Philistine city-states, as does an Aramaic letter from the ruler of Ekron to Nekau II.[41] In this text, Adon of Ekron implores Nekau II to defend the city of Ekron, invoking the mutual protection clause of his vassal treaty with Egypt:

---

39. Wiseman, *Chronicles of Chaldaean Kings*, 68–69; Grayson, *Assyrian and Babylonian Chronicles*, 100. For the restoration of the toponym ⸢uru⸣iš-qi⸣-il-lu-nu see I. Finkel cited in Lawrence E. Stager, "Ashkelon and the Archaeology of Destruction: Kislev 604 BCE," *ErIsr* 25 (1996): 72*, and Ran Zadok cited in Alexander Fantalkin, "Why Did Nebuchadnezzar Destroy Ashkelon in Kislev 604 BCE?," in *The Fire Signals of Lachish: Studies in the Archaeology and History of Israel in the Late Bronze Age, Iron Age, and Persian Period in Honor of David Ussishkin*, ed. Israel Finkelstein and Nadav Na'aman (Winona Lake, IN: Eisenbrauns, 2011), 87.

40. Stager, "Ashkelon and the Archaeology of Destruction"; Lawrence E. Stager et al., "Stratigraphic Overview," in *Ashkelon 1: Introduction and Overview (1985–2006)*, ed. Lawrence E. Stager, J. David Schloen, and Daniel M. Master (Winona Lake, IN: Eisenbrauns, 2008), 279–83, 309–12; Fantalkin, "Why Did Nebuchadnezzar Destroy Ashkelon in Kislev 604 BCE?," 100.

41. Nadav Na'aman, "Nebuchadnezzar's Campaign in Year 603 B.C.E.," *BN* (1992): 41–44; Seymour Gitin, "The Philistines in the Prophetic Texts: An Archaeological Perspective," in *Hesed Ve-Emet: Studies in Honor of Ernest S. Frerichs*, ed. Jodi Magness and Seymour Gitin, BJS 320 (Atlanta: Scholars Press, 1998), 276n2; Fantalkin, "Meẓad Ḥashavyahu," 132. For a different interpretation of these archaeological remains see Lipiński, *On the Skirts of Canaan*, 160, and Oded Lipschits, *The Fall and Rise of Jerusalem: Judah and Babylonian Rule* (Winona Lake, IN: Eisenbrauns, 2005), 52n55. Although we lack direct archaeological or literary evidence for Nebuchadnezzar's capture of Gaza in 604 BCE, Herodotus furnishes some indirect evidence for this event. According to Herodotus, *Hist.* 2.159 (see section 2.5. below), Nekau II captured Gaza in 601 BCE, which suggests that it was under Babylonian control at the time.

2. In the Shadow of Empire

The reason that [I have sent to the Lord of Kings is to inform him that the armies] of the king of Babylon have come (and) reach[ed] Aphek and ... they have seized ... For the Lord of Kings Pharaoh knows that [your] servant ... to send an army to rescue m[e]. Do not abandon m[e, for your servant did not contravene the treaty of the Lord of Kings] and your servant preserved his good relations.

זי [שלחת על מרא מלכן הו להודעתה זי חילא] זי מלך בבל אתו מטא[ו] אפק ו[...] אחזו
[...] כי מרא מלכן פרעה ידע כי עבד[ך...] למשלח חיל לחצלתנ[י] אל [י]שבקנ[י כי שקר
עבדך בעדי מרא מלכן] וטבתה עבדך נצר⁴²

We do not have the text of Nekau II's reply, but he apparently ignored Adon's request and let Ekron fall to Babylon. Most likely, Nekau II also recalled the Egyptian garrison at Meṣad Ḥashavyahu in the face of Nebuchadnezzar's advance. There is no evidence within the archaeological record to suggest that the fortress was destroyed but it is hard to imagine Nebuchadnezzar leaving an Egyptian fortress intact as he advanced on Ashkelon.[43]

2.5. NEKAU II STRIKES BACK: 601–598 BCE

In November or December of 601 BCE, Nebuchadnezzar attempted to invade Egypt for the first time. Two textual sources refer to this event, each with a slightly different emphasis. According to Herodotus, Nekau II emerged as the clear victor of these battles: "Then Nekau, having engaged the Syrians [= the Babylonians] with his army, defeated them at Migdol. After the battle, he took Cadytis [= Gaza], the great city of the Syrians" (καὶ Συρίοισι πεζῇ ὁ Νεκῶς συμβαλὼν ἐν Μαγδώλῳ ἐνίκησε, μετὰ δὲ τὴν μάχην Κάδυτιν πόλιν τῆς Συρίης ἐοῦσαν μεγάλην εἷλε, *Hist.* 2.159). The Babylonian Chronicle, by contrast, claims that the Egyptian and Babylonian armies fought to a stalemate:

> In the month of Kislev he [= Nebuchadnezzar] took the lead of his army and went to Egypt. The king of Egypt heard and ⌈mustered⌉ his army. They struck each other on the breast in battle and inflicted much

---

42. For the text of this letter and the identity of its sender, see Bezalel Porten, "The Identity of King Adon," *BA* 44 (1981): 36–52, who restores the missing words and letters on the basis of contemporary Akkadian parallels. In addition to the Aramaic text, the verso of the letter also bears a short sentence in Demotic, which reads "what the ruler of Ekron sent to the king…" (r.dj pꜣ wr ʿgrn n nsw…) according to Günter Vittmann, "Kursivhieratische und frühdemotische Miszellen," *Enchoria* 25 (1999): 124–27.

43. Fantalkin, "Meṣad Ḥashavyahu," 144.

carnage on each other. The king of Babylon (and) his army turned back and [returned] to Babylon.

ina ⁱᵗⁱGAN pa-ni ERIN₂.ME-šú iṣ-bat-ma ana ᵏᵘʳmi-ṣir DU-ik LUGAL ᵏᵘʳmi-ṣir iš-me-e-ma ERIN₂.ME-šú ⌈id-ki-e-⌉[ma] ina ME₃ EDIN GABA a-ḫa-meš im-ḫa-ṣu-ma BAD₅-BAD₅ a-ḫa-meš ma-a-diš GAR.MEŠ LUGAL URIᵏⁱ ERIN₂.ME-šú GUR-am-ma a-na TIN.TIRᵏⁱ [GUR]⁴⁴

Of the two, Herodotus preserves the most plausible account. The Babylonian Chronicle is a friendly source that seeks to glorify Nebuchadnezzar at every opportunity, but even here it acknowledges that the Babylonian army suffered heavy losses—so heavy, in fact, that Nebuchadnezzar did not undertake a campaign the following year. Herodotus's account also receives partial corroboration from the Masoretic Text of Jer 47:1, which may allude to the capture of Gaza: "That which was the word of Yahweh to the prophet Jeremiah concerning the Philistines before Pharaoh attacked Gaza" (אשר היה דבר יהוה אל ירמיהו הנביא אל פלשתים בטרם יכה פרעה את עזה). Ultimately, Nebuchadnezzar's failure to capture Egypt in 601 BCE is not particularly surprising. As Kahn and Tammuz point out, invading Egypt was a monumental undertaking in the ancient world, fraught with both natural and contrived dangers. Of the nine Babylonian attempts to invade Egypt between 754 BCE and 539 BCE, only two were successful.⁴⁵

Ultimately, the Egyptian victories at Migdol and Gaza prompted Jehoiakim to switch allegiance from Babylon to Egypt, an event that is described in 2 Kgs 24:1 and in Josephus's *Ant.* 10.88–89. The account in Josephus explicitly links Jehoiakim's treachery to Egyptian military actions in the Levant: "But in the third year, he [Jehoiakim] did not pay him [Nebuchadnezzar] tribute because he heard that the Egyptians were advancing against the Babylonian [king]. But he [Jehoiakim] was deprived of hope, for the Egyptians did not dare to undertake the campaign" (τῷ δὲ τριτῷ στρατεύειν τοὺς Αἰγυπτίους ἀκούσας ἐπὶ Βαβυλώνιον καὶ τοὺς φόρους αὐτῷ μὴ δοὺς διεψεύσθη τῆς ἐλπίδος· οἱ γὰρ Αἰγύπτιοι ποιήσασθαι τὴν στρατείαν οὐκ ἐθάρρησαν).⁴⁶ This passage stands at odds with Herodotus's claim in *Hist.* 2.159 that Nekau II campaigned against Nebuchadnezzar in the Levant in 601 BCE and recaptured Gaza. We can perhaps rec-

---

44. Wiseman, *Chronicles of Chaldaean Kings*, 70–71; Grayson, *Assyrian and Babylonian Chronicles*, 101.

45. Dan'el Kahn and Oded Tammuz, "Egypt Is Difficult to Enter: Invading Egypt—A Game Plan (Seventh–Fourth Centuries BCE)," *JSSEA* 35 (2008): 58.

46. Flavius Josephus, *Jewish Antiquities*, vol. 4: *Books 9–11*, trans. Ralph Marcus, LCL (Cambridge: Harvard University Press, 1937), 206–7. See also Christopher Begg, *Josephus' Story of the Later Monarchy (AJ 9,1–10,185)*, BETL 145 (Leuven: Leuven University Press, 2000), 507.

oncile the two passages by hypothesizing that *Ant.* 10.88–89 refers to Egyptian military aid in defense of Judah rather than Egyptian attempts at recapturing the Philistine city-states.

The Egyptian victories at Migdol and Gaza must have been fairly decisive because Nebuchadnezzar did not take to the battlefield again in a sustained way for another three years. According to the Babylonian Chronicle, Nebuchadnezzar stayed in Babylon in 600 BCE repairing his chariot force, and in the following year he campaigned in the Syrian desert and plundered the Arab tribes living there.[47] Only in November or December of 598 BCE did Nebuchadnezzar move to recapture the Levant and secure Judah's obedience. Second Kings 24:7 describes the Babylonian reconquest of the Levant as follows: "the king of Egypt did not come out of his land again because the king of Babylon had taken all that had belonged to the king of Egypt, from the Wadi of Egypt to the river Euphrates" (ולא הסיף עוד מלך מצרים לצאת מארצו כי לקח מלך בבל מנחל מצרים עד נהר פרת כל אשר היתה למלך מצרים).[48] The placement of this verse between the announcement of Jehoiakim's death in 2 Kgs 24:6 and the reference to his brother Jehoiachin's ascension in 2 Kgs 24:8 is strange and could indicate that Nebuchadnezzar's military actions took place during the transition of power in Judah. Whatever the case, 2 Kgs 24:10–16 reports that Jehoiachin surrendered to Nebuchadnezzar and was deported to Babylon along with members of the royal family, high-ranking officials, and craftsmen. Nebuchadnezzar then appointed Zedekiah as king over Judah. The Babylonian Chronicle, by contrast, focuses solely on the siege of Jerusalem:

> In the seventh year, in the month of Kislev, the king of Babylon mustered his army and went to Ḥatti-land, encamped against the city of Judah and on the second day of Adar took the city. He captured (its) king. He appointed a king of his own choice. He re[ceive]d its heavy tribute and brought it back to Babylon.

---

47. Israel Eph'al, "Nebuchadnezzar the Warrior: Remarks on His Military Achievements," *IEJ* 53 (2003): 181; Dan'el Kahn, "Some Remarks on the Foreign Policy of Psammetichus II in the Levant (595–589)," *JEH* 1 (2008): 142.

48. This verse provides a convenient snapshot of Egyptian territorial holdings in the Levant and Syria prior to the Babylonian victory at Carchemish in 605 BCE and most likely inspired the statement in *Ant.* 10.85 that Nekau II controlled all of Syria prior to the battle of Carchemish. Additional evidence for the Babylonian reconquest of the Levant comes from the Istanbul Prism, which mentions that the king of Gaza provided raw materials for the renovation of the Ezida temple in 598 BCE. For the text and translation of this prism, see Eckhard Unger, *Babylon: Die heilige Stadt nach der Beschreibung der Babylonier*, 2nd ed. (Berlin: de Gruyter, 1970), 286.

MU.7.KAM₂ ⁱᵗⁱGAN LUGAL URIᵏⁱ ERIN₂.ME-šú id-ki-ma a-na ᵏᵘʳḫat-tú DU-ma ina UGU URU ia-a-aḫ-u-du ŠUB-ma ina ⁱᵗⁱŠE UD.2.KAM₂ URU iṣ-ṣa-bat LUGAL ik-ta-šad LUGAL šá ŠA₃-šú ina ŠA₃-bi ip-te-qid bi-lat-sa DUGUD il-[qa-am-m]a ana TIN.TIRᵏⁱ KU₄-ib⁴⁹

2.6. THE TWILIGHT OF JUDAH: 598–586 BCE

Babylonian control over the Levant proved short-lived, however. Beginning in 596 BCE, Nebuchadnezzar became embroiled in a series of wars in Elam and Mesopotamia and effectively ceded the Levant to Egyptian control.⁵⁰ His Egyptian counterpart did not fare much better. Nekau II died in 595 BCE and his son Psamtik II succeeded him. The new pharaoh devoted the first three years of his reign to subduing the Nubian kingdom of Napata to the south of Egypt in order to prevent a re-run of Tanutamani's 664 BCE invasion of Egypt. In 593 BCE, Psamtik II decisively defeated the Nubians at Pnoubs (modern-day Kerma-Doukki Gel in northern Sudan) and turned his attention to Syria-Palestine.⁵¹ In the Petition of Pediese (Papyrus Rylands 9) dated to 513 BCE, the eponymous author claims that his grandfather accompanied Psamtik II on a trip to the Levant in 592 BCE.⁵² The purpose of this trip remains unclear, but as Dan'el Kahn points out, Psamtik II could not have traveled to the Levant unless he was secure in his control of the area or was prepared to confront Babylonian resistance.⁵³ Judah may have

---

49. Wiseman, *Chronicles of Chaldaean Kings*, 72–73; Grayson, *Assyrian and Babylonian Chronicles*, 102.

50. Eph'al, "Nebuchadnezzar the Warrior," 181–82; Kahn, "Some Remarks on the Foreign Policy of Psammetichus II," 143.

51. Kahn, "Some Remarks on the Foreign Policy of Psammetichus II," 146–48.

52. For this papyrus see Günter Vittmann, *Der demotische Papyrus Rylands 9*, ÄAT 38, 2 vols. (Wiesbaden: Harrassowitz, 1998).

53. Kahn, "Some Remarks on the Foreign Policy of Psammetichus II," 150–51. For various interpretations of this trip see Kenneth S. Freedy and Donald B. Redford, "The Dates in Ezekiel in Relation to Biblical, Babylonian, and Egyptian Sources," *JAOS* (1970): 479–81; Anthony J. Spalinger, "Egypt and Babylon: A Survey (620 B.C.–550 B.C.)," *SAK* (1977): 233–34; Schipper, *Israel und Ägypten*, 242–43; and Günter Vittmann, *Ägypten und die Fremden im ersten vorchristlichen Jahrtausend* (Mainz: Philipp von Zabern, 2003), 40, among others. A stela base from either Heliopolis or Sais may allude to a clash between Egypt and Babylon as part of this trip when it refers to Psamtik II as "victor over the Asiatics" (ḥwj sṯ.tjw) (Kahn, "Some Remarks on the Foreign Policy of Psammetichus II," 151n50; M. Henri Gauthier, "Un monument nouveau du roi Psamtik II," *ASAE* 34 [1934]: 129–34). Caution is necessary, however, since claiming victory over the Asiatics was a well-known trope in ancient Egyptian royal inscriptions. It need not indicate that a battle occurred.

2. In the Shadow of Empire

made diplomatic overtures to Egypt at this time as well. According to Ezek 17:15, Zedekiah rebelled against Nebuchadnezzar by "sending his messengers to Egypt so that they might give him horses and a large army" (לשלח מלאכיו מצרים לתת לו סוסים ועם רב). Taken together, these two texts suggest that Judah had reentered the Egyptian orbit by 592 BCE.[54]

Egypt exercised control over Judah for only four years. Psamtik II fell ill shortly after his trip to Syria and died in 589 BCE, leaving his successor Apries to deal with Babylonian recriminations.[55] In 588 BCE, Nebuchadnezzar overcame the rebellions in Mesopotamia and Elam, recaptured the Levant, and undertook a siege of Jerusalem. According to Jer 37:5, 7, and 11, however, Nebuchadnezzar suspended the siege of Jerusalem after Apries led a military expedition into the Levant. But, while Jer 37:5 states that "pharaoh's army had gone out from Egypt" (חיל פרעה יצא ממצרים), it does not specify where and for what purpose the Egyptian army was mobilized. Only verse 7 explicitly states that Apries intended to help Judah. Nevertheless, both Josephus (*Ant.* 10.110) and most modern scholars suggest that Apries intervened to save Zedekiah from the Babylonian army.[56] Later Greek sources, however, may indicate that Nebuchadnezzar's withdrawal from Jerusalem was an unintended consequence of Apries's campaign rather than its primary goal. According to the Greek historians Herodotus (*Hist.* 2.161) and Diodorus Siculus (*Bib. hist.* 1.68.1), Apries fought against either Tyre and Sidon or Cyprus, Sidon, and other Phoenician cities at some point during his reign.[57] Based on these accounts, Schipper hypothesizes that

---

54. Freedy and Redford and T. G. H. James suggest that Psamtik II's trip to Syria-Palestine encouraged Judah to rebel against Babylon (Freedy and Redford, "Dates in Ezekiel," 480; T. G. H. James, "Egypt: The Twenty-Fifth and Twenty-Sixth Dynasties," in *The Assyrian and Babylonian Empires and other States of the Near East: From the Eighth to the Sixth Centuries BC*, vol. 3.2 of *The Cambridge Ancient History*, ed. John Boardman et al. [Cambridge: Cambridge University Press, 1991], 718).

55. Kahn, "Some Remarks on the Foreign Policy of Psammetichus II," 152.

56. Begg, *Josephus' Story of the Later Monarchy*, 543. See Kahn, "Some Remarks on the Foreign Policy of Psammetichus II," 152, for a survey of scholarship on this topic.

57. There are several problems with these accounts, however: neither author provides a date for these military campaigns and, according to A. T. Reyes and Maria Iacovou, the archaeological record has not yielded any evidence for Egyptian control over Cyprus at this time (Andres T. Reyes, *Archaic Cyprus: A Study of the Textual and Archaeological Evidence* [Oxford: Clarendon, 1994], 78; Maria Iacovou, "Cyprus during the Iron Age through the Persian Period: From the Eleventh Century BC to the Abolition of the City-Kingdoms (c. 300 BC)," in *The Oxford Handbook of the Archaeology of the Levant c. 8000–332 BCE*, ed. Mar-

Apries exploited Nebuchadnezzar's involvement in Judah to recapture the coastal trade routes linking Egypt and the Aegean.[58] Such a move would have been more consistent with Saite interests in the region than a direct confrontation with Nebuchadnezzar outside of Jerusalem. After all, the Saite pharaoh's primary interest in the Levant lay in controlling the local trade routes and maintaining a buffer state between Egypt and Babylon. There would be little strategic value in fighting a pitched battle with the Babylonian army over a commercially and strategically unimportant site like Jerusalem.

Whatever Apries's motivation for deploying Egyptian troops to the Levant, he eventually withdrew them, allowing Nebuchadnezzar to resume the siege of Jerusalem. Nevertheless, Judahite officials continued to hope for a second Egyptian intervention. A letter from the Judahite city of Lachish written on the eve of Jerusalem's destruction reports that a military official named Koniah traveled to Egypt and attempted to recall a group of Judahite soldiers stationed there: "The commander of the army, Koniah son of Elnathan, has gone down to enter Egypt and has sent to take Hodawiah son of Ahiah and his men from there" (. ירד שר הצבא, כניהו בן אלנתן לבא . מצרימה . ואת הודויהו בן אחיהו ואנשו שלח לקחת . מזה Lachish 3:14–16, 1'–2').[59] Judging from the frequent condemnations of Egyptian aid as worthless in Jer 37:1–10, Ezek 17:17; 29:1–17; 30:20–25;

---

greet L. Steiner and Ann E. Killebrew [Oxford: Oxford University Press, 2014], 809).

58. Schipper, *Israel und Ägypten*, 244; see also Freedy and Redford, "Dates in Ezekiel," 482–83; H. Jacob Katzenstein, *The History of Tyre: From the Beginning of the Second Millennium BCE until the Fall of the Neo-Babylonian Empire* (Beer-Sheva: Ben-Gurion University of the Negev Press, 1997), 318–19. Alan B. Lloyd, by contrast, dates this campaign to the period between 574 and 570 BCE, reasoning that the Babylonian siege of Tyre mentioned in Ezek 26 ended in Babylonian victory in 574 BCE (Alan B. Lloyd, *Herodotus Book II: Commentary 99–182*, EPRO 43/3 [Leiden: Brill, 1988], 170–71; David Asheri, Alan Lloyd, and Aldo Corcella, *A Commentary on Herodotus Books I–IV*, ed. Oswyn Murray and Alfonso Moreno, trans. Barbara Graziosi, Matteo Rossetti, Carlotta Dus, and Vanessa Cazzato [Oxford: Oxford University Press, 2007], 363). Apries then moved to reassert control over the Phoenician city-states. But, as Ezek 29:18–19 makes clear, the Babylonian siege of Tyre failed and so there was no need for Apries to campaign against Tyre.

59. Shmuel Aḥituv, *Echoes from the Past: Hebrew and Cognate Inscriptions from the Biblical Period* (Jerusalem: Carta, 2008), 63. Richard C. Steiner and Bezalel Porten suggest that Koniah was son of the same Elnathan sent to extradite Uriah the prophet from Egypt according to Jer 26:22 (Richard C. Steiner, "The Two Sons of Neriah and the Two Editions of Jeremiah in the Light of Two Atbash Code-Words for Babylon," *VT* 46 [1996]: 78; Bezalel Porten, "Settlement of the Jews at Elephantine and the Arameans at Syene," in *Judah and the Judeans in*

32:1–16, and Lam 4:17, it seems likely that Koniah's embassy was unsuccessful, just as Adon's request for Egyptian aid went unanswered in 604 BCE. Without Egyptian help, Jerusalem proved no match for the Babylonian army. In 586 BCE, Nebuchadnezzar overran Jerusalem, sacked the temple and palace, and once again deported several thousand Judahites to Babylon.

2.7. FURTHER CLASHES BETWEEN EGYPT AND BABYLON: 586–568 BCE

The conflict between Egypt and Babylon did not end with the capture of Jerusalem in 586 BCE. According to an Egyptian stela found at Daphnae, Nebuchadnezzar attempted to invade Egypt a second time in 582 BCE, perhaps in connection with his military campaign in the Transjordan and with the third wave of deportations from Judah and Jerusalem.[60] The stela is broken, but it describes how Apries leveraged a crucial piece of military intelligence from a Babylonian deserter to repel the Babylonian advance at Daphnae (see fig. 4).[61] Josephus also mentions this campaign in *Ant.* 10.182, but he has confused some of the details. According to his account, Nebuchadnezzar successfully invaded Egypt in 582 BCE, deposed Apries, and installed a new king in his place.[62] Because Egyptian records indicate that Apries continued to reign until 570 BCE, however, Josephus probably conflated the

---

the *Neo-Babylonian Period*, ed. Oded Lipschits and Joseph Blenkinsopp [Winona Lake, IN: Eisenbrauns, 2003], 457).

60. Nebuchadnezzar may have sacked the Egyptian site of Tell el-Ghaba, located in the eastern Nile Delta, during this campaign. Although Susana Basílico and Silvia Lupo link the destruction of this site to the first Babylonian invasion of Egypt in 601 BCE, that campaign floundered at Migdol before ever reaching Tell el-Ghaba (Susana Basílico and Silvia Lupo, "The Final Stage and Abandonment of Tell el-Ghaba, North Sinai: A Site on the Egyptian Eastern Border," in *Proceedings of the Ninth International Congress of Egyptologists*, ed. Jean-Claude Goyon and Christine Cardin, OLA 150 [Leuven: Peeters, 2007], 144; Silvia Lupo, *Tell el-Ghaba III: A Third Intermediate-Early Saite Period Site in the Egyptian Eastern Border; Excavations 1995–1999 and 2010 in Areas I, II, VI and VIII*, BARIS 2756 [Oxford: Archaeopress, 2015], 9; Silvia Lupo, "The Argentine Archaeological Mission at Tell el-Ghaba: A Third Intermediate-Early Saite Period Site on the Ancient Egyptian Eastern Border. Remarks and Main Results," *TdE* 7 [2016]: 108). To reach the outskirts of Daphnae in 582 BCE, however, Nebuchadnezzar and his army would need to bypass or subdue several Egyptian sites within the eastern Nile Delta, including Tell el-Ghaba.

61. Abd el-Maksoud and Valbelle, "Une stèle de l'an 7 d'Apriès," 12.

62. Begg, *Josephus' Story of the Later Monarchy*, 617.

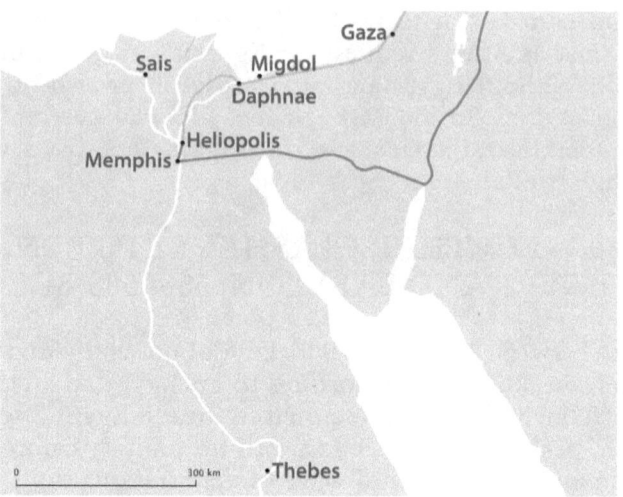

FIGURE 4 Key sites in the second Babylonian invasion of Egypt in 582 BCE

582 BCE campaign with the Babylonian involvement in the later Egyptian civil war between Apries and Amasis in 568 BCE, discussed below. According to Israel Eph'al, Josephus's account probably comes from a later tradition that sought to explain how Jeremiah got from Egypt to Babylon, where he was thought to have composed Ps 137.[63]

Following the second Babylonian invasion, Babylon and Egypt maintained an uneasy stalemate for twelve years. In 570 BCE, however, Egypt descended into civil war, providing an opening for Nebuchadnezzar to stage a third invasion of Egypt. According to Herodotus (*Hist.* 2.161–63, 169) and Diodorus Siculus (*Bib. hist.* 1.68.2–5), the civil war broke out in the wake of a disastrous military campaign against the Greek colony of Cyrene on what is today the eastern coast of Libya, in which Apries's native Egyptian troops suffered heavy losses. The survivors renounced Apries and installed their general, Amasis, as a rival king.

The details of the ensuing civil war remain unclear. Herodotus, Diodorus Siculus, and the Amasis Stela all telescope the war into a single, decisive battle. They also exhibit internal disagreements. Although all three sources pit Apries and his foreign mercenaries against Amasis and his Egyptian troops, they disagree on the location of the battle and the nature of Apries's fate: Herodotus places the battle at the town of Momemphis and reports that Apries was captured and later executed

---

63. Eph'al, "Nebuchadnezzar the Warrior," 184.

by Amasis; Diodorus Siculus locates the battle at the village of Marea and claims that Apries died in battle; and the Amasis Stela states that the battle took place at *jmȝw*—perhaps Kom el-Hisn in the western Nile Delta—with Apries evading capture or death.[64] The Greek accounts appear to reflect later pro-Amasis propaganda.[65] If Amasis had succeeded in killing or capturing Apries in 570 BCE, we would expect him to mention it in his victory stela. It seems likely, therefore, that Apries eluded Amasis for some time. This still leaves the problem of the civil war's geographic scope, however. The claims made by Herodotus, Diodorus Siculus, and the Amasis Stela are difficult to reconcile, but Anthony Leahy has made a good case for the following reconstruction: after the initial munity, Amasis captured Sais, Apries's capital city, from the delta, forcing Apries to retreat to Memphis (see fig. 5).[66] Apries then launched a counterattack but was repelled at Momemphis or *jmȝw*[67] and may have fled south. As the date formula in a legal papyrus (BM 10113) shows, Apries continued to be recognized as the legitimate king of Egypt at Thebes for at least eight months after Amasis's coronation.[68] Eventually, however, Amasis consolidated control over Upper Egypt and Apries was forced to seek refuge with his former enemy Nebuchadnezzar.

Two years later, in 568 BCE, Nebuchadnezzar exploited the recent Egyptian civil war to stage a third invasion of Egypt, a campaign that is mentioned in a fragmentary Babylonian inscription (BM 33041), the Amasis Stela from Elephantine, and Ezek 29:18–19. BM 33041 claims that:

[In th]e 37th year, Nebuchadnezzar king of Bab[ylon] w[ent to] Egypt to wage war. [Ama]sis king of Egypt [mustered his ar]my. [...]*ku*-troops from Cyrene, [... troops from] distant islands in the midst of the sea, [... troops from] other (places) in the midst of Egypt, [carryi]ng weapons, horses, and ch[ario]ts he called [to h]is aid.

[M]U.37.KAM₂ ¹ᵈAG₃-NIG₂-DU-ŠEŠ LUGAL TIN.[TIRᵏⁱ] [...] *mi-ṣir a-na e-piš* ME₃ *il-*[*lik-ma...*]*su* LUGAL *mi-ṣir um*ʔ-*ma-*[*ni-šú id-ki-ma...*]-*ku-ú šá* ᵘʳᵘ*pu-ṭu-ia-a-man* [... *n*]*a-gi-i ne-su-tú*

---

64. Jansen-Winkeln, "Die Siegesstele des Amasis," 136; Blöbaum, *"Denn ich bin ein König, der die Maat liebt,"* 13.

65. Lloyd, *Herodotus Book II: Commentary 99–182*, 202; Asheri, Lloyd, and Corcella, *Commentary on Herodotus Books I–IV*, 367.

66. Anthony Leahy, "The Earliest Dated Monument of Amasis and the End of the Reign of Apries," *JEA* 74 (1988): 192.

67. Leahy identifies the two sites (Leahy, "Earliest Dated Monument of Amasis," 192).

68. Leahy, "Earliest Dated Monument of Amasis," 188. For the text of this papyrus, see Nathaniel Reich, *Papyri juristischen Inhalts in hieratischer und demotischer Schrift aus dem British Museum* (Vienna: A. Hölder, 1914), 5–8.

šá qé-reb tam-ti[m...] šá ki ma-du-tú šá qé-reb ᵏᵘʳ*mi-ṣir* [...]-*ši* ᵍᶦˢTUKUL ANŠE.KUR.RAᵐᵉˢ
ᵍᶦˢ[GIGIR]ᵐᵉˢ [...*r*]*e-ṣu-ti-šú id-kam-ma*⁶⁹

Unfortunately, the name of Nebuchadnezzar's foe falls within a lacuna in the text, but it can be restored on the basis of the Elephantine stela, which mentions an Asiatic (*sṭ.tjw*) invasion of Egypt via the Ways of Horus during the reign of Amasis. According to this stela, Apries provided naval support for the invading Babylonian army and sailed a fleet of Aegean mercenary ships down the Canopic branch of the Nile in order to threaten the Egyptian capital at Sais. Amasis, however, defeated this two-pronged assault and later found Apries's corpse floating in the waves of the Nile.⁷⁰ Ezekiel 29:18–19, which may date to 571 BCE (cf. Ezek 29:17),⁷¹ describes Egypt as Nebuchadnezzar's recompense for the abortive siege of Tyre:

Ezekiel 29:18–19

¹⁸ Mortal, Nebuchadnezzar king of Babylon made his army work hard against Tyre. Every head was made bald and every shoulder was rubbed raw, but neither he nor his army received a wage from Tyre for their work. ¹⁹ Therefore, thus says the Lord Yahweh, "I am about to give the land of Egypt to Nebuchadnezzar king of Babylon and he will carry off its wealth, and plunder it, and despoil it. And it will be a wage for his army."

בן אדם נבכדראצר מלך בבל העביד את חילו עבדה גדלה אל צר כל ראש מקרח וכל כתף
מרוטה ושכר לא היה לו ולחילו מצר על העבדה לכן כה אמר אדני יהוה הנני נתן לנבכדראצר
מלך בבל את ארץ מצרים ונשא המנה ושלל שללה ובזז בזה והיתה שכר לחילו

Because these verses incorrectly predict that Nebuchadnezzar would capture Egypt in 568 BCE, they most likely predate the invasion itself.⁷²

Nebuchadnezzar's third invasion of Egypt met with the same fate as the first two: he failed to win every pitched battle—one of the prerequi-

---

69. For the text of BM 33041 see Stephen Langdon, *Die neubabylonischen Königsinschriften*, trans. Rudolf Zehnpfund (Leipzig: J. C. Hinrichs, 1912), 207, and Elmar Edel, "Amasis und Nebukadrezar II," *GöMisz* 29 [1978]: 14.

70. Jansen-Winkeln, "Die Siegesstele des Amasis," 135–37; Blöbaum, *"Denn ich bin ein König, der die Maat liebt,"* 13.

71. Freedy and Redford, "Dates in Ezekiel," 472–73.

72. On the importance of unfulfilled prophecies for dating prophetic texts, see Reimer, "Jeremiah before the Exile?," 209; Grabbe, "'The Lying Pen of the Scribes'?," 197, 200; and Konrad Schmid, "Prognosis and Postgnosis in Biblical Prophecy," *SJOT* 31 (2018): 112–13.

2. *In the Shadow of Empire* 33

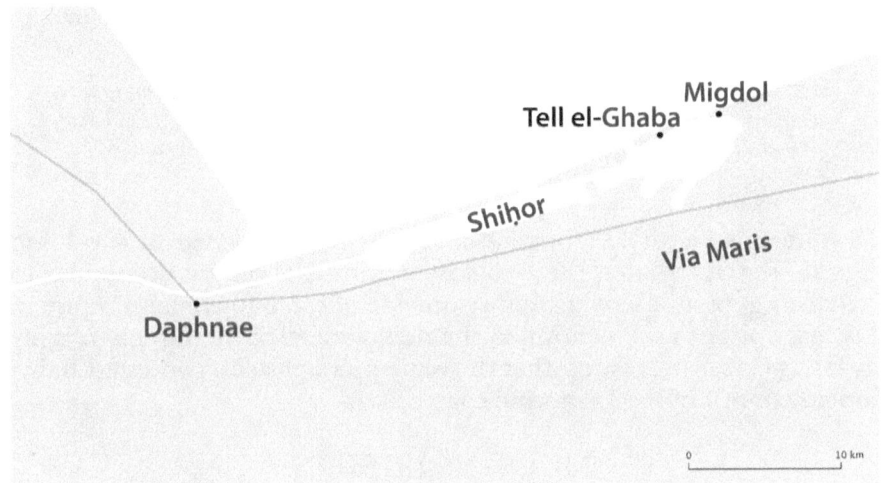

FIGURE 5 Key sites from the three Babylonian attempts to invade Egypt, 601–568 BCE

sites for conquering Egypt identified by Kahn and Tammuz[73]—and was forced to retreat. Nevertheless, Nebuchadnezzar continued to contest Egyptian power in the Levant. Sometime between 572 and 562 BCE,[74] he succeeded in recapturing Sidon and mainland Tyre from Amasis as mentioned in the Wadi Brisa Inscription from modern-day Lebanon:

> (As for Lebanon) where a foreign enemy had exercised rulership and taken its produce so that its inhabitants fled and went far away: by the strength of Nabu (and) Marduk my lords, I regularly sent (armies) to

---

73. Based on their analysis of attested invasions of Egypt between 754 and 306 BCE, Kahn and Tammuz propose three prerequisites for the successful conquest of Egypt: (1) the invader must decisively win all field battles; (2) the invading army must capture Memphis; and (3) if necessary, the invader must pursue the defender into Upper Egypt (Kahn and Tammuz, "Egypt Is Difficult to Enter," 37). The defender can succeed merely by thwarting one of these goals.

74. According to Ezek 29:18–19, Nebuchadnezzar failed to capture Tyre despite a prolonged siege. We can infer from this account that Nebuchadnezzar did not recapture Tyre until sometime after 571 BCE and, if the Babylonian documents referring to military operations in Tyre are any indication, probably not until the end of his reign. Several Babylonian documents from Uruk and Sippar dated between 564 and 562 BCE refer to allocations of military personnel and equipment to Tyre and most likely refer to a second, successful siege of Tyre. For these documents, see Stefan Zawadski, "Nebuchadnezzar and Tyre in the Light of New Texts from the Ebabbar Archive in Sippar," *ErIsr* 27 (2003): 276*–81*, and Eph'al, "Nebuchadnezzar the Warrior," 186–87.

Lebanon for battle. [My armies] expelled its enemy above and below and I made the land happy.

ša ᵗᵘ²KUR₂ a-ḫu-ú i-bi-lu-[ma] i-ki-mu-u ḫi-ṣi-ib-[šu] ni-šá-a-šu ip-pa-ar-ša-a-ma i-ḫu-za né-s[i-i]š i-na e-mu-qu ᵈAG ᵈAMAR.UTU EN.EN-e-a a-na ᵏᵘʳla-ab-na-nu a-na [ta-ḫa]-˹za˺ ú-sa-ad-di-ru [ᵗᵘ²ERIN₂ᵐᵉˢ-ya] na-ka-ar-šu e-li-iš ù ša-ap-li-iš as-su-uḫ-ma li-ib-ba ma-a-ti ˹ú-ṭi₄-ib˺[175]

Despite this victory, Nebuchadnezzar never succeeded in subduing Egypt. Ten years later, the Babylonian king Nabonidus continued to refer to Egypt as a separate entity outside of the Babylonian Empire in his inscriptions and mentioned the deployment of the Egyptian army as far as Gaza, suggesting that the Saite pharaohs still contested Babylonian control of the Levantine coast.[76]

2.8. CONCLUSION

Overall, the Saite pharaohs exercised control over Judah for approximately twenty-three years—from 620 to 604 BCE, from 601 to 598 BCE, and from 592 to 588 BCE. As a result, Egypt remained a viable alternative to Babylon for Judah during much of the late seventh and early sixth centuries BCE. Egypt also played a much bigger role in Judahite life during this period than previously recognized: the Saite pharaohs interfered in Judahite sucession, employed Judahite soldiers in their armies, and imposed tribute on Judah's kings. These interactions—along with others described in the following chapter—shaped Judahite attitudes toward Egypt and left their mark in the book of Jeremiah.

---

75. Rocío Da Riva, *The Inscriptions of Nebuchadnezzar at Brisa (Wadi esh-Sharbin, Lebanon): A Historical and Philological Study*, AfOB 32 (Wien: Institut für Orientalisk der Universität Wien, 2012), 62–63. Nebuchadnezzar does not identify this enemy explicitly, but Amasis is the most plausible option.

76. Eph'al, "Nebuchadnezzar the Warrior," 188.

3.
Winners and Losers: Varieties of Judahite Experience during the Saite Period

Egyptian control over Judah during the late seventh and early sixth centuries BCE had a profound effect on Judahite life. At the top of the social hierarchy, certain members of the Judahite elite were integrated into the Egyptian administration of the Levant and enjoyed access to Egyptian prestige items. The average Judahite, by contrast, bore the brunt of Saite policies: they paid Saite taxes, provided food for the foreign mercenaries that the Saite pharaohs stationed in the Levant, and served as auxiliaries in the Egyptian army. The two groups also suffered different fates following the fall of Jerusalem in 586 BCE: while the majority of the Judahite elite were exiled to Babylon, many non-elite Judahites fled to Egypt to escape Babylonian retribution or reunite with family members stationed there. In this chapter, I will survey these differences in order to shed new light on the historical background of the book of Jeremiah.

The experiences of Judahites under Saite rule reflect the larger strategic goals of the Saite state. As argued in the previous chapter, the Saite pharaohs were primarily concerned with maintaining access to the trade routes of the Arabian Peninsula and the Aegean and with preserving a territorial buffer between the Egyptian heartland and the Babylonian Empire. To meet these goals, the Saite pharaohs employed both offensive and defensive tactics. Until 605 BCE they regularly deployed armies to the middle and upper Euphrates to contest Babylonian power in the region; they also campaigned against the Nubian kingdom to their south until 592 BCE, when Psamtik II scored decisive victories at Pnoubs and Napata. As part of these campaigns, the Saite pharaohs employed both foreign mercenaries and auxiliaries recruited from their Levantine vassals.¹

On the defensive side, the Saite pharaohs built or co-opted fortresses at strategic points within the Levant and fortified them with foreign mercenaries and Judahite auxiliary troops.² At least three of these fortresses were located in Judahite territory. The fortress at Meṣad Ḥashavyahu guarded the coastal waters linking the Nile Delta with northern Syria and the Aegean, while the fortresses at Arad and Kadesh Barnea protected the overland trade routes running from northern Arabia to Syria.³

The layout, ethnic makeup, and command structure of these fortresses differed from site to site. According to Alexander Fantalkin, Psamtik I constructed the fortress at Meṣad Ḥashavyahu on an Egyptian model and stationed Ionian mercenaries there.⁴ Forty-six percent of the everyday pottery—cooking ware and lamps—is of Ionian manufacture, reflecting the presence of this foreign population.⁵ The site has also produced a small quantity of local Egyptian cookware (about 1 percent of the everyday pottery), attesting to the presence of a few Egyptian officers stationed at the fortress.⁶ This find fits with other data regarding the integration of Greek troops into the Egyptian military. According to an inscribed libation vessel from Coppa Nevigata in southwestern Italy,

---

1. The Greek and Phoenician mercenaries in Psamtik II's service left graffiti on the colossus of Ramesses II at Abu Simbel (André Bernard and Olivier Masson, "Les inscriptions grecques d'Abou-Simbel," *REG* 70 [1957]: 5–6; Philip C. Schmitz, "The Phoenician Contingent in the Campaign of Psammetichus II against Kush," *JEH* 3 [2010]: 321–37), while Let. Aris. 1.13 and Berossus (cited in *Ag. Ap.* 1.136–37) refer to Judahite auxiliaries fighting on behalf of Egypt in Nubia and Mesopotamia (Pelletier, *Lettre d'Aristée à Philocrate*, 108–9; Wright, *Letter of Aristeas*, 121; *BNJ* 680; Barclay, *Flavius Josephus: Against Apion*, 83).

2. Fantalkin, "Meẓad Ḥashavyahu," 95–100.

3. The locations of these fortresses on the margins of Judah shows that the Saite pharaohs were not interested in controlling Judah for its own sake but rather for the access it provided to the wider ancient Near East.

4. Fantalkin, "Meẓad Ḥashavyahu," 49–52, 139–40. Wenning, "Griechische Söldner in Palästina," 263, suggests that Jehoiakim hired the Greek mercenaries stationed at Meṣad Ḥashavyahu to guard a newly liberated Judah, but, as demonstrated in the previous chapter, Jehoiakim was an Egyptian or Babylonian vassal for his entire reign. It is unlikely, therefore, that he would have been able to hire mercenaries on his own initiative.

5. Fantalkin, "Meẓad Ḥashavyahu," 103. Wolf-Dietrich Niemeier suggests that this figure is slightly too high, arguing that moratoria and basket-handled amphorae from Meṣad Ḥashavyahu are of Cypriote rather than Ionian manufacture (Wolf-Dietrich Niemeier, "Greek Mercenaries at Tell Kabri and Other Sites in the Levant," *TA* 29 [2002]: 330).

6. Fantalkin, "Meẓad Ḥashavyahu," 103.

an Egyptian officer named Bakenref (bȝk-n-rn.f) served as "commander of the Aegean troops" (ḥrj mšꜥ n ḥȝ.w nb.wt) during Psamtik II's campaign against Nubia.[7] There is no evidence that Judahite troops were ever stationed at Meṣad Ḥashavyahu.

The fortresses at Arad and Kadesh Barnea were different. Judging from the epigraphic and material remains, a Judahite officer named Eliashib commanded a largely Judahite garrison at Arad.[8] Kadesh Barnea stratum II has also yielded a primarily Judahite assemblage, and excavators attribute its construction to Josiah.[9] Nevertheless, the presence of a hieratic ostracon at Arad and several hieratic scribal exercises at Kadesh Barnea attest to Egyptian oversight of these fortresses and many of the Arad ostraca refer to foreign troops temporarily garrisoned at the Arad fortress.

The Saite pharaohs faced a massive logistical challenge while pursuing their strategic goals in Mesopotamia, Nubia, and the Levant: they had to fund and feed soldiers located hundreds of miles from the Egyptian heartland. To do so, they outsourced many of the day-to-day tasks involved in this process to their Levantine vassals. In Judah, this approach affected different social classes in different ways. Certain members of the Judahite elite assisted with the collection of taxes and the distribution of rations to Egypt's mercenary troops, and served as messengers and diplomats. Non-elites, by contrast, paid taxes that funded Egypt's mercenary armies (and enriched the Egyptian elite and their Judahite collaborators), grew and harvested food for Egypt's foreign mercenaries, and served as auxiliaries in the Egyptian army. In the following sections, I will summarize the available evidence for the experiences of both groups.

---

7. Massimo Pallotino, "Vaso egiziano inscritto proveniente dal villaggio preistorico di Coppa Nevigata," *Atti dell'Accademia Nazionale dei Lincei, Classe di Scienze morali, storiche e filosofiche* 6 (1952): 580–90; Pierre-Marie Chevereau, *Prosopographie des cadres militaires égyptiens de la Basse Époque: Carrières militaires et carrières sacerdotales en Égypte du XIe au IIe siècle avant J.-C.* (Paris: Antony, 1985), 129; Sergio Perignotti, *I Greci nell'Egitto della XXVI dinastia*, PBE 4 (Bologna: La Mandragora, 1999), 87–89.

8. Aharoni, *Arad Inscriptions*, 5–8; Niemeier, "Archaic Greeks in the Orient," 22.

9. Rudolph Cohen and Hannah Bernick-Greenberg, *Excavations at Kadesh Barnea (Tell El-Qudereit) 1976–1982*, IAA Reports 34.1–2 (Jerusalem: IAA, 2007), 15–17.

3.1. ELITE EXPERIENCE

None of the Judahite officials mentioned in the textual record ever states outright that they collaborated with Egypt. Nevertheless, onomastics, scribal practice, and material culture provide indirect evidence for the participation of elite Judahites in the Egyptian administration of the Levant.

Adoption of Egyptian Personal Names

Egyptian names experienced an upsurge among the Judahite elite during the Saite period with individuals like מיאמן (< Egyptian *mry-jmn* "beloved of Amun") and פבמת (< Egyptian *pꜣ-kꜣ-mwt* "the one who belongs to the Ka of Mut") appearing in the textual record of this time.[10] While the majority of these names most likely reflect the Egyptianizing tastes of the era, the name Pashḥur, I argue, provides evidence for the participation of Judahites into the Saite administration. This name comes from Egyptian *pꜣ-šrj-n-ḥr* "the son of Horus" and is by far the most popular Egyptian name in Judah during this period.[11] At least four different individuals bore this name, two of whom were high officials in the Judahite court: Pashḥur son of Immer, the chief overseer in the Jerusalem temple (פקיד נגיד בבית יהוה), and Pashḥur son of Malkiah, a priest and official (שר) in Zedekiah's court.[12]

Comparative material suggests that these individuals were named after an important figure in the Egyptian administration in order to signal allegiance to the Saite state. The most popular Egyptian names

---

10. David Calabro, "Personal Names with Egyptian Elements in Preexilic Hebrew Inscriptions," in *These Are the Names*, ed. Aaron Demsky, Studies in Jewish Onomastics 5 (Ramat-Gan: Bar-Ilan University Press, 2011), 95–118.

11. For the etymology of this name see Shmuel Aḥituv, "Pashḥur," *IEJ* 20 (1970): 95–96; for the distribution of Egyptian names in the Judahite onomasticon see Calabro, "Personal Names with Egyptian Elements," 118.

12. The other Pashḥurs are Pashḥur son of Aḥimoh (פשחר בן אחאמה) from Burnt Bullae Archive 151 and Pashḥur son of Menaḥem (פשחר בן מנחם) from Burnt Bullae Archive 152 (Nahman Avigad, *Hebrew Bullae from the Time of Jeremiah: Remnants of a Burnt Archive*, trans. R. Grafman [Jerusalem: Israel Exploration Society, 1986], 97–98). The name Pashḥur, without a patronymic, also appears in Arad Ostracon 54, the Aroer Ostracon, Jer 38:1, and in bullae from the city of David (Aharoni, *Arad Inscriptions*, 86; André Lemaire, "Notes d'épigraphie nord-ouest sémitique," *Semitica* 30 [1980]: 19–20; Eilat Mazar and Reut Livyatan Ben-Arie, "Hebrew and Non-Indicative Bullae," in *Area G*, vol. 1 of *The Summit of the City of David Excavations 2005–2008, Final Reports*, ed. Eilat Mazar [Jerusalem: Shoham, 2015], 307–8).

3. Winners and Losers 39

among Greek and Carian mercenaries during the Saite period all refer to the Saite pharaohs in some way. This pattern is not accidental. As Damien Agut-Labordère observes, first-generation Greek mercenaries often named their sons after the reigning pharaoh in the hope that their descendants would continue to serve the Saite state.[13] In several cases, this strategy worked. Psammetichos son of Theokles, for example, served as a navigator on Psamtik II's Nubian campaign of 593 BCE and left a graffito on the colossus of Ramesses II at Abu Simbel.[14] And Wahibra-em-akhet (wȝḥ-jb-rꜥ-m-ȝḫ.t) son of Zenodote (zntty) and Alexikles (ȝrkzkrz)—whose name incorporates either Psamtik I's prenomen or Apries's nomen—may have served as "Chancellor of Upper Egypt" (ḫtm bjty).[15] Carian mercenaries pursued a similar naming strategy. Judging from the graffiti they left at Abu Simbel as well as from additional Egyptian and Carian inscriptions from Buhen and Mit Rahina, five different Carian mercenaries bore names referring to Psamtik I.[16] One of these men, Psamtik-ewi-Neith, served as leader of the Carian troops during Psamtik II's Nubian campaign.[17]

A similar explanation may account for the abundance of Pashḥurs among the Judahite elite of the early sixth century BCE. The fathers of these men—Malkiah, Immer, Aḥimoh, and Menaḥem—served the Saite pharaohs in some capacity and wanted their sons to follow in their foot-

---

13. Agut-Labordère, "Plus que des mercenaires!," 303; see also Damien Agut-Labordère, "The Saite Period: The Emergence of a Mediterranean Power," in *Ancient Egyptian Administration*, ed. Jaun Carlos Moreno García, HdO 104 (Leiden: Brill, 2013), 994; Kaplan, "Cross-Cultural Contacts among Mercenary Communities," 19; Haider, "Epigraphische Quellen zur Integration von Griechen," 201, 205.

14. Bernard and Masson, "Les inscriptions grecques," 5–6.

15. Pieter A. A. Boeser, *Die Denkmäler der saïtischen, griechisch-römischen, und koptischen Zeit* (Leiden: Brill), 1915, 2; Marie-Louise Buhl, *The Late Egyptian Anthropoid Stone Sarcophagi* (Copenhagen: Nationalmuseet, 1959), 31, 33–34; Perignotti, *I Greci nell'Egitto della XXVI dinastia*, 98–99; Vittmann, *Ägypten und die Fremden*, 203.

16. M. Georges Daressy, "Une trouvaille des bronzes à Mit Rahineh," *ASAE* 3 (1902): 143–44; Frank Kammerzell, *Studien zu Sprache und Geschichte der Karer in Ägypten*, GOF 4.27 (Wiesbaden: Harrassowitz, 1993), 124–27; Ignacio J. Adiego, *The Carian Language*, HdO 86 (Leiden: Brill, 2007), 116–17, 122–23. The name Psamtik also appears in Carian inscriptions from Memphis, Thebes, and Silsilis, but the context of these inscriptions is poorly understood (Adiego, *Carian Language*, 74, 99–100, 111–13).

17. Carian mercenaries also adopted names referring to Pharaohs Nekau II and Amasis. Adiego, *Carian Language*, 49; Kaplan, "Cross-Cultural Contacts among Mercenary Communities," 12n53.

steps.[18] To do so, they named their sons after an important figure in the Egyptian administration as a means of currying favor and signaling their allegiance to the Saite state.[19]

In the case of Pashḥur son of Immer and Pashḥur son of Malkiah, this onomastic gambit appears to have paid off. Judging from the book of Jeremiah, both men occupied high positions within the Judahite court and belonged to the anti-Babylonian, pro-Egyptian faction of the Judahite elite. In Jer 20:1-6, Pashḥur son of Immer has Jeremiah put in stocks for proclaiming that Jerusalem would fall to the Babylonians, while in Jer 38:1, Pashḥur son of Malkiah reports Jeremiah to Zedekiah for seditious (i.e., pro-Babylonian) oracles and recommends that he be put to death. As represented in the book of Jeremiah, the actions of these men suggest that they favored Egyptian rule over Judah, reflecting an affinity with the Egypt that went beyond their personal names. Based on their behavior and personal names, I argue that these individuals played some role in the Egyptian administration of Judah.[20]

Training in Egyptian Scribal Practices

Apart from harassing pro-Babylonian prophets, it is unclear what duties Pashḥur son of Immer and Pashḥur son of Malkiah performed for the Saite state. Changes in Judahite scribal practice, however, suggest that certain members of the Judahite elite worked as scribes in

---

18. It is also possible that these individuals adopted the name Pashḥur later in life in order to signal allegiance to or support for the Egyptian administration in the Levant.

19. Intriguingly, the Egyptian onomasticon preserves a potential candidate for this Saite official. A vase fragment from Tyre mentions a "priest of Amun-Re, King of the Gods, Overseer of the Seal of the Lord of the Two Lands" (ḥm-nṯr n jmn-rʿ nswt nṯr.w jmj-r ḥtm.t nb tȝ.wj) whose name begins with the sequence pȝ-šrj- before disappearing into a lacuna in the text (William A. Ward, "The Egyptian Objects," in *The Pottery of Tyre*, ed. Patricia M. Bikai [Warminster: Aris and Phillips, 1978], 82-83; see also Schipper, "Egypt and the Kingdom of Judah," 213). The remains of this name coincide with the first half of pȝ-šrj-n-ḥr. Schipper identifies this individual as a Saite official stationed in the Levant. William Ward, however, argues that the vase comes from the Twenty-Fifth Dynasty and may not have originated in the Levant (Ward, "Egyptian Objects," 83). If Schipper is correct in his interpretation and dating of the vase, then pȝ-šrj- could have been the namesake of the many Pashḥurs attested in the Judahite onomasticon of the early sixth century BCE.

20. Manfred Görg, "Der Spiegeldienst der Frauen (Ex 38,8)," *BN* 23 (1984): 11-13, also argues that Pashḥur son of Immer served in the Egyptian administration.

the Egyptian administration of the Levant. The Judahite inscriptions from Lachish, Arad, and Kadesh Barnea—many of which date to the Saite period—show an increased use of hieratic numerals and commodity signs compared to inscriptions from earlier time periods. Schipper links this change to Egyptian administrative needs, as Judahite scribes recorded the collection of tribute and the distribution of rations using the Egyptian system of accounting instead of the earlier Judahite one.[21] Furthermore, as Stefan Wimmer has shown, some of the hieratic signs employed in Judah during the Saite period resemble contemporaneous signs from Egypt, which suggests that Judahite scribes received training in hieratic during this period.[22] Supporting evidence for this claim comes from Kadesh Barnea Ostracon 5, which dates to the late seventh or early sixth century BCE and contains numbers written in the Hebrew alphabet alongside their hieratic equivalents.[23] André Lemaire and Pascal Vernus interpret this text as a school exercise in hieratic numerals produced by a Judahite scribe.[24] Arad Ostracon 34, which records the distribution of rations in hieratic, provides additional evidence for hieratic scribal activity in Judah during the Saite period.[25]

Diplomatic Service

Other members of the Judahite elite may have worked as messengers or diplomats within the Saite administration. Ezekiel 17:15, for example, condemns Zedekiah for rebelling against Nebuchadnezzar "by sending his messengers to Egypt so that they might give him horses and a larger army" (וימרד בו לשלח מלאכיו מצרים לתת לו סוסים ועם רב). And according to Jer 26:20–23, Jehoiakim dispatched Elnathan son of Achbor to Egypt

---

21. Schipper, "Egypt and the Kingdom of Judah," 211.
22. Stefan Wimmer, *Palästinisches Hieratisch*, ÄAT 75 (Wiesbaden: Harrassowitz, 2008), 279. The Judahite hieratic script differed from its Saite counterpart in several ways, however. As David Calabro points out, some of the hieratic signs from Saite-period Judah do not have any parallels in Egyptian texts (David Calabro, "The Hieratic Scribal Tradition in Preexilic Judah," in *Evolving Egypt: Innovation, Appropriation, and Reinterpretation in Ancient Egypt*, ed. Kerry Muhlstein and John Gee [Oxford: Archaeopress, 2012], 82–83). Wimmer suggests that these signs are hold-overs from an earlier hieratic tradition within Judah, which was subsequently modified in the Saite period (Wimmer, *Palästinisches Hieratisch*, 279).
23. Cohen and Bernick-Greenberg, *Excavations at Kadesh Barnea*, 247.
24. André Lemaire and Pascal Vernus, "Le ostraca paleo-hébreux de Qadesh Barnéa," *Orientalia* 49 (1980): 345.
25. For this text see Shmuel Yeivin, "A Hieratic Ostracon from Tel Arad," *IEJ* 16 (1966): 153–59; and Aharoni, *Arad Inscriptions*, 62–64.

in order to extradite the pro-Babylonian prophet Uriah. Most likely, he could not have done so without prior Saite approval. So even if Elnathan was not himself a diplomat, it is likely that Jehoiakim negotiated his entry into Egypt beforehand.[26]

A Twelfth-Dynasty statue from the Baltimore Museum may provide more direct evidence for Judahite messengers working on behalf of the Saite pharaohs. This statue bears a later inscription which dates to sometime during the Twenty-Second to Twenty-Sixth Dynasties (945–525 BCE). It contains a standard Egyptian prayer and identifies the owner of the statue as "the messenger of Canaan and Philistia, Pediese son of Opay" (*wpw.tj n pʒ knʿʿn n prsṭ pʒ-dj-jst zʒ ʿpy*).[27] This individual seems to have been a Judahite with an Egyptian name, like Pashḥur son of Malkiah. Pediese is an Egyptian name meaning "the one given by Isis," while Opay is a native Hebrew name that appears in Jer 40:8, Burnt Bullae Archive 88, and two seventh-century BCE tomb inscriptions from Khirbet el-Qôm.[28] If, therefore, Pediese's inscription dates to the Twenty-Sixth Dynasty, it suggests that Judahites served in the Egyptian diplomatic corps and adopted aspects of Egyptian culture, including the use of hieroglyphic writing and Egyptian religious formulae.

---

26. This episode may hint at the existence of a vassal treaty binding Jehoiakim to Nekau II similar to the one that Adon king of Ekron mentions in his letter to the same pharaoh. As David Elgavish notes, the extradition of fugitives is a common topic in vassal treaties: vassal kings were required to extradite fugitives back to their suzerain, but suzerains were not always subject to the same obligation (David Elgavish, "Extradition of Fugitives in International Relations in the Ancient Near East," in *The Jerusalem 2002 Conference*, ed. Hillel Gamoran, *Jewish Law Association Studies* 14 [Binghampton, NY: Global Academic Publishing, 2004], 40–46). Nekau II's willingness to extradite a fugitive back to Judah may indicate that Jehoiakim enjoyed Nekau II's favor.

27. Émile Chassinat, "Un interprète égyptien pour les pays chananéens," *BIFAO* 1 (1900): 99; Georg Steindorff, "The Statuette of an Egyptian Commissioner in Syria," *JEA* (1939): pl. VII. For the history of scholarship on this object and the different proposals regarding its dating see Schipper, *Israel und Ägypten*, 194. See also Shirly Ben-Dor Evian, "Egypt and the Levant in the Iron Age I–IIA: The Ceramic Evidence," *TA* 38 (2011): 98.

28. Avigad, *Hebrew Bullae from the Time of Jeremiah*, 69; André Lemaire, "Les inscriptions de Khirbet el-Qôm et l'ashérah de YHWH," *RB* (1977): 596. Calabro suggests that this name could be a Semitic rendering of Egyptian ʿpr "to provide" found in personal names such as *ptḥ-ʿpr.f* and *ʿpr-bʿr* (Calabro, "Personal Names with Egyptian Elements," 104–5). In Pediese's inscription, however, ʿpy is written with the throw stick determinative T13, which marks it as a foreign name. Interestingly, עפי appears on Burnt Bullae Archive 88 as the father of מ]יאמן] (< Egyptian *mry-jmn* "beloved of Amun"), another Judahite with an Egyptian personal name. Perhaps מ]יאמן] and Pediese were brothers.

Material Rewards

In exchange for their loyalty to the Saite pharaohs, certain members of the Judahite elite enjoyed access to Egyptian goods and services. Jeremiah 36:22, for example, locates an Egyptian brazier in King Jehoiakim's winter palace: "the king was sitting in the winter palace [[...]] and a fire was burning on the brazier before him" (והמלך יושב בית החרף {אש}ו האח לפניו מבערת [[...]]).[29] The word for "brazier" here is an Egyptian loanword into Hebrew, which suggests that the brazier itself may have been imported from Egypt.[30]

The Silwan Monolith may provide an additional example of this dynamic. As Bernd Schipper notes, this late seventh-century BCE rock-cut tomb resembles Egyptian pyramid graves from New Kingdom Thebes.[31] It takes the form of a cube with overhanging eaves and was originally capped by a pyramidal structure. According to David Ussishikin, the exceptional quality of the stonemasonry suggests foreign artistry.[32] Despite these foreign elements, the Silwan Monolith most likely served as the final resting place of a Judahite rather than of an Egyptian. Like many Judahite tombs, but unlike Egyptian pyramid graves, the Silwan Monolith incorporates a rock-hewn bench for displaying the deceased's earthly remains.[33] It also features the remains of a monumental Hebrew inscription above the entrance cursing would-be tomb-robbers, like other, more typically Judahite tombs from the Silwan necropolis (e.g., the tomb of the Royal Steward).[34] If this line of reasoning proves correct, then the Silwan Monolith provides further evidence for the

---

29. Reading את האח "the brazier" as אש האח "the fire of the brazier" with the Septuagint, Peshitta, and Targum and omitting the phrase בחדש התשיעי "in the ninth month" as a gloss from verse 9 with the Septuagint (Janzen, *Studies in the Text of Jeremiah*, 52).

30. Thomas O. Lambdin, "Egyptian Loanwords in the Old Testament," *JAOS* 73 (1953): 146, 153; Maximilian Ellenbogen, *Foreign Words in the Old Testament* (London: Luzac, 1962), 21, 117; Yoshiyuki Muchiki, *Egyptian Proper Names and Loanwords in Northwest Semitic*, SBLDS 173 (Atlanta: Scholars Press, 1999), 238, 251; Benjamin J. Noonan, *Non-Semitic Loanwords in the Hebrew Bible: A Lexicon of Language Contact*, LSAWS 14 (Winona Lake, IN: Eisenbrauns, 2019), 47–48. For the dissimilation of ʿ to ʾ in the Egyptian antecedent of this word see Jürgen Ossing, "Zum Lautwechsel l ↔ ʿ unter Einfluss von ḥ," *SAK* 8 (1980): 217–25.

31. Schipper, *Israel und Ägypten*, 259–61.

32. David Ussishkin, *The Village of Silwan: The Necropolis from the Period of the Judean Kingdom* (Jerusalem: Israel Exploration Society, 1993), 331.

33. Ussishkin, *Village of Silwan*, 47–60.

34. Gabriel Barkay, "The Tomb of Pharaoh's Daughter: A Reconsideration"

availability of Egyptian goods and services to the Judahite elite of the Saite period. Its owner had the means and standing to commission an Egyptian-style funerary monument for themselves and may have hired an Egyptian stonemason to do so.

Several other upper-class Judahite tombs from the Saite period have yielded a mix of Egyptian and Judahite prestige items. The grave goods from the Ketef Hinnom burial caves, for example, include a Wadjet eye bead, an Egyptian terracotta amulet shaped like a woman's head, and two silver scrolls bearing a variant of the priestly blessing known from Num 6:24–26.[35] The juxtaposition of Egyptian prestige items and a Hebrew text later incorporated into the Priestly source offers a striking material parallel to the figures of Pashḥur son of Immer and Pashḥur son of Malkiah. These men served as both priests in the Jerusalem temple and officials within the Egyptian administration of Judah.[36]

Ultimately, the participation of the Judahite elite in the Egyptian administration of the Levant helps explain why Judah switched allegiance between Egypt and Babylon so many times over the course of the late seventh and early sixth centuries BCE. Certain members of the Judahite elite owed their power to the Saite pharaohs and would only relinquish it under the threat of violence. We can see this dynamic play out several times in the last two decades of Judah's existence. In 604, 598, and 586 BCE, Nebuchadnezzar II won Judah's allegiance through armed conflict: his overwhelming victories over the Philistine city-

---

[Hebrew], in *City of David Studies of Ancient Jerusalem: Proceedings of the Sixth Conference*, ed. Eyal Miron (Jerusalem: Megalim, 2005), 148–50.

35. Gabriel Barkay, *Ketef Hinnom: A Treasure Facing Jerusalem's Walls* (Jerusalem: The Israel Museum, 1986), 7, 28–31.

36. For more general examples of Egyptian influence on Judahite material culture during the Saite period see Duncan MacKenzie, *Excavations at Ain Shems (Beth-Shemesh)*, Palestine Exploration Fund Annual 2 (Manchester: Palestine Exploration Fund, 1912), pl. XXXVIII:2, XLIII:4; Olga Tufnell, *Lachish III (Tell ed-Duweir): The Iron Age*, The Wellcome-Marston Archaeological Research Expedition to the Near East 3 (London: Oxford University Press, 1953), pl. 34:7, 12–14; 35:43, 46; 36:48; Chester Charlton McCown, *Archaeological and Historical Results*, vol. 1 of *Tell en-Naṣbeh: Excavated under the Direction of the Late William Frederic Badè* (Berkeley: The Palestine Institute of Pacific School of Religion, 1947), pl. 55:77; Kathleen M. Kenyon, *Excavations at Jericho II: The Tombs Excavated in 1955–1956* (London: British School of Archaeology in Jerusalem, 1965), fig. 261: 1, 2, 5; Gregory D. Mumford, "International Relations between Egypt, Sinai and Syria-Palestine in the Late Bronze Age to Early Persian Period (Dynasties 18–26: c. 1550–525 BC)" (PhD thesis, University of Toronto, 1998), 1965–66, 2369–90, 2440; Bernard Couroyer, "Menues trouvailles à Jérusalem," *RB* 77 (1970): 248.

states in 604 BCE convinced Jehoiakim to switch sides; and in 598 and 586 BCE, he secured Judah's submission after undertaking a prolonged siege of Jerusalem. But there is no evidence that the Saite pharaohs compelled Judah to rejoin the Egyptian orbit through force of arms. When Nebuchadnezzar was preoccupied with other parts of his empire or appeared weak, the Judahite elite simply gravitated back toward Egypt. In 601 BCE Jehoiakim withheld tribute from Nebuchadnezzar after the Babylonian defeats at Migdol and Gaza, and in 592 BCE Zedekiah resumed diplomatic relations with Egypt following Nebuchadnezzar's prolonged absence from the Levant. Both men were connected to Egypt in some way. Jehoiakim was placed on the throne by Nekau II and—even though Zedekiah himself was a Babylonian appointee—his court included several pro-Egyptian officials such as Pashḥur son of Malkiah and Pashḥur son of Immer. Perhaps these men convinced Zedekiah to throw his lot in with Egypt just as they convinced him to imprison Jeremiah for sedition according to Jer 38:4–5. Whatever the case, Jehoiakim, Zedekiah, and other members of the pro-Egyptian elite were so committed to Egypt that they were willing to risk military conflict with Babylon—even after hearing of Nebuchadnezzar's brutal campaign against the Philistine city-states.[37]

3.2. NON-ELITE EXPERIENCE

The lives of non-elite Judahites were decidedly less glamorous under the Saite pharaohs. As I will demonstrate in this section, they paid taxes which funded the pharaohs' military campaigns, grew food to feed the foreign mercenaries employed by the Saite pharaohs, and served as auxiliaries in the Egyptian army in Mesopotamia, the Levant, and Egypt.

Taxation

Non-elite Judahites experienced an increased tax burden under the Saite pharaohs. Upon the ascension of Jehoiakim, Nekau II imposed a punitive tribute (ענשׁ) on Judah, which Jehoiakim subsequently passed on to the populace: "He [= Nekau II] imposed a tribute of one hundred

---

37. Of course, not all members of the Judahite elite collaborated with the Saite pharaohs or supported Egyptian control over Judah. As the book of Jeremiah demonstrates, other members of the elite backed Babylon in the struggle for control of the Levant (see, e.g., Jer 26:20–24; 38:14–24) and may have sympathized with the plight of non-elite Judahites. These individuals may have had a hand in composing the anti-Egyptian oracles discussed in the following chapters.

talents of silver and one talent of gold on the land ... Jehoiakim gave the silver and gold to Pharaoh, but he taxed the land in order to meet pharaoh's demand for money. He collected silver and gold from the people of the land to give to Pharaoh Nekau" (ויתן ענש על הארץ מאה ככר כסף וככר זהב ... והכסף והזהב נתן יהויקים לפרעה אך העריך את הארץ לתת את הכסף על פי פרעה איש כערכו נגש את הכסף ואת הזהב את עם הארץ לתת לפרעה נכה, 2 Kgs 23:33, 35). This punitive tribute served a dual purpose. It provided funds for Nekau II's ongoing campaigns along the upper Euphrates and served to punish the people of the land, who had placed Jehoiakim's ill-fated predecessor on the throne against Nekau II's wishes.

Comparative data from other regions of the Saite empire suggests that Nekau II's punitive tribute was not a one-off affair. According to a stela from the Apis temple in Memphis dated to 612 BCE, the Phoenician city-states were dependent on Egypt and paid taxes to the pharaoh. The stela also mentions an Egyptian administrator stationed in the region: "Their chiefs were subjects of the palace, with a royal official standing over them, assessing their taxes for the capital as in Egypt" (wrw.sn m nḏ.t ḥꜥ.t smr nswt ꜥḥꜥ ḥr.sn ḥtr bꜣk.w.sn r ḫnw mj tꜣ mrj.t).[38] Nebuchadnezzar's Wadi Brisa Inscription—dated between 572 and 562 BCE—may also allude to the taxation of the Phoenician city-states. In this inscription, Nebuchadnezzar boasts of liberating Lebanon from "an enemy" (^{lu_2}KUR$_2$) who had taken Lebanon's produce by force, a possible reference to taxation:

> (As for Lebanon) where a foreign enemy had exercised rulership and taken its produce so that its inhabitants fled and went far away: by the strength of Nabu (and) Marduk my lords I regularly sent (armies) to Lebanon for battle. [My armies] expelled its enemy above and below and I made the land happy.
>
> ša ^{lu_2}KUR$_2$ a-ḫu-ú i-bi-lu-[ma] i-ki-mu-u ḫi-ṣi-ib-[šu] ni-šá-a-šu ip-pa-ar-ša-a-ma i-ḫu-za né-s[i-i]š i-na e-mu-qu ^{d}AG ^{d}AMAR.UTU EN.EN-e-a a-na ^{kur}la-ab-na-nu a-na [ta-ḫa]-ˈzaˈ ú-sa-ad-di-ru [^{lu_2}ERIN$_2^{meš}$-ya] na-ka-ar-šu e-li-iš ù ša-ap-li-iš as-su-uḫ-ma li-ib-ba ma-a-ti ˈú-ṭi$_4$-ibˈ[139]

The identity of this enemy goes unmentioned, but Egypt is the most plausible option.[40] Based on these parallels, we can imagine a similar system of taxation and administration for Judah.

---

38. Émile Chassinat, "Textes provenant du Sérapéum de Memphis," *RT* 22 (1900): 166; August Mariette, *Œuvres divers*, Bibliothèque égyptologique 18 (Paris: Ernest Leroux, 1904), 249.

39. Da Riva, *Inscriptions of Nebuchadnezzar at Brisa*, 20, 62–63.

40. Herodotus (*Hist.* 2.161, 182) and Diodorus Siculus (*Bib. hist.* 1.68.1) claim that Apries captured Tyre and Sidon around 589 BCE and until the Wadi

3. Winners and Losers

Corvée Labor

Non-elite Judahites were also responsible for producing and distributing food to the foreign mercenaries stationed in the Levant. The presence of stone vessels for food processing at Meṣad Ḥashavyahu, for example, suggests that the fortress served as an administrative center whose soldiers received preprocessed agricultural goods from Judahite farmers.[41] This conclusion receives further support from an ostracon recovered from the site that records the complaint of a field hand against an overseer named Hoshavyahu:

> May my lord the official hear the word of his servant! As for your servant, your servant was reaping in Ḥaṣar Asam and your servant reaped and measured and stored as usual before the sabbath. When your [se]rvant finished reaping and storing as usual, Hoshavyahu son of Shobay came and took your servant's cloak. When I finished my reaping as usual, he took your servant's cloak. All of my brothers will vouch for me—those reaping with me in the heat of [the] s[un]. My brothers will vouch for me truly: I am innocent of gu[ilt. Now, please return] my garment. I call out to the official to re[turn the cloak of] your se[rvant. So gran]t him mer[cy and retu]rn [the cloak of your] servant...[42]

ישמע אדני . השר את דבר עבדה . עבדך קצר . היה . עבדך . בחצר אסם . ויקצר עבדך
ויכל ואסם כימם . לפני שבת כאשר כל [ע]בדך את קצר ואסם כימם ויבא הושביהו בן
שבי . ויקח . את בגד עבדך כאשר כלת את קצרי זה ימם לקח בגד עבדך וכל אחי . יענו .
לי . הקצרם אתי בחם . [ה]ש[מש] אחי . יענו . לי אמן נקתי . מא[שם . ועת השב נא את]
בגדי ואמלא . לשר להש[ב את בגד] עב[דך ותת]ן אלו . רח[מם והש]בת את [בגד ע]בדך

The ostracon does not say what prompted Hoshavyahu to confiscate the field hand's cloak.[43] But, as Nadav Na'aman points out, such a punishment is more fitting for a corvée laborer than a hired hand.[44] If the field hand were a wage laborer, Hoshavyahu could simply dock his pay. The ostracon thus provides evidence that Judahite corvée laborers produced food for the garrison at Meṣad Ḥashavyahu.

Brisa Inscription itself, there is no evidence that control of the Phoenician city-states changed hands.
    41. Fantalkin, "Meṣad Ḥashavyahu," 127.
    42. Aḥituv, *Echoes from the Past*, 156–63.
    43. Perhaps Hoshavyahu accused the field hand of failing to meet the daily quota of grain. Such a scenario would explain the field hand's insistence that Hoshavyahu came at the end of the working day, after he had finished measuring and storing.
    44. Na'aman, "Kingdom of Judah under Josiah," 47; see also Fantalkin, "Meṣad Ḥashavyahu," 127.

The Arad ostraca provide additional evidence for the distribution of resources to foreign mercenaries employed by the Saite pharaohs. Ostracon 1, for example, instructs the commander of the fortress to supply a group known as the Kittim with wine and flour:

> To Eliashib: And now, give to the Kittim 1 bat and 3 (hin) of wine and write the name of the day. And from the surplus of the best flour you should load 1 kor of flour to make bread for them. You should give from the wine of the amphorae.
>
> אל . אלישב . ועת . נתן . לכתים . יין ב 1 3 וכתב . שם הים . ומעוד הקמח הראשן . תרכב
> K . קמח לעשת . לחם . להם . מיין . האגנת . תתן[45]

Ostracon 18, on the other hand, refers to a group of individuals known as קרסי:

> And now, give to Shemariah a lethech (?) and to the קרסי you should give a homer (?).
>
> ועת תן . לשמריהו L ולקרסי תתן . Ḥ [46]

Both כתים and קרסי most likely refer to foreign mercenaries temporarily housed and provisioned at Arad at the behest of the Saite pharaohs.[47] As later Phoenician evidence shows, כתים designated the inhabitants of Kition on the southern coast of Cyprus. During the Saite period, the population of Kition included both indigenous Cypriotes and the descendants of earlier Phoenician settlers—two groups that served as mercenaries under the Saite pharaohs.[48] The referent of קרסי proves more elusive. Yosef Garfinkel identifies these individuals as Cypriotes, while Ran Zadok treats them as Carians.[49] I favor Zadok's proposal for

---

45. Aharoni, *Arad Inscriptions*, 12.
46. Aharoni, *Arad Inscriptions*, 37.
47. The absence of Aegean pottery from Arad may suggest that the Aegean mercenaries mentioned in the epigraphic record were simply passing through the region, as Thomas Braun argues (T. F. R. G. Braun, "The Greeks in the Near East," in *The Expansion of the Greek World: Eighth to Sixth Centuries BC*, vol. 3,3 of *The Cambridge Ancient History*, 2nd ed., ed. John Boardman and N. G. L. Hammond [Cambridge: Cambridge University Press, 1982], 22).
48. Iacovou, "Cyprus during the Iron Age through the Persian Period," 813; Vittmann, *Ägypten und die Fremden*, 44–83; Schmitz, "Phoenician Contingent," 321–37. In addition to the evidence collected by Schmitz, Meṣad Ḥashavyahu has yielded an ostracon bearing a potentially Phoenician name (Joseph Naveh, "More Hebrew Inscriptions from Meṣad Ḥashavyahu," *IEJ* 12 [1962]: 30–31; Fantalkin, "Meẓad Ḥashavyahu," 114).
49. Yosef Garfinkel, "MLṢ HKRSYM in Phoenician Inscriptions from Cy-

3. Winners and Losers

linguistic reasons.[50] But, whatever the case, both Cypriotes and Carians served as mercenaries in the Egyptian army during the Saite period.[51]

Several passages in the Hebrew Bible hint at further contact between Judahites and the foreign mercenaries employed by the Saite pharaohs. Jeremiah 46:9 depicts Nubian, Cyrenian, and Lydian mercenaries fighting in the Egyptian army at the battle of Carchemish, while the Septuagint text of Ezek 30:5 numbers Nubians, Cyrenians, Lydians, and Libyans among Egypt's armed forces.[52] Most likely, these passages reflect on-going contact between Judahites and the foreign mercenaries employed by the Saite state. Judahite farmers, soldiers, and scribes all worked to distribute rations to the foreign mercenaries stationed in Judah, and as I will argue in the following section, Judahite auxiliaries fought alongside these mercenaries in the Egyptian army.

Military Service

Both at home and abroad, non-elite Judahites served as auxiliaries in the Egyptian army. The Egyptian-controlled fortresses at Arad and Kadesh Barnea featured primarily Judahite garrisons and, as both classical and epigraphic sources attest, the Saite pharaohs recruited Judahite soldiers for their campaigns in Mesopotamia, Nubia, and Egypt. The Babylonian historian Berossus (cited in Josephus, *Ag. Ap.* 1.137) mentions that Nebuchadnezzar captured Judahites, Phoenicians, and Assyrians after his 605 BCE victory at Carchemish, which suggests that Judahite soldiers

---

prus, the QRSY in Arad, HKRSYM in Egypt, and BNY QYRS in the Bible," *JNES* 47 (1988): 29–30; Ran Zadok, "On Anatolians, Greeks, and Egyptians in 'Chaldean' and Achaemenid Babylonia," *TA* 32 (2005): 80.

50. Except for the initial ק, קרסי closely resembles the term for Carian found in Babylonian sources of the sixth century BCE, Karsaya (^{lu_2}kar-sa-a-a) (Wilhelm Eilers, "Kleinasiatisches," *ZDMG* [1940]: 189–233). The discrepancy between the two forms can be explained by reference to Carian phonology. The Carian self-designation *qrit* features an initial voiceless uvular stop, a sound that was absent from both Akkadian and Hebrew, but resembled both the Akkadian voiceless velar stop and the Hebrew ejective velar stop (Adiego, *Carian Language*, 244).

51. Vittmann, *Ägypten und die Fremden*, 44–83, 155–79; Hélène Cassimatis, "Des Chypriotes chez les pharaons," *Les cahiers du centre d'études chypriotes* 1 (1984): 33–38.

52. The Table of Nations in Gen 10 may also reflect Egyptian reliance on Aegean mercenaries when it depicts Egypt as the father of the Lydians (לודים) and the Cretans (כפתרים). Because Egypt only enjoyed a close relationship with Lydia during the Saite period, these verses might originate during this time. Siegfried Herrmann, "Lud, Luditer," *BHH* 2:1108.

fought in the Egyptian army in Mesopotamia.⁵³ The Letter of Aristeas 1.13, on the other hand, claims that Judahite soldiers accompanied Pharaoh Psamtik on a campaign against the Ethiopians.⁵⁴ The exact date of this campaign remains disputed, but, as mentioned in the previous chapter, Kahn makes a good case that Josiah supplied Psamtik I with Judahite soldiers sometime between 620 and 610 BCE.⁵⁵ Lachish Letter 3:14–16, 1'–2' also alludes to the presence of Judahite soldiers in Egypt when it states: "The commander of the army, Koniah son of Elnathan, has gone down to enter Egypt and has sent to take Hodawiah son of Ahiah and his men from there" (. ירד שר . הצבא . כניהו בן אלנתן לבא . מצרימה .ואת הודויהו בן אחיהו ואנשו שלח לקחת . מזה).

3.3. THE EARLY HISTORY OF THE JUDAHITE DIASPORA IN EGYPT

While certain members of the Judahite elite enjoyed power and prestige during the Saite period, non-elite Judahites endured increased taxes, forced labor, and conscription. The experiences of the two groups continued to diverge with the Babylonian conquest of Jerusalem. According to 2 Kgs 25:11–12, Nebuzaradan—Nebuchadnezzar's point man in the Levant—exiled much of the Jerusalem elite to Babylon but left the poorest of the land to be vinedressers and tillers of the soil. From that point onward, we lose sight of non-elite Judahites since the elite perspective dominates so many of the exilic and postexilic texts that are preserved in the Hebrew Bible. As I will argue in this section, however, some non-elite Judahites—particularly soldiers—formed an important component of the Judahite diaspora in Egypt. To make this argument, I will draw on data from the book of Jeremiah, the later Elephantine papyri, and material culture to reconstruct the formation and early history of the Egyptian diaspora.

The primary evidence for Judahite diaspora communities in Egypt comes from three passages in the book of Jeremiah: Jer 44:1, 24:8, and 43:5–7. The most detailed description appears in Jer 44:1, which lists four Judahite enclaves in Egypt: "The word which came to Jeremiah for all the Judahites living in the land of Egypt—those living in Migdol, in Daphnae, in Memphis, and in the land of Patros" (הדבר אשר היה אל ירמיהו אל כל היהודים הישבים בארץ מצרים הישבים במגדל ובתחפנחס ובנף ובארץ פתרוס). At first glance, this verse attests to the presence of Judahite communities at four sites within Egypt. Four pieces of evidence, however, suggest that

---

53. *BNJ* 680; Barclay, *Flavius Josephus: Against Apion*, 83.
54. Pelletier, *Lettre d'Aristée à Philocrate*, 108–9; Wright, *Letter of Aristeas*, 121.
55. Kahn, "Judean Auxiliaries," 513–14.

the place names Migdol, Daphnae, and Memphis are a later addition to the text and might not, therefore, refer to communities founded in the wake of the Saite period. First, these sites play no further role in the remainder of the narrative; in particular, they are absent from verse 15, the only other verse to describe the origin of Jeremiah's interlocutors. Second, the place name "Memphis" lacks an equivalent in the Septuagint translation of this verse.[56] Third, the repetition of the participle הישבים "dwelling" looks suspiciously like a resumptive repetition signaling the addition of new material especially when compared to the lone participle in verse 15: "all the people dwelling in the land of Egypt—namely, in Patros" (כל העם הישבים בארץ מצרים בפתרוס). Fourth, Migdol, Daphnae, and Memphis are cities in Egypt while Patros refers to Upper Egypt as a whole.[57] Taken together, these four factors suggest that Jer 44:1 once read "all the Judahites living in Egypt ... and in the land of Patros" with Patros and Egypt denoting Upper and Lower Egypt respectively.[58] In this form, Jer 44:1 did not locate the Egyptian diaspora at specific sites, but depicted it as dispersed throughout all of Egypt.[59]

The textual and redactional history of Jer 44:1 casts doubt on its value as a historical source. Because the additions to this verse cannot be dated with certainty, they could refer to Judahite communities founded under different historical circumstances than the ones prevailing in the early sixth century BCE.[60] It is even possible that the

---

56. It is also possible that the omission of this community is due to parablepsis in the *Vorlage* of the Septuagint (ובתחפנחס ... ובארץ פתרוס).

57. Hermann-Josef Stipp, *Jeremia 25–52*, HAT I/12,2 (Tübingen: Mohr Siebeck, 2019), 607. פתרוס is a Hebrew transcription of the Egyptian term for Upper Egypt, pȝ-tȝ-rsj (literally, "the southern land") (Muchiki, *Egyptian Proper Names and Loanwords*, 234–35; Francis Beyer, *Ägyptische Namen und Wörter im Alten Testament*, ÄAT 93 [Münster: Zaphon, 2019], 95–98).

58. Stipp, *Jeremia 25–52*, 608. Compare, for example, the use of מצרים to refer to Lower Egypt in TAD A3 3 and the juxtaposition of Egypt and Patros in Isa 11:11.

59. Karl-Friedrich Pohlmann offers a similar solution to this problem by treating all of the individually named communities including Patros as a later addition (Karl-Friedrich Pohlmann, *Studien zum Jeremiabuch: Ein Beitrag zur Frage nach der Entstehung des Jeremiabuches*, FRLANT 118 [Göttingen: Vandenhoeck & Ruprecht, 1978], 168). Robert P. Carroll, by contrast, treats the phrase "all the Judahites dwelling in the land of Egypt" as a gloss because it would be historically implausible for all of the Judahite communities in Egypt to attend Jeremiah's sermon (Robert P. Carroll, *Jeremiah: A Commentary*, OTL [Philadelphia: Westminster Press, 1986], 734).

60. As I will argue in chapter 5, the earliest form of Jer 44:1–28 most likely predates the mid-sixth century BCE. But this conclusion does not allow us to establish a firm date for the additions to verse 1.

additions to Jer 44:1 were not historically motivated: the redactors may have simply harmonized the verse with its immediate context and the other references to Egypt in the book of Jeremiah. The inclusion of Daphnae, for example, could represent an attempt to reconcile Jer 44 with the preceding oracle against Daphnae in 43:9–13. And the inclusion of Daphnae, in turn, could have prompted the addition of Migdol and Memphis based on Jer 2:16 and 46:14.

Nevertheless, there are two indications that the redactors of Jer 44:1 were familiar with the distribution of the Egyptian diaspora. First, harmonization alone cannot account for the addition of Migdol. The textual evidence from the Septuagint suggests that Jer 44:1 developed in two or three stages—i.e., Daphnae > Migdol > Memphis or Daphnae and Migdol > Memphis—with the connection between Daphnae and Migdol triggering the initial expansion.[61] But Migdol and Daphnae never appear together to the exclusion of Memphis in the entire Hebrew Bible. Jeremiah 2:16 links Daphnae with Memphis, while Jer 46:14 combines Migdol and Memphis in the Septuagint and Migdol, Memphis, and Daphnae in the Masoretic Text. Using only the texts found in the Hebrew Bible, a redactor could not add Migdol to Jer 44:1 without also adding Memphis. This analysis suggests that at least the addition of Migdol was based on historical data. Second, the final list of sites follows a north-to-south order—beginning with Migdol in the eastern delta and ending with Patros near the first cataract—which could indicate that the redactor or redactors of this verse were familiar with Egyptian geography.

Jeremiah 24:8 also displays knowledge of the diaspora communities living in Egypt when it includes "those who live in the land of Egypt" (הישבים בארץ מצרים) alongside "Zedekiah king of Judah, his officials, and the remnant of Jerusalem who remain in this land" (את צדקיהו מלך יהודה ואת שריו ואת שארית ירושלם הנשארים בארץ הזאת) among those destined for punishment.[62] As many scholars point out, however, the phrase "those

---

61. Janzen, *Studies in the Text of Jeremiah*, 57; William L. Holladay, *Jeremiah 1: A Commentary on the Book of the Prophet Jeremiah, Chapters 1–25*, Hermeneia (Philadelphia: Fortress Press, 1989), 277; McKane, *Commentary on Jeremiah 26–52*, 728.

62. Werner H. Schmidt claims that the reference to Judahite communities in Egypt in Jer 24:8 is anachronistic since such communities were not established until after the fall of Judah in 586 BCE (Werner H. Schmidt, *Das Buch Jeremia: Kapitel 1–20*, ATD 20 [Göttingen: Vandenhoeck & Ruprecht, 2008], 56). The historical record does not necessarily support this conclusion, however. While it is unclear whether Egypt featured permanent Judahite communities before 586 BCE, Lachish Letter 3 shows that Judahite soldiers were stationed in Egypt before 586 BCE.

who live in the land of Egypt" appears to be a gloss which disrupts the logic of Jer 24:1–10. In the beginning of the passage, Jeremiah sees two baskets of figs standing outside the Jerusalem temple—one containing fresh figs and the other containing rotten, inedible figs—which Yahweh identifies as various social groups. According to verses 5 and 8 respectively, the fresh figs represent the Judahites exiled to Babylon in 597 BCE, while the rotten figs represent the remnant of Judah *and* those living in Egypt. It is unclear why the oracle would represent two different communities with a single basket of figs, and so the reference to the Egyptian community most likely represents a gloss.[63]

The date of this gloss and the circumstances surrounding its insertion remain debated for several reasons. For one, the gloss does not contain any historical information that would allow us to date it precisely, which means we must rely on the base text of Jer 24:1–10 to supply a *terminus post quem*. But the date of Jer 24:1–10 itself is highly contentious. Some scholars take the date formula in verse 1 at face value and assign the oracle as a whole to 597 BCE, while others see Jer 24:1–10 as an exilic or postexilic composition long since divorced from historical facts.[64] Therefore, the most we can say is that the gloss attests to the existence of Judahite diaspora communities in Egypt at some point in time.

Jeremiah 43:5–7 presents the most detailed account of Judahite migration to Egypt in the wake of the Saite period. According to this passage, several military officers led a group of Judahite refugees to the

---

63. William L. Holladay, *Jeremiah 2: A Commentary on the Book of the Prophet Jeremiah, Chapters 26–52*, Hermeneia (Philadelphia: Fortress Press, 1989), 659; Susan Niditch, *The Symbolic Vision in Biblical Tradition*, HSM 30 (Chico: Scholars Press, 1983), 61; Schmidt, *Das Buch Jeremia: Kapitel 21–52*, 56. Paradoxically, the gloss undermines itself. It bears witness to the ongoing existence of the Judahite communities in Egypt even as it claims that they were marked for destruction in 597 BCE (Jaeyoung Jeon, "Egyptian Gola in Prophetic and Pentateuchal Traditions: A Socio-Historical Perspective," *JAEI* 18 [2018]: 13).

64. Jeremiah 24:1–10 acts as if the Babylonian deportations of 586 and 582 BCE never happened. This potential historical inaccuracy suggests two possibilities for dating: either Jer 24:1–10 was composed before the second wave of deportations in 586 BCE as the heading in verse one states or it was written long after the events it purports to depict and could afford to take liberties with historical data; see Schmid, "Book of Jeremiah," 443–44; Hermann-Josef Stipp, "Jeremiah 24: Deportees, Remainees, Returnees, and the Diaspora," in *Centres and Peripheries in the Early Second Temple Period*, ed. Christoph Levin and Ehud Ben Zvi (Tübingen: Mohr Siebeck, 2016), 376–77; Christl M. Maier, "The Nature of Deutero-Jeremianic Texts," in *Jeremiah's Scriptures: Production, Reception, Interaction and Transformation*, ed. Hindy Najman and Konrad Schmid (Leiden: Brill, 2016), 120.

Daphnae following the fall of Jerusalem and the assassination of the Babylonian-appointed governor of Judah:

Jeremiah 43:5–7

⁵Johanan son of Kareah and all the commanders of the armies took the remnant of Judah which had returned to settle in the land of Judah from all the nations to which they had been driven—⁶the men, the women, the children, the princesses and everyone whom Nebuzaradan captain of the guard had left in the care of Gedaliah son of Ahikam son of Shaphan—as well as Jeremiah the prophet and Baruch son of Neriah. ⁷And they came to the land of Egypt because they did not listen to the voice of Yahweh. And they came to Daphnae.

⁵ויקח יוחנן בן קרח וכל שרי החילים את כל שארית יהודה אשר שבו מכל הגוים אשר נדחו שם לגור בארץ יהודה ⁶את הגברים ואת הנשים ואת הטף ואת בנות המלך ואת כל הנפש אשר הניח נבוזראדן רב טבחים את גדליהו בן אחיקם בן שפן ואת ירמיהו הנביא ואת ברוך בן נריהו ⁷ויבאו ארץ מצרים כי לא שמעו בקול יהוה ויבאו עד תחפנחס

In its present form in the Masoretic Text, this passage contains several potential expansions. For one, Hermann-Josef Stipp has argued that the phrases "as well as Jeremiah the prophet and Baruch son of Neriah" and "and they came to Daphnae" are later additions to the text intended to forge a link between the preceding narrative and the oracle against Daphnae in verses 9–12. His reason for this is simple. The placement of Jeremiah and Baruch after the long relative clause in verse 6 is stylistically awkward and implies that the two men stand under the judgment proclaimed in verse 7ab. But this characterization conflicts with the portrayal of Jeremiah as a true prophet in the majority of chapters 41–43.[65] At the same time, the phrase "they came to Daphnae" in verse 7c appears redundant after the statement "they came to Egypt" in verse 7a and makes for an anticlimactic conclusion to the story after the sweeping condemnation of the Judahite migrants in 7b.[66] In the end, however, these expansions do not significantly alter the core of the story: following the fall of Jerusalem, Judahite soldiers and those in their care sought refuge in Egypt in order to escape Babylonian retribution.

The origin and viewpoint of Jer 37–43 raise a more serious hurdle to treating Jer 43:5–7 as a historical source. As Stipp has shown, several

---

65. Stipp, *Jeremia 25–52*, 584.

66. Hermann-Josef Stipp, "The Concept of the Empty Land in Jeremiah 37–44," in *The Concept of Exile in Ancient Israel and Its Historical Contexts*, ed. Ehud Ben Zvi and Christopher Levin, BZAW 404 (Berlin: De Gruyter, 2010), 119n36; Hermann-Josef Stipp, "Legenden der Jeremia-Exegese (II): Die Verschleppung Jeremias nach Ägypten," *VT* 64 (2014): 654–63; Stipp, *Jeremia 25–52*, 586.

3. Winners and Losers

lines of evidence suggest that Jer 37–43 was composed in the Babylonian diaspora and reflects the viewpoint of a particularly pro-Babylonian segment of this community.[67] These chapters consistently depict other Judahite communities negatively: they condemn the Egyptian diaspora to suffer and die in their new home along the Nile and discount the existence of a Palestinian community entirely. The prophecy in Jer 42:12 even appears to address the Babylonian diaspora directly.[68] But these biases do not appreciably color the depiction of Judahite migration to Egypt in Jer 43:5–7, I would argue. While some aspects of the story are ideologically motivated—such as the insistence that the entire population of Judah relocated to Egypt[69]—it is hard to imagine an ideological motive for other elements in the narrative, such as the role of Judahite soldiers in leading the migration. Indeed, external evidence renders this aspect of the story plausible. As Lachish Letter 3 indicates, Judahite soldiers did travel between Judah and Egypt during this time period and would have been familiar with the military roads linking the two countries. Furthermore, Judahite soldiers had a good reason for leaving Judah. In order to prevent future rebellions, victorious generals in the ancient Near East often massacred enemy combatants and Nebuchadnezzar was no exception. In the description of the battle of Carchemish found in the Babylonian Chronicle, for example, he boasts that he

> ... defeated [and] utterly annihilated them. The Akkadian troops overtook the survivors of the Egyptian army who had escaped and whom the weapons had not reached and decimated them in the district of Hamath. Not one man [returned] to his country.
>
> [BAD₅-BAD₅]-šú-nu iš-kun EN ⌈la⌉ ba-še-e i[g-mu]r-šú-nu-tú šit-ta-a-tú ERIN₂.ME ᵏᵘʳ[mi-ṣir ... šá ina] BAD₅-BAD₅ iš-ḫi-ṭu-ma ᵍⁱˢTUKUL la ik-šu-du-šú-nu-tú ina pi-ḫat ᵏᵘʳḫa-ma-a-t[ú] ERIN₂.ME ᵏᵘʳURIᵏⁱ ik-šu-du-šu-nu-ti-m[a BAD₅]-BAD₅-šú-nu iš-ku-nu e-du LU₂ ana KUR-šú [ul GUR][70]

---

67. Stipp, "Concept of the Empty Land," 133.
68. Stipp, "Concept of the Empty Land," 126–29; see also Pohlmann, *Studien zum Jeremiabuch*, 148, 157.
69. Stipp, "Concept of the Empty Land," 109–10.
70. Wiseman, *Chronicles of Chaldaean Kings*, 66–67; Grayson, *Assyrian and Babylonian Chronicles*, 99. It is possible that some of these statements are simply rhetorical, as Charlie Trimm argues (Charlie Trimm, *Fighting for the King and the Gods: A Survey of Warfare in the Ancient Near East*, RBS 88 [Atlanta: SBL Press, 2017], 379). But the massive drop in Judah's population from the preexilic to the exilic periods—almost two-thirds according to some estimates—hints at an incredibly high death toll during the Babylonian conquest and its aftermath (Charles E. Carter, *The Emergence of Yehud in the Persian Period: Social and Demographic Study*, JSOTSup 294 [Sheffield: Sheffield Academic Press, 1999], 246–48;

In light of this evidence, it seems likely that Jer 43:5–7 reflects the migration of soldiers and other Judahites to Egypt in the wake of the Babylonian conquest.

The Elephantine papyri may provide some indirect evidence for the formation of Judahite diaspora communities in Egypt during the Saite period. Although these texts date to the fifth and fourth centuries BCE, they contain several references to the earlier history of the Judahite garrison at Elephantine.[71] In a letter to the governor of Judah dated to 407 BCE, the leaders of the community request permission to rebuild their temple and claim that the Judahite community at Elephantine predates Cambyses's invasion of Egypt in 525 BCE: "During the days of the king(s) of Egypt, our fathers built that temple on Elephantine, the fortress. And when Cambyses entered to Egypt, he found that temple built" (ומן יומי מלך מצרין אבהין בנו אגורא זך ביב בירתא וכזי כנבוזי על למצרין אגורא זך בנה השכחה) (TAD A4 7:13–14; see also A4 8:12–13). This claim receives support from Isa 49:12, which forms part of Second Isaiah and is conventionally dated to 539 BCE. In this text, the anonymous prophet includes the "land of the Syenians" among the locations from which Judahite exiles will return: "these shall come from afar; and these shall come from the north and from the west; and these shall come from the land of Syenians" (הנה אלה מרחוק יבאו והנה אלה מצפון ומים ואלה מארץ {סונים}).[72] Syene was Elephantine's "sister city," situated on the bank of the Nile across from the island of Elephantine. The "land of the Syenians" in this passage may, therefore, allude to the Elephantine community. If this is the case, then TAD A4 7:13–14 and Isa 49:12 provide a *terminus ante quem* of approximately 539 BCE for the foundation of the Judahite community at Elephantine.[73]

The circumstances that led to the foundation of the Elephantine community are more difficult to ascertain, but it is possible that the Elephantine community represents a lost Judahite legion deployed to Upper Egypt during the Saite period.[74] According to the Letter of

---

Lipschits, *Fall and Rise of Jerusalem*, 270, 368, 372; Rainer Albertz, *Die Exilszeit: 6. Jahrhundert v. Chr.*, BE 7 [Stuttgart: Kohlhammer, 2001], 80). Stipp attributes this demographic decline to Babylonian pacification techniques and their lingering after-effects (Stipp, "Concept of the Empty Land," 137–47).

71. Karel van der Toorn, *Becoming Diaspora Jews: Behind the Story of Elephantine*, ABRL (New Haven: Yale University Press, 2019), 94.

72. Reading סונים with 1Q Isaᵃ 49:12 (Donald W. Parry and Elisha Qimron, *The Great Isaiah Scroll (1QIsaᵃ): A New Edition*, DJD 32 [Leiden: Brill, 1999], 83). For the use of the related ethnonym סונכן at Elephantine, see TAD A4 10:6.

73. Porten, "Settlement of the Jews at Elephantine," 452, 456.

74. For different variations on this historical scenario see Porten, "Settlement of the Jews at Elephantine," 3; Kaplan, "Cross-Cultural Contacts among

3. Winners and Losers

Aristeas, Judahite soldiers participated in one of the Saite pharaohs' campaigns against Nubia during the late seventh or early sixth centuries BCE and then remained in Egypt.[75] The Letter of Aristeas does not mention where these soldiers settled, but Elephantine would be a logical choice since it served as a bastion against Nubia aggression, according to Herodotus, *Hist.* 2.30. If some of these soldiers remained in Elephantine to guard Egypt's southern border, they may have found themselves trapped in Egypt following the fall of Jerusalem in 586 BCE. Because Elephantine is 550 miles south of Jerusalem, it would take months for news of Judah's fall to reach Elephantine; at that point, the remaining soldiers may have opted to remain in Egypt rather than risk returning to Judah.

The Elephantine papyri also provide evidence for a Judahite community located at Migdol, in the Eastern Delta. In TAD A3 3:1–4, a certain Osea writes to his son Shelomam, who is stationed at Elephantine, to say that his salary has not been disbursed in Migdol:

> [Peace of the te]mple of Yaho in Elephantine to my son, Shelomam, [fr]om your brother, Osea. Greetings of peace and strength [I send to you] ... [and now] from the day that you left Lower Egypt, salary has not been g[iven ... and when] we complained to the officials concerning your salary here in Migdol ...

> [שלם ב]ית יהו ביב אל ברי שלמם [מ]ן אחוך אושע שלם ושררת [הושרת לך] ... [וכעת]
> מן יום זי נפקתם מן מצרין פרס לא י[היב ... וכזי] קבלן לפחותא על פרסכן תנה במגדל ...

It is unclear, however, whether the Judahite community at Migdol represents a hold-over from the Saite period due to the complicated settlement history of the site. During the Saite period, Migdol was located at Tell el-Qedua. But, following the Persian invasion of Egypt under Cambyses and the destruction of Tell el-Qedua in 525 BCE, it was relocated to the neighboring site of Tell el-Herr.[76] If the local garrison survived the Persian attack, Cambyses may have incorporated it into his army and redeployed it to Tell el-Herr.[77]

Mercenary Communities," 8; Schipper, "Egyptian Imperialism after the New Kingdom," 284; and the summary and analysis of previous scholarship in Angela Rohrmoser, *Götter, Tempel und Kult der Judäo-Aramäer von Elephantine: Archäologische und schriftliche Zeugnisse aus dem perserzeitlichen Ägypten*, AOAT 396 (Münster: Ugarit-Verlag, 2014), 73–81. For an alternative theory see van der Toorn, *Becoming Diaspora Jews*, 61–88.

75. Pelletier, *Lettre d'Aristée à Philocrate*, 108–9; Wright, *Letter of Aristeas*, 121.

76. Eliezer D. Oren, "Migdol: A New Fortress on the Edge of the Eastern Nile Delta," *BASOR* 256 (1984): 31, 35.

77. According to Pierre Briant, the Achaemenid kings did occasionally

Material culture may provide additional evidence for Judahites living in Egypt in the late seventh and early sixth centuries BCE. In a 2003 survey, Aren M. Maier writes that "there is quite compelling testimony of finds of apparent Palestinian origin from sites throughout late Iron age (Saite) Egypt" including Migdol, Daphnae, Saqqara, Kafr Ammar, and Lahun.[78] Maier also notes that the distribution of these finds agrees in part with the list of Judahite communities found in Jer 44:1: Migdol and Daphnae are both represented, while Saqqara and Kafr Ammar are located in the vicinity of Memphis.[79] He concludes that these could hint at the presence of Judahites in Egypt during the Saite period but are more likely to reflect trade between Egypt and Judah.[80] John S. Holladay, by contrast, offers a more optimistic interpretation of the evidence: he argues for the presence of a Judahite trading diaspora in Egypt during the early sixth century BCE on the basis of distinctive Judahite wine-decanters from Daphnae, Migdol, Pithom, and Tell Tebilla.[81]

As this survey of the data shows, military service forms a common theme uniting the three main sources of evidence bearing on the Judahite diaspora in Egypt. Jeremiah 43 depicts a group of military officers leading Judahite refugees to Egypt; the Elephantine community most likely had its origins in a Judahite regiment deployed to Upper Egypt during the Saite period; and at least one of the Egyptian sites to yield Palestinian artifacts—Migdol—served a military function.[82] I argue,

---

absorb defeated enemies into their armies (Pierre Briant, "The Achaemenid Empire," in *War and Society in the Ancient and Medieval Worlds: Asia, The Mediterranean, Europe, and* Mesoamerica, ed. Kurt Raaflaub and Nathan Rosenstein [Cambridge: Harvard University Press, 1999], 116–20; Pierre Briant, *From Cyrus to Alexander: A History of the Persian Empire* [Trans. Peter T. Daniels; Winona Lake, IN: Eisenbrauns, 2002], 195–98; see also Herodotus, *Hist.* 1.76, 6.6.) This strategy may also explain the continued presence of Judahite soldiers at Elephantine during the Persian period.

78. Aren M. Maier, "The Relations between Egypt and the Southern Levant during the Late Iron Age: The Material Evidence from Egypt," *Ägypten und Levant* 12 (2003): 240.

79. Maier, "Relations," 242.

80. Maier, "Relations," 243.

81. John S. Holladay, "Judeans (and Phoenicians) in Egypt in the Late Seventh to Sixth Centuries B.C.," in *Egypt, Israel, and the Ancient Mediterranean World: Studies in Honor of Donald B. Redford*, ed. Gary N. Knoppers and Antoine Hirsch, PAe 20 (Leiden: Brill, 2004), 405–29.

82. Migdol was the westernmost Egyptian fortress located along the Ways of Horus, the highway linking Egypt and the Levant. Its 15–20-meter-high mudbrick walls served as the first line of defense against invading armies that managed to cross the Sinai desert. Oren identifies Migdol with the Στρατόπεδα that Psamtik I erected along the Ways of Horus to house the Ionian and Carian

therefore, that Judahite soldiers formed an important component—if not the nucleus—of the Egyptian diaspora. Some of these soldiers may have become "trapped" in Egypt after the fall of Jerusalem in 586 BCE. Others may have relocated to Egypt in order to escape Babylonian retribution or reunite with family members stationed there.[83]

Apart from Elephantine, the location of the Judahite diaspora communities in Egypt remains uncertain. If the final version of Jer 44:1 does contain accurate information about Judahite settlement in Egypt, then Migdol, Daphnae, and Memphis may have featured Judahite communities. Archaeological evidence provides some limited support for the presence of Judahites at Migdol, Daphnae, and Memphis and may hint at the presence of Judahites at additional sites such as Ilahun, Pithom, and Tell Tebilla.

The transitory nature of military service makes it difficult to determine when the Judahite communities in Egypt were "founded." As Lachish Letter 3—and to a lesser extent the Elephantine papyri—suggest, Judahite soldiers were stationed in Egypt before the fall of Jerusalem. But the mere presence of Judahite soldiers in Egypt does not necessarily imply the existence of permanent Judahite communities along the Nile. We do not know whether these soldiers hoped to return home once their tour of duty was finished, like the Ionian and Carian mercenaries stationed in Egypt.[84] These Judahite garrisons may not have become permanent settlements until the fall of Jerusalem left them trapped in a foreign land.

Judging from the available evidence, the Egyptian diaspora consisted primarily of non-elite individuals. The Judahite soldiers stationed in Egypt were drawn from the ranks of the lower classes and may have been joined by other non-elite Judahites after the fall of Jerusalem in 586 BCE. According to 2 Kgs 25:11–12, Nebuzaradan exiled the majority of the Jerusalem elite to Babylon but "left the poorest of the land ... to be vinedressers and tillers of the soil" (ומדלת הארץ השאיר ... לכרמים

---

mercenaries in his employ according to Herodotus (*Hist.* 2.154) and Diodorus Siculus (*Bib. hist.* 1.67.1) (Oren, "Migdol," 38). The semantics of Στρατόπεδα do not fit this identification, however. Henry George Liddell and Robert Scott list the main meaning of στρατόπεδον as "camp" or "encampment" rather than a "fortress," and so Στρατόπεδα most likely refers to a series of temporary military camps along the Ways of Horus (LSJ, 1653). The Hebrew toponym פי החירת in the Exodus itinerary, which I have recently argued is a native Hebrew phrase meaning "at the entrance of the camps," may refer to these structures (Aren M. Wilson-Wright, "Camping along the Ways of Horus: A Central Semitic Etymology for *pî ha-ḥîrot*," *ZAW* 129 [2017]: 261–64).

83. Holladay, "Judeans (and Phoenicians) in Egypt," 423–24.
84. Kaplan, "Cross-Cultural Contacts among Mercenary Communities," 16.

וליגבם) in Judah. Thus, after the fall of Jerusalem, only non-elite individuals would have been left in Judah and able to migrate to Egypt. But the Judahite diaspora in Egypt did not necessarily consist entirely of non-elite individuals. If Jer 43:5–12 is to be believed, several Judahite princesses joined Johanan's group of migrants after the Babylonian conquest of Judah.

Despite the presence of a few elite individuals, the Egyptian diaspora skewed toward the lower class compared to the Babylonian diaspora. Judging from the brief notices in 2 Kgs 24:12, 14–16, 2 Kgs 25:7, and Jer 29:2, the Babylonian diaspora consisted primarily of elite individuals with ties to the Jerusalem court, such as officials (שרים), officers (סריסים), the queen mother (הגבירה, אם המלך), the king's wives (נשי המלך), artisans (החרש), smiths (המסגר), the citizens of the land (אולי הארץ), and two former kings. Some of these individuals, such as Pashḥur son of Malkiah, belonged to the pro-Egyptian faction of the Judahite court.[85] In a final ironic twist, Judahite collaborators—those who benefitted the most from Egyptian control over Judah—were exiled to Babylon, while non-elite Judahites—those who had suffered the most under the Saite pharaohs—wound up in Egypt. No doubt members of the Egyptian diaspora harbored conflicting emotions about their new home: they had suffered under the policies of the Saite pharaohs, but now lived in Egypt for the foreseeable future.

3.4. CONCLUSION

Egyptian control over Judah profoundly altered Judahite life during the late seventh and early sixth centuries BCE, but it affected elite and non-elite Judahites differently. Certain members of the Judahite elite supported the Saite pharaohs' strategic goals by serving as scribes and diplomats and, in return, enjoyed access to Egyptian prestige goods. Their experiences help explain why Judah vacillated between Egypt and Babylon so many times during the late seventh and early sixth centuries BCE. While the Judahite elite feared Nebuchadnezzar's military might, they owed their power and prestige to the Saite pharaohs. When Nebuchadnezzar was absent from the Levant or appeared weak, they simply gravitated back to Egypt. Non-elite Judahites, by contrast, languished under the Saite pharaohs. They paid the taxes that funded the Saite pharaohs' mercenary armies, fed and housed foreign troops deployed to

---

85. Ezra, Nehemiah, and 1 Chronicles treat Pashḥur son of Malkiah as the founder of a priestly lineage whose descendants eventually returned to Judah. In doing so, they presuppose that Pashḥur son of Malkiah was exiled to Babylon.

Judah, and served as auxiliaries in the Egyptian army in Mesopotamia, Judah, and Egypt. The two groups also suffered different fates following the fall of Jerusalem in 586 BCE. Nebuchadnezzar exiled many members of the upper class, including Judahite collaborators like Pashḥur son of Malkiah, to Babylon. Non-elite Judahites, by contrast, fled to Egypt to escape Babylonian retribution or became "trapped" in Egypt following the fall of Jerusalem in 586 BCE. These differences inform the depiction of Egypt in the book of Jeremiah, which forms the subject of the following two chapters.

4.
Fulminating against the Pharaoh: Anti-Saite Oracles in the Book of Jeremiah

As shown in the previous chapter, the burdens of Saite control disproportionally fell on the shoulders of non-elite Judahites. This injustice, in turn, fostered resentment toward the Saite pharaohs and their Judahite collaborators and informed many of the depictions of Egypt in the book of Jeremiah. In this chapter, for example, I will argue that the historical overview in Jer 2:14–19, the "cup of wrath" oracle in Jer 25:15–29, and the oracles against Egypt in Jer 46:2–26 all express dissatisfaction with Egyptian rule. Jeremiah 2:14–19 critiques Judahite collaborators for their short-sighted selfishness. While they reaped the benefits of Egyptian rule, their compatriots were conscripted into the Egyptian army and often died in far-flung locales like Carchemish and Elephantine at the behest of the Saite pharaohs. The "cup of wrath" oracle, on the other hand, provides a map of the Saite empire and its neighbors on the eve of the battle of Carchemish in 605 BCE and expresses the hope that Babylon will liberate Judah from Egyptian control. Finally, the oracles against Egypt in Jer 46:2–26 contain a pastiche of prophetic material reflecting on at least three different military encounters between Nebuchadnezzar II and the Saite pharaohs. Verses 3–12 celebrate the devastating Egyptian defeat at Carchemish; verses 14–24 applaud the attempted Babylonian invasion of Egypt in 601 BCE; and the two fragmentary oracles preserved in verses 25–26 cheer on either the second Babylonian invasion of Egypt in 582 BCE or the third Babylonian invasion of 568 BCE. Along the way, I will propose several new text-critical and redactional proposals regarding Jer 2:14–19, 25:15–29, and 46:2–26 and note how a historical approach to dating these texts can supplement existing redaction-critical approaches.

4.1. JEREMIAH 2:14–19: NO BLOOD FOR EGYPT!

The short oracle in Jer 2:14–19 provides a precis of Judahite history:

Jeremiah 2:14–19

[14] Is Israel a slave? Or is he a house-born servant? Why has he become plunder? [15] Lions have roared against him; they have raised their voice. They made his land into a waste and his cities are ruined, without inhabitant. [16] The people of Memphis and Daphnae too have broken[1] your head. [17] Have you not done this to yourself by abandoning Yahweh your god? [[...][2] [18] What then do you gain by going to Egypt to drink the waters of Shiḥor? And what do you gain by going to Assyria to drink the waters of the Euphrates?[3] [19] Your wickedness will punish you and your apostasies will reprove you. Know and see that your abandoning Yahweh your god is bad and bitter. You do not fear me, says the Lord, Yahweh of Armies.[4]

[14] העבד ישראל אם יליד בית הוא מדוע היה לבז [15] עליו ישאגו כפרים נתנו קולם וישיתו ארצו לשמה עריו נצתה מבלי ישב [16] גם בני נף ותחפנס ירעוך קדקד [17] הלוא זאת תעשה לך עזבך את יהוה אלהיך [[...][18] ועתה מה לך לדרך מצרים לשתות מי שחור ומה לך לדרך אשור לשתות מי נהר [19] תיסרך רעתך ומשבותיך תוכחך ודעי וראי כי רע ומר עזבך את יהוה אלהיך ולא פחדתי אליך נאם אדני יהוה צבאות

The oracle opens with a series of rhetorical questions highlighting Judah's current subjugation before seguing into a historical overview of

---

1. Emending יְרָעוּךְ "they will shepherd you" to יְרֹעוּךְ on the basis of the Peshitta, which reads *nerʿonek* "they will break you."

2. The Septuagint lacks a counterpart to the phrase מוליכך בדרך בעת "when he led you in the way" found in the Masoretic Text (Janzen, *Studies in the Text of Jeremiah*, 10).

3. The common noun נהר with or without the definite article often designates the Euphrates River within the Hebrew Bible (e.g., Gen 31:21; 36:37; Mic 7:12; Zech 9:10; Isa 7:20; Ps 72:8). Only in the case of Dan 10:4 does it refer to the Tigris, most likely as the result of an erroneous gloss. In Jer 2:18, Targum Jonathan explicitly translates נהר as פרת "Euphrates."

4. Emending וְלֹא פָחְדְּתִי אֵלָיִךְ "and fear of me is not in you" to וְלֹא פָחַדְתְּ אֵלַי "you did not fear me" on the basis of the Peshitta, which reads *w-lo dḥelt men*. In this context, פָחַדְתְּ represents the rare second-person feminine singular form of the suffix conjugation (see also Jer 32:21; Mic 4:13; Ruth 3:3, 4), which may have proven confusing to a later scribe and triggered the change in the pointing and consonantal structure of the verse. William McKane, *Commentary on Jeremiah 1–25*, vol. 1 of *A Critical and Exegetical Commentary on Jeremiah*, ICC (Edinburgh: T&T Clark International, 1986), 39; Schmidt, *Das Buch Jeremia: Kapitel 1–20*, 82. For this form of the verb, see GKC, §44h; Joüon, §42f.

4. Fulminating against the Pharaoh

Judah's political fortunes during the eighth and seventh centuries BCE: "Lions have roared against him; they have raised their voice. They made his land into a waste and his cities are ruined, without inhabitant. The people of Memphis and Daphnae too have broken your head."[5] The lions in verse 15 appear to symbolize Assyria, as they often do in other prophetic works (e.g., Amos 3:12; Isa 5:29; Nah 2:12–13; Jer 4:7), while the people of Memphis and Daphnae in verse 16 represent Egypt.[6] In this way, the oracle evokes the transition between Assyrian and Egyptian control over Judah in the mid- to late seventh century BCE. Verse 17 links Judah's political subordination to its apostasy: "Have you not done this to yourself by abandoning Yahweh your god?" The prophet then asks Judah what it stands to benefit from the current state of affairs—"What then do you gain by going to Egypt to drink the waters of Shiḥor? And what do you gain by going to Assyria to drink the waters of the Euphrates?"—before pronouncing judgment on Judah for abandoning Yahweh in verse 19.

With the exception of verse 18—which links imperial powers with specific bodies of water—the oracle condemns Judah for the timeless sin of apostasy. The complex metaphor of verse 18, by contrast, refers to the current state of affairs at the time the oracle was first proclaimed and must, therefore, allude to a more specific, historically grounded transgression. The meaning of this metaphor thus depends on the historical context in which it was first deployed and the feelings that the

---

5. A shift in gender and person occurs between verses 15 and 16. Verses 14–15 address Israel using third-person masculine singular pronouns, while verses 16–19 employ second-person feminine singular pronouns to refer to the same entity. Oliver Glanz attributes this grammatical shift to the polyvalence of ישראל as both a masculine *Volksname* and a feminine *Landesname*, while Robert P. Carroll associates it with a change in social function (Oliver Glanz, *Understanding Participant-Reference Shifts in the Book of Jeremiah: A Study of Exegetical Method and Its Consequences for the Interpretation of Referential Incoherence*, SSN 60 [Leiden: Brill, 2013], 136; Carroll, *Jeremiah*, 592). Christoph Levin and Mark E. Biddle, by contrast, treat the change in address as a redactional seam separating an earlier communal lament from a later theological commentary on Judah's political subordination (Christoph Levin, *Die Verheißung des neuen Bundes in ihrem theologiegeschichtlichen Zusammenhang ausgelegt*, FRLANT 137 [Göttingen: Vandenhoeck & Ruprecht, 1985], 156; Mark E. Biddle, *A Redaction History of Jeremiah 2:1–4:2*, AThANT 77 [Zurich: Theologischer Verlag, 1990], 55).

6. Holladay, *Jeremiah 1*, 78; Peter Machinist, "Assyria and Its Image in First Isaiah," *JAOS* 103 (1983): 728–29; Brent A. Strawn, *What Is Stronger than a Lion? Leonine Image and Metaphor in the Hebrew Bible and Ancient Near East*, OBO 212 (Freiburg: Academic Press, 2005), 178–79.

key terms "Egypt," "Shiḥor," "Assyria," and "the Euphrates" would have evoked at this time. In the following sections, I will argue that Jer 2:14–19 dates between 620 and 610 BCE—the first decade of Saite control over Judah—and condemns Judahite collaborators for their complacency with the political and military order of the time. They created the conditions for Egyptian control by abandoning Yahweh and now benefit from Egyptian domination at the price of Judahite lives. The same system that rewards them with power and prestige throws non-elite Judahites into the meat grinder of foreign wars.

Dating

In its current form, Jer 2:14–19 contains two potential historical references that can help us date this oracle more precisely—one in verse 16 and one in verse 18. The statement that "the people of Memphis and Daphnae too have broken your head" in verse 16 alludes to Egyptian aggression towards Judah.[7] Historical and literary considerations suggest that this statement refers to the beginning of Saite control over Judah around 620 BCE.[8] Other than Sheshonq I's Levantine campaign in the late tenth century BCE—which may not have affected the Southern Kingdom at all—the only other Egyptian action against Judah that is attested in the historical record is the annexation of Judahite territory during the Saite period.[9] Furthermore, the literary structure of the oracle mirrors Judah's historical experiences: the reference to Egypt in verse 16 follows the allusion to Assyria in verse 15 just as Saite control of Judah followed on the heels of Assyrian domination.

Some scholars question the historical import of verse 16, however. William McKane, for example, argues that the reference to Memphis

---

7. McKane and Holladay suggest that verse 16 refers to the death of Josiah at the hands of Nekau II in 609 BCE with the term קדקד serving as a metaphor for the ill-fated king (McKane, *Commentary on Jeremiah 1–25*, 37; Holladay, *Jeremiah 1*, 95). Such a reference is unlikely, however, because the Neo-Assyrian Empire ceased to be an independent political entity in the previous year, the most plausible *terminus a quo* for Jer 2:14–19 as I will argue below.

8. Rüdiger Liwak makes a similar argument but dates the beginning of Egyptian control over Judah to 626 BCE (Rüdiger Liwak, *Der Prophet und die Geschichte: Eine literar-historische Untersuchung zum Jeremiabuch*, BWANT 121 [Stuttgart, Kohlhammer, 1987], 173).

9. Martin Noth, *Könige I, 1. Könige 1–16*, BKAT 9.1 (Neukirchen-Vluyn: Neukirchener, 1983), 330–31; Mordechai Cogan, *1 Kings*, AB 10 (New York: Doubleday, 2000), 390–91; Schipper, *Israel und Ägypten*, 119–32; Schipper, "Egypt and Israel," 35–36; Ben-Dor Evian, "Past and Future of 'Biblical Egyptology,'" 4.

and Daphnae in this verse is paradigmatic rather than historical; it serves only to highlight the problem of cultivating an alliance with Egypt.[10] Robert P. Carroll, on the other hand, claims that "the reference to Tahpanhes in v. 16 may reflect the experiences of the people who fled there after the fall of Jerusalem, but the reference is too allusive to be given a specific meaning."[11] In making these arguments, McKane and Carroll focus on terminology to the exclusion of context. While they are correct that the geographical terms Memphis and Daphnae by themselves cannot help date the oracle—Memphis and Daphnae, after all, remained important sites for large swathes of Egyptian history—the context of the verse as a whole points toward the Saite period.[12] Verse 16 refers to Egyptian aggression against Judah following the decline of the Neo-Assyrian Empire.

The second historical reference in the oracle appears in verse 18, which questions the wisdom of Judah's entanglement with Egypt and Assyria: "What do you gain by going to Egypt to drink the waters of Shihor? And what do you gain by going to Assyria to drink the waters of the Euphrates?" (ועתה מה לך לדרך מצרים לשתות מי שחור ומה לך לדרך אשור לשתות מי נהר). The reference to Assyria in this verse suggests that the oracle predates the fall of the Assyrian capital at Harran in 610 BCE and the demise of the Assyrian Empire as an independent political power, but once again, some scholars question the historical reliability of this reference. William L. Holladay, for example, suggests that Assyria serves a stand-in for Babylon in Jer 2:18 and points to several verses where the Hebrew term אשור refers to a geopolitical entity other than Assyria.[13] As supporting evidence, he notes that verse 18 associates Assyria with the Euphrates River, even though the Assyrian heartland centered on the Tigris. Carroll, on the other hand, notes that Egypt and Assyria form a word pair in prophetic texts like Hos 7:11, 9:3, 6, 11:5, 11, 12:2, Zech 10:10–11, Isa 7:18, 19:23–25, and 52:4, some of which date long after the fall of the Neo-Assyrian Empire.[14] Such a poetic device—he argues—preserved the name of Assyria well into the Persian period and

---

10. McKane, *Commentary on Jeremiah 1–25*, 37.

11. Carroll, *Jeremiah*, 129.

12. According to Leclère, Memphis was occupied from the pre-dynastic period onward, while Daphnae was founded in the Saite period and inhabited until the end of the Persian period (François Leclère, *Les villes de Basse Égypte au Ier millénnaire av. J. C.: Analyse archéologique et historique de la topographie urbaine*, BdE 144 [Cairo: Institut français d'archéologie orientale, 2008], 39, 510).

13. Holladay, *Jeremiah 1*, 63, 93, 98. In Lam 5:6, for example, אשור denotes Babylon, while in Ezra 6:22 אשור refers to Persia.

14. Carroll, *Jeremiah*, 129; Holladay, *Jeremiah 1*, 78.

so the reference to Assyria in Jer 2:18 need not indicate a date before 610 BCE.

Neither of these arguments holds much force, however. Following the sack of Nineveh in 612 BCE, the remainder of Assyrian territory was situated along the upper Euphrates and Orontes Rivers rather than along its historical heartland on the Tigris. The association of Assyria and the Euphrates in verse 18 could, therefore, reflect the territorial extent of the Neo-Assyrian Empire after 612 BCE. Indeed, most of the Egyptian campaigns in aid of Assyria focused on the Euphrates River, and the Judahite soldiers who fought in these battles could have brought information about Assyria's diminished boundaries back to Judah (see below).

Furthermore, most of the prophetic texts that juxtapose Egypt and Assyria predate the fall of the Neo-Assyrian Empire and reflect the antagonism between the Assyrian kings and the Nubian pharaohs of the Twenty-Fifth Dynasty in the late eighth century BCE. Hosea 7:11, 9:3, 6, 11:5, 11, 12:2 and Isa 7:18, 19:23–25 all plausibly date to this time period.[15] Only Isa 52:4 and Zech 10:10–11—both of which date broadly to the Persian period (539–333 BCE)—postdate the fall of the Assyrian Empire. Yet Isa 52:4 treats Egypt and Assyria as historical threats rather than contemporary political powers, while Zech 10:10–11 refers to diaspora communities located in Egypt and the former Assyrian Empire.

This survey of the evidence suggests two conclusions. First, the Twenty-Fifth Dynasty and the early Saite period provide the most plausible historical context for the development of the Assyria-Egypt word pair. Second, the poetic parallelism between Egypt and Assyria that developed during this period did not lead later authors to treat Assyria as a political power after the fall of Harran in 610 BCE. Therefore, I would treat the reference to Assyria in Jer 2:18 as historically grounded and date Jer 2:14–19 sometime between the advent of Egyptian control over Judah in 620 BCE and the fall of Assyria in 610 BCE. The association of Assyria with the Euphrates River in verse 18 may suggest an even narrower date range for this passage if it reflects the fall of Nineveh and the loss of Assyrian territory along the Tigris in 612 BCE.

This historically based date stands at odds with redaction-critical attempts to date Jer 2:14–16. According to Christoph Levin and Mark E.

---

15. Heath D. Dewrell, "Depictions of Egypt in the Book of Hosea and Their Implications for Dating the Book," *VT* 71 (2021): 503–30; J. J. M. Roberts, "Isaiah's Egyptian and Nubian Oracles," in *Israel's Prophets and Israel's Past: Essays on the Relationship of Prophetic Texts and Israelite History in Honor of John H. Hayes*, ed. Bard E. Kelle and Megan Bishop Moore, LHBOTS 446 (New York: T&T Clark, 2006), 201, 206.

4. Fulminating against the Pharaoh

Biddle, the earliest passages in Jer 2–10 consist of communal laments, such as Jer 4:29, which were written in the immediate aftermath of the Babylonian conquest of Jerusalem and bewail Judah's fate.[16] Over time, these laments were supplemented with a series of additions reflecting on the theological significance of the exile. The first of these redactional layers—the *Schuldübernahme* redaction—addresses Jerusalem in the second person feminine singular and lays the blame for the exile on Judah's persistent apostasy.[17] Levin and Biddle divide Jer 2:14–19 between the oldest form of the text and the *Schuldübernahme* redaction: verses 14–15 constitute a communal lament addressed to Israel in the third person masculine singular, while verses 16–19 contain several accusations of apostasy addressed toward a second-person feminine singular entity (verses 17 and 19).[18] If they are correct, then Jer 2:14–19 dates sometime after 586 BCE, several decades after the date range 620–610 BCE suggested by my historical analysis.

Levin and Biddle's conclusions raise one important question, however. If the two literary layers in Jer 2:14–19 reflect on the Babylonian exile, then why do they cast Assyria and Egypt rather than Babylon as Israel's primary antagonists? This discrepancy suggests that the literary development of Jer 2:14–19 that may have begun in the preexilic period was spurred, in part, by the events of the late seventh and early sixth centuries BCE. Undoubtedly, the advent of Egyptian control over Judah constituted a disaster on a par with the Babylonian exile and prompted the development of both communal lament and theological speculation on Judah's reduced status. Recognition of this possibility allows us to push the literary development of Jer 2:14–19 back into the preexilic period while keeping the series of redactional stages posited by Levin and Biddle intact. Alternatively, one could posit a slightly more complicated redactional history for Jer 2:14–19, in which an early communal lament about Assyrian aggression in verses 14–15 was updated to reflect the dawn of Egyptian hegemony with the addition of verses 16 and 18 and further modified by the inclusion of verses 17 and 19.

---

16. Levin, *Die Verheißung des neuen Bundes*, 156; Biddle, *Redaction History of Jeremiah 2:1–4:2*, 55, 82; see also Schmid, "Book of Jeremiah," 438–39.

17. Levin, *Die Verheißung des neuen Bundes*, 157–59; Biddle, *Redaction History of Jeremiah 2:1–4:2*, 57–58.

18. Levin, *Die Verheißung des neuen Bundes*, 157; Biddle, *Redaction History of Jeremiah 2:1–4:2*, 55.

Interpretation

If I am correct in dating Jer 2:14–19 to the first decade of Saite control over Judah, then the terms "Egypt," "Shihor," "Assyria," and "the Euphrates" most likely held a militaristic connotation for the earliest readers and auditors of this oracle. Both bodies of water mentioned in verse 18 would have been a familiar sight to Judahite soldiers fighting on behalf of the Saite pharaohs. According to Berossus (cited in Josephus's *Ag. Ap.* 1.137), Nebuchadnezzar captured Judahite prisoners of war at the battle of Carchemish in 605 BCE, which indicates that Judahite auxiliaries fought in the Egyptian army along the Euphrates River. Archaeological evidence, on the other hand, may attest to the presence of Judahite soldiers at Migdol on the banks of Shihor[19] during the Saite period.[20] As this evidence shows, Judahite soldiers fought and died in what is now northern Syria and the eastern delta of the Nile at the behest

---

19. Shihor (שחור) comes from Egyptian *šj-ḥr* "the waters of Horus" and referred to a fresh-water lagoon in the eastern Nile Delta that was guarded by several Egyptian border fortresses (Manfred Bietak, *Tell el-Dab'a II* [Vienna: Österreichischen Akademie der Wissenschaft Wien, 1975], 137; Manfred Bietak, "Comments on the 'Exodus,'" in *Egypt, Israel, and Sinai: Archaeological and Historical Relationships in the Biblical Period*, ed. Anson F. Rainey [New York: Syracuse University Press, 1987], 167; James K. Hoffmeier, *Ancient Israel in Sinai: The Evidence for the Authenticity of the Wilderness Tradition* [Oxford: Oxford University Press, 2005], 82). Many biblical scholars, however, treat שחור as a synonym for יאור "Nile" based on the juxtaposition of these two terms in Isa 23:3: "its revenue was the grain of Shihor, the harvest of the Nile" (זרע שחר קציר יאור תבואתה) (Nadav Na'aman, "The Shihor of Egypt and Shur That Is before Egypt," *TA* 7 [1980]: 96; Holladay, *Jeremiah 1*, 96; Jack R. Lundbom, *Jeremiah 1–20: A New Translation with Introduction and Commentary*, AB 21A [New Haven: Yale University Press, 1999], 273; Liwak, *Der Prophet und die Geschichte*, 171; Carroll, *Jeremiah*, 128; McKane, *Commentary on Jeremiah 1–25*, 38). Yet the parallelism between these two terms in Isaiah need not imply that they were synonymous any more than the parallelism between Gath and Ashkelon in 2 Sam 1:20 serves to identify these two cities. The two terms could easily refer to separate bodies of water that nourished Egypt's crops. Furthermore, all of the other references to שחור in the Hebrew Bible suggest that this term designated a lagoon in the eastern Nile Delta rather than the Nile itself. Joshua 13:3 locates the boundary of Canaan at שחור "which is east of Egypt"—that is, outside of the Egyptian heartland along the Nile valley—while 1 Chr 13:5 treats שחור as the southern boundary of Israel at its maximal extent. Because Migdol, the eastern-most Egyptian border fortress, sat on the banks of שחור, Shihor would have been a logical term for designating the boundary between Egypt and Canaan (Josh 13:3) or Israel (1 Chr 13:5) (Hoffmeier, *Ancient Israel in Sinai*, 104).

20. Oren, "Migdol," 13.

of their Egyptian overlords, where they would have quite literally drunk the waters of the Euphrates and the waters of Shiḥor.²¹ Jeremiah 2:14–19 reflects the experiences of these soldiers. And while the evidence only indicates the presence of Judahite soldiers in the Egyptian army after the fall of the Assyrian Empire in 610 BCE—i.e., after the most plausible date for the composition of Jer 2:14–19—Judahite soldiers were most likely integrated into the Egyptian army by 610 BCE at the latest. According to Dan'el Kahn, the Letter of Aristeas indicates that Judahite troops took part in one of Psamtik I's Nubian campaigns sometime between 620 and 610 BCE.²²

Based on this historical overview I suggest that verses 16–19 highlight the plight of non-elite Judahites under the Saite administration: while a few elite Judahites, like Pashḥur son of Immer, owed their power and prestige to Egypt, far more Judahites died on the banks of the Euphrates and Shiḥor to insure Egypt's security. The rhetorical question in verse 18, therefore, censures the Judahite elite for acquiring power and prestige at the cost of their compatriots' lives. The surrounding verses emphasize this point by depicting foreign domination as the result of apostasy, removing any possible excuse the Judahite elite could muster. According to verses 16 and 17, the Judahite elite created the conditions for Egyptian domination by abandoning Yahweh and now profit from this situation at the price of Judahite lives: "The people of Memphis and Daphnae too have broken your head. Have you not done this to yourselves by abandoning Yahweh your god?" In this regard, Jer 2:14–19 resembles other prophetic passages that side with the masses against the elite, such as Amos 2:6–8.

4.2. JEREMIAH 25:15–29: AN ORACLE OF LIBERATION

In its current form in the Masoretic Text, the "cup of wrath" oracle in Jer 25:15–29 proclaims judgment on the nations of the world:

---

21. Thus, I do not agree with McKane, Maier and Allen's suggestion that verse 18 critiques Judah for vacillating between Assyria and Egypt (McKane, *Commentary on Jeremiah 1–25*, 38; Michael P. Maier, *Ägypten—Israels Herkunft und Geschick: Studie über einen theo-politischen Zentralbegriff im hebräischen Jeremiabuch*, ÖBS 21 [Frankfurt: Peter Lang, 2002], 48; Leslie C. Allen, *Jeremiah: A Commentary*, OTL [Louisville: Westminster John Know, 2008], 4). Such a choice would have been historically impossible since Assyrian domination gave way to Egyptian sovereignty with the decline of the Neo-Assyrian Empire.

22. Kahn, "Judean Auxiliaries," 513–14.

Jeremiah 25:15–29

¹⁵ For thus said Yahweh, the god of Israel, to me, "Take this cup of wine—that is, wrath—from my hand and make all the nations to whom I am sending you drink it. ¹⁶ And they will drink and sway and go mad because of the sword I am sending among them." ¹⁷ So I took the cup from Yahweh's hand and made all the nations to whom he sent me drink: ¹⁸ Jerusalem and the cities of Judah and its kings and officials to make them a desolation and a waste, a curse, and an object of hissing like they are today; ¹⁹ Pharaoh king of Egypt, his servants, his officials, all his people ²⁰ and all the mixed people; all the kings of the land of Uz; all the kings of the land of the Philistines—Ashkelon, Gaza, Ekron, and the remnant of Ashdod; ²¹ Edom, Moab, and the Ammonites; ²² all the kings of Tyre and all the kings of Sidon and the kings of the island which is across the sea; ²³ Dedan, Tema, and Buz, all those with shaven temples; ²⁴ all the kings of Arabia; and all the kings of the mixed people who dwell in the desert; ²⁵ all the kings of Zimri, all the kings of Elam and all the kings of Media; ²⁶ all the kings of the north, near and far, one after the other—all the kingdoms of the earth which are upon the face of the earth. And the king of Sheshach shall drink after them. ²⁷ Then you will say to them, "Thus says Yahweh of Armies, the god of Israel, 'Drink, become drunk, and vomit! Fall over, never to rise because of the sword I am sending among you!'" ²⁸ And if they refuse to take the cup from your hand to drink, you will say to them, "Thus says Yahweh of Armies, 'You will certainly drink! ²⁹ Indeed, I am beginning to do evil to the city that is called by my name. Shall you remain innocent?! You will not remain innocent because I am summoning a sword against all the inhabitants of the earth,' says Yahweh of Armies."

¹⁵ כי כה אמר יהוה אלהי ישראל אלי קח את כוס היין החמה הזאת מידי והשקיתה אתו את כל הגוים אשר אנכי שלח אותך אליהם ¹⁶ ושתו והתגעשו והתהללו מפני החרב אשר אנכי שלח בינתם ¹⁷ ואקח את כוס מיד יהוה ואשקה את כל הגוים אשר שלחני יהוה אליהם ¹⁸ את ירושלם ואת ערי יהודה ואת מלכיה ואת שריה לתת אתם לחרבה לשמה לשרקה ולקללה כיום הזה ¹⁹ את פרעה מלך מצרים ואת עבדיו ואת שריו ואת כל עמו ²⁰ ואת כל הערב ואת כל מלכי ארץ העוץ ואת כל מלכי ארץ פלשתים ואת אשקלון ואת עזה ואת עקרון ואת שארית אשדוד ²¹ את אדום ואת מואב ואת בני עמון ²² ואת כל מלכי צר ואת כל מלכי צידון ואת מלכי האי אשר בעבר הים ²³ ואת דדן ואת תימא ואת בוז ואת כל קצוצי פאה ²⁴ ואת כל מלכי ערב ואת כל מלכי הערב השכנים במדבר ²⁵ ואת כל מלכי זמרי ואת כל מלכי עילם ואת כל מלכי מדי ²⁶ ואת כל מלכי הצפון הקרבים והרחקים איש אל אחיו ואת כל הממלכות הארץ אשר על פני האדמה ומלך ששך ישתה אחריהם ²⁷ ואמרת אליהם כה אמר יהוה צבאות אלהי ישראל שתו ושכרו וקיו ונפלו ולא תקומו מפני החרב אשר אנכי שלח ביניכם ²⁸ והיה כי ימאנו לקחת הכוס מידך לשתות ואמרת אליהם כה אמר יהוה צבאות שתו תשתו ²⁹ כי הנה בעיר אשר נקרא שמי עליה אנכי מחל להרע ואתם הנקה תנקו לא תנקו כי חרב אני קרא על כל ישבי הארץ נאם יהוה צבאות

The discrete list of nations in verses 18–25, however, belies the universal scope of this passage and suggests that the oracle originally referred to a specific historical context. The identification of this context remains debated due in part to the numerous text-critical and redactional issues affecting this passage.[23] In the following sections, I will undertake a new text-critical and redactional analysis of the oracle, demonstrating that the list of nations was initially limited to the territory of the Saite empire, its trading partners, and potential allies. I will then argue that the earliest form of the oracle dates to 605 BCE and expressed the hope that Babylon—symbolized by the cup of wine—would destroy the Saite empire and liberate Judah.

Textual and Redactional Criticism of the Oracle

The oracle opens with a divine command: "〚...〛 Thus said Yahweh, the god of Israel, 〚...〛, 'Take this cup of wine—that is, wrath—from my hand and make all the nations to whom I am sending you drink it.'"[24] In this regard, the oracle recalls other texts in the Hebrew Bible where the act of serving alcohol serves a metaphor for Yahweh's wrath, such as Isa 51:17, 22, Jer 49:12, 51:7, Ezek 23:31–34, Hab 2:16, Ps 11:6, 75:9, and Lam 4:21.[25] Of these passages, Jer 51:7 is particularly relevant for the interpretation of Jer 25:15–29 because it exhibits verbal parallels with Jer 25:16 (יתהללו, התהללו) and also belongs to the Jeremianic tradition. Intriguingly, this passage explicitly identifies Babylon with the cup used

---

23. Holladay, *Jeremiah 1*, 676; Jack R. Lundbom, *Jeremiah 21–36: A New Translation with Introduction and Commentary*, AB 21B (New Haven: Yale University Press, 2004), 588; McKane, *Commentary on Jeremiah 1–25*, 645; Igor Mikhailovich Diakonoff, "The Near East on the Eve of Achaemenian Rule (Jeremiah 25)," in *Variatio Delectat. Iran und der Westen: Gedenkschrift für Peter Calmeyer*, ed. Reinhard Dittman et al., AOAT 272 (Münster: Ugarit-Verlag, 2000), 228.

24. The Septuagint lacks a counterpart to the initial כי "for" and subsequent אלי "to me" found in the Masoretic Text of this verse (Carolyn J. Sharp, "'Take Another Scroll and Write': A Study of the LXX and MT of Jeremiah's Oracles against Egypt and Babylon," *VT* 47 [1997]: 510). The absence of כי suggests that a later scribe or editor added this word to the source text of the Masoretic Text in order to link the "cup of wrath" episode to the preceding oracles against Judah in Jer 25:1–14. Georg Fischer, *Jeremia 1–25*, HThKAT (Freiburg: Herder, 2005), 746.

25. For more information on this motif see William McKane, "Poison, Trial by Ordeal and the Cup of Wrath," *VT* 30 (1980): 474–92; Gisela Fuchs, "Das Symbol des Bechers in Ugarit und Israel: Vom 'Becher der Fülle' zum 'Zornesbecher,'" in *Verbindungslinien: Festschrift für Werner H. Schmidt zum 65. Geburtstag*, ed. Axel Graupner, Holger Delkurt, and Alexander B. Ernst (Neukirchen-Vlyun: Neukirchener, 2000), 65–84; and Theodor Seidl, *Der Becher in der Hand des Herrn: Studie zu den prophetischen "Taumelbecher"-Texten*, ATSAT 70 (St. Ottlien: EOS, 2001).

to punish the nations: "Babylon was a golden cup in Yahweh's hand, making all the world drunk. The nations drank of its wine; therefore, the nations went mad" (כוס זהב בבל ביד יהוה משכרת כל הארץ מיינה שתו גוים על כן יתהללו גוים). Based on this parallel, I argue that the cup of wine also represents Babylon in Jer 25:15–29, a conclusion that receives support from the omission of Babylon from the list of nations in its earliest form (see page 82–83 below).[26]

The Masoretic Text describes Yahweh's cup of wine using the grammatically difficult expression "this cup of wine—that is, wrath" (כוס היין החמה הזאת). As it stands, this phrase cannot mean "this cup of the wine of wrath," because היין bears the definite article and cannot govern החמה as the head of a construct chain. To elucidate this difficult construction, most commentators suggest that the word wrath (החמה) originally stood in apposition to the word wine (היין).[27] It is unclear, however, whether the word wrath represents an integral part of the verse or a later addition to the text. Maier and Schmidt argue for its originality, while Holladay and McKane treat it as a later addition. Whatever the case, the appositional use of the word wrath serves to identify the cup of wine with Yahweh's anger.

In verse 16, Yahweh explains the effect the cup of wine will have on its victims: "they will sway and go mad because of the sword I am sending among them" (והתגעשו והתהללו מפני החרב אשר אנכי שלח בינתם). The reference to a sword at this point is unexpected, especially since the verbs "to sway" (התגעשו) and "to go mad" (התהללו) describe the symptoms of drunkenness rather than terror.[28] According to a similar passage in Jer 51:7, the nations go mad (יתהללו) simply by drinking from the cup; Yahweh does not have recourse to a sword. Because of this discrepancy, I agree with McKane, Beat Huwyler, and Werner H. Schmidt that a later editor added the reference to the sword in verse 16 from verse 27, where the word for "sword" is well integrated into context.[29]

---

26. Smelik and Allen come to a similar conclusion (Smelik, "Function of Jeremiah 50 and 51," 93–94; Allen, *Jeremiah*, 290, 460).

27. GKC §131k; McKane, *Commentary on Jeremiah 1–25*, 641; Holladay, *Jeremiah 1*, 670; Huwyler, *Jeremia und die Völker*, 350; Maier, *Ägypten*, 252; Schmidt, *Das Buch Jeremia: Kapitel 1–20*, 66; Stipp, *Jeremia 25–52*, 67. Carroll and Driver, by contrast, adopt the reading of the Septuagint (τὸ ποτήριον τοῦ οἴνου τοῦ ἀκράτου τούτου "this cup of unmixed wine") and repoint הַחֵמָה as הַחֹמָה, a masculine participle from the root חמה "to be hot" denoting strong wine (Carroll, *Jeremiah*, 499; G. R. Driver, "Linguistic and Textual Problems: Jeremiah," *JQR* 28 [1937]: 119). This emendation is problematic, however, because the root חמה is not attested in Biblical Hebrew with this meaning.

28. Stipp, *Jeremia 25–52*, 68.

29. McKane, *Commentary on Jeremiah 1–25*, 636; Huwyler, *Jeremia und die*

4. Fulminating against the Pharaoh

In verse 17, Jeremiah carries out Yahweh's command and brings the cup of wine to the nations that are enumerated in verses 18–25. According to Holladay and Allen, the list of nations is a secondary addition to the oracle that developed over the course of the late seventh and early sixth centuries BCE and reflects the events of this time period.[30] But as Huwyler and Fischer rightly note, the phrase "all the nations to whom I send you" (את כל הגוים אשר אנכי שלח אותך אליהם) in verse 15 and the comparable expression "all the nations to whom Yahweh sent me" (את כל הגוים אשר שלחני יהוה אליהם) in verse 17 anticipates a discrete list of nations.[31] I would argue, therefore, that the list of nations is, in part, original to the oracle.

In both the Masoretic Text and the Septuagint, the list of nations opens with Judah, represented by "Jerusalem and the towns of Judah, its kings and its officials" (את ירושלם ואת ערי יהודה ואת מלכיה את שריה). The oracle further specifies that drinking from the cup will turn Judah into "a desolation and a waste, and an object of hissing [...] like today" (לחרבה לשמה לשרקה [...] כיום).[32] The phrase "like today" in verse 18 is missing from the Septuagint and presupposes a date in the exilic period.[33] Most likely, it represents a later addition to the Masoretic Text that was added during the Babylonian exile when Judah could rightly be described as "a desolation and a waste."

Many commentators go further and treat the inclusion of Judah at the beginning of the list as a later addition to the text as well. McKane, Carroll, and Maier, for example, argue that the use of the phrase "the nations" (הגוים) in verses 15 and 17 precludes the inclusion of Judah in verse 18 because the Hebrew word גוי can only refer to foreign nations.[34] As Aelred Cody points out in his study of the term גוי, however, גוי can refer to Judah when it is the object of judgment (e.g., Jer 5:9, 29; 7:28), which is the case here.[35] Nevertheless, there are several other clues that verse 18 is secondary. First and foremost, the form of this entry deviates from the common format employed throughout the list: all of the other entries in the list consist of either a general geographic designation (e.g., Moab) or a political designation such as "all the kings of [geographic

---

Völker, 351; Schmidt, *Das Buch Jeremia: Kapitel 1–20*, 66.

30. Holladay, *Jeremiah 1*, 670–72; Allen, *Jeremiah*, 289.

31. Huwyler, *Jeremia und die Völker*, 359; Fischer, *Jeremia 1–25*, 747.

32. The Septuagint lacks an equivalent of ולקללה "and a curse" (Janzen, *Studies in the Text of Jeremiah*, 45).

33. Janzen, *Studies in the Text of Jeremiah*, 45; Fischer, *Jeremia 1–25*, 762.

34. McKane, *Commentary on Jeremiah 1–25*, 637; Carroll, *Jeremiah*, 499; Maier, *Ägypten*, 255.

35. Aelred Cody, "When Is the Chosen People Called a *Gôy*?," *VT* 14 (1964): 1–2.

name]" or "Pharaoh king of Egypt." The entry for Judah, by contrast, identifies Judah through its constituent parts, "Jerusalem and the towns of Judah" (את ירושלם ואת ערי יהודה). This phrase recalls the parallelism between "Jerusalem" and "the towns of Judah" in the woe oracle preserved in Jer 9:10 and could represent an adaptation or borrowing from this passage: "I will make Jerusalem into heaps of ruins, the abode of jackals, and I will make Judah a wasteland, without inhabitant."[36] Second, none of the other entries describe the effect of Yahweh's cup of wine on its drinker, unlike verse 18. Third, the phrase "its kings and its officials" (ואת מלכיה את שריה) differs from similar expression found in the list.[37] Unlike the phrase "his servants and his officials" (ואת עבדיו ואת שריו) found in the entry for Egypt, "its kings and its officials" refers back to Jerusalem and the towns of Judah rather than the political leaders of the nation.

The Masoretic Text and Septuagint ring slight variations on the word ערב "mixed people," which appears in the entry for Egypt in verses 20 and 24. The Masoretic Text reads "all of the mixed people" (וְאֵת כָּל־הָעֶרֶב), while the Septuagint reflects a Hebrew source text that read "all his [= Pharaoh's] mixed people" (καὶ πάντας τοὺς συμμίκτους αὐτοῦ = וְאֵת כָּל־עַרְבּוֹ) in parallel with the phrases "his servants" (ואת עבדיו), "his officials" (ואת שריו), and "all his people" (ואת כל עמו). The reading of the Masoretic Text seems to have developed from the Septuagint reading through a two-step process of scribal error and correction. First, a scribe misread ואת כל ערב ואת כל מלכי ארץ ... ואת כל ערבו ואת כל מלכי ארץ as ... by skipping over the first ו of the words כל ערבו ואת. A later editor or scribe then corrected the semantically difficult expression "each mixed person" (כל ערב) to "all the mixed people" by inserting a definite article before ערב.[38]

In Biblical Hebrew, ערב refers to a variety of mixed populations, including the mixed multitude that accompanied the Israelites out of Egypt during the Exodus (Exod 12:38) and the resident foreigners in Jerusalem at the time of Nehemiah (Neh 13:3). Here, ערב most likely refers to the non-Egyptian mercenaries employed by the Saite pharaohs. Several of the versions understood this word in military terms. The Sep-

---

36. Huwyler identifies verse 18 as an explicitly Deueteronomistic addition to the oracle (Huwyler, *Jeremia und die Völker*, 352).

37. Huwyler plausibly suggests that the use of the plural reflects a synoptic view of Judah's history as seen from the perspective of the exile (Huwyler, *Jeremia und die Völker*, 352).

38. When כל modifies an indefinite noun, it takes a distributive sense that is semantically inappropriate in the context of Jer 25:19. Bruce K. Waltke and M. O'Connor, *An Introduction to Biblical Hebrew Syntax* (Winona Lake, IN: Eisenbrauns, 1990), 289.

4. Fulminating against the Pharaoh 77

tuagint translates ערב with σύμμικτος, a term that often refers to irregular troops, while Targum Jonathan simply renders ערב as סמכותא "troops." The term ערב also appears in a list of military personnel employed by the Saite pharaohs in Ezek 30:5: "Cush, Cyrene, Lydia, Lybia, and all of the mixed troops and the people of the allied land."[39]

The Masoretic Text includes "all the kings of the land of Uz" (ואת כל מלכי ארץ העוץ) in verse 20 after the description of Egypt in verse 19. Huwyler and Stipp suggest that this entry represents an insertion from Lam 4:21, which reads "Rejoice and be happy, O daughter Edom, who dwells in the land of Uz. To you as well, the cup will pass. You will become drunk and be stripped naked" (שישי ושמחי בת אדום יושבתי בארץ עוץ גם עליך תעבר כוס תשכרי ותתערי).[40] But if a later editor did copy this phrase from Lam 4:21, it is unclear why they would insert this phrase here rather than in verse 21 following the entry for Edom. Instead, I suggest that a later editor misinterpreted כל הערב in the Masoretic Text as "all the Arabs" and inserted a more specific term following this blanket designation.

The Septuagint and the Masoretic Text differ in their treatment of verse 22. The Septuagint reflects a consonantal source text that read "the kings who are across the sea" (βασιλεῖς τοὺς ἐν τῷ πέραν τῆς θαλάσσης = את מלכים אשר בעבר הים), while the Masoretic Text reads את מלכי האי בעבר הים "the kings of the island that is across the sea." Many scholars adopt the reading of the Septuagint and identify "the kings who are across the sea" as the rulers of the various Phoenician colonies dotting the Mediterranean basin.[41] But this identification creates a historical problem: other than Kition on Cyprus there is no evidence that the Phoenician colonies were involved in the events convulsing the ancient Near East in the late seventh and early sixth centuries BCE, and so it is unclear why the author of this oracle would have included them. Therefore, I would argue that the phrase "the kings who are across the sea" does not refer to the Phoenician colonies but rather to the island of Cyprus with its variegated political and linguistic landscape.[42] The Masoretic Text made

---

39. Following the Septuagint, which reflects a Hebrew source text that read ולוד ולוב וכל הערב (καὶ Λυδοὶ καὶ Λίβυες καὶ πάντες ἐπίμικτοι) as opposed to the jumbled reading of the Masoretic Text (ולוד וכל הערב וכוב). Most likely, the reading of the Masoretic Text resulted from the transposition of וכל הערב and ולוב and the mistaken writing of כוב for לוב under the influence of כל.

40. Huwyler, *Jeremia und die Völker*, 355; Stipp, *Jeremia 25–52*, 70.

41. McKane, *Commentary on Jeremiah 1–25*, 638; Holladay, *Jeremiah 1*, 674; Maier, *Ägypten*, 253; Diakonoff, "Near East," 225–26; Fischer, *Jeremiah 1–25*, 750; Stipp, *Jeremia 25–52*, 70.

42. For the political and linguistic diversity of Cyprus in the late seventh and early sixth centuries BCE, see Maria Iacovou, "Historically Elusive and In-

this identification more explicit by adding the word הָאִי after מלכים and by changing the absolute form מלכים to the construct. Alternatively, it is possible that the Masoretic Text preserves a better reading of verse 20 and that a later scribe accidentally omitted הָאִי from the Hebrew source text of Septuagint Jeremiah due to homoeoteleuton—i.e., by skipping from מלכי to אשר since מלכי and הָאִי end in the same consonant: מלכֵי הָאִי אשר > מלכי אשר. A later editor then corrected the grammatically anomalous expression מלכי אשר to מלכים אשר.[43]

The list of Arabian cities and desert dwelling groups in verses 23 and 24 also exhibits variation in the Masoretic Text and the Septuagint. The Masoretic Text reads "Dedan, Tema, Buz, and all who have shaven temples, all the kings of Arabia, and all of the kings of the mixed people who live in the desert" (ואת דדן ואת תימא ואת בוז ואת כל קצוצי פאה ואת כל מלכי ערב ואת כל מלכי הערב השכנים במדבר), while the Septuagint omits the phrase "all the kings of Arabia." Huwyler and Stipp suggest that this phrase represents either a summary statement secondarily attached to the list of Arabian cities in verse 23 or an accidental repetition of כל מלכי הערב.[44] But even without this phrase verse 23 shows signs of expansion. The entry for "all the kings of the mixed people" interrupts the stock phrase "all those who have shaven temples and live in the desert" (ואת כל קצוצי פאה השכנים במדבר), which appears in the list of uncircumcised nations in Jer 9:25 (cf. Jer 49:22).[45] This phenomenon suggests that the

---

ternally Fragile Island Polities: The Intricacies of Cyprus's Political Geography in the Iron Age," *BASOR* 370 (2013): 31–34; Iacovou, "Cyprus during the Iron Age through the Persian Period," 797–98.

43. During the late seventh and early sixth centuries BCE, the Phoenician city-states were distinct entities each ruled by a single king (Guy Bunnens, "Phoenicia in the Late Iron Age: Tenth Century BCE to the Assyrian and Babylonian Periods," in *The Oxford Handbook of the Phoenician and Punic Mediterranean*, ed. Brian R. Doak and Carolina López-Ruiz [Oxford: Oxford University Press, 2019], 67–69). It is unclear, therefore, why the author or compiler of the list described these geographic entities using the phrase "all the kings of" (את כל מלכי). Perhaps they assimilated Tyre and Sidon to Philistia, Cyprus, and Elam, which were home to multiple polities each ruled by a separate king (Iacovou, "Cyprus during the Iron Age through the Persian Period," 795; Elynn Gorris and Yasmina Wicks, "The Last Centuries of Elam: The Neo-Elamite Period," in *The Elamite World*, ed. Javier Álvarez-Mon, Gian Pitero Basello, and Yasmina Wicks [London: Routledge, 2018], 254, 256). Or perhaps the plural reflects the "theoretical" nature of the oracle, as Stipp suggests (*Jeremia 25–52*, 70).

44. Huwyler, *Jeremia und die Völker*, 355; Stipp, *Jeremia 25–52*, 70.

45. Herodotus also notes that the Arabs shaved their temples: "they say that they [the Arabians] cut their hair as Dionysus had his cut, cutting round about, and shaving the temples" (καὶ τῶν τριχῶν τὴν κουρὴν κείρεσθαι φασι κατά

4. Fulminating against the Pharaoh

phrase "all the kings of the mixed people" is itself an early textual addition. Based on this analysis, I reconstruct the earliest form of verses 23 and 24 as "Dedan, Tema, Buz: all who have shaven temples and live in the desert" and would treat the phrase "all the kings of the Arabs" as a marginal gloss on Dedan, Tema, and Buz that was later inserted into the text in the wrong place and accidentally repeated in the Masoretic Text tradition.

In verse 25, the Masoretic Text includes "all the kings of Zimri" (ואת כל מלכי זמרי) alongside the kings of Elam and Media. Scholars have explained the enigmatic name זמרי in one of two ways. It is either a mistake for גמרי, the gentilic for Cimmerian—a semi-nomadic Iranian population that inhabited the area north of the Caucus and the Black Sea[46]—or a mistake for זמכי, an *atbaš* cipher for Elam.[47] The first option presents several problems. For one, the name זמרי does not bear a definite article like a gentilic adjective normally would.[48] Furthermore, the Cimmerians suffered defeat at the hands of Alyattes king of Lydia in 626 BCE and subsequently disappeared from the historical record.[49] So either גמרי represents a seventh-century addition to an even earlier list of nations, or the Cimmerians continued to be politically relevant after 626 BCE but do not appear in the historical record. We can rule out the first possibility because the list of nations in Jer 25:15–29 does not mention Assyria and hence dates after the fall of the Neo-Assyrian Empire in 610 BCE.[50]

περ αὐτὸν τὸν Διόνυσον κεκάρθαι· κείρονται δὲ περιτρόχαλα, ὑποξυρῶντες τοὺς κροτάφους, Herodotus, *Hist.* 3.8).

46. Diakonoff, "Near East," 228.

47. Janzen, *Studies in the Text of Jeremiah*, 14; McKane, *Commentary on Jeremiah 1–25*, 639; Huwyler, *Jeremia und die Völker*, 355; Stipp, *Jeremia 25–52*, 71. Fischer treats זמרי as original, while Schmidt suggests that it designates Babylon (Fischer, *Jeremia 1–25*, 751; Schmidt, *Das Buch Jeremia: Kapitel 21–52*, 66). In an *atbaš* cipher, the first letter of the Hebrew alphabet maps onto the last letter, the second letter maps onto the penultimate letter, and so on.

48. GKC, §125e; Joüon, §137c; Waltke and O'Connor, *Introduction to Biblical Hebrew Syntax*, 245.

49. Askold Ivantchik, "Cimmerians," *EBR* 5:323.

50. One could argue that the news of Assyria's final downfall did not reach Judah until after 610 BCE, which would permit a later *terminus post quem* for Jer 25:15–29. But if my interpretation of Jer 2:14–19 is correct, then Judahite soldiers fought in the Egyptian army in an attempt to defend the remains of the Neo-Assyrian Empire from Babylonian and Median predation between 620 and 610 BCE. If Judahite soldiers fought at Harran in 610 BCE, they could have carried news of Assyria's demise back to Jerusalem within a short period of time.

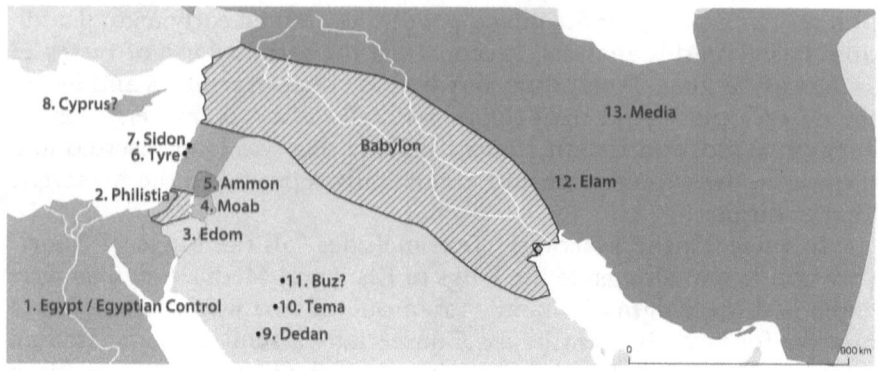

FIGURE 6 Geographic distribution of the nations included in the earliest form of Jeremiah 25:15–29 (the numbers 1 to 13 refer to the order in which the geographic locations are mentioned in the text)

Treating זמרי as a mistake for זמכי, an *atbaš* cipher for Elam, proves more plausible. Text-critically, it is easier to explain a change from זמכי to זמרי than a change from גמרי to זמרי since ר and כ are fairly similar in the Aramaic square script.[51] כ differs from ר only in the presence of a second horizontal stroke adjoining the vertical. A change from ג to ז, by contrast, would require several scribal mistakes in either the square script (ג > ז) or the paleo-Hebrew script (𐤂 > 𐤆).[52] Furthermore, it is easier to account for the addition of an *atbaš* cipher for Elam historically than a reference to the Cimmerians. A scribe or editor working in the Persian period may have interpreted Elam as a reference to the Persian Empire and thought it best to disguise the name of the ruling power with a cipher, which they wrote as a marginal gloss on Elam. A second editor could have then inserted the gloss into the text itself. We can perhaps date the emergence of this variant to the early Persian period since the earliest Persian kings most likely originated from an Elamo-Iranian milieu, as Wouter Henkelman has argued in detail.[53]

---

51. Alternatively, Allen suggests that זמכי was assimilated to the more common personal name זמרי (Allen, *Jeremiah*, 281).

52. Emanuel Tov does not include ג and ז in his list of commonly confused letters (Emanuel Tov, *Textual Criticism of the Hebrew Bible* [3rd rev. ed.; Minneapolis: Fortress Press, 2012], 228–31).

53. Wouter F. M. Henkelman, "Cyrus the Persian and Darius the Elamite: A Case of Mistaken Identity," in *Herodot und das Persische Weltreich: Akten des 3. Internationalen Kolloquiums zum Thema "Vorderasien im Spannungsfeld klassischer und altorientalischer Überlieferungen" Innsbruck, 24.–28. November 2008*, ed. Robert Rollinger, Brigitte Truschnegg, and Reinhold Bichler (Wiesbaden:

4. Fulminating against the Pharaoh

Verse 26 exhibits several textual and redactional problems. In the Masoretic Text, verse 26 opens with the summary statement "all the kings of the north, near and far, one after the other" (את כל מלכי הצפון הקרבים והרחקים), while in the Septuagint it begins with the phrase "all the kings of the east, far and near" (καὶ πάντας βασιλεῖς ἀπὸ ἀπηλιώτου τοὺς πόρρω καὶ τοὺς ἐγγύς). The correspondence between north and east here is unexpected. Hermann-Josef Stipp attributes this discrepancy to the geographic location of this passage's translator, who adjusted verse 26a in order to cater to the Egyptian audience for whom they produced their translation.[54] This explanation proves problematic, however. Because any nation to the north of Judah also lay to the north of Egypt, the translator would not need to adjust their translation to reflect the geographic position of their audience. Furthermore, it is unclear why the Septuagint translators would adjust Jer 32:26a but not any of the twenty-three other verses in their Hebrew source text that contained the word "north" (צפון) (Jer 1:13, 14, 15; 3:12, 18; 4:6; 6:1, 22; 10:22; 13:20; 15:12; 16:15; 23:8; 25:9; 31:8; 46:6, 10, 20, 24; 47:2; 50:3, 9, 41).

To solve this problem, I suggest that verse 26a originally read "all the kings of the east and all the kings of the north" (ואת כל מלכי הקדם ואת כל מלכי צפון), reflecting the predominantly west-to-east and south-to-north progression of the nations in the earliest reconstructible form of the oracle (see fig. 6).[55] According to the geographic ordering of the list, which proceeds north and east from Egypt, any kingdoms omitted from the list would lie either to the east of Elam or to the north of the Phoenician city-states. Subsequently, a later scribe omitted the phrase "all the kings of the east" from the Masoretic Text by skipping from the first ואת כל מלכי to ואת כל מלכי הצפון due to the similarity of the phrases ואת כל מלכי הקדם and ואת כל מלכי הצפון. The translator of Septuagint Jer 25 or a later scribe made a similar error with "all the kings of the north" in the Septuagint. Alternatively, it is possible that the correspondence between north and east in the different versions of verse 26a is simply a quirk of translation since the Septuagint does not always render Hebrew directional terms correctly. Genesis 28:14 LXX, for example, translates "east" (קדמה) as

---

Harrassowitz, 2011), 584–86. To cite one possible example of Elamite influence on the Persian court, the name Cyrus (*kuraš*) has a plausible Elamite etymology, "(DN) has protected." For a similar dating of verse 25, see Huwyler, *Jeremia und die Völker*, 356.

54. Hermann-Josef Stipp, *Studien zum Jeremiabuch: Text und Redaktion*, FAT 96 (Tübingen: Mohr Siebeck, 2015), 193.

55. Fischer and Stipp note that the nations mentioned in Jer 25 follow a roughly west-to-east order (Fischer, *Jeremia 1–25*, 748; Stipp, *Jeremia 25–52*, 74). Fischer also makes a similar observation concerning the oracles against the nations in Jer 46–51 (Fischer, "Jer 25 und die Fremdvölkersprüche," 494).

"south" (λίβα) and "south" (נגבה) as "east" (ἀνατολάς). Yet the rarity of the correspondence between the Hebrew term for "north" (צפון) and the Greek term for "east" (ἀπηλιώτης) argues against this possibility. In only one other case—Exod 27:11—does the Septuagint translate צפון as ἀπηλιώτης, motivated most likely by the use of the multivalent directional term λίψ "south, west" two verses earlier.[56] Without the presence of λίψ or a similarly multivalent term in verse 26a to confuse later scribes, scribal error remains the most likely solution to this problem.

Verse 26b contains a second summary statement that extends the scope of Yahweh's judgment from a limited set of nations to the entire world: as his final act, Jeremiah must bring the cup of wrath to "all of the kingdoms 〚...〛 that are upon the earth."[57] This statement stands at odds with the rest of the oracle. If the cup of wrath were originally intended for "all the kingdoms 〚...〛 that are upon the earth," there would be no need to enumerate specific nations in verses 18–25. It also renders the summary statement "all the kings of the east and all the kings of the north," which serves as a catch-all for any nations omitted from the oracle's "world map" in verse 26a, superfluous. For these reasons, I follow Stipp in seeing verse 26b as a later addition to the oracle.[58]

The Masoretic Text of verse 26 includes an additional nation that is not found in the Septuagint: "and after them the king of Sheshach will drink" (ומלך ששך ישתה אחריהם).[59] Several shifts in content and grammar mark this phrase as a later addition to the Masoretic Text, including a change from the first person to the third person and change in genre from execution to prediction.[60] The placement of the phrase after the dueling summary statements in verses 26a and 26b also supports this conclusion.

The name Sheshach is an *atbaš* cipher for Babylon, the significance of which remains debated. Some scholars treat it as a cipher intended to disguise a sharp critique of Babylon, while others identify it as a play on words used for rhetorical or magical effect, discombobulating the Mesopotamian empire just as the letters of its name were rearranged.[61]

---

56. LSJ, 188, 1055; GELS, 68, 432.

57. Omitting the grammatically anomalous הארץ "the land" with the Septuagint (Hermann-Josef Stipp, *Das masoretische und alexandrinische Sondergut des Jeremiabuches: Textgeschichtlicher Rang, Eigenarten, Triebkräfte*, OBO 136 [Göttingen: Vandenhoeck & Ruprecht], 68).

58. Stipp, *Jeremia 25–52*, 73.

59. Janzen, *Studies in the Text of Jeremiah*, 122; Stipp, *Das masoretische und alexandrinische Sondergut*, 85.

60. McKane, *Commentary on Jeremiah 1–25*, 641.

61. Lundbom argues that the *atbaš* cipher in verse 26 represents a play on words rather than a cryptogram because Jer 25:9, 11, and 12 all mention Baby-

4. Fulminating against the Pharaoh

Either way, the reference to Babylon at the end of verse 26 most likely represents a later addition made during the exilic period when Babylon ruled much of the ancient Near East.[62] It reflects the belief, common to Jer 25:1–14 and Jer 27:1–11, that Babylonian control over Judah would eventually come to an end and Babylon would receive its just deserts.

The final three verses of the "cup of wrath" oracle in Jer 25:27–29 address the possibility that the nations could simply refuse to drink from the cup of wrath and thereby avoid punishment:

Jeremiah 25:27–29

[27] You will say to them, "Thus says Yahweh of Armies, the god of Israel, 'Drink, become drunk, and vomit! Fall over, never to rise because of the sword I am sending among you!'" [28] And if they refuse to take the cup from your hand to drink, you will say to them, "Thus says Yahweh of Armies, 'You will certainly drink! [29] Indeed, I am beginning to do evil to the city that is called by my name—shall you remain innocent?! You will not remain innocent because I am summoning a sword against all the inhabitants of the earth,' says Yahweh of Armies."

[27] ואמרת אליהם כה אמר יהוה צבאות אלהי ישראל שתו ושכרו וקיו ונפלו ולא תקומו מפני החרב אשר אנכי שלח ביניכם [28] והיה כי ימאנו לקחת הכוס מידך לשתות ואמרת אליהם כה אמר יהוה צבאות שתו תשתו [29] כי הנה בעיר אשר נקרא שמי עליה אנכי מחל להרע ואתם הנקה תנקו לא תנקו כי חרב אני קרא על כל ישבי הארץ נאם יהוה צבאות

In terms of both grammar and content, these verses diverge from the preceding unit. Grammatically, the *we-qatal* verb ואמרת that opens verse 27 cannot continue the string of consecutive preterit verbs found in verse 17. Thematically, verses 27–29 represent a switch in content from the fulfillment of Yahweh's initial command to the articulation of a new directive. They also expand Yahweh's judgment from a set list of nations to "all the inhabitants of the earth" like verse 26b and link the fate of the nations to Judah's fortunes. In this regard, verses 27–29 presuppose the inclusion of Judah among the list of nations in verse 18,

---

lon openly (Lundbom, *Jeremiah 21–36*, 260). Note, however, that these verses lack the word Babylon in the Septuagint—which means that they did not address Babylon openly in their original form—and belong to a separate textual unit within chapter 25 that may reflect a period of composition outside of the Neo-Babylonian period. Carroll and Fischer, by contrast, argue that the cipher was intended to have a "magical effect" on Babylon (Carroll, *Jeremiah*, 503; Fischer, *Jeremia 1–25*, 753).

62. Stipp dates this addition to the postexilic period, but questions why a later redactor would disguise Babylon under a cryptogram since it was no longer politically relevant (Stipp, *Jeremia 25–52*, 73).

which itself represents a later addition to the oracle, as I have argued above. Based on this evidence, I suggest that the author of verses 27–29 also added verses 18 and 26b to the list of nations.[63] Such a hypothesis represents the most parsimonious reconstruction of the oracle's redaction history, but—of course—it is always possible that verses 18, 26b, and 27–29 represent independent additions to the oracle.

Taking these text-critical and redactional considerations into account, I reconstruct the earliest form of the "cup of wrath" oracle as follows:

Jeremiah 25:15–26

[15] 〚...〛 Thus said Yahweh, the god of Israel, 〚...〛, "Take this cup of wine—that is, wrath—from my hand and make all the nations to whom I am sending you drink it. [16] And they will drink and sway and go mad 〚...〛" [17] So I took the cup from Yahweh's hand and made all the nations to whom he sent me drink: [18] 〚...〛 [19] Pharaoh king of Egypt, his servants, his officials, all his people [20] and all his mixed troops; 〚...〛, all the kings of the land of the Philistines: Ashkelon, Gaza, Ekron, and the remnant of Ashdod; [21] Edom, Moab, and the Ammonites; [22] all the kings of Tyre and all the kings of Sidon and the kings 〚...〛 who are across the sea; [23] Dedan, Tema, and Buz: all those with shaven temples 〚...〛 who dwell in the desert; 〚...〛 all the kings of Elam and all the kings of Media; [26] {all the kings of the east} and all the kings of the north, near and far, one after the other 〚...〛

[15] 〚...〛 כה אמר יהוה אלהי ישראל 〚...〛 קח את כוס היין החמה הזאת מידי והשקיתה אתו את כל הגוים אשר אנכי שלח אותך אליהם [16] ושתו והתגעשו והתהללו 〚...〛 [17] ואקח את כוס מיד יהוה ואשקה את כל הגוים אשר שלחני יהוה אליהם [18] 〚...〛 [19] את פרעה מלך מצרים ואת עבדיו ואת שריו ואת כל עמו [20] ואת כל ערבו 〚...〛 ואת כל מלכי ארץ פלשתים ואת אשקלון ואת עזה ואת עקרון ואת שארית אשדוד [21] את אדום ואת מואב ואת בני עמון [22] ואת כל מלכי צר ואת כל מלכי צידון ואת מלכים אשר בעבר הים [23] ואת דדן ואת תימא ואת בוז ואת כל קצוצי פאה [24] ואת 〚...〛 השכנים במדבר [25] 〚...〛 ואת כל מלכי עילם ואת כל מלכי מדי [26] {ואת כל מלכי הקדם} ואת כל מלכי הצפון הקרבים והרחקים איש אל אחיו ואת כל הממלכות 〚...〛 אשר על פני האדמה

The earliest reconstructible form of the text consisted of verses 15 (minus the word החמה), 16a, 17, and 19–26a. During the Babylonian exile, a later redactor added verses 18, 26b, and 27–29 to the oracle in order to tie the fate of the nations to Judah's suffering, which, in turn, prompted the reference to a sword in verse 16b. The encrypted reference to Babylon in verse 26c also presupposes a date in the exilic period but was not neces-

---

63. According to Stipp, this addition served to explain why the original oracle had not fully come to pass (Stipp, *Jeremia 25–52*, 66).

4. Fulminating against the Pharaoh 85

sarily added to the oracle at the same time as verses 18, 26b, and 27–29. The list of nations also underwent several expansions, one of which—the insertion of an *atbaš* cipher for Elam in verse 25—can perhaps be traced to the early Persian period.

Dating

Ultimately, the list of nations provides several clues as to the dating of the "cup of wrath" oracle as a whole. The absence of Assyria suggests that the list was composed after 610 or 609 BCE. Following the sack of Harran in 610 BCE and the failure of the Assyrian army to retake the city in 609 BCE, Assyria ceased to be an independent political entity and no longer merited a place in the oracle's world map. Furthermore, the arrangement and composition of the list itself suggests a date before the winter of 604 BCE. The first seven entries belong to the Saite empire at its greatest territorial extent[64] before Nebuchadnezzar cap-

---

64. See the previous chapter for evidence of Saite control over the Philistine and Phoenician city-states. Evidence for Saite hegemony over Edom, Moab, and Ammon is harder to come by due to a more general lack of data from late seventh and early sixth-century BCE sites in the Transjordan. Only two such sites have yielded Egyptian artifacts from the Saite period, Tell el-Mazar and Leḥun (Khair Yassine, *Tell el Mazar I: Cemetery A* [Amman: University of Jordan Press, 1984], 108–10; Denyse Homès-Fredericq, "Late Bronze and Iron Age Evidence from Lehun in Moab," in *Early Edom and Moab: The Beginning of the Iron Age in Southern Jordan*, ed. Piotr Bienkowski, SAM 7 [Sheffield: Sheffield Academic Press, 1992], 198; P. M. Michèle Daviau, "In the Shadow of a Giant: Egyptian Influence in Transjordan during the Iron Age," in *Walls of the Prince. Egyptian Interactions with Southwest Asia in Antiquity: Essays in Honour of John S. Holladay, Jr.*, ed. Timothy P. Harrison, Edward B. Banning, and Stanley Klassen [Leiden: Brill, 2015], 239, 245). Despite this lack of evidence, we can reasonably infer that Edom, Moab, and Ammon belonged to the Saite empire because they had previously been Neo-Assyrian vassals and Psamtik I assumed control over Neo-Assyrian territorial holdings in the Levant in the mid-seventh century BCE (Randall W. Younker, "Ammon during the Iron II Period," in *The Oxford Handbook of the Archaeology of the Levant c. 8000–332 BCE*, ed. Margreet L. Steiner and Ann E. Killebrew [Oxford: Oxford University Press, 2014], 760; Margreet L. Steiner, "Moab during the Iron II Period," in *The Oxford Handbook of the Archaeology of the Levant c. 8000–332 BCE*, ed. Margreet L. Steiner and Ann E. Killebrew [Oxford: Oxford University Press, 2014], 779; Piotr Bienkowski, "Edom during the Iron II Period," in *The Oxford Handbook of the Archaeology of the Levant c. 8000–332 BCE*, ed. Margreet L. Steiner and Ann E. Killebrew [Oxford: Oxford University Press, 2014], 791). Control over Edom, Moab, and Ammon would also grant the Saite pharaohs access to the rich trade routes flowing out of the Arabian Peninsula and so it would be surprising from a strategic point of view

tured the Philistine city-states and secured the allegiance of Judah, Tyre, and Sidon in 604 BCE.[65] Given the geographic ordering of the list, this arrangement is unlikely to be an accident. And while the Saite pharaohs did manage to recapture Gaza, Tyre, and Sidon over the course of the early sixth century BCE, they never secured full control of the Levant again. Thus, I would argue that both the list of nations and the earliest form of the oracle as a whole were composed before the winter of 604 BCE at a time when Babylonian victory seemed imminent. More specifically, I would point to the Egyptian defeat at Carchemish in 605 BCE as a possible impetus for the composition of the oracle.[66] Because Judahite soldiers fought on the Egyptian side at the battle of Carchemish, news of Nekau II's devastating defeat could have reached Judah within a matter of weeks.

As in the case of Jer 2:14–19, the historically based dating of Jer 25:15–29 offered above conflicts with redaction-critical approaches to dating this passage. Huwyler, for example, posits three main stages in the development of Jer 25:15–29: an original core consisting of verses 15–17 and a list of the geographically identified nations (e.g., Ashkelon, Gaza, etc.), a preliminary redaction that expanded the list of nations to include several politically identified entities (e.g., all the kings of the Philistines, all the kings of Tyre, etc.), and a Deuteronomistic redaction comprising verses 18 and 26–29.[67] According to Huwyler, the oldest form of the text must postdate 605 BCE because Judah did not experience the sort of military defeat symbolized by the cup of wrath until Nebuchadrezzar's Levantine campaign of 604 BCE.[68] The preliminary redaction, on the other hand, dates to the Achaemenid period because it presupposes a time when Elam (= Persia) and Media were a single kingdom and could be juxtaposed in verse 25.[69] If Huwy-

---

if Psamtik I did not assume control over the Transjordanian polities (Schipper, "Egypt and the Kingdom of Judah," 214; Schipper, "Egyptian Imperialism after the New Kingdom," 283–84).

65. Diakonoff and Stipp, by contrast, suggest that the original list of nations corresponded to the territory of the Babylonian Empire (Diakonoff, "Near East," 228; Stipp, *Jeremia 25–52*, 72). But the Babylonian Empire did not include Egypt, Cyprus, Dedan, Elam or Media, and Babylon itself does not appear among the list of affected nations in the earliest reconstructible form of the oracle.

66. So too Stipp, *Jeremia 25–52*, 72.

67. Huwyler, *Jeremia und die Völker*, 354, 357–58.

68. Huwyler, *Jeremia und die Völker*, 359.

69. Huwyler, *Jeremia und die Völker*, 56. Similarly, McKane and Schmidt argue that the reference to the Medes in verse 25 presupposes a date for the "cup of wrath" oracle in the Persian period, but it is important to distinguish

ler's analysis proves correct, then the earliest form of the "cup of wrath" oracle cannot provide a snapshot of the Saite empire around 605 BCE as I have claimed.

Huwyler's analysis suffers from several problems, however. For one, it is unclear why Judah's historical experiences are relevant for dating the earliest form of the text because—according to Huwyler's own redactional schema—the reference to Judah in verse 18 is part of a later Deuteronomistic redaction.[70] And if Judah did not appear in the earliest form of the text, then there is no obstacle to dating the literary core of the "cup of wrath" oracle to 605 BCE. Second, the simple juxtaposition of Elam and Media in verse 25 does not necessarily indicate that they were united into a single kingdom identifiable with the Achaemenid Empire. The only other time that Elam and Media appear in parallel in the Hebrew Bible is in Isa 21:2, which forms part of an early seventh-century BCE oracle against Sennacherib.[71] Persian and post-Persian period texts, by contrast, use the phrase "Persia and Media" (פרס ומדי) to refer to the Achaemenid Empire.[72] Third, it is unclear whether Huwyler's preliminary redaction is even a redaction at all. The geographically and politically identified nations could stem from different sources used in composing verses 19–25 rather than different redactional layers. As I have shown, the combination of politically and geographically identified nations in Jer 25:19–25 forms a coherent, geographically arranged whole. Splitting this section into two redactional stages destroys this arrangement. In light of these difficulties, the Saite period represents the most likely date for the earliest version of the "cup of wrath" oracle.

Interpretation

Read in light of Saite history and of the battle of Carchemish in 605 BCE in particular, the "cup of wrath" oracle presents an anti-Egyptian, pro-Babylonian message. In particular, it depicts Babylon destroying

---

the Medes from the later Achaemenids (McKane, *Commentary on Jeremiah 1–25*, 645; Werner H. Schmidt, *Das Buch Jeremia: Kapitel 21–52*, ATD 21 [Göttingen: Vandenhoeck & Ruprecht, 2013], 69).

70. Huwyler, *Jeremia und die Völker*, 359.

71. J. J. M. Roberts, *First Isaiah*, Hermeneia (Minneapolis: Fortress Press, 2015), 277; cf. Joseph Blenkinsopp, *Isaiah 1–39*, AB 19 (Yale: Yale University Press, 2000), 326.

72. In the book of Esther, this phrase is always governed by a single *nomen regens* (e.g., שרי פרס ומדי "officials of Persia and Media" in Esth 1:14). If the preliminary redaction of Jer 25:14–29 did date to the Persian period, we would expect verse 25 to read את כל מלכי עילם ואת כל מלכי ומדי rather than את כל מלכי עילם ואת כל מלכי מדי.

the Saite empire, its trading partners, and potential allies, and liberating Judah from Egyptian control. To substantiate this argument, I will show that the cup of wine most likely represents Babylon, that the earliest lists of nations in Jer 19–25 are all related to Saite Egypt in some way, and that the absence of Judah from this list is meaningful.

The "cup of wrath" oracle does not explicitly identify the cup of wine with a particular individual or nation. Judging from the parallels between Jer 25:15–16 and 51:7, however, the cup of wine most likely symbolizes Babylon in its role as Yahweh's instrument of punishment. In both passages, the cup of wine causes the nations to become drunk and go mad, but Jer 51:7 identifies this cup with Babylon:

Jeremiah 25:15–16

[15] ⟦...⟧ Thus said Yahweh, the god of Israel, to me, "Take this cup of wine—that is, wrath—from my hand and make all the nations to whom I am sending you drink it. [16] And they will drink and sway and go mad."

[15] ⟦...⟧ כה אמר יהוה אלהי ישראל אלי קח את כוס היין החמה הזאת מידי והשקיתה אתו
את כל הגוים אשר אנכי שלח אותך אליהם [16] ושתו והתגעשו והתהללו

Jeremiah 51:7

Babylon was a golden cup in Yahweh's hand, making all the world drunk. The nations drank of its wine; therefore, the nations went mad.

כוס זהב בבל ביד יהוה משכרת כל הארץ מיינה שתו גוים על כן יתהללו גוים

In this way, the oracle depicts Babylon meting out punishment on the nations enumerated in verses 19–25.

These nations were all related to the Saite empire in some way. Egypt itself appears first in the list and receives the most detailed description of any individual nation. Where the other entries in the list consist of simple place names or the phrase "all the kings of [geographic name]," the entry for Egypt includes various political and military figures alongside "Pharaoh king of Egypt"—namely, "his servants, his officials, his people, and his mixed troops." Furthermore, almost all of the remaining nations were relevant to the Saite pharaohs' strategic interests in some way. Gaza, Ashkelon, Ashdod, Ekron, Edom, Moab, Ammon, Tyre, and Sidon were all Egyptian vassals during the late seventh century BCE, whose territory provided access to the trade routes of the Aegean and the Arabian Peninsula and a buffer against Babylonian aggression. Together with Judah and Egypt itself, they formed the bulk of the Saite empire. The kings who are across the sea as well as Dedan, Tema, and

Buz correspond to Egypt's Aegean and Arabian trading partners, while Elam and Media could represent potential allies of the Saite pharaohs.[73] Although the Median king Cyaraxes helped Nabopolassar defeat the Assyrians, he also carved out an empire of his own in northern Mesopotamia, effectively pinning Babylon between Median and Egyptian territory.[74] The inclusion of Elam and Media in the oracle could express the fear that the Medes would eventually turn on the Babylonians and prevent them from defeating Egypt.

The list of nations does not include every kingdom that was relevant to the Saite pharaohs' strategic interests, however. Judah is conspicuously absent from the group of Saite vassal states in verses 20–22.[75] This omission is difficult to explain. Stipp suggests that the oracle omitted Judah because it was still possible for the inhabitants of Judah to repent and avoid punishment.[76] But it is unclear why Judah as a whole would merit punishment alongside Egypt, its trading partners, and potential allies. Members of the Judahite elite were certainly complicit in the Saite pharaohs' oppressive policies, but the destruction of the Saite empire described in the oracle would remove them from power without unnecessary collateral damage. I suggest, therefore, that Judah does not appear in the earliest form of the oracle because the author of this text saw the Babylonians as liberators rather than conquerors. Nebuchadnezzar himself cultivated this image in some of the inscriptions he left in the Levant. In his Wadi Brisa Inscription, for example, he boasts that

> [my armies] expelled its [= Lebanon's] enemy above and below and I made the land happy
>
> [^{lu_2}ERIN$_2^{meš}$-ya] na-ka-ar-šu e-li-iš ù ša-ap-li-iš as-su-uḫ-ma li-ib-ba ma-a-ti ⌈ú-ṭi$_4$-ib⌉

and

> I caused the people of Lebanon to lie down in green pastures and did not permit anyone to frighten them. So that no one may oppress them, I installed a statue of my eternal kingship.

---

73. Gorris and Wicks, "Last Centuries of Elam," 255.
74. Wiseman, *Chronicles of Chaldaean Kings*, 10, 14, 44–45; Grayson, *Assyrian and Babylonian Chronicles*, 93.
75. These nations were added in subsequent redactions, as mentioned above.
76. Stipp, *Jeremia 25–52*, 72.

UN^meš qé-re-eb ^kurla-ab-na-nu a-bu-ri-iš ú-šar-bi-iṣ-ma ⌜mu⌝-ga-al-li-tu la u-šar-ši-ši-[na-ti] aš-šum ma-na-ma la ḫa-ba-li-[ši-na] [ṣ]a-lam šar-ru-ti-ya da-rí-⌜a⌝-[ti] [ú-ša]-⌜aṣ-bi-it⌝[77]

The author of the "cup of wrath" oracle may have held a similar attitude toward Babylonian military intervention: there was no need to include Judah in the list of affected nations, because it was being freed, not punished. If the Babylonians did succeed in defeating the Egyptians, then the average Judahite would no longer be subject to conscription and corvée labor.

The "cup of wrath" oracle offers a populist spin on the pro-Babylonian message that pervades the book of Jeremiah. Later texts like Jer 27 and 38 present submission to Babylon as a fundamentally pragmatic choice: in these texts, Jeremiah urges the Judahite elite to surrender to Babylon in order to save the city and its inhabitants from destruction, for example, in Jer 38:2: "the one who remains in this city shall die by the sword, by famine and by pestilence, but the one who goes out to the Chaldeans shall live. They will have their life as a prize of war and live" (הישב בעיר הזאת ימות בחרב ברעב ובדבר והיצא אל הכשדים יחיה והיתה לו נפשו לשלל וחי). The "cup of wrath" oracle, by contrast, has its roots in an earlier, more optimistic reading of international politics. If my interpretation of the text proves correct, then it presents Babylon as the key to escaping the injustices of Egyptian rule and is animated by a spirit of liberation rather than self-preservation.[78] The oracles against Egypt in Jer 46:2–26—to which I now turn—develop this idea further.

4.3. JEREMIAH 46:2–26: CELEBRATING EGYPT'S DOWNFALL

Like the "cup of wrath" oracle, the oracles against Egypt in Jer 46:2–26 celebrate Babylonian victory over Egypt and cast Babylon as a potential liberator. But while the "cup of wrath" oracle focuses on a singular historical moment, Jer 46:2–26 reflects a variety of historical situations within the broader Saite period. The first oracle in verses 3–12 applauds the Babylonian victory at the battle of Carchemish in 605 BCE, while the second oracle in verses 14–24 predicts that Nebuchadnezzar's first invasion of Egypt in 601 BCE would result in an overwhelming Babylonian victory. Verses 25–26 contain a patchwork of prophetic

---

77. Da Riva, *Inscriptions of Nebuchadnezzar at Brisa*, 62–63.

78. It is unclear why the author of this passage put so much faith in yet another imperial power. Perhaps they wagered that Babylonian control would be less oppressive to the average Judahite than the Saite regime.

4. Fulminating against the Pharaoh

material—ranging in date from 601 to 568 BCE—which comments on the first and third Babylonian invasions of Egypt. Although these passages may stem from different historical moments, they all reflect the idea that Babylon could serve as a counterweight to the Saite pharaohs and lessen the burden of Saite policies on Judah.

In their current form in the Masoretic Text, the oracles against Egypt read as follows:

Jeremiah 46:2-26

[2] Concerning Egypt. Concerning the army of Pharaoh king of Egypt that was by the river Euphrates in Carchemish, which Nebuchadnezzar king of Babylon smote in the fourth year of Jehoiakim son of Josiah king of Judah: [3] Ready buckler and shield and advance for battle! [4] Harness the horses and mount the steeds! Take your stations in your helmets! Whet your lances and don your coats of mail! [5] Why do I see them terrified and turning back? Their warriors are beaten and flee swiftly. They do not turn—terror is all around—oracle of Yahweh. [6] The swift cannot flee and the warrior cannot escape. In the north by the river Euphrates they have stumbled and fallen. [7] Who is this that rises like the Nile, like rivers whose waters surge? [8] Egypt rises like the Nile, like rivers that surge with water. It said, "Let me rise, let me cover the earth, let me destroy cities and their inhabitants." [9] Advance, O horses! And dash madly, O chariots! Let the warriors go forth: Cush and Cyrene, who grasp the shield, and the Lydians, who wield the bow. [10] That day is a day of vengeance for my lord Yahweh of Armies to take vengeance on his foes. The sword will eat and be sated and drink its fill of their blood for my lord Yahweh of Armies holds a sacrifice in the land of the north by the river Euphrates. [11] Go up to Gilead and take balm, O virgin daughter Egypt! In vain you multiply medicines, but there is no healing for you. [12] The nations have heard of your shame and the earth is full of your cry, for warrior has stumbled upon warrior and both have fallen together.

[13] The word that Yahweh spoke to Jeremiah the prophet about the coming of Nebuchadnezzar king of Babylon to strike the land of Egypt:

[14] Declare in Egypt and proclaim in Migdol, proclaim in Memphis and say in Daphnae: "take a stand and be firm, because a sword will devour all around you!" [15] Why has your mighty one been swept away? He did not stand because Yahweh pushed him. [16] Stumbling increased. Each man said to his companion, "Arise! Let us return to our people, to the land of our birth because of the oppressor's sword." [17] Give Pharaoh king of Egypt the name "Loudmouth Who Lets the Appointed Time Pass By." [18] As I live, says the king—Yahweh of Armies is his name—he is coming like Tabor among the mountains and like Carmel on the sea.

¹⁹ Pack your bags for exile, O prostrate daughter Egypt! For Memphis will become a waste, a ruin without inhabitant. ²⁰ Egypt is a beautiful heifer. An insect from the north lands on her. ²¹ Even her mercenaries in her midst are like fatted calves. Indeed, they too have turned and fled together. They did not stand because the day of their calamity has come upon them, the time of their punishment. ²² Her voice goes forth like a snake, for they come with an army and they bring axes against her like hewers of trees. ²³ They cut down her forest, says Yahweh, even though it is impenetrable, for they are more numerous than locusts. They are without number. ²⁴ Daughter Egypt is put to shame. She is given into the hand of a people from the north. ²⁵ Yahweh of Armies, the god of Israel, said, "I am about to punish Amun from Thebes and Pharaoh and Egypt and its gods and its kings and Pharaoh and those who trust in him. ²⁶ And I will give them into the hand of those who seek their life, into the hand of Nebuchadnezzar king of Babylon and into the hand of his servants. But afterwards she will be inhabited as in the days of old," says Yahweh.

² למצרים על חיל פרעה נכו מלך מצרים אשר היה על נהר פרת בכרכמש אשר הכה נבוכדראצר מלך בבל בשנת הרביעית ליהויקים בן יאשיהו מלך יהודה ³ ערכו מגן וצנה וגשו למלחמה ⁴ אסרו הסוסים ועלו הפרשים והתיצבו בכובעים מרקו הרמחים לבשו הסרינת ⁵ מדוע ראיתי חתים נסגים אחור וגבוריהם יכתו ומנוס נסו ולא הפנו מגור מסביב נאם יהוה ⁶ אל ינוס הקל ואל ימלט הגבור צפונה על יד נהר פרת כשלו ונפלו ⁷ מי זה כיאר יעלה כנהרות יתגעשו מימיו ⁸ מצרים כיאר יעלה וכנהרות יתגעשו מים ויאמר אכסה ארץ אבידה עיר וישבי בה ⁹ עלו הסוסים והתהללו הרכב ויצאו הגבורים כוש ופוט תפשי מגן ולודים תפשי דרכי קשת ¹⁰ והיום ההוא לאדני יהוה צבאות יום נקמה להנקם מצריו ואכלה חרב ושבעה ורותה מדמם כי זבח לאדני יהוה צבאות בארץ צפון אל נהר פרת ¹¹ עלי גלעד וקחי צרי בתולת בת מצרים לשוא הרביתי רפאות תעלה אין לך ¹² שמעו גוים קלונך וצוחתך מלאה הארץ כי גבור בגבור כשלו יחדיו נפלו שניהם

¹³ הדבר אשר דבר יהוה אל ירמיהו הנביא לבוא נבוכדראצר מלך בבל להכות את ארץ מצרים ¹⁴ הגידו במצרים והשמיעו במגדול והשמיעו בנף ובתחפנחס אמרו התיצב והכן לך כי אכלה חרב סביביך ¹⁵ מדוע נסחף אביריך לא עמד כי יהוה הדפו ¹⁶ הרבה כושל גם נפל איש אל רעהו ויאמרו קומה ונשבה אל עמנו ואל ארץ מולדתנו מפני חרב היונה ¹⁷ קראו שם פרעה מלך מצרים שאון העביר המועד ¹⁸ חי אני נאם המלך יהוה צבאות שמו כי כתבור בהרים וככרמל בים יבוא ¹⁹ כלי גולה עשי לך יושבת בת מצרים כי נף לשמה תהיה ונצתה מאין יושב ²⁰ עגלה יפה פיה מצרים קרץ מצפון בא בא ²¹ גם שכריה בקרבה כעגלי מרבק כי גם המה הפנו נסו יחדיו לא עמדו כי יום אידם בא עליהם עת פקדתם ²² קולה כנחש ילך כי בחיל ילכו ובקרדמות באו לה כחטבי עצים ²³ כרתו יערה נאם יהוה כי לא יחקר כי רבו מארבה ואין להם מספר ²⁴ הבישה בת מצרים נתנה ביד עם שפון ²⁵ אמר יהוה צבאות אלהי ישראל הנני פוקד אל אמון מנא ועל פרעה ועל אלהיה ועל מלכיה ועל פרעה ועל הבטחים בו ²⁶ ונתתים ביד מבקשי נפשם וביד נבוכדראצר מלך בבל וביד עבדיו ואחרי כן תשכן כימי קדם

Two prose superscriptions—one in verse 2 and one in verse 13—divide the oracles against Egypt into two sections and purport to describe the historical background of each subdivision. These verses appear to be

4. Fulminating against the Pharaoh

a later addition. Most of the oracles against the nations in the book of Jeremiah begin with a simple, prepositional superscription of the form "concerning X" (e.g., X-ל) (Moab, Ammon, Edom, Damascus, and Kedar). The superscription in verse 2, by contrast, combines the simple prepositional formula "concerning Egypt" with a lengthy relative clause: "Concerning Egypt. Concerning the army of Pharaoh Nekau that was by the river Euphrates in Carchemish which Nebuchadnezzar king of Babylon smote in the fourth year of Jehoiakim, ⟦...⟧[79] king of Judah" (למצרים על חיל פרעה נכו מלך מצרים אשר היה על נהר פרת בכרכמש אשר הכה נבוכדראצר מלך בבל בשנת הרביעית ליהויקים ⟦...⟧ מלך יהודה). This discrepancy suggests that the bulk of verse 2 is a later supplement to the initial prepositional phrase "concerning Egypt" (למצרים), which was added early enough to be preserved in the source texts of both the Masoretic Text and the Septuagint. The exact date of this addition remains unclear, but a historical error provides a clue as to its relative date. According to verse 2, Nebuchadnezzar was king of Babylon during the battle of Carchemish; according to the Babylonian Chronicle, however, he did not ascend the throne until the following year.[80] This error suggests that the longer superscription was composed after Judah's incorporation into the Babylonian Empire in 604 BCE since Nebuchadnezzar's father, Nabopolassar, never exercised dominion over Judah. Looking back from the perspective of Babylonian hegemony under Nebuchadnezzar, the author of the superscription may have assumed that Nebuchadnezzar had become king before the battle of Carchemish.

Verses 3–12: The First Oracle against Egypt

The first oracle opens in *medias res*, with an officer shouting orders to his subordinates, urging them to prepare for battle: "Ready buckler and shield and advance for battle! Harness the horses and mount the steeds! Take your stations in your helmets! Whet your lances and don your coats of mail" (ערכו מגן וצנה וגשו למלחמה אסרו הסוסים ועלו הפרשים והתיצבו בכובעים מרקו הרמחים לבשו הסירנת). At this point in the oracle, the ethnicity of the commanding officer and his subordinates remains unclear as does the timing of his commands.[81] As many commentators have pointed

---

79. The Septuagint reflects a Hebrew source text without the phrase בן יאשיהו "son of Josiah" (Sharp, "'Take Another Scroll and Write,'" 510).

80. Wiseman, *Chronicles of Chaldaean Kings*, 25–27; Grayson, *Assyrian and Babylonian Chronicles*, 99; Schmidt, *Das Buch Jeremia: Kapitel 21–52*, 285; Stipp, *Jeremia 25–52*, 646.

81. Georg Fischer, *Jeremia 26–52*, HThKAT (Freiburg: Herder, 2005), 472; Stipp, *Jeremia 25–52*, 647.

out, the final command appears to be out of order since soldiers usually sharpen their weapons and put on their armor *before* advancing into battle. Holladay, McKane, and Huwyler attempt to solve this problem by emending מרקו "whet" to either רמו "throw" or הריקו "draw" on the basis of the Septuagint, which reads "throw the spears" (προβάλετε τὰ δόρατα).[82] Such an emendation cannot solve the problem of the verse's ordering, however. Even with the emendation, the command to "don your coats of mail" appears after the order to advance for battle, leaving some soldiers unprotected. Lundom, by contrast, argues that the order of the commands does not have to appear in a strictly logical order because the author of the oracle was free to exercise poetic license in the composing his account.[83] Alternatively, the order of the commands could reflect the confusion of battle with some soldiers fumbling for weapons while their comrades advance into battle.[84] This interpretation would provide a fitting introduction to verse 5, which describes the rout of the soldiers addressed in verses 3 and 4.

In verse 5, the narrator asks why the soldiers from the previous verses are terrified (מדוע [[...]] המה חתים).[85] The oracle then skips over the battle itself in order to describe its aftermath. The soldiers from verses 3 and 4 have fallen back and broken into headlong flight, but to no avail. In verse 6, the narrator underscores the futility of retreat: "The swift cannot flee and the warrior cannot escape. In the north by the [[...]] Euphrates they have stumbled and fallen" (אל ינוס הקל ואל ימלט הגבור צפונה על יד [[...]] פרת כשלו ונפלו).[86] The second half of verse 6 locates the battle along the Euphrates, which agrees with the superscription in verse 2.

Verse 7 exchanges the military imagery of the preceding verses for an aquatic metaphor in order to highlight Egypt's power. The narrator asks, "Who is this that rises like the Nile, like rivers whose waters surge?" (מי זה כיאר יעלה כנהרות יתגעשו מימיו) before answering their question in the

---

82. McKane, *Commentary on Jeremiah 26–52*, 1113; Holladay, *Jeremiah 2*, 314; Huwyler, *Jeremia und die Völker*, 80.

83. Jack R. Lundbom, *Jeremiah 37–52: A New Translation with Introduction and Commentary*, AB 21C (New Haven: Yale University Press, 2004), 191.

84. Stipp, *Jeremia 25–52*, 645.

85. The Septuagint lacks an equivalent to the verb ראיתי "I saw" found in the Masoretic Text (Sharp, "'Take Another Scroll and Write,'" 510).

86. Omitting the word נהר "river" here as an expansion from verses 2 and 20 with the Septuagint (Janzen, *Studies in the Text of Jeremiah*, 58). For the use of the negated jussive "to express the conviction that something cannot or should not happen," see GKC §109e; Joüon, §114j. The translator of verse 6 apparently did not understand this subtlety of Hebrew grammar and translated verse 6 as: "let not the swift flee and let not the strong escape" (μὴ φευγέτω ὁ κοῦφος, καὶ μὴ ἀνασωζέσθω ὁ ἰσχυρός).

4. Fulminating against the Pharaoh

following verse: "Egypt rises like the Nile, like rivers that surge with water" (מצרים כיאר יעלה וכנהרות יתגעשו מים).[87] In the second half of verse 8, the figure of Egypt adopts the narrator's aquatic metaphor to describe its imperial ambitions: "let me rise, let me cover the earth, let me destroy [[...]] those who inhabit it" (ישבי בה [[...]] אכסה ארץ אבידה).[88] At this point in the oracle, the identity of the defeated soldiers from verses 3–5 remains unknown, and so Egypt's self-aggrandizing speech may lead the reader to believe that Egypt has put these soldiers to flight.[89] In verse 9, Egypt issues orders to the soldiers fighting under its command, including several mercenary groups known to have served the Saite pharaohs: "Advance, O horses! And dash madly, O chariots! Let the warriors go forth: Cush and Cyrene,[90] who grasp the shield, and the Lydians, [[...]] who wield the bow!" (עלו הסוסים והתהללו הרכב ויצאו הגבורים כוש ופוט תפשי מגן ולודים [[...]] דרכי קשת).[91]

The final three verses of the oracle offer a theological interpretation of the military imagery in verses 3–9 and identify Egypt as the defeated party. Verse 10 interprets the battle "as a day of vengeance" (יום נקמה) and an opportunity for Yahweh "to take vengeance on his foes" (להנקם מצריו) and states that "Yahweh [[...]] holds a sacrifice in the land of the north by the river Euphrates" (זבח ל[[...]]יהוה [[...]] בארץ צפון אל נהר פרת).[92] Verses 11 and 12 then implicitly identify Egypt as the defeated

---

87. It is unclear whether the reading מימיו from verse 7 or מים from verse 8 is more original. Stipp treats verse 8a as a later addition to the text because it repeats verse 7 almost verbatim (Stipp, *Jeremia 25–52*, 650).

88. Omitting ועיר "city and" with the Septuagint (Sharp, "'Take Another Scroll and Write,'" 510).

89. Allen, *Jeremiah*, 463.

90. Although normally translated as Libya, Hebrew פוט can be identified with the Graeco-Libyan city of Cyrene in these passages on the basis of BM 33041, Herodotus (*Hist.* 2.181), Nah 3:9 and Ezek 30:5 LXX. According to the fragmentary Babylonian text BM 33041, Amasis mustered soldiers from *pūṭu-iaman* in preparation for Nebuchadnezzar's invasion in 568 BCE. As Elmar Edel points out, *pūṭu-iaman* is a compound phrase meaning "Pūṭu of the Greeks," and probably refers to the Greek colony at Cyrene (Edel, "Amasis und Nebukadrezar II," 15–16). This interpretation receives support from Herodotus, *Hist.* 2.181, which mentions that Amasis made an alliance with Cyrene and took a Cyrenian wife. Furthermore, the collocation of פוט and לובים "Libyans" in Nah 3:9 and Ezek 30:5 LXX implies that פוט and לובים are not synonymous. I suggest, therefore, that פוט refers to Cyrene, a Libyan city that supplied the Egyptian army with troops. See also Stager, "Ashkelon and the Archaeology of Destruction," 61*.

91. Omitting the second תפשי "carrying" with the Septuagint (Sharp, "'Take Another Scroll and Write,'" 510).

92. Stipp, *Jeremia 25–52*, 653. Huwyler suggest that מצריו "from his foes"

party, thus contradicting Egypt's boastful statements in verses 8 and 9. In verse 11, the narrator instructs Egypt to seek balm in Gilead—an ironic statement given the fame of Egyptian medical knowledge in the ancient Near East—before proclaiming the uselessness of pharmaceuticals for healing Egypt's wound.[93] In verse 12, the narrator claims that news of Egypt's shameful defeat has become known internationally: "the nations have heard of your shame and the earth is full of your cry, for warrior has stumbled upon warrior and both have fallen together" (שמעו גוים קלונך וצוחתך מלאה הארץ כי גבור בגבור כשלו יחדיו נפלו שניהם). Taken together, these three verses show that Yahweh wills Egypt's defeat and, in a certain sense, fights against Egypt himself.

Taking all of the text-critical data into account, I reconstruct the earliest form of the first oracle against Egypt as follows:

Jeremiah 46:3–12

> [3] Ready buckler and shield and advance for battle! [4] Harness the horses and mount the steeds! Take your stations in your helmets! Whet your lances and don your coats of mail! [5] Why 〚...〛 are they terrified and turning back? Their warriors are beaten and flee swiftly. They do not turn—terror is all around—oracle of Yahweh. [6] The swift cannot flee and the warrior cannot escape. In the north by 〚...〛 the Euphrates they have stumbled and fallen. [7] Who is this that rises like the Nile, like rivers whose waters surge? [8] Egypt rises like the Nile, like rivers that surge with water. It said, "Let me rise, let me cover the earth, let me destroy 〚...〛 its inhabitants." [9] Advance, O horses! And dash madly, O chariots! Let the warriors go forth: Cush and Cyrene, who grasp the shield, and the Lydians, 〚...〛 who wield the bow. [10] That day is a day of vengeance for my lord Yahweh 〚...〛 to take vengeance on his foes. The sword will eat and be sated and drink its fill of their blood for my lord Yahweh 〚...〛 holds a sacrifice in the land of the north by the river Euphrates. [11] Go up to Gilead and take balm, O virgin daughter Egypt! In vain you multiply medicines, but there is no healing for you. [12] The nations have heard of your shame and the earth is full of your cry, for warrior has stumbled upon warrior and both have fallen together.

> [3] ערכו מגן וצנה וגשו למלחמה [4] אסרו הסוסים ועלו הפרשים והתיצבו בכובעים מרקו הרמחים לבשו הסירנת 〚...〛 [5] מדוע חתים נסגים אחור וגבוריהם יכתו ומנוס נסו ולא הפנו

---

could be an error for מצרים "Egypt" (Huwyler, *Jeremia und die Völker*, 90). If he is correct, then verse 10 would explicitly identify the battle as an opportunity for Yahweh "to take vengeance on Egypt." The Septuagint lacks an equivalent to the titles צבאות "of Armies" (twice) and אדני "my lord" in this verse (Sharp, "'Take Another Scroll and Write,'" 510).

93. According to Lundbom, *Jeremiah 37–52*, 203, the reference to Gilead in verse 11 could also indicate that Gilead belonged to the Saite empire.

4. Fulminating against the Pharaoh   97

מגור מסביב נאם יהוה ⁶אל ינוס הקל ואל ימלט הגבור צפונה על יד [...] פרת כשלו ונפלו ⁷מי זה כיאר יעלה כנהרות יתגעשו מימיו ⁸מצרים כיאר יעלה וכנהרות יתגעשו מים ויאמר אכסה ארץ אבידה [...] ישבי בה ⁹עלו הסוסים והתהללו הרכב ויצאו הגבורים כוש ופוט תפשי מגן ולודים [...] דרכי קשת ¹⁰והיום ההוא לאדני יהוה [...] יום נקמה להנקם מצריו ואכלה חרב ושבעה ורותה מדמם כי זבח לאדני יהוה [...] בארץ צפון אל נהר פרת ¹¹עלי גלעד וקחי צרי בתולת בת מצרים לשוא הרביתי רפאות תעלה אין לך ¹²שמעו גוים קלונך וצוחתך מלאה הארץ כי גבור בגבור כשלו יחדיו נפלו שניהם

Dating

A sense of vagueness pervades the first oracle against Egypt. Its ten verses depict an Egyptian military defeat along the Euphrates River, but they do not localize the battle more specifically and do not identify Egypt's enemy at all.[94] Fortunately, it is still possible to identify this battle because only one Egyptian defeat along the Euphrates is attested in the historical record, the battle of Carchemish in 605 BCE. If the oracle does refer to the battle of Carchemish, as both the superscription and historical probability suggest, we can account for the vagueness of the oracle in one of two ways: either the oracle was composed in the immediate aftermath of the battle of Carchemish when the details of the conflict were well known and the author of the oracle could afford to be allusive, or the oracle was composed long after the battle of Carchemish when historical details about this military encounter were scarce. I opt for the first scenario because the oracle preserves at least one historical detail that a later writer would be unlikely to know, namely, that Cushite, Cyrenian, and Lydian mercenaries fought in the Egyptian army at Carchemish.[95] In this regard, I agree with most commentators that the first oracle against Egypt dates to 605 BCE, shortly after the battle of Carchemish.[96]

Interpretation

The first oracle against Egypt represents the Egyptian defeat at Carchemish in 605 BCE as a divine punishment for the Saite pharaohs' imperial

---

94. Carroll aptly suggests that Egypt's enemy (i.e., Babylon) is absent from the oracle because Yahweh himself fights against Egypt (Carroll, *Jeremiah*, 763).

95. Given the presence of Judahite soldiers at the battle of Carchemish, the author of this oracle may have drawn on eye-witness accounts to describe the composition of the Egyptian army.

96. Carroll, *Jeremiah*, 760; Holladay, *Jeremiah 2*, 318; Huwyler, *Jeremia und die Völker*, 102; Lundbom, *Jeremiah 37–52*, 188; Grabbe, "'The Lying Pen of the Scribes'?," 194; Allen, *Jeremiah*, 461; Schmidt, *Das Buch Jeremia: Kapitel 21–52*, 286; Stipp, *Jeremia 25–52*, 647.

ambitions.[97] The pharaoh's aggressive and self-aggrandizing statements in verses 8 and 9 lead directly into the proclamation of divine condemnation in verse 10. But, as Stipp notes, the oracle applies its anti-imperialist rhetoric inconsistently; it does not condemn the imperialist policies that impelled Nabopolassar and Nebuchadnezzar to contest Egyptian control of northern Syria in the first place.[98] Why then, he asks, does the oracle condemn Egypt alone?[99] The answer to this question rests on the historical setting of the oracle: Egyptian imperialism in northern Syria held dire consequences for the average Judahite, while Babylonian imperialism did not. From 616 to 605 BCE, Judahite soldiers fought and died along the Euphrates in order to protect Saite interests in the region. I suggest, therefore, that the first oracle against Egypt applauds the Babylonian victory because it held the potential to stop Egyptian involvement in northern Syria and the associated loss of Judahite lives.[100]

This hypothesis only postpones the answer to Stipp's question, however. Once Babylon assumed control over Judah in 604 BCE, it becomes more difficult to explain why certain Judahites would continue to cheerlead Babylonian foreign policy. This problem is particularly acute in the second oracle against Egypt, to which I now turn.

Verses 14–24, 26c: The Second Oracle against Egypt

A long prose superscription in verse 13 introduces the second oracle against Egypt: "[...] What Yahweh spoke to Jeremiah [...] about the coming of [...] the king of Babylon to strike the land of Egypt" ([...] אשר דבר יהוה אל ירמיהו [...] לבוא [...] מלך בבל להכות את ארץ מצרים).[101] This

---

97. Stipp, *Jeremia 25–52*, 651.

98. The Babylonians were not victims of Egyptian aggression at Carchemish. If Lipiński and Zecchi are correct that Carchemish housed an Egyptian outpost of some sort, then the Babylonians would have been the aggressors (Lipiński, *On the Skirts of Canaan*, 157; Zecchi, "Note on Two Egyptian Seal Impressions," 205).

99. Stipp, *Jeremia 25–52*, 653.

100. In this regard, the first oracle was remarkably prescient. Following the Babylonian victory at Carchemish, the Saite pharaohs lost their foothold in northern Syria and would never again contest Babylonian power on the Euphrates.

101. The Septuagint lacks an equivalent to הדבר "the word" at the beginning of the verse and to הנביא "the prophet" and נבוכדראצר "Nebuchadnezzar" from the middle of the verse (Sharp, "'Take Another Scroll and Write,'" 510). The absence of the name Nebuchadnezzar could suggest that verse 2 and verse 13 stem from the same writer with the reference to Nebuchadnezzar in verse 2 intended to carry over into verse 13.

4. Fulminating against the Pharaoh 99

superscription links the following oracle to an impending Babylonian invasion of Egypt, which the oracle itself predicts will be successful. According to the available historical records, Nebuchadnezzar attempted to invade Egypt three times during the late seventh and early sixth centuries BCE: once in 601 BCE, once in 582 BCE, and once in 568 BCE. All three of these attempts failed. In 601 BCE, Nekau II routed Nebuchadnezzar at the delta fortress of Migdol and recaptured Gaza; in 582 BCE, Apries repelled a Babylonian invasion around Daphnae thanks to information provided by a Babylonian deserter; and in 568 BCE, Amasis defeated a joint Babylonian-Egyptian invasion led by Nebuchadnezzar and the previous pharaoh, Apries somewhere in the Nile Delta.[102] Because the second oracle incorrectly predicts that the Babylonian invasion will succeed, it most likely predates one of the three known Babylonian invasions.[103] Deciding which invasion provides the most plausible historical context for the composition of this oracle, however, requires a detailed analysis of the oracle itself.

Like the first oracle, the second oracle begins with a call to arms, directed this time at the Egyptian cities of Migdol and Memphis: "Declare [[...]] in Migdol and proclaim in Memphis [[...]]: take a stand and be firm, because a sword will devour all around you!" (הגידו [[...]] במגדול והשמיעו בנף [[...]] התיצב והכן לך כי אכלה חרב סביבך).[104] During the Saite period, Migdol was the eastern-most Egyptian border fortress along the Ways of Horus and, as such, served as the first line of defense against foreign invasion.[105] Memphis, by contrast, was an important royal-ritual center and formed a link between the cities of the Nile Delta and the remainder of Egypt.[106]

---

102. See chapter 2 for a historical overview of these invasions.

103. On the importance of unfulfilled prophecies for dating prophetic texts, see Reimer, "Jeremiah before the Exile?," 209; Grabbe, "'The Lying Pen of the Scribes'?," 197, 200; and Schmid, "Prognosis and Postgnosis in Biblical Prophecy," 112–13.

104. Here, I follow the reading of the Septuagint. The Masoretic Text, by contrast, expands verse 14 into two bicola on the basis of Jer 2:16 or 44:1: "declare in Egypt, and proclaim in Migdol and proclaim in Memphis and say in Daphnae" (הגידו במצרים והשמיעו במגדול והשמיעו בנף ובתחפנחס אמרו). This expansion may have been historically motivated. According to the recently published Apries Stela, Apries repelled Nebuchadnezzar's second invasion of Egypt outside the walls of Daphnae and so the addition of Daphnae to verse 14 may reflect the strategic importance of this site during the Babylonian invasion of 582 BCE (Abd el-Maksoud and Valbelle, "Une stèle de l'an 7 d'Apriès," 12).

105. Oren, "Migdol," 34.

106. The northern part of the city featured a large fortified palace, which dates to the reign of Apries and served as a residence for Apries and his successor Amasis (W. M. Flinders Petrie and J. H. Walker, *The Palace of Apries (Memphis II)*

As Kahn and Tammuz have shown, almost every successful invasion of Egypt between 673 and 306 BCE ended with the capture of Memphis and the loss of communication between the delta and the south.[107] The reference to Migdol and Memphis in verse 14 thus reflects the strategic importance of these sites.

Verse 15 exhibits several text-critical problems. The Masoretic Text reads, "Why has your mighty one been swept away [treating אַבִּירֶיךָ as an abstract plural]. He did not stand" (מַדּוּעַ נִסְחַף אַבִּירֶיךָ לֹא עָמָד), while the Septuagint reflects a Hebrew source text that read "Why has Apis fled? Why did your [chosen] bull not stand firm?" (διὰ τί ἔφυγεν ὁ Ἆπις; ὁ μόσχος ὁ ἐλεκτός σου οὐκ ἔμεινεν = מַדּוּעַ נָס חַף אַבִּירְךָ לֹא עָמָד).[108] With the exception of Lundbom, Galvin and Schmidt, most commentators adopt the reading of the Septuagint because it exhibits poetic parallelism and agrees more fully with the Egyptian context of the oracle.[109] The cult of the Apis bull

---

[London: School of Archaeology in Egypt, 1909], 3; Leclère, *Les villes de Basse Égypte*, 61, 69; Maria Helena Trinidade Lopes, *Mênfis: O rosto de Apriés* [Lisbon: Tinta-da-Chian, 2010], 35). To the east of the palace, there is a large, enclosed area. W. M. Flinders Petrie, J. H. Walker, and Maria Helena Trinidade Lopes identify this area as a mercenary camp intended to house the foreign soldiers serving under Apries, while François Leclère suggests that it could be a temenos separating the palace from the more mundane parts of the city (Petrie and Walker, *Palace of Apries*, 12; Maria Helena Trinidade Lopes, "The Apries Palace Project," *EA* 42 [2013]: 36–37; Lopes, *Mênfis*, 39; Leclère, *Les villes de Basse Égypte*, 66, 70). To the west of the palace, excavators uncovered a massive temple dedicated to the Apis bull, a divine being that Jer 46:15 singles out for mockery. Much of the site, however, remains unexplored (Jill Kamil, "Ancient Memphis: Archaeologists Revive Interest in a Famous Egyptian Site," *Archaeology* 38 [1985]: 30; David Jeffreys, "The Survey of Memphis, Capital of Ancient Egypt: Recent Developments," *Archaeology International* 11 [2008]: 41–44).

107. Kahn and Tammuz, "Egypt Is Difficult to Enter," 56.

108. The adjective ἐλεκτός "chosen" in the Septuagint lacks a counterpart in the Masoretic Text (Sharp, "'Take Another Scroll and Write,'" 511).

109. Carroll, *Jeremiah*, 768; McKane, *Commentary on Jeremiah 26–52*, 1128; Holladay, *Jeremiah 2*, 323; Huwyler, *Jeremia und die Völker*, 112; Stipp, *Studien zum Jeremiabuch*, 184. See also the additional citations in Lundbom, *Jeremiah 37–52*, 210. Lundbom, Galvin, and Schmidt opt for the reading of the Masoretic Text (Lundbom, *Jeremiah 37–52*, 210; Galvin, *Egypt as a Place of Refuge*, 152; Schmidt, *Das Buch Jeremia: Kapitel 21–52*, 283). Thomas Schneider, on the other hand, forges a middle ground between the Septuagint and the Masoretic Text by retaining the pointing of the Masoretic Text but separating נִסְחַף into two words like the Septuagint (Thomas Schneider, "Jeremia in Memphis: Eine Neusituierung von Jeremia 46,13–24," in *Prophetie und Psalmen: Festschrift für Klaus Seybold zum 65. Geburtstag*, ed. Beat Huwyler, Hans-Peter Mathys, and Beat Weber, AOAT 280 [Münster: Ugarit-Verlag, 2001], 80–81). According to him,

4. Fulminating against the Pharaoh

in Memphis was especially popular during the Saite period and counted the Saite pharaohs among its most ardent supporters.[110] The final clause of verse 15 attributes Apis's unsteadiness to Yahweh's intervention and sets up a clash between the Egyptian and Judahite deities that continues into the following verse: "because Yahweh pushed him" (כִּי יהוה הֲדָפוֹ).

The opening of verse 16 proves problematic. The Masoretic Text contains the nonsensical reading "the stumbler has increased" (הִרְבָּה כּוֹשֵׁל), while the Septuagint reflects a Hebrew source text that read "and your multitude stumbled" (καὶ τὸ πλῆθός σου ἠσθένησεν = וְרֻבְּךָ כָּשַׁל). McKane, Carroll, and Schneider adopt the reading of the Septuagint but struggle to account for the change from ורבך to הרבה text-critically since the Hebrew letter ה does not resemble either ו or ך.[111] Schneider, for example, argues that the Septuagint reading πλῆθός σου comes from a Hebrew source text that read רִכְבּוֹ "his chariot" based on the correspondence between πλῆθός σου "your multitude" in Nah 2:14 LXX and רִכְבָּהּ "her chariot" in Nah 2:14 MT. Accordingly, he emends הִרְבָּה to רִכְבּוֹ "its chariot" and takes רִכְבּוֹ as a reference to the cart used to transport the statue of the Apis bull during processions.[112] Yet Nah 2:14 is not necessarily relevant to the textual analysis of Jer 46:16. Although a simple interchange

---

נֹס חַף reflects the Egyptian divine title *nsw ḥp* "King Apis" commonly applied to the Apis bull. This interpretation, however, lacks linguistic and text-critical support. Elsewhere in the Hebrew Bible, Egyptian *nsw* "king" is rendered as נֵיס, not נֹס (compare תַּחְפְּנֵיס < Egyptian *tȝ-ḥm.t-pȝ-nsw* "the wife of the king" in 1 Kgs 11:19–20) and none of the textual traditions of Jer 46:16 match Schneider's reconstruction. For this interpretation of the name תַּחְפְּנֵיס see Manfred Görg, "Namen und Titel in 1 Kön 11,19f," *BN* 26 (1987): 22.

110. Artifacts recovered from the Apis temple in Memphis include votive tables dedicated by Amasis and Nekau II and several Twenty-Fifth-Dynasty building blocks repurposed by Psamtik II (Michael Jones, "The Temple of Apis in Memphis," *JEA* 76 [1990]: 142; Leclère, *Les villes de Basse Égypte*, 64). See also the description of Psamtik I's construction of the Apis temple in Herodotus, *Hist.* 2.153.

111. Carroll, *Jeremiah*, 768; McKane, *Commentary on Jeremiah 26–52*, 1128; Schneider, "Jeremia in Memphis," 81–82. Huwyler, Maier, and Schmidt, by contrast, retain the reading of the Masoretic Text since it is the *lectio difficilior* and read "he has increased stumbling" (Huwyler, *Jeremia und die Völker*, 113; Maier, *Ägypten*, 282; Schmidt, *Das Buch Jeremia: Kapitel 21–52*, 285). Rudolph and Holladay read "has the great Rahab stumbled?" by revocalizing הִרְבָּה as הֲרָבָה and inserting רהב before כשל (Wilhelm Rudolph, *Jeremia*, Handbuch zum Alten Testament 12 [3rd ed.; Tübingen: Mohr Siebeck, 1968], 250–51; Holladay, *Jeremiah 2*, 329). Such a reading, however, lacks textual support and suffers from two serious grammatical problems. We would expect the adjective הרבה to follow רהב and the participle כשל to be feminine in agreement with its antecedent.

112. Schneider, "Jeremia in Memphis," 81–82.

of כ and ב—e.g., רכבה > רבכה, which was then reinterpreted as רִבְכָה "your [masculine singular] multitude"—can explain the reading of the Septuagint in Nah 2:14, such a change cannot account for the difference between ורבך to הרבה.[113] Nor is it possible to explain the difference between the Masoretic Text and the Hebrew source text of the Septuagint by a simple confusion of letters. The letter ה does not resemble ו or כ in either the palaeo-Hebrew or Aramaic scripts (𐤄 ≠ 𐤅, 𐤊; ה ≠ ו, כ).[114] In my opinion, the simplest solution to the textual crux of Jer 46:16 is to emend בּוֹשֵׁל to כָּשַׁל following the Septuagint and treat it as the verbal complement of הרבה, which yields the phrase "he stumbled repeatedly" (הרבה כשל).[115] This reconstruction receives text-critical support from 1 Sam 2:3. In this verse, the Septuagint misunderstood the use of רבה as a verbal complement in the Masoretic Text and translated אל תרבו and תדברו as separate verbs rather than components of a single verbal phrase.[116] Similarly, I would argue that the translator of Jer 46:16 did not understand the grammatical relationship between הרבה and כשל and interpreted הרבה as the subject of כשל. If this reconstruction proves correct, then the opening of verse 16 continues the imagery of divine conflict developed in verse 15: "Why has Apis fled? Why did your bull not stand? Because Yahweh pushed him. He stumbled repeatedly and fell." Taken together, the two verses depict Yahweh quite literally pushing the Apis bull out of the picture, thereby removing Memphis's divine protection.

The remainder of verse 16 introduces new imagery: "each man said to his companion, 'Arise! Let us return to our people, to the land of our birth because of the oppressor's sword'" (איש אל רעהו ויאמרו קומה ונשבה אל עמנו ואל ארץ מולדתנו מפני חרב היונה).[117] The speakers in this verse seem to

---

113. For metathesis as a source of textual errors see Tov, *Textual Criticism*, 232–33. כָ- is the long second-person masculine singular possessive suffix, which appears 40 times in the Hebrew Bible (including in Jer 29:25) and is the usual form of this suffix in Qumran Hebrew (GKC, §91e; Joüon, §94h).

114. Tov does not include ה and ו or ה and כ in his list of commonly confused letters (Tov, *Textual Criticism*, 228–31).

115. Lundbom too understands הרבה as an auxiliary verb, but groups it with the preceding verse: כי יהוה הדפו הרבה "because Yahweh pushed him repeatedly" (Lundbom, *Jeremiah 37–52*, 210). This reconstruction is unlikely to be correct, however, since auxiliary verbs almost always precede their verbal complement in Biblical Hebrew (GKC, §120g; Joüon, §177g).

116. In Ps 51:4—the other case where רבה governs a verbal complement in the Hebrew Bible—the Septuagint renders this construction correctly.

117. Reading חֶרֶב הַיּוֹנָה "sword of the oppressor" with the Targum Jonathan (חרב סנאה "sword of the enemy") and the Peshitta (ḥarbɔ d-madwayɔ "sword of the afflicter") instead of חֶרֶב הַיּוֹנָה "sword of the dove," which makes little sense. The

4. Fulminating against the Pharaoh

be foreign mercenaries living in Egypt who hope to avoid the coming slaughter by returning home.[118] Ironically, their departure would only hasten Egypt's demise by weakening its defenses.

Verse 17 contains a textual crux that bears on the dating of the second oracle as a whole. In the Masoretic Text, either the narrator or the foreign mercenaries from verse 16 criticize the reigning pharaoh: "Give Pharaoh king of Egypt the name[119] 'Loudmouth (?) Who Lets the Appointed Time Pass By'" (קראו שם פרעה מלך מצרים שאון העביר המועד).[120] Where the Masoretic Text simply reads "Pharaoh king of Egypt" (פרעה מלך מצרים), both the Septuagint and the Peshitta reflect a Hebrew source text that read "Pharaoh Nekau king of Egypt" (Φαραω Νεχαω βασιλέως Αἰγύπτου; perʿon ḥgirɔ malkɔ d-meṣren = פרעה נכה מלך מצרים).[121] From a text-critical standpoint, the agreement between one branch of the Masoretic Text family and the Septuagint suggests that פרעה נכה is the preferred reading.[122] I would argue, therefore, that most branches of the Masoretic Text family lost נכה due to a simple scribal error: a scribe

---

Septuagint reinterprets היונה as היון "the Greek" (Sharp, "'Take Another Scroll and Write,'" 10).

118. Fischer, *Jeremia 26–52*, 480.

119. Emending קָרְאוּ שָׁם "they called there" to קִרְאוּ שֵׁם with the Septuagint.

120. The significance of this name remains obscure. James K. Hoffmeier argues that it characterizes the pharaoh as rash and foolish according to the ancient Egyptian value system, an appraisal that fits well with Herodotus' and Diodorus Siculus's portrayal of Apries (James K. Hoffmeier, "A New Insight on Pharaoh Apries from Herodotus, Diodorus and Jeremiah 46:17," *JSSEA* 11 [1981]: 168). But as Schneider points out, Herodotus and Diodorus Siculus wrote after Amasis's victory over Apries and are, therefore, not unbiased sources for Apries's character (Schneider, "Jeremia in Memphis," 83). Instead, he argues that the Hebrew phrase parodies Apries's throne name ḥʿ-jb-rʿ "he who exalts the heart of Re" and translates שאון העביר המועד as "(Fest)lärm, der das Fest verpaßt hat." Alternatively, the name may characterize the pharaoh as an ineffective general who is incapable of seizing the initiative.

121. Stipp, *Studien zum Jeremiabuch*, 169. The Peshitta reads perʿon ḥgirɔ, a derogative term employed by both the Peshitta and Targum Jonathan for Nekau II in 2 Kgs 23 and 2 Chr 35 and 36. The derivation of this nickname remains debated. Most likely, Aramaic-speaking readers of the Bible interpreted the name נכה as passive participle from the Hebrew root נכי "to strike" and translated it into Aramaic using the root חגר "to be crippled," as Begg suggests (*Josephus' Story of the Later Monarchy*, 485).

122. It is theoretically possible that the Septuagint influenced the Peshitta reading of Jer 46:17, but as Gillian Greenberg notes, the Peshitta translator only rarely had recourse to the Septuagint and only when dealing with grammatically difficult passages (Gillian Greenberg, *Translation Technique in the Peshitta to Jeremiah*, MPIL 13 [Leiden: Brill, 2002], 22–23, 147–49).

skipped from the ע of פרעה to the ה of נכה since both words end in a ה.[123] Many scholars, however, interpret the second half of verse 17 as a veiled jab at Apries and dismiss the reference to Nekau in the Septuagint and Peshitta versions of verse 17 as an addition or gloss from verse 2.[124]

Hoffmeier, Carroll, Holladay, Huwyler, and Galvin, for example, consider העביר to be a play on Apries's personal name, wꜣḥ-jb-rꜥ "the heart of Re endures," which is rendered into Hebrew as חפרע in Jer 44:30.[125] Such an interpretation is unconvincing, however. As Stipp notes, the similarities between העביר and חפרע are limited and several other Hebrew words—including רע "bad, wicked"—could have furnished a more obvious and devastating pun on the name חפרע.[126] Given these problems, I find it unlikely that a Hebrew speaker would perceive העביר as a play on חפרע, and without this play on words, there is no reason to dismiss the reading of the Septuagint and the Peshitta as a later gloss.

In Verse 18, Yahweh likens the invading general to two prominent mountains in the northern Levant, Carmel and Tabor.[127] The signif-

---

123. Nekau is spelled two different ways in the Hebrew Bible: as נכה in 2 Kgs 23:29, 33, 34, and 35 and as נכו in Jer 46:2, 2 Chr 35:20, and 36:4. The use of the spelling נכו in Jer 46:2 does not preclude the possibility that verse 17 employed the other spelling, especially since the two verses stem from different hands.

124. Janzen, *Studies in the Text of Jeremiah*, 65; Carroll, *Jeremiah*, 768; Holladay, *Jeremiah 2*, 108; Stipp, *Das masoretische und alexandrinische Sondergut*, 146; Huwyler, *Jeremia und die Völker*, 385; Galvin, *Egypt as a Place of Refuge*, 142.

125. Hoffmeier, "New Insight," 167–68; Carroll, *Jeremiah*, 768; Holladay, *Jeremiah 2*, 108; Huwyler, *Jeremia und die Völker*, 385; Galvin, *Egypt as a Place of Refuge*, 142. This interpretation goes back to Carl H. Cornhill, *Das Buch Jeremia* (Leipzig: Tauchnitz, 1905), 453. Schneider suggests that Hebrew חפרע reflects Apries's throne name ḥꜥꜥ-jb-rꜥ, but as Christoffer Theis points out, the texts of the Hebrew Bible exclusively refer to pharaohs by their personal names (Schneider, "Jeremia in Memphis," 82; Christoffer Theis, "Sollte Re sich schämen? Eine subliminale Bedeutung des Namens חפרע in Jeremia 44,30," *UF* 42 [2010]: 683, 685).

126. Stipp, *Jeremia 25–52*, 658. The two words share only two consonants, ע and ר, and differ in all other respects. While similar in place and manner of articulation, ב and פ differ in terms of voicing; ה and ח differ in place of articulation; and, other than ח and ה, the ordering of phonemes within each word does not match. Citing Carsten Peust, Theis invokes the occasional dissimilation of ח in the presence of ע to explain the ה of העביר, but this sound rule only applies in Egyptian, not Hebrew (Carsten Peust, *Egyptian Phonology: An Introduction to the Phonology of a Dead Language*, Monographien zur Ägyptischen Sprache 2 [Göttingen: Peust & Gutschmidt, 1999], 98–99; Theis, "Sollte Re sich schämen?," 685). Furthermore, the transcription of wꜣḥ-jb-rꜥ into Hebrew as חפרע in Jer 44:30 shows that this sound rule did not operate in Apries's personal name.

127. The Septuagint lacks an equivalent to צבאות "of Armies" and שמו "his

4. Fulminating against the Pharaoh

icance of this simile remains debated. Huwyler, Carroll, McKane, Schmidt, and Stipp see an allusion to Nebuchadnezzar's inexorable advance here.[128] Schneider, by contrast, opts for a historical explanation. He suggests that Carmel and Tabor allude to Nebuchadnezzar's prolonged siege of Tyre from 585 to 573 BCE—which served as a prelude to his 568 BCE invasion of Egypt—and help situate the oracle in the third decade of the sixth century BCE.[129] This interpretation, however, relies on the assumption that the oracle dates to 568 BCE, which is unlikely since Apries was not actually pharaoh during Nebuchadnezzar's 568 BCE invasion. As mentioned in chapter 2, Amasis deposed Apries in 570 BCE and defeated a joint invasion by Nebuchadnezzar and Apries in 568 BCE.[130] In the following verse, Yahweh instructs Egypt to pack her bags for exile "because Memphis will become a waste, a ruin without inhabitant" (כי נף לשמה תהיה ונצתה מאין יושב).

Verse 20 depicts Egypt as a type of heifer (עגלה יפה פיה) beset by a stinging insect (קרץ) from the north.[131] Most commentators and Semitists treat יפה פיה as reduplicated form of the feminine adjective יפה "beautiful" meaning "very beautiful," but this interpretation runs into morphological problems.[132] Because יפה comes from a III-י root, a reduplicated form of the adjective should not feature a word-internal ה: for example, *yapaypiy-at > yəpêpiyâ.[133] Schneider, by contrast, suggests

---

name" in this verse (Sharp, "'Take Another Scroll and Write,'" 511). Janzen attributes the presence of these forms in the Masoretic Text to expansion from other contexts, such as Jer 31:35 (Janzen, *Studies in the Text of Jeremiah*, 79).

128. Carroll, *Jeremiah*, 770; McKane, *Commentary on Jeremiah 26–52*, 1130; Huwyler, *Jeremia und die Völker*, 116; Schmidt, *Das Buch Jeremia: Kapitel 21–52*, 288; Stipp, *Jeremia 25–52*, 659. Lundbom, by contrast, thinks that Tabor and Carmel refer to Yahweh, while Holladay argues that the simile refers to Apries's fate (Lundbom, *Jeremiah 37–52*, 214; Holladay, *Jeremiah 2*, 324, 330).

129. Schneider, "Jeremia in Memphis," 95.

130. If one wished to maintain the allusion to Apries in verse 17, then the oracle would need to date to the second Babylonian invasion of Egypt in 582 BCE.

131. The use of a heifer to represent Egypt may have a religious dimension. Fischer, for example, identifies the heifer with the goddess Hathor, who often took the form of a cow and was the patron goddess of beauty and cosmetics (Fischer, *Jeremia 26–52*, 482).

132. GKC §84n; Aaron Michael Butts, "Reduplicated Nominal Patterns in Semitic," *JAOS* 131 (2011), 87, 103; Carroll, *Jeremiah*, 769; McKane, *Commentary on Jeremiah 26–52*, 1131; Holladay, *Jeremiah 2*, 331; Huwyler, *Jeremia und die Völker*, 118; Maier, *Ägypten*, 282; Lundbom, *Jeremiah 37–52*, 217; Schmidt, *Das Buch Jeremia: Kapitel 21–52*, 284.

133. Three Masoretic manuscripts (mss 89, 93, and 96) read יפיפיה instead of יפהפיה.

repointing יְפֵה־פִיָּה as יָפָה פִיָה—the feminine adjective יָפָה "beautiful" followed by the word for "entrance, mouth" bearing a locative ה—and reading the first colon of verse 20 as "a beautiful heifer is at the entrance to Egypt." According to him, this phrase serves to localize the cult of the Apis bull's mother in Memphis, which is often identified as "the gate of Egypt" in Egyptian texts.[134] While Schneider's interpretation fits the consonantal text of the Masoretic Text better than the traditional interpretation, it disrupts the logic of the following verses. The second half of verse 20 requires a metaphorical identification between the heifer and Egypt; otherwise, the reference to "her mercenaries" in verse 21 would make little sense. Therefore, I would repoint יְפֵה־פִיָּה as יָפָה פִיָה and treat עֶגְלָה יָפָה פִיָה as an appositional relative clause meaning "a heifer whose mouth is beautiful," i.e, "a heifer with a beautiful mouth."[135] Such an interpretation receives support from the Septuagint, which employs a passive participle of the verb καλλωπίζω "to beautify the face" to describe the heifer.[136]

Verse 21 continues the bovine metaphor by likening Egypt's foreign mercenaries (שכריה) to fatted calves.[137] The imagery of this verse is multivalent. On the one hand, it recalls the lavish gifts received by some of the foreign mercenaries employed by the Saite pharaohs.[138] A Greek inscription from western Anatolia commissioned by the Ionian mercenary Pedon states that: "the Egyptian King Psamtik gave him a bracelet of gold for his feats of prowess and a city for his valor" (ϱῶι βασιλεὺς ἔδωϙ' ὠιγύπτιος : Ψαμμήτιχος : ἀριστήιια ψίλιόν τε χρύσεον καὶ πόλιν ἀρετῆς ἕνεκα).[139] The produce generated by this city would have enabled Pedon to eat well. Although not referring to foreign mercenaries, Herodotus describes the daily rations given to Apries's Egyptian bodyguards as follows: "These men, besides their lands, each received as a daily

---

134. Schneider, "Jeremia in Memphis," 84.

135. The Hebrew Bible preserves a handful of indisputable examples of appositional relative clauses as well as several more ambiguous cases. For a summary of the evidence, see Na'ama Pat-El, "The Morphosyntax of Nominal Antecedents in Semitic and an Innovation in Arabic," in *Proceedings of the Oslo-Austin Workshop in Semitic Linguistics*, ed. Lutz Edzard and John Huehnergard (Wiesbaden: Harrassowitz, 2014), 33–34.

136. LSJ, 869; GELS, 359.

137. For the presence of mercenaries in Memphis during the Saite period see Petrie and Walker, *Palace of Apries*, 12; Lopes, "The Apries Palace Project," 36–37; Lopes, *Mênfis*, 39; Leclère, *Les villes de Basse Égypte*, 66, 70.

138. Allen, *Jeremiah*, 466–67; Lundbom, *Jeremiah 37–52*, 219.

139. Olivier Masson and Jean Yoyotte, "Une inscription ionienne mentionnant Psammétique Ier," *Epigraphica Anatolica* 11 (1988): 173; Agut-Labordère, "Plus que des mercenaires!," 297–98.

4. Fulminating against the Pharaoh

provision five minas' weight of roast grain, two minas of beef, and four cups of wine. These were the gifts received by each bodyguard" (τούτοισι ὦν τάδε πάρεξ τῶν ἀρουρέων ἄλλα ἐδίδοτο ἐπ' ἡμέρῃ ἑκάστῃ, ὀπτοῦ σίτου σταθμὸς πέντε μνέαι ἑκάστῳ, κρεῶν βοέων δύο μνέαι, οἴνου τέσσερες ἀρυστῆρες. ταῦτα τοῖσι αἰεὶ δορυφορέουσι ἐδίδοτο, *Hist.* 2.168). At the same time, verse 21 also likens Egypt's foreign mercenaries to the Apis bull itself. Like the Apis bull in verse 15, they "flee... and do not stand" (נסו ... לא עמדו). In this way, verse 21 characterizes the Egyptian army as a fighting force gone soft—their first inclination is to run and, like the Apis bull, they are easily routed by Yahweh.

The next three verses employ a kaleidoscopic array of images to depict the downfall of Egypt. In her distress, Egypt makes a noise like a snake gliding away.[140] Her enemies come against her with axes in order to cut down her impenetrable forest, an image that Schneider argues refers to the dense palm groves that surrounded Memphis during antiquity.[141] They are able to accomplish this Herculean feat because they are more numerous than locusts. At the end of this visual whirlwind, verse 24 finally alludes to the identity of Egypt's assailants: "daughter Egypt will be put to shame and handed over to a people from the north" (הבישה בת מצרים נתנה ביד עם צפון). As in the first oracle against Egypt, the second oracle does not name Babylon explicitly so that Egypt's downfall may redound to Yahweh's credit.[142]

But the oracle does not end with Egypt's subjugation and humiliation. After a series of later insertions in verses 25 and 26ab—to be discussed in the following section—it resumes in verse 26c with a promise of rehabilitation for the once mighty empire: "afterward she [= Egypt] will be inhabited as in the days of old—says Yahweh" (ואחרי תשכן כימי קדם נאם יהוה).[143] This statement comes as a surprise after the carnage of the previous verses. Its presence may suggest that the second

---

140. Grammatically, it is possible to interpret the Hebrew phrase קולה כנחש ילך in two different ways. We can either treat קולה as the subject of ילך and כנחש as a prepositional phrase modifying the verb (i.e., "her voice goes like a snake") or we treat can כנחש as both the predicate of קולה and the construct head of ילך (i.e., "her voice is like a snake that goes").

141. Schneider, "Jeremia in Memphis," 95.

142. Stipp, *Jeremia 25–52*, 652.

143. The feminine singular verb תשכן at the end of verse 26 lacks an explicit subject and stands at odds with the masculine plural nouns found in verse 25 and the first part of verse 26. The nearest antecedent for this verb is "daughter Egypt" (בת מצרים) in verse 24. This discrepancy suggests that verses 25 and 26ab are a later insertion in the oracle that severed the connection between 24 and 26c. Strangely, the Septuagint omits verse 26 altogether (Sharp, "'Take Another Scroll and Write,'" 511). The absence of this material may be due to *parablepsis*,

oracle was not directed against Egypt in general but only against the Saite pharaohs and the institutions that supported them, such as their foreign mercenary troops and the cult of the Apis bull. Once these institutions and individuals were removed from power by means of the exile predicted in verse 19, Egypt could resume life as usual.

Taking all of the redaction and text-critical data into account, I reconstruct the earliest form of the second oracle as follows:

Jeremiah 46:14–24, 26c

[14] Declare in ⟦...⟧ in Migdol and proclaim in Memphis ⟦...⟧: "Take a stand and be firm, because a sword will devour all around you!" [15] Why has Apis fled? Why did your {bull} not stand firm? Because Yahweh pushed him [16] {he stumbled} repeatedly and fell. Each man said to his companion, "Arise! Let us return to our people, to the land of our birth because of the {oppressor's} sword. [17] {Give} Pharaoh {Nekau} king of Egypt {the name} "Loudmouth Who Lets the Appointed Time Pass By." [18] As I live, says King Yahweh ⟦...⟧, he is coming like Tabor among the mountains and like Carmel on the sea. [19] Pack your bags for exile, O prostrate daughter Egypt! For Memphis will become a waste, a ruin without inhabitant. [20] Egypt is a heifer {with a beautiful mouth}. An insect from the north lands on her. [21] Even her mercenaries in her midst are like fatted calves. Indeed, they too have turned and fled together. They did not stand because the day of their calamity has come upon them, the time of their punishment. [22] Her voice goes forth like a snake, for they come with an army and they bring axes against her like hewers of trees. [23] They cut down her forest, says Yahweh, even though it is impenetrable, for they are more numerous than locusts. They are without number. [24] Daughter Egypt is put to shame. She is given into the hand of a people from the north. ⟦...⟧ [26c] But afterwards she will be inhabited as in the days of old, says Yahweh.

[14] הגידו ⟦...⟧ במגדול והשמיעו בנף ⟦...⟧ התיצב והכן לך כי אכלה חרב סביבך [15] מדוע {נָס} חַף אַבִּירְךָ} לא עמד כי יהוה הדפו [16] הרבה {כָּשַׁל} גם נפל איש אל רעהו ויאמרו קומה ונשבה אל עמנו ואל ארץ מולדתנו מפני חרב {הַיּוֹנָה} [17] {קראוּ שֵׁם} פרעה {נכה} מלך מצרים שאון העביר המועד [18] חי אני נאם המלך יהוה ⟦...⟧ כי כתבור בהרים וככרמל בים יבוא [19] כלי גולה עשי לך יושבת בת מצרים כי נף לשמה תהיה ונצתה מאין יושב [20] עגלה {יְפֵה־פִיָּה} מצרים קרץ מצפון בא בא [21] גם שכריה בקרבה כעגלי מרבק כי גם המה הפנו נסו יחדיו לא עמדו כי יום אידם בא עליהם עת פקדתם [22] קולה כנחש ילך כי בחיל ילכו ובקרדמות באו לה כחטבי עצים [23] כרתו יערה נאם יהוה כי לא יחקר כי רבו מארבה ואין להם מספר [24] הבישה בת מצרים נתנה ביד עם צפון ⟦...⟧ [26c] ואחרי כן תשכן כימי קדם

---

with the translator skipping from the או of וְאַחֲרֵכן in verse 26c to the או of וַאֲמַר that begins verse 27.

Dating

The dating of the second oracle against Egypt hinges on the textual history and interpretation of verse 17. In the Septuagint and the Peshitta, this verse identifies the defending pharaoh as Nekau II, while the latter half of the verse could contain a pun on Apries's personal name חפרע. These two data points assume different historical settings: if the reading of the Septuagint and the Peshitta is preferred, then the oracle most likely refers to the first Babylonian invasion of Egypt in 601 BCE; if the verb העביר alludes to Apries, then the oracle most likely dates to the second Babylonian invasion of Egypt in 582 BCE. Of the two options, I find the first to be more plausible. The agreement between the Septuagint and one branch of the Masoretic Text family—the Peshitta—suggests that פרעה נכה is the preferred reading, while the words חפרע and העביר are too dissimilar to form an easily recognizable pun. If this line of reasoning proves cogent, then the attempted Babylonian invasion of 601 BCE represents the most plausible setting for the second oracle since it is the only historically attested Babylonian invasion during Nekau II's reign.[144]

It may be possible to date the second oracle even more precisely. Overall, this text envisions the first Babylonian invasion of Egypt as a divinely ordained surgical strike: at the beginning of hostilities, Yahweh places the Apis bull *hors de combat* with a well-timed shove, removing any divine protection that the city of Memphis might enjoy (verses 15–16); Nekau II fails to seize the initiative in the face of Nebuchadnezzar's inexorable advance (17–18); Egypt's foreign mercenaries—gone soft through decadent living—turn and flee (verse 21); and the invading army hews down the palm groves surrounding the city of Memphis (verse 22). In real life, none of this came to pass. Nekau II routed the Babylonian army at the delta fortress of Migdol and then launched a successful counter attack on Gaza. Because the oracle incorrectly predicts the outcome of the invasion, it most likely predates the beginning of this campaign in November or December 601 BCE.[145] Instead, it may reflect the lead-up to the invasion as the Babylonian army mustered in the southern Levant.

---

144. So too Stipp, *Jeremia 25–52*, 655.
145. Wiseman, *Chronicles of Chaldaean Kings*, 70–71; Grayson, *Assyrian and Babylonian Chronicles*, 101.

Interpretation

Like the first oracle, the second oracle against Egypt comments on the ongoing conflict between Egypt and Babylon, but with one crucial difference: it most likely comes from a time when Judah was under Babylonian control and Nebuchadnezzar was preparing to invade Egypt.[146] Seen in this light, the overwhelming Babylonian victory depicted in the oracle appears suspiciously like Babylonian propaganda. Was the author of the second oracle a Babylonian apologist? Not necessarily. Rather, the interests of anti-Egyptian voices within Judah may have aligned with Babylonian policy toward Egypt.

Although the battle of Carchemish and Nebuchadnezzar's Levantine campaign left Egypt weakened, it still represented a formidable threat to both Babylon and Judah as the history of the early sixth century BCE shows. Egypt's proximity to the Levant meant that it could foment rebellion in Babylon's Levantine vassals with impunity. And, as long as Egypt remained a viable alternative to Babylon, there was always the temptation for pro-Egyptian factions within Judah to repledge their loyalty to Egypt—as they would do in 601 and 592 BCE—and resume the callous policies of the Saite regime. The only way to prevent this from happening was to remove the Saite pharaohs from power and the only person capable of doing so was Nebuchadnezzar. I claim, therefore, that the second oracle expresses the hope that Nebuchadnezzar would score a knock-out blow against the Saite state and render it incapable of ever subjugating Judah again. This sentiment finds explicit expression in Ezek 29:15, which describes the post-destruction fate of the Saite kingdom: "It shall be the lowliest of the kingdoms and will never again vaunt itself over the nations. I will make them too small to rule over the nations" (מן הממלכות תהיה שפלה ולא תתנשא עוד על הגוים והמעטתים לבלתי רדות בגוים). Similarly, the second oracle describes the defeat and exile of the Saite elite and their supporters but ends with a promise of rehabilitation for the rest of Egypt.

Verses 25–26b: A Prophetic Patchwork

Verses 25 and 26 show signs of extensive editorial activity. As mentioned in the previous section, verses 25 and 26ab represent a later insertion into the second oracle that severs the connection between "daughter Egypt" in verse 24 and the feminine singular verb in verse 26c. In addition, the Septuagint lacks a counterpart to verse 26 as a whole and the phrase "and upon Egypt and upon its gods and upon its kings and

---

146. Stipp, *Jeremia 25–52*, 661.

upon Pharaoh" (ועל מצרים ועל אלהיה ועל מלכיה ועל פרעה) in verse 25.[147] The absence of this material in the Septuagint coupled with the repetition of "and upon Pharaoh" in the Masoretic Text of verse 25 suggests that these sections are a later addition.[148] Based on the textual data, I argue that verses 25 and 26 developed in two stages. First, a redactor inserted the shorter form of verse 25 between what is now verses 24 and 26c. Then, a second redactor added verse 26ab to the source text of the Masoretic Text and expanded verse 25.[149] In the following paragraphs, I will examine the dating of and motivation for these expansions.

Verse 25 contains a textual crux that that proves crucial for contextualizing the insertion of this verse into the second oracle against Egypt: the Masoretic Text family and the Hebrew source text of the Septuagint utilize different prepositions to express the relationship between Thebes and the Egyptian god Amun. Where the Masoretic Text uses the preposition מן "from,"[150] the Septuagint reads "See, I am avenging Amun, her son upon Pharaoh and those who trust in him" (ἰδοὺ ἐγὼ ἐκδικῶ τὸν Αμων τὸν υἱὸν αὐτῆς ἐπὶ Φαραω καὶ ἐπὶ τοὺς πεποιθότας ἐπ' αὐτῷ), reflecting a Hebrew source text that read אמון בנא "Amun in Thebes." Presumably, the Septuagint translator of verse 25 misinterpreted the consonantal sequence בנא in their source text as variant form of בנה "her son," which is unsurprising given the use of בא for בה "in her" in verse 20. The reading of the Septuagint is preferable to the reading of the Masoretic Text because it coheres better with religious data from the ancient Near East. The name "Amun in Thebes" (אמון בנא) matches other geographically determined divine names found in the Hebrew Bible and in Northwest Semitic inscriptions, such as "Yahweh in Hebron" (יהוה בחברון) in 2 Sam 15:7 and "Tannit in Lebanon" (תנת בלבנן) in *KAI* 81:1,[151] while the reading of the

---

147. Sharp, "'Take Another Scroll and Write,'" 511.
148. Janzen, by contrast, attributes the absence of this material in the Septuagint to haplography (Janzen, *Studies in the Text of Jeremiah*, 118).
149. Alternatively, a third redactor could have expanded verse 25 independently of the additions in verse 26ab.
150. The Peshitta reflects a source text with the preposition מן when it reads Hebrew מנא as "Ammon of the water" (ʾamon d-mayyo).
151. For additional examples of "DN ב-GN" names see P. Kyle McCarter, "Aspects of the Religion of the Israelite Monarchy: Biblical and Epigraphic Data," in *Ancient Israelite Religion: Essays in Honor of Frank Moore Cross*, ed. Patrick D. Miller, Paul D. Hanson, and S. Dean McBride (Philadelphia: Fortress Press, 1987), 140–41. For a different analysis of this class of divine names see Spencer L. Allen, "An Examination of Northwest Semitic Divine Names and the *Bet*-locative," *JESOT* 2 (2013): 61–82; Spencer L. Allen, *The Splintered Divine: A Study of Ištar, Baal, and Yahweh Divine Names and Divine Multiplicity in the Ancient Near East*, SANER 5 (Berlin: De Gruyter, 2015), 297–308.

Masoretic Text lacks clear parallels.[152] The Septuagint reading also exhibits parallels with other passages from the book of Jeremiah.

Thematically, verse 25 envisions Yahweh fighting against Amun directly, in an ancient Near Eastern clash of the titans that recalls Yahweh's shoving match with the Apis bull in verses 15–16: "I am about to punish Amun in Thebes" (הנני פוקד אל אמון בנא). In this regard, verse 25 closely resembles the opening lines of Jer 51:44, where Yahweh states that "I will punish Bel [= Babylon's national god, Marduk] in Babylon" (ופקדתי על בל בבבל). In both verses, Yahweh states his intention to punish the head god of the enemy pantheon using almost identical language. The two verses differ only in the form of the verb (participle versus prefix conjugation) and the choice of preposition (אל versus על).[153] Unlike verse 25, however, the opening statement of Jer 51:44 forms part of a larger series of hostile actions taken against Babylon that includes references to military conflict and invasion, for example, "the wall of Babylon has fallen" (גם חומת בבל נפלה). Ultimately, this connection between Yahweh's conflict with Bel and the invasion and conquest of Babylon in Jer 51:44 may have inspired a later redactor to attach verse 25 to the second oracle against Egypt. Just as Yahweh's battle with Bel presaged the downfall of Babylon, so too Yahweh's battle with Amun could be connected with the invasion of Egypt predicted in Jer 46:14–24. This does not mean, of course, that verse 25 also referred to the first Babylonian invasion of Egypt in 601 BCE. It could also refer to the second or third invasion.

Because verse 25 represents a later insertion into the second oracle against Egypt, it does not necessarily date to 601 BCE like the rest of the oracle. The content of verse 25, however, suggests a relatively early date for the original composition of this verse, if not its insertion into Jer 46. Because verse 25 is directed against Egypt, it would make little

---

152. Most likely, the reading of the Masoretic Text developed through harmonization with Nah 3:8, which reads "Are you better than Thebes that dwells in the midst of rivers, surrounded by water, whose rampart is the sea, whose wall is water [following the Septuagint]?" (התטבי מנא אמון הישבה ביארים מים סביב לה אשר חיל ים מים חומתה) and is the only other text in the Hebrew Bible to mention the Egyptian god Amun. נא אמון in Nah 3:8 transcribes Egyptian *njw.t jmn* "city of Amun," one of several Egyptian names for Thebes.

153. As Aaron D. Hornkohl notes, the shift of על to אל in Jer 46:25 is a feature of Transitional and Late Biblical Hebrew (Aaron D. Hornkohl, *Ancient Hebrew Periodization and the Language of the Book of Jeremiah: The Case for a Sixth-Century Date of Composition*, SSLL 74 [Leiden: Brill, 2014], 227–37). The expressions פקד על and פקד אל are thus semantically equivalent.

4. Fulminating against the Pharaoh

sense for it to be written after Egypt ceased to be relevant in Judahite political life. Judah finally escaped Saite control in 587 BCE when they were conquered by Babylon, and so verse 25 most likely dates before this time.[154]

Following the addition of verse 25 to the second oracle against Egypt, a second redactor added verse 26ab between verses 25 and 26c in order to more explicitly connect Yahweh's battle with Amun to the Babylonian invasion of Egypt predicted in verses 14–24. The language of verse 26ab recalls Jer 44:30, which predicts that Apries will be given into the hands of his enemies during either the Egyptian civil war of 570 BCE or the third Babylonian invasion of 568 BCE as I demonstrate in the following chapter. In Jer 44:30, Yahweh declares: "I will hand them over to those who seek their life, to Nebuchadnezzar and his servants" (ונתתים ביד מבקשי נפשם וביד נבוכדראצר מלך בבל וביד עבדיו), while in Jer 46:26 he states: "I am about to hand over Pharaoh Apries king of Egypt into the hand of his enemies and into the hands of those who seek his life" (הנני נתן את פרעה חפרע ביד איביו וביד מבקשי נפשו).[155] Based on these similarities, I hypothesize that the addition of verse 26ab dates to the third Babylonian invasion of Egypt in 568 BCE.[156] The addition of the phrase "and upon Egypt and upon her gods and upon her kings" in verse 25, by contrast, proves harder to date and may ultimately precede the addition of verse 26ab to the oracle. Kahn, for example, suggests that the reference to multiple kings in verse 25 may reflect the early stages of the Egyptian civil war of 570 BCE when Apries and Amasis were still vying for power.[157]

Like the two preceding oracles, the fragmentary oracles in verses 25 and 26 express antipathy toward Egypt and its supporters. In its earliest reconstructible form, verse 25 singled out three individuals or groups for punishment: "Amun in Thebes, Pharaoh [[...]] and those who trust in him" (אל אמון בנא ועל פרעה [[...]] על הבטחים בו). If this verse dates to the first Babylonian invasion of Egypt, then the phrase "those who trust in him" in verse 25 could include members of the Judahite elite as in the anti-Saite oracle found in Ezek 29. According to Ezek 29:16, Egypt

---

154. Theoretically, verse 25 could condemn the Egyptians for failing to lift the siege of Jerusalem in 588 BCE sometime after the fact, but I would not date verse 25 significantly later than 587 BCE.

155. Janzen, *Studies in the Text of Jeremiah*, 41.

156. If I am correct, then the Babylonian invasion of Egypt in 568 BCE may have insured the continuing relevance of the second oracle against Egypt even though it incorrectly predicted that the Babylonian invasion of 601 BCE would succeed.

157. Kahn, "Nebuchadnezzar and Egypt," 74.

"will no longer be a source of trust for the house of Israel" (לא יהיה עוד לבית ישראל למבטח) implying that Egypt *did* serve as a source of trust for the Judahite elite during the Saite period. Verse 26ab then expands on verse 25 by specifying how Yahweh will punish these individuals: he will hand them over to Nebuchadnezzar king of Babylon and his officers. As in the preceding oracles, Babylon serves as a counterweight to Egyptian imperial ambitions and works to insure that Judah is never subject to Egyptian control ever again.

4.4. CONCLUSION

A better understanding of the Saite period provides new insight into Jer 2:14–19, 25:15–29, and 46:2–26. According to my analysis, Jer 2:14–19 dates between 620 or 612 and 610 BCE and condemns certain members of the Judahite elite for ignoring the plight of their compatriots. While a few Judahite collaborators like Pashḥur son of Immer reaped the benefits of Egyptian control, Judahite soldiers were fighting and dying on the banks of the Euphrates and Shiḥor in pursuit of the pharaohs' strategic goals. The earliest reconstructible form of Jer 25:15–29 dates to 604 BCE and provides a map of the Saite empire on the eve of the Babylonian conquest of the Levant. According to the logic of the oracle, Yahweh uses Babylon, represented by a cup of wine, to punish Egypt and free Judah from Saite control. Finally, the oracles against Egypt in Jer 46:2–26 consistently applaud Babylonian victories over Egypt—both real and imagined. The first oracle in verses 3–12 celebrates the Babylonian victory at the battle of Carchemish in 605 BCE; the second oracle in verses 14–24 predicts that the first Babylonian invasion of Egypt would be an overwhelming success; and verses 25–26 contain additional material from the Saite and Neo-Babylonian periods, some of which exhibits verbal and thematic parallels with Jer 44, to be discussed in the next chapter.

5.
At Home Abroad: Texts Relating to the Egyptian Diaspora in the Book of Jeremiah

Although Egyptian control over Judah ended in 588 BCE with Nebuchadnezzar II's third invasion of the Levant, Egypt did not immediately lose its relevance for Judahite life. Several Judahite diaspora communities in Egypt continued to live under Saite rule, and their experiences, I argue, shaped the book of Jeremiah. Two passages in particular—Jer 43:8–13 and Jer 44:16–19, 24–25—reflect ongoing contact between Judah and various diaspora communities in Egypt already in the early exilic period. Jeremiah 43:8–13, I claim, was composed in Daphnae around 582 BCE and reflects the experiences of Judahites living in Lower Egypt during Nebuchadnezzar's second invasion of Egypt, while Jer 44:16–19, 24–25 attests to contact between Judah and the Judahites living in Upper Egypt around 570 BCE. The book of Jeremiah thus preserves the earliest evidence for Judahite communities living in Egypt and provides evidence of contact between Judah and the Judahite communities in Daphnae and Upper Egypt at an early date.

5.1. JEREMIAH 43:8–13: FROM THE FRONTLINES TO THE FRONTIER

Jeremiah 43:8–13 constitutes the sole textual evidence, biblical or otherwise, for a Judahite community at Daphnae.[1] The unique character of

---

[1]. For potential archaeological evidence of a Judahite community at Daphnae see Maier, "Relations," 237–38; Holladay, "Judeans (and Phoenicians) in Egypt," 407; Jeffrey Spencer, "Egyptian Pottery and Imported Transport Amphorae from Tell Dafana: Types and Distribution," in *Tell Dafana Reconsidered:*

this passage has led some scholars to question its historicity.² But new archaeological evidence from Daphnae suggests that it is grounded in historical events. In this section, I will argue that Jer 43:8–13 reflects the experiences and concerns of the Judahite community in Daphnae in the lead-up to Nebuchadnezzar's second invasion of Egypt in 582 BCE. I will also explore how these verses came to be incorporated into the book of Jeremiah, concluding that they provide evidence for early contact between Judah and the Judahite diaspora communities in Egypt.

In the current arrangement of the book of Jeremiah, the oracle in Jer 43:1–13 forms part of a larger narrative. The preceding verses, Jer 42:1–43:7, describe the relocation of the entire population of Judah to Egypt in 586 BCE following the assassination of Gedaliah, the Babylonian-appointed governor of Judah. The military commanders Johanan and Azariah, along with the people of Judah, ask Jeremiah to consult Yahweh on their behalf. Earlier, in Jer 41:17, the people had broached the possibility of traveling to Egypt and they now wish to know "the road we should take and what we should do" (את הדרך אשר נלך בה ואת הדבר אשר נעשה). The community swears to obey Yahweh's commands and, after a ten-day interlude, Jeremiah informs the people that Yahweh wants them to remain in Judah. He also warns them not to go to Egypt and states that war, famine, and pestilence will follow them if they disobey Yahweh's commands. In 43:2–3, the people claim that Jeremiah is telling a lie in Yahweh's name and they accuse Baruch—who has gone unmentioned until this point of the story—of inciting Jeremiah against them. They then head to Egypt with Jeremiah and Baruch in tow and settle in Egypt.³ According to the current form of the text, Jeremiah delivers the oracle in Jer 43:8–13 immediately upon arriving in Daphnae:

The Archaeology of an Egyptian Frontier Town, ed. François Leclère and Jeffrey Spencer (London: The British Museum, 2014), 94–95; Jeffrey Spencer, "Catalogue of Egyptian Pottery, Transport Amphorae and Ostraca from Tell Dafana in the British Museum," in *Tell Dafana Reconsidered: The Archaeology of an Egyptian Frontier Town*, ed. François Leclère and Jeffrey Spencer (London: The British Museum, 2014), 107.

2. Lundbom, *Jeremiah 37–52*, 144; Allen, *Jeremiah*, 439; Schmidt, *Das Buch Jeremia: Kapitel 21–52*, 258.

3. Although chapters 42–44 reflect a tradition that Jeremiah fled to Egypt following the assassination of Gedaliah, the historical basis of this tradition remains debated. Hermann-Josef Stipp, for example, argues that Jeremiah and Baruch are a late addition to Jer 43:6 and that there is no evidence that Jeremiah and Baruch ever traveled to Egypt (Stipp, "Legenden der Jeremia-Exegese (II)," 654–63).

5. At Home Abroad

Jeremiah 43:8–13

⁸And the word of Yahweh came to Jeremiah in Daphnae: ⁹"Take some large stones in your hand and hide them in the presence of the Judahite men בְּמֶלֶט בַּמַּלְבֵּן which is at the entrance of Pharaoh's palace in Daphnae. ¹⁰And say to them, 'Thus says Yahweh of Armies, the god of Israel, "I am about to send for Nebuchadnezzar king of Babylon my servant. And he will set his throne above these stones which you hid and he will spread his שפרור above them. ¹¹And he will come and strike the land of Egypt. Those destined for death to death, those destined for exile into exile, and those destined for the sword to the sword. ¹²And he will kindle a fire in the temples of the Egyptian gods and burn them. And he will carry them off. And he will pluck the land of Egypt like a shepherd plucks (lice) from his cloak. And he will depart from there in peace. ¹³He will break the pillars of Beth Shemesh which is in Egypt and the temples of the Egyptian gods he will burn with fire."'"

⁸ויהי דבר יהוה אל ירמיהו בתחפנחס לאמר ⁹קח בידך אבנים⁴ גדלות וטמנתם במלט במלבן אשר בפתח בית פרעה בתחפנחס לעיני אנשים יהודים ¹⁰ואמרת אליהם כה אמר יהוה צבאות אלהי ישראל הנני שלח ולקחתי את נבכדראצר מלך בבל עבדי ושמתי⁵ כסאו ממעל לאבנים האלה אשר טמנתי ונטה את שפרורו [Q שפרירו] עליהם ¹¹ובאה [Q ובא] והכה את ארץ מצרים אשר למות למות ואשר לשבי לשבי ואשר לחרב לחרב ¹²והצתי אש בבתי אלהי מצרים ושרפם ושבם ועטה את ארץ מצרים כאשר יעטה הרעה את בגדו ויצא משם בשלום ¹³ושבר את מצבות בית שמש אשר בארץ מצרים ואת בתי אלהי מצרים ישרף באש

---

4. The word for stones exhibits gender disparity throughout the oracle. At the beginning of verse 9, it is modified by a feminine plural adjective, but in the rest of the oracle, it is referred to using masculine plural pronouns (e.g., טמנתם in verse 9, עליהם in verse 10). Most likely, this disparity reflects the neutralization of final nasal consonants that took place in later Hebrew, which led to a loss of distinction between masculine and feminine plural possessive suffixes: הם-, הן- -hĩ, ם-, ן- -ã. For more on this linguistic phenomenon, see section 5.2. below.

5. The Masoretic Text gives credit to Yahweh for some of Jeremiah and Nebuchadnezzar's actions by using first-person singular verbal forms in certain sections of the oracle (e.g., הצתי, שמתי). The Septuagint, by contrast, employs third-person masculine singular verb forms throughout the text of the oracle. Most scholars treat the Masoretic Text as secondary and interpret the reading of the Masoretic Text as a theologically motivated change intended to more explicitly credit Yahweh for Egypt's downfall (Janzen, *Studies in the Text of Jeremiah*, 133; Pohlmann, *Studien zum Jeremiabuch*, 160; Holladay, *Jeremiah 2*, 277; Stipp, *Das masoretische und alexandrinische Sondergut*, 126–27; Lundbom, *Jeremiah 37–52*, 146–47).

Textual and Redactional Criticism of the Oracle

Verses 9 and 10 contain several difficult words that affect the interpretation of the oracle as a whole. In verse 9, Yahweh instructs Jeremiah to "Take some large stones in your hand and hide them במלט במלבן which is at the entrance of Pharaoh's palace in Daphnae in the presence of the Judahite men" (קח בידך אבנים גדלות וטמנתם במלט במלבן אשר בפתח בית פרעה בתחפנחס לעיני אנשים יהודים).⁶ The terms מלט and מלבן are both obscure, which makes it difficult to understand Jeremiah's symbolic actions and to assess the historical context of the oracle. Because במלט lacks an equivalent in the Septuagint and could be a gloss on במלבן, I will begin with a linguistic analysis of the latter.⁷ Most cognate and inner-biblical evidence suggests that מלבן meant "a mold for bricks," but such a meaning does not make sense in the context of Jer 43:8–13, which states that Nebuchadnezzar will place his throne on top of the מלבן.⁸ Late Hebrew, Palmyrene, Syriac, and modern Arabic cognates of this word, however, can refer to anything rectangular—usually a door or window frame, but also a porch or portico.⁹ As Jacob Levy points out, these terms under-

---

6. Lundbom, *Jeremiah 37–52*, 144; Allen, *Jeremiah*, 439; and Schmidt, *Das Buch Jeremia: Kapitel 21–52*, 258 claim that Daphnae did not feature a royal palace during the Saite period and argue that the author of Jer 43:8–13 was either ignorant of the conditions in Daphnae or used the phrase בית פרעה to refer to an administrative building. Later literary evidence, however, supports Jer 43:8–13 in locating a royal palace at Daphnae. The Coptic Cambyses Romance mentions both a royal palace and a temple to Amun-Re located in Daphnae, while the eponymous narrator of the Instructions of Chashesonqy states that he received rations from the royal palace while imprisoned in Daphnae (H. Ludin Jansen, *The Coptic Story of Cambyses' Invasion of Egypt: A Critical Analysis of Its Literary Form and Its Historical Purpose* [Oslo: Dybwad, 1950], 64, 69; Heinz-Josef Thissen, *Die Lehre des Anchscheschonqi (P. BM 10508)*, PTA 32 [Bonn: Habelt, 1984], 10, 18).

7. Janzen, by contrast, attributes the absence of במלט in the Septuagint to haplography (Janzen, *Studies in the Text of Jeremiah*, 183).

8. Compare Akkadian *nalbanu* "brick mold" (*CAD* 11.1:199–200) and Jewish Babylonian Aramaic *malbānā* "brick mold" (Michael Sokoloff, *A Dictionary of Jewish Babylonian Aramaic of the Talmudic and Geonic Periods* [Ramat Gan: Bar Ilan University Press, 2002], 357) as well as 2 Sam 12:31 and Nah 3:14.

9. Marcus Jastrow, *Dictionary of the Targumim, the Talmud Babli and Yerushalmi, and the Midrashic Literature* (Peabody, MA: Hendrickson, 2006), 786; Robert Payne-Smith, *Thesaurus Syriacus* (Oxford: Clarendon, 1878–1901), 2:1187; Delbert R. Hillers and Eleonora Cussini, *Palmyrene Aramaic Texts* (Baltimore: Johns Hopkins University Press, 1996), 381; Basile Aggoula, "Remarques sur l'inventaire des inscriptions de Palmyre, Fasc XI et XII," *Sem* 29 (1979): 117.

went a semantic shift from "brick mold" to "any rectangular object."[10] The Septuagint also understood מלבן in this way and translated it with πρόθυρον "doorway, porch, or portico."[11] Based on this cognate and translational evidence, I would identify the מלבן as a rectangular architectural feature located near the entrance of Pharaoh's palace.[12]

Context allows us to narrow down the possibilities for interpretation even further. Verse 10 implies that מלבן refers to some sort of flat, horizontal surface when it states that Nebuchadnezzar will place his throne over the stones hidden by Jeremiah. Even a powerful Mesopotamian king like Nebuchadnezzar would have difficulty setting his throne on an uneven or vertical surface. The context of the verse also cautions against interpreting מלבן as doorway, as some of the cognate terms would indicate. Although the Mesopotamian king's throne may have fit in the doorway to Pharaoh's palace, it would have impeded movement in and out of the building. Therefore, I would interpret מלבן as a flat, rectangular surface, such as a courtyard or terrace.

The archaeological remains from Daphnae may even preserve a potential candidate for this architectural feature. As W. M. Flinders Petrie discovered in 1888, Saite-period Daphnae featured two large casemate structures which served as the foundation for additional buildings.[13] These structures consisted of a network of partially filled mud brick cells that could be used for storage and may have served to counteract

---

10. Jacob Levy, *Wörterbuch über die Talmudim und Midraschim* (2nd ed.; Berlin: Harz, 1924), 3:121.

11. LSJ, 1481; *GELS*, 586.

12. The term מלבן is especially well suited for describing a brick terrace. Not only are brick terraces usually rectangular, they also form a negative image of a large brick mold.

13. W. M. Flinders Petrie, *Tanis: Nebesheh (Am) and Defenneh (Tahpanhes)*, Memoir of the Egypt Exploration Fund 4 (London: Trübner & Co., 1888), 53–54. See also François Leclère, "Tell Dafana: Identity, Exploration and Monuments," in *Tell Dafana Reconsidered: The Archaeology of an Egyptian Frontier Town*, ed. François Leclère and Jeffrey Spencer (London: The British Museum, 2014), 11–16. Beginning with Petrie in the late nineteenth century, scholars have identified Daphnae as a military fortress like Migdol inspired, in part, by the description of Daphnae as a bulwark against Arabian and Assyrian aggression in Herodotus, *Hist.* 2.30 (Petrie, *Tanis: Nebesheh (Am) and Defenneh (Tahpanhes)*, 53). Recent archaeological work, along with a re-evaluation of the material from Petrie's excavation, however, indicates that Daphnae was a temple town rather than a fortress during the Saite period (Leclère, "Tell Dafana," 9). It is located at the modern site of Tell Dafana and features a temple and a palace (Leclère, "Tell Dafana," 21).

dampness in the humid Nile Valley.¹⁴ Several of the cells featured a vaulted roof, but others were closed by means of a loose paving stone, which granted access to the network of chambers below. Petrie identified the larger casemate structure as the foundation of the royal palace at Daphnae.¹⁵ More recent excavations have uncovered the entrance to this building. Along the northern face of the casemate structures, excavators discovered the remains of a paved road and a monumental limestone staircase. The staircase terminates in a rectangular landing, with a door to the first casemate structure on the right and a second staircase leading to the entrance of the second casemate structure on the left. To the right of the paved road, there is a brick terrace, which Petrie identified as the מלבן.¹⁶ The bricks of this terrace sat directly on top of loose sand, which would make it easy for Jeremiah to hide stones underneath them—or at least for an author to imagine him doing so.¹⁷ Verse 10 may, therefore, reflect this architectural feature.

Interpreting מלבן as "pavement" or "terrace" also helps us determine whether מלט is a secondary addition to the Masoretic Text. This term is cognate with Syriac *mlɔṭɔ* "mortar" and Classical Arabic *milāṭ* "plaster, cement" and probably referred to a type of fixative.¹⁸ As mentioned above, the Septuagint lacks a counterpart to the phrase במלט, which suggests one of two possibilities: either the Septuagint translator omitted a difficult word that they did not understand or they were working with a Hebrew source text that did not contain the phrase במלט. I prefer the second option and would interpret the prepositional phrase במלט in the Masoretic Text as a later explanatory gloss made by an editor who was

---

14. Oren, "Migdol," 13. One of these cavities yielded a seal of Psamtik I (Leclère, "Tell Dafana," 14).

15. Petrie, *Tanis: Nebesheh (Am) and Defenneh (Tahpanhes)*, 50–51; Leclère, *Les villes de Basse Égypte*, 514; Leclère, "Tell Dafana," 17.

16. Leclère, "Tell Dafana," 17.

17. Holladay suggests that the stones hidden by Jeremiah were meant to serve as a stabilizing platform for Nebuchadnezzar's throne (Holladay, *Jeremiah 2*, 302). But if I am correct in identifying the location of Jeremiah's sign act with the brick terrace in front of the casemate structures at Daphnae, then there would be no need for Jeremiah to level the ground in preparation for Nebuchadnezzar's throne.

18. Payne-Smith, *Thesaurus Syriacus*, 2:2137; William Edward Lane, *An Arabic-English Lexicon* (London: Williams & Norgate, 1863–1893), 7:2737; Albert de Biberstein-Kazimirski, *Dictionnarie arabe-français* (Paris: Maison-neuve, 1860), 2:1149; Georg Wilhelm Friedrich Freytag, *Lexicon Arabico-Latinum* (Halle: Schwetscke, 1830–1837), 4:207. For a slightly different analysis of the relationship between Hebrew מלט, Syriac *mlɔṭɔ* and Classical Arabic *milāṭ* see Noonan, *Non-Semitic Loanwords in the Hebrew Bible*, 146–47.

unfamiliar with the urban geography of Daphnae. If, for example, a later reader did not know that the terrace outside of the casemate structures at Daphnae sat directly on loose sand—and instead imagined Jeremiah performing his sign act on a paved terrace—then it would be difficult for the reader to envision Jeremiah's symbolic actions. The prophet could not simply lift up one of the bricks as the author of Jer 43:8–13 seems to have imagined, but would instead need to insert the stones into the structure of the terrace using a fixative. Therefore, I argue that a later editor added the prepositional phrase במלט in order to explain how Jeremiah hid the stones in the terrace outside the royal palace.

Verse 10 contains a third cryptic word. At the end of this verse, Jeremiah states that Nebuchadnezzar will "stretch out his שפרור over them [i.e., the stones]" (ונטה את שפרורו Q] שפרירו [עליהם]). The versions offer little help in interpreting this cryptic *hapax legomenon*. Both the Septuagint and the Peshitta translate שפרור as "weapon" (τὰ ὅπλα αὐτοῦ and *zēneh*, respectively), while the Vulgate and Targum Jonathan interpret it as another word for "throne" (*solium suum* and אודנה, respectively), neither of which make much sense in context.[19] There is no reason for the oracle to mention Nebuchadnezzar's throne twice in the same verse using different words, and neither weapons nor thrones appear as the direct object of the verb נטה elsewhere in the Hebrew Bible.[20] Despite these difficulties, the context of the verse offers two clues for interpreting שפרור. It was an object that could be spread or unfurled (נטה) and, because it is associated with the Babylonian king, it stands a good chance of having an Akkadian etymology. Based on these criteria, I argue that שפרור ultimately comes from the Akkadian verb *šuparruru* "to spread" and refers to a sunshade or parasol placed above Nebuchadnezzar's royal throne.[21]

---

19. According to Robert Hayward, some Targumic manuscripts (b g o) translate שפריר using אפדנא, an Old Persian loanword into Aramaic that denotes a type of palace (Robert Hayward, *The Targum of Jeremiah: Translated, with Critical Introduction, Apparatus, and Notes*, The Aramaic Bible 12 [Wilmington, DE: Michael Glazier, 1987], 162; Claudia A. Ciancaglini, *Iranian Loanwords in Syriac*, Beiträge zur Iranistik 28 [Wiesbaden: Dr. Ludwig Reichert, 2008], 113–14).

20. In the book of Joshua, Yahweh commands Joshua to "point with the spear that is in your hand" (נטה בכידרון אשר בידך) (Josh 8:18, 26), but here, spear is part of a prepositional phrase modifying נטה and not the direct object of the verb.

21. *CAD* 17.3:317. Unfortunately, Akkadian does not preserve any nominal derivatives of *šuparruru*, which complicates the comparison of שפרור and *šuparruru*. Carroll, Holladay, Lundbom, Allen, and Schmidt identify Nebuchadnezzar's שפרור as a sunshade or tent based on context, but, as far as I am aware, no one has made the linguistic connection between Hebrew שפרור and Akkadian *šuparruru* (Carroll, *Jeremiah*, 725; Holladay, *Jeremiah 2*, 277; Lundbom,

As Oscar White Muscarella points out, such sunshades served primarily as royal status symbols in Mesopotamia.[22] The oracle thus envisions Nebuchadnezzar placing the symbols of his authority outside of the royal palace at Daphnae in preparation for executing judgment on the city and its inhabitants.[23]

According to verse 11, Nebuchadnezzar will punish the residents of Daphnae, giving "those destined for death to death, those destined for exile into exile, and those destined for the sword to the sword" (אשר למות למות ואשר לשבי לשבי ואשר לחרב לחרב). Then, in verse 12, the focus of the oracle shifts from the human population of Daphnae to its divine inhabitants. In the first half of this verse, the figure of Jeremiah claims that Nebuchadnezzar will burn down the temples of Egypt and abduct the divine images housed in them: "and he will kindle a fire in the temples of the Egyptian gods and burn them. And he will carry them off" (והצתי אש בבתי אלהי מצרים ושרפם). He then employs an evocative simile to describe Nebuchadnezzar's systematic removal of Daphnae's population—"he shall pluck the land of Egypt like a shepherd plucks (lice) from his cloak" (ועטה את ארץ מצרים כאשר יעטה הרעה את בגדו)[24]—before stating that Nebuchadnezzar will depart from Egypt unopposed.

Verse 13 makes the surprising claim that Nebuchadnezzar will continue to mete out punishment on Egypt even after his departure: "He will break the pillars of Beth Shemesh which is in Egypt and the temples

---

Jeremiah 37–52, 146; Allen, *Jeremiah*, 426; Schmidt, *Das Buch Jeremia: Kapitel 21–52*, 258). Naftali Herz Tur-Sinai argues that שפרור is related to the Akkadian adjective *šuparruru* and designates a net that Nebuchadnezzar will spread over Jeremiah's audience upon his arrival in Daphnae (Naftali Herz Tur-Sinai, *Die Heilige Schrift* [Frankfurt: J. Kaufmann, 1937], 1416). This interpretation suffers from several problems, however. Although the adjective *šuparruru* can modify other Akkadian words for net, such as *sapārša*, it never refers to a net by itself. Furthermore, Tur-Sinai's interpretation assumes that the suffix on עליהם refers to the members of Jeremiah's audience, but it is unclear why Jeremiah would refer to the men of Judah in the third person as part of a direct address.

22. Oscar White Muscarella, "Parasols in the Ancient Near East," *Notes in the History of Art* 18 (1999): 6.

23. Compare, also, Jer 1:15: "because I am about to call all 〚...〛 the kings of the north, says Yahweh. And they will come and each one will set his throne at the entrance to the gates of Jerusalem" (כי הנני קרא לכל 〚...〛 ממלכות צפונה נאם יהוה ובאו ונתנו איש כסאו פתח שערי ירושלם). Here, I omit the word משפחות "tribes" with the Septuagint (Janzen, *Studies in the Text of Jeremiah*, 10).

24. For the translation of עטה as "to pluck (lice)" see John Adney Emerton, "Lice or a Veil in Song of Songs 1:7?," in *Understanding Poets and Prophets: Essays in Honour of George Wishart Anderson*, ed. A. Graeme Auld, JSOTSup 152 (Sheffield: JSOT Press, 1993), 134–38.

of the Egyptian gods he will burn with fire" (ושבר את מצבות בית שמש אשר באש ישרף מצרים אלהי בתי ואת מצרים בארץ). This logical inconsistency has led many scholars to treat verse 13 as a later addition to the oracle or relocate it after verse 11, which describes Nebuchadnezzar's judgment.²⁵ Of the two solutions, I prefer the first. Relocating verse 13 after verse 11 leads to a repetition of the claim that Nebuchadnezzar will burn the temples of the Egyptian gods using only slightly different vocabulary and phrasing: "and he will kindle a fire in temples of the Egyptian gods and burn them / and the temples of the Egyptian gods he will burn with fire" (והצבתי אש בבתי אלהי מצרים ושרפם / ואת בתי אלהי מצרים ישרף באש).²⁶ Treating verse 13 as a secondary addition, by contrast, is consistent with the literary development of oracles in the ancient Near East in general and in ancient Israel in particular: oracles on the same subject matter tend to be combined over time.²⁷

Verse 13 features its own text-critical riddle that affects the interpretation of the oracle: the Masoretic Text family and the Septuagint gloss the place name בית שמש in different ways. In the Masoretic Text, the Peshitta, the Targum, and the Vulgate, the second half of the verse reads "and he [= Nebuchadnezzar] will break the pillars of Beth Shemesh, which is in Egypt" (ושבר את מצבות בית שמש אשר בארץ מצרים), while the Septuagint states that "and he will shatter the pillars of Heliopolis, namely, those in On" (καὶ συντρίψει τοὺς στύλους Ἡλίου πόλεως τοὺς ἐν Ων = ושבר את מצבות בית שמש אשר באון).²⁸ The divergence of the two main textual witnesses to this passage suggests that verse 13 originally ended after the geographic name בית שמש and was only later expanded in various ways to distinguish the בית שמש located in Egypt from the בית שמש located in the Levant. One of these glosses survived in the Masoretic Text family and the other survived in the Septuagint.

The Septuagint rendering of בית שמש as Heliopolis most likely presupposes the gloss "which are in On." Without this identifying gloss,

---

25. Pohlmann, *Studien zum Jeremiabuch*, 160; Holladay, *Jeremiah 2*, 277; Lundbom, *Jeremiah 37–52*, 139. In theory, verse 13 could serve as a coda to the oracle, but it introduces new information not found in the preceding verses— namely, that Nebuchadnezzar will break the pillars of Beth Shemesh.
26. Kahn, "Nebuchadnezzar and Egypt," 74.
27. Martti Nissinen, for example, notes that Neo-Assyrian prophecies were occasionally grouped into larger compilations dealing with a single topic (Martti Nissinen, *Ancient Prophecy: Near Eastern, Biblical, and Greek Perspectives* [Oxford: Oxford University Press, 2018], 99–100). See also Reinhard G. Kratz, *The Prophets of Israel*, trans. Anselm C. Hagedorn and Nathan MacDonald, CrStHB 2 (Winona Lake, IN: Eisenbrauns, 2015), 31–32.
28. The translator of this passage apparently interpreted את מצבות as the antecedent of אשר באון rather than בית שמש.

however, it is unclear what בית שמש refers to in the context of verse 13 and the oracle against Egypt in Jer 43:8–13 as a whole. One thing is certain, however: בית שמש probably did not refer to Heliopolis in the oldest version of this text for two reasons. First, the standard Hebrew name for Heliopolis was אן, a Hebrew transcription of Egyptian *jwnw*.[29] Second, it would be strange for the oracle to threaten a city that goes unmentioned in the rest of Jer 42–43 and is irrelevant from a narrative point of view. For these reasons, I would follow Holladay in translating בית שמש as "temple of the Sun" and treat it as a reference to the temple of the sun god Amun-Re found in the northern precinct of Daphnae.[30] If this interpretation proves correct, then verse 13 represents an independent oracle on the fate of Daphnae that was appended to verses 8–12 sometime before the integration of Jer 43:8–13 into its present context.

The identification of בית שמש as Heliopolis in the Septuagint may reflect the events of the early Achaemenid period. The later Greek historians Strabo (*Geogr.* 17.1.27–28) and Diodorus Siculus (*Bib. hist.* 1.46) both claim that the Persian king Cambyses mutilated the obelisks of Heliopolis when he captured Egypt in 525 BCE, and this event may have motivated the gloss found in the Septuagint. The religious architecture of Heliopolis may have played a role in this re-identification as well. Verse 13 associates בית שמש with "pillars" (מצבות), and Heliopolis was so famous for its obelisks in antiquity that its Egyptian name, *jwnw*, literally means "pillars." To date, excavators have uncovered the remains of numerous obelisks at Heliopolis, dating from the New Kingdom until the Saite period.[31]

Based on this text-critical and redactional analysis, I reconstruct the earliest forms of Jer 43:8–12 and 13 as follows:

Jeremiah 43:8–12, 13

[8] And the word of Yahweh came to Jeremiah in Daphnae: [9] "Take some large stones in your hand and hide them 〚...〛 in the terrace which is

---

29. Muchiki, *Egyptian Proper Names and Loanwords*, 229–30; Beyer, *Ägyptische Namen und Wörter im Alten Testament*, 80.

30. Holladay, *Jeremiah 2*, 320; Leclère, *Les villes de Basse Égypte*, 128–29, 527; Leclère, "Tell Dafana," 20. In addition to the archaeological evidence presented by Leclère, the Coptic Cambyses Romance also locates a temple of Amun-Re in Daphnae during the reign of Apries (Jansen, *Coptic Story of Cambyses' Invasion of Egypt*, 64).

31. W. M. Flinders Petrie and Ernest McKay, *Heliopolis, Kafr Ammar and Shurafa* (London: School of Archaeology in Egypt, 1915), 5–6; Abdel-Aziz Saleh, *Excavations at Heliopolis: Ancient Egyptian Ounû* (Cairo: Cairo University Faculty of Archaeology, 1981–1983), 1:39–41.

at the entrance of Pharaoh's palace in Daphnae in the presence of the Judahite men. ¹⁰ And say 〚...〛, 'Thus says Yahweh 〚...〛, "I am about to send for Nebuchadnezzar king of Babylon 〚...〛. And {he} will set his throne above these stones which {you} hid and he will spread his parasol above them. ¹¹ And he will come and strike the land of Egypt. Those destined for death to death, those destined for exile into exile, and those destined for the sword to the sword. ¹² And {he} will kindle a fire in the temples of {their} gods and burn them. And he will carry them off. And he will pluck the land of Egypt like a shepherd plucks (lice) from his cloak. And he will depart 〚...〛 in peace.
¹³ He will break the pillars of Beth Shemesh 〚...〛 and the temples of {their} gods he will burn with fire.""³²

⁸ ויהי דבר יהוה אל ירמיהו בתחפנחס לאמר ⁹ קח בידך אבנים גדלות וטמנתם 〚...〛 במלבן אשר בפתח בית פרעה בתחפנחס לעיני אנשים יהודים ¹⁰ ואמרת אליהם כה אמר יהוה צבאות אלהי ישראל הנני שלח ולקחתי את נבכדראצר מלך בבל 〚...〛 ו{שם} כסאו ממעל לאבנים האלה אשר {טָמָנְתָּ} ונטה את שפרורו [Q שפרירו] עליהם ¹¹ ובאה [Q ובא] והכה את ארץ מצרים אשר למות למות ואשר לשבי לשבי ואשר לחרב לחרב ¹² ו{הצב} אש בבתי {אלהיהם} ושרפם ושבם ועטה את ארץ מצרים כאשר יעטה הרעה את בגדו ויצא משם בשלום
¹³ ושבר את מצבות בית שמש 〚...〛 ואת בתי {אלהיהם} ישרף באש

Dating

Several clues within Jer 43:8–13 allow us to reconstruct the historical context of 43:8–12 and 43:13 with a high degree of accuracy. Both oracles predict that Nebuchadnezzar would successfully invade Egypt and punish its inhabitants, but as mentioned in the previous chapters, all three of Nebuchadnezzar's Egyptian campaigns failed. Because Jer 43:8–12 and 43:13 both make an incorrect prediction, they most likely predate one of Nebuchadnezzar's attempts to invade Egypt. Of the three invasions, the content of Jer 43:8–12 and 43:13 best fits Nebuchadnezzar's second campaign against Egypt in 582 BCE, in which Daphnae played a pivotal role.³³ According to the Apries Stela, Apries received advanced warning of Nebuchadnezzar's invasion plans from a

---

32. Here, I follow the Septuagint in omitting אליהם "to them," צבאות "of Armies," and עבדי "my servant" in verse 10 and משם "from there" from verse 13 (for an evaluation of these textual variants, see Janzen, *Studies in the Text of Jeremiah*, 54–57, 74). I also split the difference between the Masoretic Text and the Septuagint and read בתי אלהיהם "the temples of their gods" in verses 12 and 13 instead of בתי אלהי מצרים "the temples of the gods of Egypt" or οἰκίαις θεῶν αὐτῶν "the temples of their gods" and οἰκίαις αὐτῶν "their temples."

33. Holladay and Hermann-Josef Stipp, by contrast, connect the oracle in Jer 43:8–13 to Nebuchadnezzar's third Egyptian campaign of 568 BCE (Holladay, *Jeremiah 2*, 302; Stipp, "Concept of the Empty Land," 123). Such

deserter and was able to rout the Babylonian army in the eastern delta outside of Daphnae.³⁴ At that point, however, Nebuchadnezzar's forces had already bypassed or subdued the Egyptian fortresses farther to the east, which would have left plenty of time for a Judahite observer to compose an oracle (or oracles) predicting Babylonian victory at Daphnae before the final confrontation outside the city.

The content of the two oracles also help us pinpoint their likely place of composition. Both Jer 43:8–12 and 43:13 display familiarity with the urban geography of Daphnae: Jer 43:8–12 mentions the brick terrace located at the entrance of the royal palace and appears to be familiar with specific details of its construction (i.e., that it sat on loose sand), while Jer 43:13 refers to the temple of Amun-Re located in Daphnae. The specificity of these details suggest that the two oracles originated in Daphnae. This conclusion receives support from the thematic focus of the oracles. Of all the Judahite communities in the early sixth century BCE, the Daphnae community would be the most interested in the fate of this city. For the communities in Babylon and Judah, Nebuchadnezzar's second invasion of Egypt would be a notable event, but for the community in Daphnae it was a matter of survival—would they be forced to relocate for the second time in a decade? Moreover, the Daphnae community would have had the best grasp on the military developments taking place in the vicinity of their city. An observer based in Babylon or Judah would have a hard time piercing the fog of war hanging over Egypt in 582 BCE and issuing a plausible prediction about Nebuchadnezzar's movements.³⁵

Interpretation

Neither Jer 43:8–12 nor 43:13 offer a rationale for the anticipated sack of Daphnae.³⁶ It is not explicitly identified as a punishment for the sins of the Judahite community; it is just something that will happen. It is tempting, therefore, to treat Jer 43:8–12 and 43:13 as anti-Egyptian oracles on a par with Jer 25:15–29 and 46:2–26. Both oracles, after all,

---

a historical reconstruction is unlikely, however, since Daphnae did not play a critical role in that military conflict.

34. Abd el-Maksoud and Valbelle, "Une stèle de l'an 7 d'Apriès," 12.

35. It is also possible, although less likely, that Jer 43:8–13 was composed in Judah using information about Daphnae gleaned from an Egyptian source, such as a letter from Daphnae.

36. The later juxtaposition of Jer 42:1–43:7 and 43:8–13 makes it appear that Nebuchadnezzar's invasion of Egypt is a punishment for the Judahite remnant. In 42:16, Jeremiah proclaims that the sword, feminine, and pestilence will follow the Judah remnant to Egypt, and 43:8–13 explains how this will occur.

focus primarily on the destruction of Egyptian religious monuments. And, as argued in chapter 3, the Judahite diaspora in Egypt consisted primarily of non-elite individuals—those who had suffered the most under the Saite administration of Judah. Perhaps they felt that Egypt should undergo further punishment for the injustices they had suffered. At the same time, however, these individuals had recently relocated to Egypt to escape the horrors of the Babylonian conquest of Judah. It is hard to imagine that the Judahite community in Daphnae would hope for an encore of this gruesome event, which would—at best—drive them from their new home. Life in the diaspora may have tempered earlier anti-Egyptian sentiment among the Judahite inhabitants of Daphnae and led to a re-evaluation of Nebuchadnezzar's ongoing military actions. They were no longer hoping for Babylonian liberation from Egyptian rule but rather sought a reprieve from the ravages of war. Thus I would interpret Jer 43:8–12 and 43:13 as a warning to the Judahite inhabitants of Daphnae about the coming invasion.

A Note on the Compositional History of Jeremiah 42–43

If I am correct in attributing Jer 43:8–12 and 43:13 to the Judahite community in Daphnae, then the historical and geographic context of these oracles stands at odds with the rest of Jer 42–43. As Karl-Friedrich Pohlmann and Hermann-Josef Stipp point out, these chapters seek to discredit the Egyptian community as disobedient and depict the land of Judah as empty and ripe for reinhabitation following the departure of the remnant of Judah.[37] They thus reflect the perspective of those who were deported to Babylon in 586 BCE as punishment for Gedaliah's death.[38] Stipp refers to chapters 42:1–43:7 and their larger literary context in Jer 37–43 as the "Narrative of Judah's Downfall in Palestine."[39] Most likely, these chapters were composed in Babylon itself shortly after the events they depict. Thematic differences between Jer 42:1–43:7 and

---

37. Pohlmann, *Studien zum Jeremiabuch*, 157; Carolyn J. Sharp, *Prophecy and Ideology in Jeremiah: Struggles for Authority in the Deutero-Jeremianic Prose* (London: T&T Clark, 2003), 90; Stipp, "Concept of the Empty Land," 108–14.

38. Stipp, Rainer Albertz, Miller and Hayes, and Joel Weinberg, by contrast, argue that chapters 42 and 43 were written in 582 BCE and telescope the events of the early exilic period into a single narrative beginning with the assassination of Gedaliah in 586 BCE and ending with Nebuchadnezzar's invasion of the Transjordan in 582 BCE (Stipp, "Concept of the Empty Land," 115, 126, 128; Albertz, *Die Exilszeit*, 83–84; Miller and Hayes, *History of Ancient Israel and Judah*, 486; Joel Weinberg, "Gedaliah, the Son of Ahikam in Mizpah: His Status and Role, Supporters and Opponents," *ZAW* 119 [2007]: 357).

39. Stipp, "Concept of the Empty Land," 115.

Jer 43:8–13 support this conclusion. Where Jer 42:1–43:7 attributes Nebuchadnezzar's attack on Egypt to the perfidy of the Judahites living within its borders, Jer 43:8–13 merely predicts a Babylonian attack on Daphnae; it does not pass judgment on the Judahite refugees living in the city. And where Jer 42:1–43:7 claims that Nebuchadnezzar will annihilate the Judahite community in Egypt (e.g., "they shall have no survivor or refugee from the misfortune that I am bringing upon them," Jer 42:17 ולא יהיה להם שריד ופליט מפני הרעה אשר אני מביא עליהם), Jer 43:8–13 allows for the possibility of survivors when it states that the Mesopotamian king will give "those destined for exile into exile" (ואשר לשבי לשבי).[40]

If Jer 43:8–13 was composed in Daphnae and Jer 42:1–43:7 originated some 1,100 miles away in Babylon, how and when did these textual units come to be combined? We can safely rule out a postexilic date for several reasons. For one, it would be strange for members of the Egyptian community to preserve a historically inaccurate oracle for over four decades and then bring it back with them to the land of Judah. And while the third Babylonian invasion of Egypt in 568 BCE may have temporarily reawakened interest in prophecies of doom directed at Daphnae, it cannot account for the preservation of this oracle for another three decades until the first wave of exiles returned to Judah from Babylon. A postexilic date would also require the Babylonian returnees to maintain the claim that the Egyptian community ceased to exist shortly after 586 BCE, while at the same time co-opting an oracle from this community.

This conclusion leaves the exile as the most plausible context for the combination of Jer 43:8–13 and Jer 42:1–43:7. More specifically, I argue that the Judahite remnant transmitted Jer 43:8–13 from Egypt to Babylon in the early exilic period, perhaps not long after 582 BCE,[41]

---

40. Despite these differences, Jer 43:8–13 complements Jer 42:1–43:7 by describing the gruesome fate of the Daphnae community in detail.

41. See also Stipp, "Concept of the Empty Land," 151. Pohlmann's treatment of Jer 43:8–13 allows for a third possibility. He argues that Jer 43:8–13 was originally composed in Judah in order to dissuade certain Judahites from relocating to Egypt (Pohlmann, *Studien zum Jeremiabuch*, 163). If he is correct, then the exiles from 586 BCE could have carried a copy of Jer 43:8–13 with them to Babylon and used this oracle in constructing their polemic against the Egyptian community. This reconstruction, however, does not fit the historical context of Jer 43:8–13 proposed above: the oracle in Jer 43:8–13 was composed four years after the events depicted in Jer 42:1–43:7 and could not serve to dissuade the inhabitants of Judah from emigrating to Egypt. And even if Jer 42:1–43:7 dates to 582 BCE as some scholars have argued, it still stands at odds with Pohlmann's historical reconstruction. As I have argued above, the most plausible setting for the oracle in Jer 43:8–13 was Nebuchadnezzar's initial foray into Egypt when

as part of the ongoing contact between Judah and Babylon in the early exilic period.⁴² If the Babylonian community co-opted Jer 43:8–13 at an early date, then it becomes much easier to explain why this historically inaccurate oracle was preserved: it supported the larger claim of chapters 42 and 43 that the Egyptian diaspora was or would be destroyed regardless of its historical accuracy. And given Nebuchadnezzar's tendency to downplay military defeats in official records and replace them with descriptions of mutual destruction, we need not impute willful ignorance or self-deception to the Babylonian community.⁴³ Influenced by Babylonian propaganda, they may have believed that the Egyptian community *was* wiped out in 582 BCE.

Ultimately, Jer 42–43 shows signs of intercultural textual development. Jeremiah 43:8–13, I argue, originated in the Egyptian temple town of Daphnae in 582 BCE during Nebuchadnezzar's second invasion of Egypt. From there, it was sent to Babylon via Judah, where it was integrated into Jer 42:1–43:7 as a proof text describing the fate of the Egyptian community. If this hypothesis regarding the textual genesis of Jer 42–43 proves correct, then Jer 43:8–13 attests to ongoing contact between Judah and the diaspora community in Daphnae in the early exilic period.

---

fears ran high that the Babylonian army would capture Daphnae. But at that point, it would be illogical for the inhabitants of Judah to relocate to Egypt for safety. The Babylonian army had already meted out punishment to Judah en route to Egypt and had transformed the formerly safe haven of the eastern delta into a war zone.

42. Holladay, *Jeremiah 2*, 118–19, 434–35; Mark Leuchter, *The Polemics of Exile in Jeremiah 26–45* (Cambridge: Cambridge University Press, 2008), 224; Stipp, "Concept of the Empty Land," 136.

43. Nebuchadnezzar's first campaign against Egypt provides a good example of this practice. Although Herodotus (*Hist.* 2.159) depicts Nebuchadnezzar's Egyptian campaign of 601 BCE as an unmitigated disaster—the Babylonian army was routed at Migdol and Nekau II recaptured Gaza—the Babylonian Chronicle for 601 BCE simply states that Babylonian and Egyptian armies inflicted great losses on one another (Wiseman, *Chronicles of Chaldaean Kings*, 70–71; Grayson, *Assyrian and Babylonian Chronicles*, 101). And while the Babylonian Chronicle breaks off after 594 BCE, it is reasonable to assume that the lost portion of the chronicle described Babylonian defeats in a similar manner.

5.2. JEREMIAH 44: STRANGE GODS IN A STRANGE LAND

Lower Egypt was not the only home-away-from-home for Judahites during the Saite period. As part of their military service on behalf of Egypt, Judahite soldiers campaigned as far as the first cataract where some of them settled down and formed the nucleus of later Judahite communities. The earliest reference to one of these communities dates to approximately 539 BCE. In this section, I will argue that Jer 44:16–19, 24–25 preserves even earlier evidence for the existence of the Upper Egyptian diaspora. These verses, I claim, reflect contact between the Judahite diaspora community or communities in Upper Egypt and Judah sometime before 568 BCE.

Jeremiah 44:16–19, 24–25 forms part of a large narrative in Jer 44. In this text, the figure of Jeremiah delivers a speech to all of the Judahite inhabitants of Egypt and then enters into a theological debate with the community from Upper Egypt (פתרוס < Egyptian *pꜣ-tꜣ-rsj* "the southern land"). The speech itself contains fairly standard Deuteronomistic motifs: Jeremiah reminds the Egyptian communities that Yahweh brought disaster on Judah in the form of invasion and exile because the inhabitants of Judah offered incense to other gods.[44] He then asks the Egyptian communities why they continue to court disaster by worshiping foreign deities in the land of Egypt: "Why are you doing great evil to yourselves ... by angering me with the works of your hands, by making offerings to other gods in the land of Egypt?" (למה אתם עשים רעה גדולה אל נפשתכם ... להכעסני במעשי ידיכם לקטר לאלהים אחרים בארץ מצרים, Jer 44:7–8). In verses 16–19, the members of the Upper Egyptian community respond to Jeremiah's accusations and invert his arguments. They claim to have experienced hardship only when they stopped worshiping the Queen of Heaven—presumably as a result of Josiah's reforms—and vow to resume worshiping this goddess in Egypt as a means of insuring their prosperity. In response, Jeremiah ironically commands the women of Upper Egypt to keep their vows to the Queen of Heaven and promises that Yahweh's name will never again be uttered in the land Egypt. He also promises that Yahweh will watch over the Egyptian community "for harm and not

---

44. William McKane, "Worship of the Queen of Heaven (Jer 44)," in *Wer ist wie du, Herr, unter den Göttern? Studien zur Theologie und Religionsgeschichte Israels: Für Otto Kaiser zum 70. Geburtstag*, ed. Ingo Kottsieper (Göttingen: Vandenhoeck & Ruprecht, 1994), 321; Stipp, "Concept of the Empty Land," 131; Winifred P. Thiel, *Die deuteronomistische Redaktion von Jeremia 26–45: Mit einer Gesamtbeurteilung der deuteronomistischen Redaktion des Buches Jeremia*, WMANT 52 (Neukirchen-Vluyn: Neukirchener Verlag, 1981), 74–75.

5. At Home Abroad

for good. All the men of Judah who are in the land of Egypt will perish by the sword and famine until they are annihilated" (לרעה ולא לטובה ותמו כל איש יהודה אשר בארץ מצרים בחרב וברעב עד כלותם, Jer 44:27). The chapter closes with a sign that Yahweh's words will come to pass.

Text-Critical and Source-Critical Analysis

Fragmentary as they are, Jer 44:16–19 and 24–25 do not preserve any historical references that would allow us to date them more accurately. Instead, we must rely on the literary context of these verses in Jer 44 for help with dating. Unfortunately, however, chapter 44 is riddled with text-critical difficulties and logical inconsistencies that affect the interpretation of the text as a whole. William McKane rightly wonders "whether this [chapter] is not a long pastiche which has taken as its topic the idolatry of Judeans in Egypt."[45] In this section, I will attempt to resolve some of these difficulties and improve our understanding of the relationship between verses 16–19, 24–25 and the surrounding text. Building on the work of Hermann-Josef Stipp, I argue that the creator of chapter 44 combined two or three existing sources to form a narrative of Jeremiah's confrontation with the Judahite communities living in Egypt.

As argued in chapter 3, the earliest form of Jer 44:1 addressed the Judahites living in the land of Egypt and the land of Patros as a whole rather than in a series of individual communities. But even this more general characterization of Jeremiah's audience stands at odds with the following 13 verses, which presuppose a different setting and a different audience. In verse 7b, for example, Jeremiah asks: "Why are you doing great harm to yourselves to cut off man and woman, child and infant from the midst of Judah?" (למה אתם עשים רעה גדולה אל נפשתכם להכרית לכם איש ואשה עולל ויונק מתוך יהודה). Such a question only makes sense if Jeremiah's audience has not yet departed for Egypt but was still located in the land of Judah. It also puts the following verses into a different perspective: in particular, the phrase "in the land of Egypt where you are coming to settle" (בארץ מצרים אשר אתם באים לגור שם) in verse 8 (cf. v. 14) appears prospective rather than retrospective. The pronouncement of judgment in verse 12 also presupposes a setting in Judah:

---

45. McKane, "Worship of the Queen of Heaven," 321.

Jeremiah 44:12a

I will take the remnant of Judah who are determined to come to the land of Egypt to sojourn there and they shall perish in the land of Egypt.

ולקחתי את שארית יהודה אשר שמו פניהם לבוא ארץ מצרים לגור שם ותמו כל בארץ מצרים

Elsewhere in the Hebrew Bible, the idiom "to set one's face to do X" (שים פנים ל-) usually indicates that a decision has been made but has not been carried out yet (e.g., 2 Kgs 12:18; Dan 11:17). Jeremiah 42:15–17 furnishes two particularly clear examples of this usage:

Jeremiah 42:15–17

[15] Now, therefore, hear the word of Yahweh, O remnant of Judah! Thus says Yahweh of Armies, the god of Israel, "If you are indeed determined to go to Egypt and you come to sojourn there, [16] the sword which you fear will overtake you there in the land of Egypt, and the famine which you dread will follow you to Egypt and there you will die. [17] All of the people who have decided to go to Egypt to sojourn there will die by the sword, by famine, and by pestilence. They will not have a remnant or survivor from the harm which I am bringing upon them."

[15] ועתה לכן שמעו דבר יהוה שארית יהודה כה אמר יהוה צבאות אלהי ישראל אם אתם שום תשמון פניכם לבא מצרים ובאתם לגור שם [16] והיתה החרב אשר אתם יראים ממנה שם תשיג אתכם בארץ מצרים והרעב אשר אתם דאגים ממנו שם ידבק אחריכם מצרים ושם תמתו [17] ויהיו כל האנשים אשר שמו את פניהם לבוא מצרים לגור שם ימותו בחרב ברעב ובדבר ולא יהיה להם שריד ופליט מפני הרעה אשר אני מביא עליהם

In these verses, Jeremiah uses the expression שים פנים ל- to refer to the Judahite remnant because they are still located in the land of Judah. And since Jer 44:12 also uses this idiom, it most likely takes place in the land of Judah as well. Verse 12—as well as verse 14—also agrees with Jer 42:15–17 against Jer 44:1 in another way as well. In these verses, Jeremiah addresses himself to "the remnant of Judah" rather than the "Judahites living in the land of Egypt and the land of Patros."

These differences suggest that verses 2–14 belong to a different source than verse 1. At the same time, these verses exhibit thematic and verbal parallels with the "downfall of Judah in Palestine" narrative found in Jer 37:1–43:7. Both stories take place in Judah before the Judahite remnant has relocated to Egypt. Furthermore, verse 7b echoes the claim found in Jer 41–42 that the remnant's primary sin was relocating to Egypt, while Jer 44:12 employs phrasing reminiscent of Jer 42:15

and 17. These similarities suggest that verses 2–14 come from a source similar—although not outright identical—to the "downfall of Judah in Palestine" source. They also point toward a possible geographic origin for verses 2–14. According to Stipp, "the downfall of Judah in Palestine" narrative was composed in Babylon, and so it is possible that Jer 44:2–14—and any other verses affiliated with them—may have originated in Babylon as well.

The cast and setting of the narrative change abruptly in verse 15, signaling a potential change in source.[46] Here Jeremiah's interlocutors are no longer the remnant of Judah but rather "all the men who knew that their wives were making offerings to other gods, and all the women standing by, a great congregation and all the people living in the land of Egypt—namely, in Patros" (כל האנשים הידעים כי מקטרות נשיהם לאלהים אחרים וכל הנשים העמדות קהל גדול וכל העם הישבים בארץ מצרים בפתרוס).[47] In this regard, verse 15 agrees with verse 1 against verses 2–14 in placing Jeremiah and his addressees in Egypt. It differs slightly from verse 1, however, in changing Jeremiah's audience from "the Judahites living in the land of Egypt ... and in the land of Patros" to "the Judahites living in the land of Egypt—namely, in Patros." This discrepancy could signal a change in focus from the Judahite communities living in Egypt as a whole to the communities found in Upper Egypt alone. Nevertheless, verses 1 and 15 most likely stem from the same pen.

A second change of cast occurs in verse 16, again indicating a potential change in source. Despite the protestations of verse 15, several clues indicate that "all the women standing by" were the primary speakers in verses 16–19.[48] First, verse 15 contains several redundancies: "all the men" and "all the women" are subsets of the "all the people living in the land of Egypt—namely, in Patros." There is no need to include them here except to reconcile several mutually contradictory sources. Second, the reference to "our husbands" in the Masoretic Text of verse 19 does not make sense if "all the men who knew that their wives were making offerings to other gods" and "all the people living in the land of Egypt—namely, in Patros" are speaking in verse 15. The Peshitta and

---

46. As Joel Baden notes in a discussion of Pentateuchal source criticism, narrative contradictions are the most reliable indication of a change in source (Joel S. Baden, *The Composition of the Pentateuch: Renewing the Documentary Hypothesis*, ABRL [New Haven: Yale University Press, 2012], 30).

47. The Septuagint lacks an equivalent to the participle העמדות "standing by," but this textual variant does not affect my broader argument.

48. Thiel, *Die deuteronomistische Redaktion von Jeremia 26–45*, 70; Christl M. Maier, *Jeremia als Lehrer der Tora: Soziale Gebote des Deuteronomiums in Fortschreibungen des Jeremiabuches*, FRLANT (Göttingen: Vandenhoeck & Ruprecht, 2002), 100.

the Lucianic recension of the Septuagint sidestep this problem by prefacing verse 19 with an introductory phrase in order to indicate a change in speaker from the entire community to the women of the community ("and all the women answered and said" wa-ʿnay kolhēn nešeʾ wǝ-ʾmrǝn / "and the women said" καὶ αἱ γυναῖκες εἶπον). But these phrases are different and, therefore, likely to be secondary.[49] Third, the reference to "all the men who knew that their wives were making offerings to other gods" deprives verse 19 of its rhetorical force: "Was it without our husbands that we made cakes for her [[...]] and poured libations for her?" (המבלעדי אנשינו עשינו לה כונים [[...]] והסך לה נסכים).[50] Based on these inconsistencies, I argue that verses 16–19 were spoken by a group of women and, therefore, belong to a different source than verse 15.

Verses 16–19 also differ from verses 2–14. Where verses 2–14 condemn the remnant of Judah for offering incense to an anonymous group of other gods in the land of Judah, verses 16–19 preserve an alternative explanation for Judah's downfall set in an unspecified locale. A group of women claim that they only experienced hardship when they stopped performing various ritual actions (offering incense, pouring libations, making special cakes) for a goddess known as the Queen of Heaven (מלכת השמים).[51] They then vow to resume these ritual actions.

Verse 20 once again addresses multiple constituencies: "all the people," "the men," "the women," and "all the people answering him [= Jeremiah] this way." Although these redundancies are less extreme than in verse 15—and could be rhetorical—they do serve to modulate between verses 16–19 where Jeremiah's interlocutors are a group of women and verses 21–23 where Jeremiah addresses the remnant of Judah. This verse signals a transition between different sources and, as such, most likely belongs to the same source as verses 1 and 15.

---

49. See also Stipp, *Das masoretische und alexandrinische Sondergut*, 137n44.

50. Pohlmann, *Studien zum Jeremiabuch*, 172; McKane, "Worship of the Queen of Heaven," 319. For the omission of the difficult word להעצבה, see the excursus at the end of the chapter.

51. The Masoretic Text treats מלבת as if it were derived from מְלָ(א)כָה "handiwork," thus transforming the reference to an individual goddess into an allusion to the heavenly host. Some Masoretic manuscripts even include an א in between the ל and כ in order to further disguise the reference to a named goddess. The Septuagint, however, renders מלכת השמים as τῇ βασιλίσσῃ τοῦ οὐρανοῦ "the Queen of Heaven" in Jer 44:17–19, while Symmachus, Aquila, and Theodotion employ the translation τῇ βασιλίσσῃ τοῦ οὐρανοῦ "the Queen of Heaven" in both Jer 7:18 and 44:17–19. The Vulgate likewise renders מלכת השמים as *regina caeli* "Queen of Heaven" in both Jer 7:18 and 44:17–19. The agreement between the Septuagint, Symmachus, Aquila, Theodotion, and the Vulgate suggests that Jer 7:18 and 44:19 originally referred to the Queen of Heaven and not to the heavenly host.

Verses 21–23 return to the themes of verses 2–14: Yahweh brought disaster on Judah because the people of Judah burned incense for other gods. They also exhibit several verbal parallels with verses 2–14 including the accusation that the Judahites "did not walk in his [= Yahweh's] law, statues, and ordinances" (בתרתו ובחקתיו ובעדותיו לא הלכתם) in verse 23 (cf. ולא הלכו בתורתי ובחקתי in verse 10), and the characterization of the land of Judah as "a desolation and a waste and a curse [[...]] as it is to this day" (ותהי ארצכם לחרבה לשמהו לקללה [[...]] כהיום הזה) in verse 22 (cf. ותיינה לחרבה לשממה כיום הזה in verse 6).[52] These verbal and thematic parallels suggest that verses 21–23 belong to the same source as verse 2–14.

Verses 24–25, by contrast, continue the conversation begun in verses 16–19. They preserve Jeremiah's sarcastic reply to the Queen of Heaven's worshipers—albeit altered by later editorial interventions. Verse 24, in particular, shows signs of extensive editing. In its present form in the Masoretic Text, it addresses three partially overlapping groups: "all the people" (כל העם), "all the women" (כל הנשים), and "all of Judah which is in the land of Egypt" (כל יהודה אשר בארץ מצרים). Logic dictates that "all the people" and "all of Judah which is in the land of Egypt" are later additions to the verse.[53] If Jeremiah had originally addressed "all of the people" in verse 24, it would be unnecessary to add "all of the women," since women are a subset of "all of the people." Similarly, if he had addressed "all of Judah which is in the land of Egypt," it would be unnecessary to add "all of the people" and "all of the women" since "all of Judah" includes both of these two groups. It follows, therefore, that verse 24 originally addressed "all the women" and was only later expanded in order to smooth the transition from verses 20–23 to verse 25. Text-critical evidence provides further support for this conclusion. The Septuagint lacks an equivalent to the phrase "all of Judah which is in the land of Egypt," which suggests that this group is a later addition to the verse, taken perhaps from verse 26.[54]

Verse 25 also shows signs that it was originally addressed to a group of women. In the Masoretic Text, verse 25 employs a series of feminine plural prefix conjugation verbs with the masculine plural subject "you and your wives" (אתם ונשיכם) alongside masculine plural suffix conjugation verbs and possessive pronouns:

---

52. Omitting the phrase מאין יושב "without inhabitant" as a gloss from verse 2 with the Septuagint (Janzen, *Studies in the Text of Jeremiah*, 58).

53. Thiel, *Die deuteronomistische Redaktion von Jeremia 26–45*, 74, 76.

54. The Septuagint also lacks a counterpart to the title צבאות "of Armies" in this verse (Janzen, *Studies in the Text of Jeremiah*, 58).

Jeremiah 44:25

... What you have spoken with your mouths, you have fulfilled with your hands, saying, "We shall surely perform our vows which we vowed—to offer incense to the Queen of Heaven and pour libations for her." By all means, keep your vows and perform them!

... ותדברנה בפיכם ובידיכם מלאתם לאמר עשה נעשה את נדרינו אשר נדרנו לקטר למלכת השמים ולהסך לה נסכים הקים תקימנה את נדריכם ועשה תעשינה {אתם}...⁵⁵

As Teresa Ann Ellis points out, the alternation of masculine and feminine plural forms in this verse is too systematic to be an accident. She suggests that the use of feminine verbs with a grammatically masculine subject represents a gender-based attack on the men of the community for worshiping a goddess.⁵⁶ While I agree that verse 25 in its current form can be interpreted as a polemic, the apparent gender discrepancy in the verse is amenable to a combination of text-critical and linguistic solutions. In the Septuagint version of verse 25, Jeremiah addresses a group consisting only of women (ὑμεῖς γυναῖκες = אתנה נשים "you women") and I would argue that the Septuagint preserves the better reading here.⁵⁷ There is no obvious motive for a deliberate change of "you and your wives" to "you women," but there is a motivation for the opposite change—harmonization with the surrounding narrative. Nor is it clear how אתנה נשים could have morphed into אתם ונשיכם through scribal error.

Both logic and text-critical data suggest that Jeremiah's comments in verse 25 were originally addressed to a group of women. In such a context, the alternation between masculine and feminine forms becomes more comprehensible since masculine plural forms often replace feminine plural forms in Biblical Hebrew.⁵⁸ The second-person feminine plural suffix conjugation and the second-person feminine plural pronouns are particularly susceptible to replacement, due perhaps to the similarity between the masculine and feminine forms (e.g., כתבתם vs. כתבתן, כם- vs. כן-) and the neutralization of nasal consonants in word-final position in Late Hebrew (e.g., כתבתן, כתבתם > *katabtî*).⁵⁹ Another example

---

55. Reading תעשינה אתם "perform them" with the Septuagint in place of the Masoretic Text's repetitive תעשינה את נדריכם "perform your vows" (Janzen, *Studies in the Text of Jeremiah*, 58).

56. Teresa Ann Ellis, "Jeremiah 44: What if 'the Queen of Heaven' Is Yhwh?," *JSOT* 33 (2009): 481.

57. McKane, "Worship of the Queen of Heaven," 320.

58. GKC §135o, 144a; Joüon §149b, 150ab.

59. Elisha Qimron, *The Hebrew of the Dead Sea Scrolls*, HSS 29 (Atlanta: Scholars Press, 1986), 27–28; Richard C. Steiner, *Disembodied Souls: The Nefesh in Israel and Kindred Spirits in the Ancient Near East, with an Appendix on the Katumuwa*

of this phenomenon occurs in Ruth 1:8 where Naomi instructs Ruth and Orpah as follows: "Go, return each of you to her mother's house. May Yahweh show loyalty to you just as you have done with the dead and with me" (לכנה שבנה אשה לבית אמה יעשה [Q יעש] יהוה עמכם חסד כאשר עשיתם עם המתים ועמדי). In this verse, the imperatives appear in the feminine plural, but the suffix conjugation verb and the possessive suffix are masculine plural.[60] Based on this analysis, I reconstruct the earliest form of verses 24–25 as follows: "Jeremiah said 〚…〛 to all the women, 'Hear the word of Yahweh 〚…〛! Thus says Yahweh, 〚…〛 the god of Israel: "As for {you women}, what you have spoken with your mouths, you have fulfilled with your hands, saying, 'We shall surely perform our vows which we vowed—to offer incense to the Queen of Heaven and pour libations for her.' By all means, keep your vows and perform {them}!""" (ויאמר ירמיהו 〚…〛 אל כל הנשים שמעו דבר יהוה 〚…〛 כה אמר יהוה 〚…〛 אלהי ישראל לאמר {אתנה נשים} ותדברנה בפיכם ובידיכם מלאתם לאמר עשה נעשה את נדרינו אשר נדרנו לקטר {לְמַלְכַּת} השמים ולהסך לה נסכים הקים תקימנה את נדריכם ועשה תעשינה {אתם}).

Verses 26–29 once again locate Jeremiah's interlocutors in the land of Egypt. Verses 26 and 27 address "all the Judahites living in the land of Egypt," and verse 28 speaks of a return from Egypt to Judah. Such a setting suggests that this section comes from the same source as verses 1, 15, and 20. But where verses 1, 15, and 20 serve primarily to structure chapter 44 and resolve the discrepancies between its constituent sources, verses 26–29 pronounce judgment on the Judahites living in Egypt. According to verses 26–27, Yahweh will annihilate the Egyptian diaspora so that his name shall no longer be invoked in Egypt. This promise of total annihilation stands in tension with the promise of (limited) redemption in the following verse, a discrepancy that may indicate a different pedigree for verse 28. Perhaps a later editor who knew that the Judahite diaspora in Egypt had survived added verse 28 to the narrative.

Jeremiah 44 concludes with a prophecy about Apries, whose fate at the hands of unnamed enemies serves as a sign for Judahites living in Egypt:

Jeremiah 44:30

Thus says Yahweh, "I am about to give Pharaoh Apries into the hand of his enemies and into the hand of those who seek his life, just as I

Inscription, ANEM 11 (Atlanta: SBL Press, 2015), 141–43. More specifically, final ם and ן nasalized the preceding vowel and then were lost.

60. Thus, there is no need to posit partial linguistic updating in verse 25 as McKane suggests ("Worship of the Queen of Heaven," 321).

TABLE Source division of the book of Jeremiah 44

Source	Verses
Compiler	1, 15, 20, 26–27, 29 Minus the phrase "those living in Migdol, Daphnae, and Memphis" (הישבים במגדל ובתחפנחס ובנף) in verse 1
Downfall of Judah in Palestine	2–14, 21–23 Minus the phrase "except for fugitives" (כי אם פלטים) in verse 14
Queen of Heaven	16–19, 24–25 minus the phrases "to all the people and" (אל כל העם ו) and "all of Judah which is in the land of Egypt" (כל יהודה אשר בארץ מצרים) in verse 24 reading "you women" (אתנה נשים) with the Septuagint in verse 25
Unclear	28, 30

gave Zedekiah king of Judah into the hand of Nebuchadnezzar king of Babylon, his enemy and the one who was seeking his life.

כה אמר יהוה הנני נתן את פרעה חפרע מלך מצרים ביד איביו וביד מבקשי נפשו כאשר נתתי את צדקיהו מלך יהודה ביד נבוכדראצר מלך בבל איבו ומבקש נפשו

The affiliation of this verse is unclear. It may belong with verses 26–29 or represent a fourth source.[61] Whatever the case, the references to Apries, Nebuchadnezzar, and Zedekiah in verse 30 provide a potential historical anchor for the chapter as a whole as well as its component parts.

To summarize the discussion so far, Jer 44 consists of three contradictory sources. The first source—consisting of verses 1, 15, 20, 26–27, 29—condemns the Judahites living in Egypt to destruction for their aberrant religious practices. It also introduces and concludes the chapter as a whole and attempts to harmonize the differences between the remaining sources. These last two features suggest that the author of the first source also created Jer 44 as a whole: their viewpoint receives pride of place in the narrative and serves as the standard to which the other sources must conform.[62] In the second source—consisting of verses 2–14, 21–23—Jeremiah condemns the remnant of Judah for offering incense

---

61. Stipp opts for the latter possibility (Stipp, *Jeremia 25–52*, 617–18).

62. It is also possible that a later editor combined the three sources and made tweaks to verses 15 and 20 in order to harmonize them.

to other gods in the land of Judah, much like the final chapters of the "downfall of Judah in Palestine" narrative preserved in Jer 37:1–43:7. The third source consists of verses 16–19 and 24–25 and depicts a dispute between Jeremiah and a group of women over the worship of the Queen of Heaven. The affiliation of verses 28 and 30 is less clear—they could represent independent compositions or creations of the compiler. The table above illustrates my proposed source division of Jeremiah 44.

Dating

The final two verses of chapter 44 allow us to date the earliest form of this chapter and hence the "Queen of Heaven" source in verses 16–19 and 24–25. In verse 30, Jeremiah provides a prophetic sign that Yahweh's words will come to pass, which alludes to historical events:

Jeremiah 44:29–30

²⁹"This will be the sign for you," says Yahweh, "that I am about to punish you in this place in order that you may know that my words will surely stand against you for calamity." ³⁰Thus says Yahweh, "I am about to give Pharaoh Apries into the hand of his enemies and into the hand of those who seek his life, just as I gave Zedekiah king of Judah into the hand of Nebuchadnezzar king of Babylon, his enemy and the one who was seeking his life."

²⁹וזאת לכם האות נאם יהוה כי פקד אני עליכם במקום הזה למען תדעו כי קום יקומו דברי עליכם לרעה ³⁰כה אמר יהוה הנני נתן את פרעה חפרע מלך מצרים ביד איביו וביד מבקשי נפשו כאשר נתתי את צדקיהו מלך יהודה ביד נבוכדראצר מלך בבל איבו ומבקש נפשו

As Winifred Thiel notes, the change in number from third person masculine plural to third person masculine singular in verse 30 suggests that the author of these verses did not consider Nebuchadnezzar to be Apries's foe.[63] This observation, in turn, opens the door for other identifications, the most plausible of which is to treat Amasis and his troops as Apries's unnamed enemies.[64] In January 570 BCE, Amasis—who had served as a general in the Egyptian army—staged a coup against Apries and captured the Saite capital of Sais. The two rival pharaohs then

---

63. Thiel, *Die deuteronomistische Redaktion von Jeremia 26–45*, 81n23.
64. Schmidt, *Das Buch Jeremia: Kapitel 21–52*, 267. Holladay, by contrast, argues that verse 30 identifies Nebuchadnezzar as Apries's foe (Holladay, *Jeremiah 2*, 305). If he is correct, then we could perhaps date chapter 44 to the period immediately preceding the second Babylonian invasion of Egypt in 582 BCE. As mentioned above, this invasion failed, and so texts that predict Babylonian success most likely predate the invasion itself.

clashed at Momemphis, Marea, or *jꜣmw* with Amasis emerging as the victor. Apries fled south to Thebes, where he continued to be recognized as pharaoh until October 570 BCE, before ultimately fleeing to Babylon.[65] Two years later, Apries accompanied Nebuchadnezzar during the third Babylonian invasion of Egypt—hoping, no doubt, to regain his throne—but died in battle along the banks of the Nile.[66] This historical overview of Apries's last years suggests that Jer 44 was either written during the Egyptian civil war of 570 BCE (when Amasis sought to capture Apries) or during the aftermath of the third Babylonian invasion of Egypt in 568 BCE (after Apries died in battle).

These two scenarios suggest different options for dating chapter 44. If verse 30 has the Egyptian civil war as its historical background, then chapter 44 most likely dates sometime between Amasis's initial coup in January of 570 BCE and Apries's flight to Babylon some nine months later.[67] After that point, Apries was safe from Amasis's machinations and it would be unreasonable to predict that he would fall into the hands of his former general. If, on the other hand, verse 30 refers to the third Babylonian invasion of Egypt and Apries's death on the banks of the Nile, then chapter 44 could date any time after 568 BCE. Deciding between the two options is difficult, but the vagueness of the prophetic sign offered in verse 30 seems to support a date in 570 BCE before the identity of Apries's enemy was well known.[68] It would be strange, after all, for a prophecy composed after Apries's flight to Babylon to omit the names of his enemies.[69] But even if verse 30 presupposes the third Babylonian invasion of Egypt, it seems unlikely that the composition of verse 30—and thus Jer 44 as a whole—would date much later than 568 BCE. After a certain point, the significance of Apries's death would be lost on the text's audience. I would, therefore, date Jer 44 sometime between 570 and circa 558 BCE and its component parts to an even earlier period.

---

65. Leahy, "Earliest Dated Monument of Amasis," 188.

66. Leahy, "Earliest Dated Monument of Amasis," 190.

67. So Lundbom, *Jeremiah 37–52*, 169; Allen, *Jeremiah*, 449; Schmidt, *Das Buch Jeremia: Kapitel 21–52*, 267.

68. This criterion cannot necessarily support a late date after the name of Apries's enemy was forgotten because then we would need to explain how and why the name Apries survived.

69. Contra Thiel, *Die deuteronomistische Redaktion von Jeremia 26–45*, 80.

5. At Home Abroad

Interpretation

In its current form, the "Queen of Heaven" source begins *in medias res*; it does not mention where the confrontation between Jeremiah and the group of women took place or why it occurred:

Jeremiah 44:16–19, 24–25

[16] As for the word that you have spoken to us in the name of Yahweh, we are not listening to you. [17] Rather we will do everything that has gone forth from our mouths—offering incense to the Queen of Heaven and pouring libations for her just as we, our ancestors, our kings, and our officials did in the cities of Judah and the streets of Jerusalem. Then we were sated with bread and were well and did not see misfortune. [18] But from the time that we ceased offering incense to the Queen of Heaven and pouring libations (for her) we have lacked everything and we have perished by the sword and by famine. [19] Indeed, we are going to offer incense to the Queen of Heaven and pour libations for her. Was it without our husbands that we made cakes for her [[…]] and poured libations for her …? [24] Then Jeremiah said [[…]] to all the women, "Hear the word of Yahweh [[…]] [25] Thus says Yahweh, [[…]] the god of Israel, 'As for {you women}, what you have spoken with your mouths, you have fulfilled with your hands, saying, "We shall surely perform our vows which we vowed—to offer incense to the Queen of Heaven and pour libations for her." By all means, keep your vows and perform {them}!'"

[16] הדבר אשר דברת אלינו בשם יהוה איננו שמעים אליך [17] כי עשה נעשה את כל הדבר אשר יצא מפינו לקטר {לְמַלְכַּת} השמים והסיך לה נסכים כאשר עשינו אנחנו ואבתינו מלכינו ושרינו בערי יהודה ובחצות ירושלם ונשבע לחם ונהיה טובים ורעה לא ראינו [18] ומן אז חדלנו לקטר {לְמַלְכַּת} השמים והסך נסכים חסרנו כל וחרב וברעב תמנו [19] וכי אנחנו מקטרים {לְמַלְכַּת} השמים ולהסך לה נסכים המבלעדי אנשינו עשינו לה כונים [[…]] והסך לה נסכים … [24] ויאמר ירמיהו [[…]] אל כל הנשים שמעו דבר יהוה [[…]] [25] כה אמר יהוה [[…]] אלהי ישראל לאמר {אתנה נשים} ותדברנה בפיכם ובידיכם מלאתם לאמר עשה נעשה את נדרינו אשר נדרנו לקטר {לְמַלְכַּת} השמים ולהסך לה נסכים הקים תקימנה את נדריכם ועשה תעשינה {אתם}

In this section, I will argue that the references to the Queen of Heaven in these verses indicate that Jeremiah's interlocutors—and perhaps the "Queen of Heaven" source itself—came from Upper Egypt. These five fragmentary verses thus reflect contact between the Judahite diaspora in Upper Egypt and the land of Judah in the first third of the sixth century BCE.

The most distinctive feature of these verses is their focus on a non-Yahwistic deity. In verses 16–19 and 24–25, Jeremiah confronts a group of women for worshiping a goddess known only as the Queen of Heaven (מלכת השמים). The identity of this goddess remains an important interpretational crux in the study of Jer 44 and the history of Israelite religions more generally. Neither Jer 44 nor its companion text in Jer 7:16–20 explicitly identify the Queen of Heaven with a known goddess, forcing scholars to glean what little information they can from these two texts. Most scholars focus on the title "Queen of Heaven" itself and identify the Queen of Heaven with one of the celestial goddesses known from the first millennium BCE.[70] Such an approach is problematic, however, because many ancient Near Eastern goddesses could be described using a combination of royal and celestial language. In Mesopotamia, the title "lady of heaven" (*bēlet šamê*) could be applied to the goddesses Ishtar, Ishtaritu, and Sarpanitu, and in Egypt, almost every major goddess could bear the title "lady of the sky" (*nb.t p.t*).[71] As a result, scholars have identified the Queen of Heaven with a wide variety of goddesses—ranging from Anat to Shamash—with Astarte and Ishtar being the most popular options.[72] To escape this interpretive morass, we should focus on cognate titles—titles consisting of cognate words—rather than semantically similar ones. By doing so, we increase the chances that we are dealing with the same goddess and not a slew of different celestial deities.

Focusing on cognate titles also reduces the amount of data available for comparison. Only two other texts preserve an exact parallel to the title Queen of Heaven (מלכת השמים) found in Jer 7 and 44: the Hermopolis papyri and Papyrus Amherst 63, both of which associate the Queen of Heaven with Upper Egypt. In Hermopolis Papyrus 1 (TAD A2 1:1), a man named Nabusha sends greetings to the temple of the Queen of Heaven (בית מלכת שמין) in a letter bound for Syene, a city located across from Elephantine on the eastern bank of the Nile. And in his recent

---

70. Saul M. Olyan, "Some Observations Concerning the Identity of the Queen of Heaven," *UF* 19 (1987): 166.

71. Knut Tallquist, *Akkadische Götterepitheta: Nach den Stämmen ihrer Anfangswörter alphabetisch geordnet*, SO 1 (Helsinki: Societas Orientalis Fennica, 1938), 64; Olyan, "Some Observations," 164.

72. It is beyond the scope of this chapter to review all of the different proposals that have been made regarding the identity of the Queen of Heaven. For a survey of scholarship up to 1995, see Renate Jost, *Frauen, Männer und die Himmelskönigin: Exegetische Studien* (Gütersloh: Gütersloher, 1995), 27–29. For more recent scholarship see Gerda de Villiers, "Where Did She Come from and Where Did She Go? (the *Queen of Heaven* in Jeremiah 7 and 44)," *OTE* 15 (2002): 623–25; Ellis, "Jeremiah 44," 465–88; and Renate Jost, "Kuchen für die Himmelskönigin in Jer 17,17f. und Jer 44,15–25," in *Essen und Trinken in der Bibel: Ein literarisches Festmahl für Rainer Kessler zum 65. Geburtstag*, ed. Michaela Geiger, Christl M. Maier, and Uta Schmidt (Gütersloh: Gütersloher, 2009), 239–41.

edition of Papyrus Amherst 63, which many scholars associate with either Upper Egypt or the Elephantine community itself,[73] Karel van der Toorn argues that the title Queen of Heaven (mʾlʾ[kʾt] šʾmʾyn⁶) appears as an epithet of the Babylonian goddess Nanay in column II:11.[74] If van der Toorn's reading proves correct, then Papyrus Amherst 63 is the first text to associate the Queen of Heaven with a named goddess.[75]

---

73. See, for example, Richard C. Steiner, "The Aramaic Text in Demotic Script," in *Canonical Compositions from the Biblical World*, vol. 1 of *The Context of Scripture*, ed. William W. Hallo (Leiden: Brill, 1997), 310; Porten, "Settlement of the Jews at Elephantine," 451–70; Tawny L. Holm, "Nanay and Her Lover: An Aramaic Sacred Marriage Text from Egypt," *JNES* 76 (2017): 3; Karel van der Toorn, *Papyrus Amherst 63*, AOAT 448 (Münster: Ugarit-Verlag, 2018), 37.

74. Van der Toorn, *Papyrus Amherst 63*, 35, 47. The cult of Nanay is attested from the third millennium BCE until the eighth century CE and spread beyond Mesopotamia to Syria, Egypt and Central Asia during the mid-first millennium BCE. Joan Goodnick Westenholz, "Trading the Symbols of the Goddess Nanaya," in *Religions and Trade: Religious Formation, Transformation and Cross-Cultural Exchange between East and West*, ed. Peter Wick and Volker Rabens, Dynamics in the History of Religions 5 (Leiden: Brill, 2014), 167–98. For more on the goddess Nanay, see Paul-Alain Beaulieu, *The Pantheon of Uruk during the Neo-Babylonian Period*, CM 25 (Leiden: Brill, 2003), 182–216; Olga Drewnoska-Rymarz, *Mesopotamian Goddess Nanāja* (Warsaw: Agade, 2008); Michael P. Streck and Nathan Wasserman, "More Light on Nanāya," *ZA* 102 (2012): 183–201; and Julia M. Asher-Greve and Joan Goodnick Westenholz, *Goddesses in Context: On Divine Powers, Roles, Relationships and Gender in Mesopotamian Textual and Visual Sources*, OBO 259 (Freiburg: Academic Press, 2013), 104–31. Although Nanay was a Babylonian goddess, the title "Queen of Heaven" (מלכת השמים, מלכת שמין) itself is Northwest Semitic. This discrepancy can be explained in several ways. Perhaps the Judahite or Aramean inhabitants of Upper Egypt coined the title "Queen of Heaven" to refer to Nanay. Or perhaps they created this title as calque of the Akkadian epithet *šarrat šamê*. It is even possible that the title is a Northwest Semitic interpretation of the hypothetical Akkadian title *malkat šamāmi* "princess of Heaven," attested in expanded form as "Princess of Heaven and Earth" (*malkat šamāmi ū kakkari*) in an Old Babylonian hymn to Ishtar (Tallquist, *Akkadische Götterepitheta*, 129).

75. As far as I am aware, no other scholar has identified the Queen of Heaven with Nanay. Van der Toorn identifies the Queen of Heaven as Anat even though Papyrus Amherst 63 explicitly refers to Nanay using this title (van der Toorn, *Papyrus Amherst 63*, 35; van der Toorn, *Becoming Diaspora Jews*, 113). He bases this conclusion on the parallelism between Bethel and the Queen of Heaven in the salutation to TAD A2 1:1 "Greetings to the temple of Bethel and the temple of the Queen of Heaven" (שלם בית בתאל ובית מלכת שמין). From this, he concludes that the Queen of Heaven was Bethel's consort, whom he identifies as Anat on the basis of Assurbanipal's treaty with Baal of Tyre (SAA 02 005 r iv 6'). But this chain of inferences represents a shaky basis on which to make an iden-

Linguistic evidence from Jer 44 and 7 provides additional support for identifying the Queen of Heaven with this Babylonian goddess: כון, the word for the cakes offered to the Queen of Heaven, is a Babylonian loanword into Hebrew.[76] It comes from Akkadian kawānu (< *kamānu),[77] which refers to a cake baked in ashes that could serve as a votive offering to various deities.[78]

Both the Hermopolis papyri and Papyrus Amherst 63 provide indirect evidence for the worship of the Queen of Heaven among the Judahites living in Upper Egypt. Although these two texts reflect the religious practices of Arameans, the distinction between Arameans and Judahites at Elephantine was remarkably fluid—the Elephantine papyri often use the term Aramean and Judahite interchangeably to refer to the same individual.[79] According to van der Toorn, this terminological fluctuation indicates that the Judahites were a subset of the Aramean population of Upper Egypt.[80] Other scholars argue that the Judahites of Elephantine could be described as Aramean because they either spoke Aramaic or belonged to an Aramean garrison.[81] Whatever the case, the Judahites of Upper Egypt lived in close contact with Arameans and

---

tification. Just because Bethel and the Queen of Heaven appear in parallel in TAD A2 1:1 does not mean that they are consorts. In TAD D7 21:3, a certain Giddel invokes both Yaho and Khnum to bless Malkiah (ברכתך ליהה ולחנום), but no one has suggested that Yahweh and Khnum were consorts. The simple pairing of deities is a poor heuristic for identifying divine couples.

76. Mathias Delcor, "Le culte de la 'reine du ciel' selon Jer 7,18; 44,17–19.25 et ses survivances: Aspects de la religion populaire féminine aux alentours de l'Exil de Juda et dans les communautés juives d'Égypte," in *Von Kanaan bis Kerala: Festschrift für Prof. Mag. Dr. Dr. J. P. M. van der Ploeg O. P. zur Vollendung des siebzigsten Lebensjahres am 4. Juli 1979*, ed. W. C. Delsman, AOAT 211 (Neukirchen-Vluyn: Neukirchener, 1982), 109; Allen, *Jeremiah*, 98.

77. As Paul V. Mankowski notes, the Biblical Hebrew form of the word, כון, most likely reflects assimilation to the *qattal* nominal pattern (Paul V. Mankowski, *Akkadian Loanwords in Biblical Hebrew*, HSS 47 [Winona Lake, IN: Eisenbrauns, 2000], 62). The transcription of כון into Greek as χαυῶνας in the Septuagint may reflect an earlier stage before assimilation took place.

78. The popularity of personal names containing the theophoric element Nanay in Syene may offer additional support for this conclusion (see, e.g., the addressee of TAD A2 1:1).

79. For the most recent summary of the data see van der Toorn, *Becoming Diaspora Jews*, 31–34.

80. Van der Toorn, *Becoming Diaspora Jews*, 39–40; see also Reuven Yaron, "Who Is Who in Elephantine?," *Iura* 15 (1964): 172.

81. Bezalel Porten, *Archives from Elephantine: The Life of an Ancient Jewish Military Colony* (Berkeley: University of California Press, 1968), 33; Anke Joisten-Pruschke, *Das religiöse Leben der Juden von Elephantine in der Achämeni-*

were far more accepting of non-Yahwistic deities than the authors of the Hebrew Bible: they made cultic donations to the Aramean deities Ashim-Bethel and Anat-Bethel (TAD C3A 15:127–28); swore oaths by Herem-Bethel (TAD B7 2:7) and Sati (TAD B2 8:5); and greeted their superiors in the name of Khnum (TAD D7 21:3).[82] It is likely, therefore, that some members of the Judahite community at Elephantine also worshiped the Queen of Heaven. And because the title "Queen of Heaven" (מלכת השמין) only appears in texts associated with Upper Egypt, Jer 44:16–19, 24–25 most likely condemns the religious practices of the Judahite community or communities living there. The author of these verses, then, must have been in contact with the Upper Egyptian community or at least they knew someone who was.[83]

There is one problem with this conclusion, however. Both Jer 44:16–19, 24–25 and its companion passage in Jer 7:16–20 attribute the worship of the Queen of Heaven to the preexilic population of Judah and, if these passages represent a cultural memory of preexilic religious practice, then Jer 44:16–19, 24–25 need not reflect contact between Judah and the Judahite community in Upper Egypt.[84] The author of this text could simply have employed existing cultural or literary data in painting their portrait of the Upper Egyptian community.

Inner-biblical data caution against this conclusion, however. If the preexilic population of Judah had worshiped the Queen of Heaven, we would expect the Deuteronomistic History—which denounces the religious failings of the Southern Kingdom at every opportunity—to explicitly condemn this practice. But the Deuteronomistic History never mentions the Queen of Heaven or Nanay even though it condemns the worship of other goddesses such as Asherah and Astarte (e.g., 1 Kgs 11:5, 33; 15:13; 2 Kgs 23:4, 6, 7, 13). The silence of the Deuteronomistic History on this topic suggests that the Queen of Heaven was not worshiped in preexilic Judah under this name. Of course, it is possible that the Judahite inhabitants of Elephantine either identified Nanay with an existing Judahite goddess, such as Asherah or Astarte, or appropriated the

---

denzeit (Wiesebaden: Harrassowitz, 2008), 84; Pierre Grelot, *Documents araméens d'Égypte*, LAPO 5 (Paris: Cerf, 1972), 174.

82. Van der Toorn, *Becoming Diaspora Jews*, 58.

83. Jeon, "Egyptian Gola," 13.

84. The exact relationship between these texts remains unclear. According to Christl Maier, the creator of Jer 44 composed Jer 7:16–20 as a proof text for the claims they make in Jer 44 (Maier, *Jeremia als Lehrer der Tora*, 104). This conclusion is particularly tempting since Jer 7:16–20 appears to depend on chapter 44 as a whole. It employs some of the key phrases found in the other sections of Jer 44 but absent from verses 16–19 and 24–25, such as "other gods" (אלהים 7:18) (אחרים; cf. 44:3, 5, 8, 15) and "to anger me" (7:18) (להכעסני; cf. 44:3, 8).

title Queen of Heaven. But such a scenario is unlikely given that several features of the Queen of Heaven's cult betray a Mesopotamian rather than Judahite origin.

This conclusion has implications for the interpretation of Jer 7:16–20 and 44:16–19, 24–25. If the cult of the Queen of Heaven were confined to Egypt, then these texts do not accurately represent the religious practices of preexilic Judah but instead retroject the religious practices of the Upper Egyptian community onto the preexilic inhabitants of Judah in order to underscore their wickedness. Interestingly, these passages are not the only section of the book of Jeremiah to mischaracterize Israelite religions for polemical purposes. Jeremiah 48:13 too engages in such historical sleight of hand when it identifies Bethel as the patron deity of the Northern Kingdom even though this deity did not arrive in Israel until after the fall of Samaria: "Then Moab will be ashamed of Chemosh, just as the House of Israel was ashamed of Bethel, their confidence" (ובש מאב מכמוש כאשר בשו בית ישראל מבית אל מבטחם).[85]

Because Jer 7:16–20 and 44:16–19, 24–25 most likely do not preserve a cultural memory of preexilic religious practice in the land of Judah, the primary way for the author of Jer 44:16–19, 23–24 to learn about the cult of the Queen of Heaven would be through contact with the Judahite diaspora community in Upper Egypt. This contact could have taken several forms. Most likely, the author of this text lived in Egypt themselves or was in contact with a member of this community.[86] They

---

85. Karel van der Toorn, "Anat-Yahu, Some Other Deities, and the Jews of Elephantine," *Numen* 39 (1992): 90. Because Bethel appears in parallel with Chemosh, the patron deity of the Moabite state, it most likely refers to the Aramean deity Bethel rather than the city of the same name.

86. Two additions to chapter 44 contradict the promise of total annihilation tendered to the Upper Egyptian community in Jeremiah's speech. In the current form of verse 14, Jeremiah states that "Not a single refugee or survivor will be left of the remnant of Judah which has come to sojourn in the land of Egypt to return to the land of Judah. Although they long to live there again, they shall not return except as fugitives" (ולא יהיה פליט ושריד לשארית יהודה הבאים לגור שם בארץ מצרים ולשוב ארץ יהודה אשר המה מנשאים את נפשם לשוב לשבת שם כי לא ישובו כי אם פליטים). Verse 28 also mitigates the promise of total annihilation: "Those who escape the sword will return from the land of Egypt to the land of Judah, few in number" (ופליטי חרב ישובון מן ארץ מצרים ארץ יהודה מתי מספר). Pohlmann, Carroll, Holladay, and Allen all argue that these additions were made by a later editor who knew that some Judahites had returned from Egypt to their homeland or—at the very least—knew that the Judahite communities in Egypt continued to thrive (Pohlmann, *Studien zum Jeremiabuch*, 172, 182; Carroll, *Jeremiah*, 730; Holladay, *Jeremiah 2*, 278; Allen, *Jeremiah*, 448). Thiel, on the other hand, suggests that verse 28 is integral to Jer 44 and stands in contrast to the threat of total annihi-

may have exchanged letters with the Judahite inhabitants of Upper Egypt, much like Jedaniah and his priestly colleagues in Elephantine corresponded with the notables of Judah two centuries later (e.g., TAD A4 7:1; A4 8:1). Or the author of Jer 44 may have traveled to Upper Egypt or known members of the Upper Egyptian community that had traveled to or relocated to Judah.

Like Jer 42–43, Jer 44 shows signs of trans-cultural textual development. Most likely, its component parts originated in two different and far-flung locations: Upper Egypt and Babylon. The "Queen of Heaven" source either came from or was inspired by the Judahite community living in Upper Egypt, while the "downfall of Judah in Palestine" source was composed in Babylon. The community in Judah mediated between these two traditions; they were in contact with both diaspora communities and facilitated the transfer of textual material from Egypt to Babylon. It is unclear, however, whether the creator of Jer 44 worked in Judah or in the Babylonian diaspora. Nevertheless, the patchwork composition of Jer 44 reflects contact between Judah and the Judahite community in Upper Egypt during the first third of the sixth century BCE, several decades before the earliest explicit reference to the Elephantine community in 1Q Isa^a 49:12.

5.3. CONCLUSION

Egyptian military policies during the Saite period led to the establishment of several Judahite communities within Egypt that continued to flourish after the final loss of Egyptian control over Judah in 588 BCE. As I have argued in this chapter, these communities remained in contact with Judah during the first third of the sixth century BCE and their experiences shaped the book of Jeremiah. Jeremiah 43:8–13 contains two oracles composed in Daphnae during Nebuchadnezzar's second Egyptian campaign, while Jer 44:16–19, 24–25 attests to contact between Judah and the Judahite community in Upper Egypt around 570 BCE. Ultimately, life in the Egyptian diaspora may have changed Judahite attitudes toward Egypt and Babylon. Although many members of the Egyptian diaspora had suffered under Saite control of Judah, Nebuchadnezzar's repeated invasions of Egypt threatened their new home. In response, they may have co-opted Egyptian imagery to condemn Babylon, as I will argue in the following chapter.

---

lation put forth in verses 2–14 and 20–23 (Thiel, *Die deuteronomistische Redaktion von Jeremia 26–45*, 78). According to his analysis, a later redactor added the final words of verse 14 in order to mitigate the tension between the base text of chapter 44 and its Deuteronomistic expansions.

EXCURSUS
ON THE MEANING OF להעצבה IN JEREMIAH 44:19

In the Masoretic Text of verse 19, the women of Upper Egypt use the strange term להעצבה to describe the cakes they bake for the Queen of Heaven. Many scholars treat this form as a defectively written hiphil infinitive from the root עצב meaning "to copy her" and argue that the cakes are made in the image of the Queen of Heaven or her symbol.[87] Yet there is little textual or material evidence for this argument. The Septuagint, the Peshitta, and the parallel passage in Jer 7:18 lack a counterpart to להעצבה, and the agreement of the Septuagint and one branch of the Masoretic Text family suggests that להעצבה is a gloss.[88] In theory, this gloss could still contain accurate information about the cult of the Queen of Heaven, but the archaeological evidence for baking cakes in the shape of a goddess or her symbol is problematic. In 1959, André Parrot published several Old Babylonian molds from the city of Mari, which took the shape of nude women.[89] Subsequently, Walter Rast and Marvin Pope claim they were used to bake votive cakes for Ishtar.[90] Both of these claims are suspect. There is no evidence that the molds were used to make cakes as opposed to other types of food[91] and no way to tell whether they represent a goddess rather than a mortal woman.[92]

Text-critical evidence suggests a different meaning for להעצבה. Both Targum Jonathan and Symmachus's Greek translation treat להעצבה as a

---

87. Carroll, *Jeremiah*, 734; McKane, "Worship of the Queen of Heaven," 319; Karel J. H. Vriezen, "Cakes and Figurines: Related Women's Cultic Offerings in Ancient Israel?," in *On Reading Prophetic Texts: Gender-Specific and Related Studies in Memory of Fokkelien van Dijk-Hemmes*, ed. Bob Becking and Meindert Dijkstra (Leiden: Brill, 1996), 260–63; Lundbom, *Jeremiah 37–52*, 164; Allen, *Jeremiah*, 447; Jost, "Kuchen für die Himmelkönigin," 243–45; Schmidt, *Das Buch Jeremia: Kapitel 21–52*, 266.

88. Greenberg notes that the deliberate omissions are rare in the Peshitta of Jeremiah (Greenberg, *Translation Technique in the Peshitta to Jeremiah*, 117).

89. André Parrot, *Mission archéologique de Mari* (Paris: Geuthner, 1959), 2:37–38, pl. 19.

90. Walter E. Rast, "Cakes for the Queen of Heaven," in *Scripture in History and Theology: Essays in Honor of J. Coert Rylaarsdam*, ed. Arthur L. Merrill and Thomas W. Overholt (Pittsburgh: Pickwick Press, 1977), 171–74; Marvin H. Pope, *Song of Songs*, AB 7C (Yale: Yale University Press, 1995), 379.

91. Parrot argues that the molds may have been used for the preparation of "pâtisseries, laitages et fromages" (Parrot, *Mission archéologique de Mari*, 2:33).

92. As André Parrot rightly noted in the initial publication of the molds, "L'identification nous échappe: simple mortelle, femme de haut rang, divinité?" (Parrot, *Mission archéologique de Mari*, 2:37).

gloss on the prepositional phrase "for her" (לה) that serves to highlight the Judahites' idolatrous ways. Targum Jonathan reads "for the female idols" (לטעותא), while Symmachus reads "for her image" (τῷ γλυπτῷ αὐτῆς). Based on these readings, I would treat להעצבה as a gloss on לה, meaning "for the female idol" (לְהָעֲצַבָּה) with an uncontracted definite article following the preposition -ל.⁹³ Not only does this interpretation avoid the linguistic problems with treating להעצבה as an infinitive, it also helps explain why the final ה- on להעצבה is not treated as a third-person feminine singular suffix in the Masoretic Text.

---

93. So too, Holladay, *Jeremiah 2*, 279, and Delcor, "Le culte de la 'reine du ciel,'" 108. Since להעצבה is a late gloss, it is not surprising that it features an uncontracted definite article following the preposition ל. According to GKC §35n and Joüon §35e, most instances of the uncontracted definite article following a preposition occur in late texts.

6.
Lions Gone Wild: Jeremiah 51:38–39, the Egyptian Destruction of Humanity Myth, and the Judahite Diaspora in Egypt

The impact of Egyptian control on Judah was so pervasive that it is even possible to detect its effects in texts that do not explicitly mention Egypt, such as Jer 51:38–39. This oracle, I argue, adapts the Egyptian Destruction of Humanity myth in order to provide a theologically powerful account of Babylon's downfall. According to these verses, Yahweh uses alcohol to pacify and kill the lion-like Babylonians and save vulnerable Judahites from destruction, much like the Egyptian god Re uses beer to restrain the deadly fury of the leonine goddess Sakhmet and avert the destruction of humanity. I will also argue that Jer 51:38–39 originated among the Judahite diaspora in the eastern Nile Delta sometime between 586 and 539 BCE and reflects a potential change in attitude toward Babylon on the part of its creator. Although Nebuchadnezzar II had liberated Judah from Saite control in 604 BCE, he overstepped his bounds by continuing to invade the Egyptian heartland—an act that threatened the Judahite diaspora communities living in the eastern Nile Delta.

6.1. THE "LIONS GONE WILD" MOTIF

Jeremiah 51:38–39 uses a striking image to describe the downfall of the Babylonians:[1] "Together they[2] will roar like young lions. They will growl like lions' whelps. When they are inflamed, I will set out their drink and make them drunk so that they become merry and sleep an eternal sleep, never to awake. Oracle of Yahweh" (יחדו ככפרים ישאגו נערו כגורי אריות בחממ אשית את משתיהם והשכרתים למען יעלזו וישנו שנת עולם ולא יקיצו נאם יהוה).[3] As in

---

1. Although Jer 51:38–39 never explicitly identifies these lions as the Babylonians, context supports such an identification, as William McKane notes (*Commentary on Jeremiah 26–52*, 1328). The two oracles that frame Jer 51:38–39 both condemn Babylon and there is nothing within Jer 51:38–39 or the introduction to Jer 51:41–44 that signals a change in subject. Furthermore, the inclusion of these verses within the oracles against Babylon suggests that the compiler of this block of prophetic material perceived Jer 51:38–39 as an oracle against Babylon. In addition, Jer 51:57—which I will argue is a later gloss on verses 38–39—explicitly identifies the "they" of verses 38–39 with high-ranking Babylonian officials and military leaders.

2. The use of plural verbs within Jer 51:38–39 suggests that these verses refer to either Babylonians as a whole or the Babylonian army rather than Babylon itself or Nebuchadnezzar.

3. These verses are almost entirely free of textual issues. The Septuagint lacks a counterpart to the verb ישאגו "they will roar" found in the Masoretic Text, but the absence of this form can be explained by to homoeoteleuton in the Hebrew source text of the Septuagint (e.g., ככפרים ישאגו נערו). There is no need to treat ישאגו as a later gloss on the rare verb נערו "they will roar" as William Holladay suggests, a text-critical move that would force the two cola that form verse 38 to share a single verb (Holladay, *Jeremiah 2*, 399). Holladay avoids this problem by repointing יַחְדּוּ at the beginning of the verse as the verb *יָחֹדּוּ "they will be quick" since יַחְדָּו "is dubious as first unit [sic] in a colon, where a verb suggests itself," but there is no textual or linguistic evidence for doing so. The versions consistently translate the consonantal sequence יחדו as "together" (e.g., ἅμα, *simul*, כחדא), and יַחְדָּו appears as the first word in a clause or colon at least 11 times within the Hebrew Bible (Isa 11:7, 14, 31:3, 52:8, Jer 46:12, Lam 2:8, 1 Sam 30:24, and Exod 26:24).

The remainder of emendations that scholars have proposed over the years are intended to correct perceived problems with the tenor or grammar of the oracle. Holladay and Robert P. Carroll, for example, repoint נֵעֹרוּ to נֵעֹרוּ "they are aroused" on the basis of the Septuagint (ἐξεγέρθησαν) because the root נער means "to growl" only in this verse (Holladay, *Jeremiah 2*, 399; Carroll, *Jeremiah*, 846). Their reasoning on this point, however, proves dubious; in essence, they advocate eliminating a *hapax legomenon* simply because it is a *hapax legomenon*. What is more, there is good linguistic evidence for reading נערו as "they will roar" in verse 38 since Akkadian and Aramaic both preserve cognate terms meaning "to roar" (*CAD* 7:150–51; *CAL*, "nʕr, 'to bray, roar,'"). The Peshitta even uses the Syr-

6. Lions Gone Wild

the "cup of wrath" episode in Jer 25:15–29, Yahweh assumes the role of divine bartender in this oracle, dispensing a draft that causes stupor, incapacitation, and death. But here, his adversaries are not the nations as a whole but rather the lion-like Babylonians. This combination of leonine imagery and alcohol as a metaphor for punishment—the "lions gone wild" motif—is unique in the Hebrew Bible and the wider ancient Near East and resembles the plot of the Egyptian Destruction of Humanity myth, a New Kingdom funerary text that was inscribed in the tombs of Seti I, Ramesses II, Ramesses III, and Ramesses VI, and in the outer shrine of Tutankhamun.[4]

The Destruction of Humanity myth takes place in the primordial era. The sun god, Re, has grown old and humanity has taken advantage of his decline to rebel against him. To punish their treachery, Re sends forth his fiery eye—a metaphor for the sun disk—in the form of the goddess Hathor. Hathor proceeds to slay the majority of humanity, stopping only to inform Re how much she enjoys the carnage: "when I exercised power over humanity, it was pleasing to my heart" (jw sḥm.n.j m rmṯ.w jw nḏm.w ḥr jb.j).[5] Hathor's bloodlust causes her to transform into the ferocious leonine goddess, Sakhmet: "Then Sakhmet came into being... in order to wade in their blood from Heracleopolis onward" (ḫpr sḫmt pw ... r rhn.t ḥr znf.sn šꜥ m ḥnn nswt).[6] Alarmed at Hathor's transformation, Re devises a plan to avert Hathor/Sakhmet's destructive fury and preserve the remainder of humanity. He instructs the priests of Heliopolis to prepare large quantities of beer mixed with djdj, a type of red dye, and flood the area of jꜣmw, forming a barrier between Sakhmet and humanity.[7] The following day Sakhmet mistakes the beer for blood, drinks it,

---

iac cognate neʿrun to render נער, while the Akkadian form is used to describe the sound produced by lions: "she (= Lamaštu) roars like a lion" (nuʾʾurat kīma nēši). In light of this cognate evidence, it seems likely that the Septuagint reading stems from a reinterpretation of the uncommon verb נער "to roar" as a Niphal form of the root עור "to wake up."

4. Erik Hornung, *Der ägyptische Mythos von der Himmelskuh: Eine Ätiologie des Unvollkommenen*, OBO 46 (2nd ed.; Göttingen: Vandenhoeck & Ruprecht, 1997), 33–36.

5. For the text of this section of the myth see Hornung, *Der ägyptische Mythos*, 1–9, 37–40, 111–14.

6. Hornung, *Der ägyptische Mythos*, 38–39. The myth does not explicitly identify Sakhmet as a lion at this point in the myth but she was almost always depicted with the head of a lion in Egyptian glyptic art, as Sigrid-Eike Hoenes and Heike Sternberg note (Sigrid-Eike Hoenes, *Untersuchungen zu Wesen und Kult der Göttin Sachmet* [Bonn: Rudolf Habelt, 1976], 13; Heike Sternberg, "Sachmet," *LÄ* 5:323).

7. See Hornung, *Der ägyptische Mythos*, 40, for various theories regarding

and becomes so drunk that she no longer recognizes humanity. She returns to Re inebriated and transforms back into Hathor, her benevolent form. The myth ends with an explanation for the preparation of beer for Hathor during the New Year's festival: "The majesty of Re said to this goddess, 'Intoxicating beverages will be prepared for her at the New Year's festival. It will be allotted to my priestesses. So the preparation of intoxicating beverages became the lot of priestesses at the festival of Hathor by all people since the first day" (ḏd.jn ḥm n rꜥ n nṯr.t tn jrj.w n st sḏr.wt m jtrw-rnpt jp.w st r ḥm.wt.j ḫpr jr.t sḏr.wt pw m jp.t ḥm.wt ḥꜣb ḥwt-ḥrw jn rmṯ.w nb ḏr hrw.w dpj). The full myth reads:

> It happened that Re, the self-created god, shone when he was king.[8] Humanity and gods were as one. Then humanity devised plots against Re since his majesty was old. His bones were of silver. His body was of gold. His hair was of genuine lapis lazuli. Then his majesty recognized the plots that were devised against him by humanity.
>
> His majesty said to those who were in his retinue, "Summon for me my eye as well as Shu, Tefnut, Geb, and Nut, together with the fathers and mothers who were with me when I was in the primordial waters, and my god Nun so that he may bring his courtiers with him. You should bring them in secret so that humanity does not see and their hearts do not flee. You should come with them to the palace so that they may give their excellent advice. I am going to the primordial waters, where I came into being."
>
> Then these gods were fetched straightaway and these gods stood at both of his sides touching the ground with their foreheads in his presence. He spoke his words in the presence of the oldest father, who made humanity for the king of the people. Then they said to him, "Speak to us so that we may hear it!"
>
> Re spoke to Nun, "O eldest god from whom I came into being, and O foremost gods: Look, humanity, the creation of my eye, has devised plots against me. Tell me what you would do about it. Look, I am searching and cannot kill them until I hear what you will say about it." Then the majesty of Nun spoke, "O my son, Re, the god who is greater than the one who made him, older than the ones who created you, take your seat. Great is the fear of you. Your eye is against those who plot evil against you."
>
> The majesty of Re spoke, "Look, they have fled to the desert. Their hearts fear what I will say to them." Then they spoke in the presence of his majesty, "Let your eye go forth so that it may expose those who have plotted as evildoers against you. There is no better eye than it to strike them for you. May it come forth as Hathor!"

---

the identification of djdj.

8. Literally, "after he was in kingship" (m-ḫt wnn.f m nswyt).

Then this goddess came back to him after she had slain humanity in the desert. The majesty of this god said to her, "Welcome in peace, Hathor, who acts on behalf of the creator when I come to her."

This goddess said, "As you live for me, when I exercised power over humanity, it was pleasing to my heart." The majesty of Re said, "I will exercise power over them as king, as the one who reduces them." Then Sakhmet, the night mash, came into being in order to wade in their blood from Heracleopolis onward.

Then Re said, "Now summon for me swift, fast-moving messengers. Let them run like the shadow of a body." These messengers were fetched straightaway. Then the majesty of this god said, "Let them go to Elephantine! Let them fetch for me djdj [dye] in abundance." djdj [dye] was fetched for him.

Then the majesty of this great god caused the braided ones, who are in Heliopolis to crush this djdj [dye] while the maidservants milled barley for beer. djdj [dye] was added to this mash so that it was like human blood. Seven hundred jars of beer were made. Then the majesty of the king of Upper and Lower Egypt, Re, came there with these gods in order to see this beer.

When the day came to kill humanity by means of the goddess as they went south,[9] the majesty of Re said, "How beautiful they are! I will save humanity by means of it [i.e., the beer]." Then Re said, "Now carry them [i.e., the jars of beer] to the place where she said she would kill humanity." The majesty of the king of Upper and Lower Egypt, Re, arose in the middle of the night to cause these intoxicating beverages to be poured out. The fields became a flood three handbreadths high, filled with fluid, by the might of the majesty of this god.

Then this goddess went forth in the morning and she found these (fields) flooded. Her face became happy thereat. She drank and her heart was glad.

She came back drunk; she had not recognized humanity. Then the majesty of Re said to this goddess, "Welcome in peace, beloved!" Then the beautiful one came into being in jȝmw.

The majesty of Re said to this goddess, "Intoxicating beverages shall be prepared for her at the New Year's festival. It shall be allotted to my priestesses." So the preparation of this intoxicating beverage became the lot of priestesses at the festival of Hathor by all of humanity since the first day.

The Destruction of Humanity myth exhibits several parallels with Jer 51:38–39 and the oracles against Babylon more generally. Although Jer 51:38–39 does not explicitly identify Babylon as Yahweh's agent of punishment, sent from Mesopotamia to wreak vengeance on the nations, several other passages in the oracles against Babylon make this

---

9. Literally, "at their times of going south" (*m sw.w.sn nw ḫntyt*).

identification clear. Jeremiah 51:7, for example, states that "Babylon was a golden cup in Yahweh's hand, making all the world drunk with its wine. The nations drank; therefore, the nations went mad" (כוס זהב בבל ביד יהוה משכרת כל ארץ מיינה שתו גוים על כן יתהללו גוים). Similarly, Jer 51:20–23 depicts Babylon or Nebuchadnezzar as Yahweh's war club, with which he clobbers the inhabitants of the earth: "You are my club, my weapon of battle. With you I smash nations; with you I ruin kingdoms ..." (מפץ אתה לי כלי מלחמה ונפצתי בך גוים והשחתי בך ממלכות ...).[10] Other texts within the book of Jeremiah pit Babylon against a specific nation—Egypt. The oracles against Egypt in Jer 46:2–26 celebrate various Babylonian victories over Egypt, both real and imagined, as do the oracles in Jer 43:8–13. And if the interpretation of Jer 25:15–29 that I proposed in chapter 4 is correct, then the earliest version of the "cup of wrath" oracle expressed the hope that Babylon would liberate Judah from Saite control by meting out punishment on the Saite empire and its vassal states in the Levant. It thus depicts Babylon as Judah's savior rather than destroyer.[11] In these three passages, Yahweh uses Babylon as an instrument of punishment against the nations/Egypt, in much the same way that Re sends Hathor/Sakhmet to punish humanity. Second, both Hathor/Sakhmet and the Babylonians take on leonine traits in their role as divinely ordained destroyer: Jeremiah 51:38–39 and several other passages in the book of Jeremiah (e.g., Jer 50:17) liken the Babylonians to lions, while

---

10. The second-person masculine singular addressee of these verses goes unidentified, which has led scholars to propose a variety of different identifications for Yahweh's war club, including Judah, Jeremiah, and Babylon's eventual destroyer. The current context of the oracle, however, strongly supports an identification with Babylon or Nebuchadnezzar. An aside about Judah's, Jeremiah's, or Babylon's future foe would make a strange interlude in a series of oracles against Babylon. Furthermore, the prose oracle attached to verses 20–23 explicitly identifies Babylon with Yahweh's war club when it states: "But I will repay Babylon and all the inhabitants of Chaldea for all of the evil they have committed against Zion before your eyes. Oracle of Yahweh" (ושלמתי לבבל ולכל יושבי כשדים את כל רעתם אשר עשו בציון לעיניכם נאם יהוה). As Holladay points out, however, the use of masculine pronouns in verses 20–23 stands at odds with the consistent identification of Babylon as grammatically feminine throughout Jer 50–51 (Holladay, *Jeremiah 2*, 406). For this reason, I would identify the addressee of verses 20–23 as Nebuchadnezzar. For the other interpretations of this passage, see Carroll, *Jeremiah*, 843; McKane, *Commentary on Jeremiah 26–52*, 1311; Holladay, *Jeremiah 2*, 406; Smelik, "Function of Jeremiah 50 and 51," 92; Lundbom, *Jeremiah 37–52*, 451; Allen, *Jeremiah*, 528; Schmidt, *Das Buch Jeremia: Kapitel 21–52*, 331.

11. For a different interpretation, see Schmidt, *Das Buch Jeremia: Kapitel 21–52*, 335.

Egyptian painters and sculptors frequently represented Sakhmet with the head of a lioness.[12] And third, Re's use of alcohol to subdue Hathor/Sakhmet and prevent the destruction of humanity parallels Yahweh's decision to save Judah by making the Babylonians drunk.

Comparison with the Destruction of Humanity myth and the character of Sakhmet more generally also helps make sense of several strange features of Jer 51:38–39. A few commentators object to the literal meaning of verse 39 found in the Masoretic Text, since it appears to depict Yahweh slaking the thirst of the parched Babylonians: "When they are hot, I [Yahweh] will prepare their drink so that they become merry."[13] Comparison with the Destruction of Humanity myth, however, suggests that Yahweh uses alcohol to appease the fiery wrath of his Mesopotamian foes. In Biblical Hebrew, the verb חמם denotes both physical heat

---

12. Hoenes, *Untersuchungen zu Wesen und Kult*, 13; Sternberg, "Sachmet," 323.

13. McKane, for example, opines that "the sense can hardly be that Yahweh will make the Babylonians drunk in order to provide a kind of boisterous bonhomie" and emends יַעֲלֹזוּ "they will be happy" to יְעֻלְּפוּ "they will faint" (McKane, *Commentary on Jeremiah 26–52*, 1329; see also Carroll, *Jeremiah*, 846; Holladay, *Jeremiah 2*, 399; Stipp, *Jeremia 25–52*, 803). Such an emendation, however, rests on tenuous textual support. An interchange of פ and ז is unlikely to have occurred in the *Vorlage* of the Masoretic Text since these letters differ significantly in both the paleo-Hebrew and Aramaic scripts (ז ≠ פ; פ ≠ ז). Of all the versions, only the Septuagint preserves a reading that approximates the semantics of Hebrew יְעֻלְּפוּ: καρωθῶσιν "they will be stupefied." Despite this seeming similarity, the Greek verb καρόω never renders עלף elsewhere in the Hebrew Bible, most likely due to a difference in meaning. The Hebrew root עלף refers primarily to faintness caused by thirst (Amos 8:13; Jonah 4:8) or mourning (Isa 51:20; Ezek 31:15)—while Greek καρόω denotes stupefaction brought on by sleep or alcohol (LSJ, 879; GELS, 363). This discrepancy suggests that the Septuagint translator, like many modern scholars, had qualms about the literal meaning of the verse—which appears to depict Yahweh doing something positive for his foes—and employed a different verb. The omission of יעלזו from the parallel passage in Jer 51:57 adds further support to this conclusion.

McKane also seeks a linguistic solution to the perceived problem with יעלזו (McKane, *Commentary on Jeremiah 26–52*, 1329–30). Following Driver, "Linguistic and Textual Problems," 127–28, he translates יעלזו as "they will shudder" on the basis of Arabic ʿalaza "to be disquieted, restless (of a sick person)." But such a reading disrupts the internal logic of verses 38–39: Yahweh's ministrations are intended to pacify and ultimately kill the Babylonians, not provoke them further. The verb linking "when they are hot" with "and sleep an eternal sleep, never to awake" must represent an intermediate stage between inflammation or anger and eternal sleep. For these reasons, I retain the reading of the Masoretic Text.

and, less commonly, anger (see, e.g., Deut 19:6).[14] Both senses of the verb are appropriate if the Babylonians are being likened to Sakhmet in Jer 51:38–39. A New Year's ritual from the Ptolemaic temple at Edfu in Upper Egypt refers to Sakhmet as *ss ḥ.t nb m33.s* which can be translated as either the one "whose gaze burns everything" or the one "who burns all that she sees," while a festal calendar from the Mut temple of Karnak speaks of the need "to appease her [Sakhmet's] fury when her majesty is (still) enraged after a massacre" (*r sḥtp nšn.s dr ḥs3 ḥm.t.s m-s3 ḫry*).[15] And in the Destruction of Humanity myth, Re uses alcohol to quell Sakhmet's fiery fury and render her happy. A similar process seems to be at work in Jer 51:38–39: Yahweh plies the Babylonians with alcohol in order to pacify and ultimately destroy them. Therefore, I would translate the first half of verse 39 as "when they are inflamed, I will set out their drink so that they become merry."

Jeremiah 51:38–39 does not correspond to the Destruction of Humanity myth in every aspect, however. It adds its own theological twist to the myth that underscores the finality of Yahweh's judgment. Unlike Sakhmet, the Babylonians do not wake up following their binge, but instead descend into a perpetual slumber. They are unworthy of transformation or salvation.

As with many of the oracles contained in the book of Jeremiah, Jer 51:38–39 does not provide a rationale for the Babylonians' harsh punishment—it was apparently self-evident to the earliest readers and auditors of the oracle. But several passages within the book of Jeremiah indicate that Babylon's fault consisted of overstepping its divine mandate to punish the nations/Egypt by harming Judahites.[16] An early

---

14. McKane emends בְּחֻמָּם אָשִׁית אֶת מִשְׁתֵּיהֶם "when they are hot/angry, I will set out their drink" to בְּחֵמָה אָשִׁית אֶת מִשְׁתֵּיהֶם "I will lace their draughts with poison" in order to make the deadly nature of Yahweh's draft more explicit (McKane, *Commentary on Jeremiah 26–52*, 1330). This suggestion, however, rests on scant textual support. Although the Peshitta renders בחמם with *ḥemmtə*, a term that can denote venom, this word more commonly refers to anger in Syriac (Payne-Smith, *Thesaurus Syriacus*, 1:1299) and, as such, is an appropriate equivalent to בְּחֻמָּם.

15. Philippe Germond, *Sekhmet et la protection du monde*, Aegyptiaca Helvetica 9 (Geneva: Éditions de Belles-Lettres, 1981), 59; Anthony J. Spalinger, "A Religious Calendar Year in the Mut Temple at Karnak," *REg* 44 (1993): 176. For more references to Sakhmet's fiery rage see Hoenes, *Untersuchungen zu Wesen und Kult*, 67–82; Sternberg, "Sachmet," 325–26; Jean-Claude Goyon, *Le ritual du sḥtp Sḫmt au changement de cycle annuel: D'après les architraves du temple d'Edfou et textes parallèles, du Nouvel Empire à l'époque ptolémaïque et romaine* (Cairo: Institut français d'archéologie orientale, 2006), 28.

16. Under this paradigm, the Babylonian crackdowns on Judah in 598 BCE

instantiation of this idea appears in Jer 51:24, the prose coda to the description of Babylon as Yahweh's war club in Jer 51:20–23. This verse modifies the claim that Babylon was Yahweh's agent of punishment by stating: "But I will repay Babylon and all the inhabitants of Chaldea for all of the evil they have committed against Zion before your eyes. Oracle of Yahweh." More explicitly, the Septuagint version of Jer 25:9–12 charts the rise and fall of the nation from the north from Yahweh's agent to Yahweh's victim: "Look! I am sending and will take a people from the north. And I will lead them against this land and against its inhabitants and all the nations around it. And I will devastate them… and when seventy years are completed I will punish that nation" (ἰδοὺ ἐγὼ ἀποστέλλω καὶ λήμψομαι τὴν πατριὰν ἀπὸ βορρᾶ καὶ ἄξω αὐτοὺς ἐπὶ τὴν γῆν ταύτην καὶ ἐπὶ τοὺς κατοικοῦντας αὐτὴν καὶ ἐπὶ πάντα τὰ ἔθνη τὰ κύκλῳ αὐτῆς καὶ ἐξερημώσω αὐτούς… καὶ ἐν τῷ πληρωθῆναι τὰ ἑβδομήκοντα ἔτη ἐκδικήσω τὸ ἔθνος ἐκεῖνο). Later additions to this passage in the Masoretic Text identify the nation from the north with Babylon: "and when seventy years are complete, I will punish the king of Babylon and that nation. Oracle of Yahweh" (והיה במלאות שבעים שנה אפקד על מלך בבל ועל הגוי ההוא נאם יהוה).[17]

6.2. POTENTIAL OBSTACLES

Although the parallels between Jer 51:38–39 and the Destruction of Humanity myth are striking, there are several obstacles to overcome before we can posit a literary relationship between the two texts. First, Jer 51:38–39 makes use of imagery found elsewhere in the book of Jeremiah, so it is possible that the author of this passage combined existing motifs to produce an otherwise unique oracle. Second, the only surviving version of the Destruction of Humanity myth predates the Saite period (664–525 BCE) by at least seven hundred years. Third, Jer 51:38–39 itself may postdate the Saite period, which would increase the chronological gap separating the two works and decrease the odds that they are ultimately related. In this section, I will address these issues and argue that a relationship between Jer 51:38–39 and the Destruction of Humanity myth is still tenable: the two texts share several unique motifs not found elsewhere; the Destruction of Humanity myth continued to be known and transmitted throughout the Saite period and beyond; and Jer 51:38–39 most likely dates sometime between 604 and 539 BCE, a period when many Judahites lived under Saite rule in either Judah itself or the Egyptian diaspora.

---

and 588 BCE and Nebuchadnezzar's repeated invasions of Egypt could be interpreted as deviations from Babylon's original mandate.

17. Gesundheit, "Question of LXX Jeremiah," 46–47.

Possible Inner-Biblical Parallels

Although the combination of leonine imagery and alcohol is unique to Jer 51:38–39, these motifs appear separately in the book Jeremiah as well as prophetic and ancient Near Eastern literature more generally. Several passages within Jeremiah, for example, use leonine imagery to depict Judah's enemies. Jeremiah 2:15 pictures the Assyrians as "young lions" roaring against Judah, while Jer 4:7 describes the nation from the north—with which Babylon was later identified in the Masoretic Text of Jer 25:1–14—as a prowling lion. Meanwhile, Jer 50:17 explicitly identifies the king of Babylon as a lion: "Israel is a sheep hunted by lions. First, the king of Assyria ate it. Afterward, [[...]] the king of Babylon gnawed its bones" ([[...]] שה פזורה ישראל אריות הדיחו הראשון אכלו מלך אשור וזה האחרון עצמו (מלך בבל).[18] All of these passages, and others like them, employ a common prophetic trope that reflects the adaptation of Neo-Assyrian royal propaganda for polemical purposes.[19] Almost all of the Neo-Assyrian kings, for example, likened themselves to lions in their royal inscriptions in order to highlight their ferocity in battle—sometimes going so far as to say "I am a lion" (labbāku) as in RIMA 2:195–96.

The consumption of alcohol serves as a metaphor for divine judgment elsewhere in the book of Jeremiah as well. In the "cup of wrath" episode in Jer 25:15–26, for example, the nations are forced to drink from a cup of wine, whose contents cause madness and death, and in an exilic addition to the oracle in verse 26b, Babylon (alias Sheshak) is said to quaff this deadly cup as well.[20] Outside of this episode, Jer 51:57 attests to the use of alcohol as a means of punishing Babylon: "I will make her [= Babylon's] officials, sages [[...]], and warriors drunk so that they sleep an eternal sleep, never to awake. Oracle of the King—Yahweh of Armies is his name" (והשכרתי שריה וחכמיה [[...]] וגבוריה וישנו שנת עולם ולא יקיצו נאם המלך יהוה צבאות שמו).[21] This verse is particu-

---

18. Omitting נבוכדראצר "Nebuchadrezzar" with the Septuagint (Janzen, *Studies in the Text of Jeremiah*, 79). In a similar vein, Jer 25:30 depicts Yahweh as a lion, roaring from on high as he punishes the nations.

19. Machinist, "Assyria and Its Image in First Isaiah," 728–29; Strawn, *What Is Stronger than a Lion?*, 178–79.

20. See chapter 3 for the date of this addition. Parallels to the "cup of wrath" episode appear in Isa 51:17, 22, Jer 49:12, 51:7, Ezek 23:31–34, Hab 2:16, Ps 11:6, 75:9, and Lam 4:21. For the interpretation of these passages see McKane, "Poison, Trial by Ordeal and the Cup of Wrath," 474–92; Fuchs, "Das Symbol des Bechers in Ugarit und Israel," 65–84; Seidl, *Der Becher in der Hand des Herrn*.

21. The Septuagint lacks a counterpart to the phrase פחותיה וסגניה "her governors and deputies" found in the Masoretic Text. Most likely, this word pair

larly important for evaluating the relationship between Jer 51:38–39 and the Egyptian Destruction of Humanity myth since it closely resembles verse 39. Theoretically, Jer 51:57 could represent a literary antecedent of Jer 51:38–39, to which leonine imagery was later added. Further consideration, however, suggests that Jer 51:57 is a gloss on Jer 51:38–39 intended to make the identity of Yahweh's enemies explicit and resolve a potential theological problem in the original oracle. Verse 57 omits the allusive leonine imagery of Jer 51:38–39 and instead identifies Yahweh's victims as various Babylonian military and civil officials. It also avoids the theologically problematic claim that Yahweh's ministrations will lift the spirits of his victims by omitting the verb יעלזו. At the same time, the focus of verse 57 on Babylon—and its detailed list of Babylonian officials—suggests that Jer 51:57 dates to the exilic period as well. Thus, if I am correct in identifying Jer 51:57 as a gloss on Jer 51:38–39, then verses 38–39 must date somewhat earlier in the Babylonian period than verse 57.[22]

The presence of these tropes elsewhere in the book of Jeremiah complicates the comparison between Jer 51:38–39 and the Destruction of Humanity myth. In theory, the author of Jer 51:38–39 could have combined existing prophetic motifs into an oracle that resembled the Destruction of Humanity myth but was not dependent on it. Two uniquely shared features found only in Jer 51:38–39 and in the Destruction of Humanity myth militate against this possibility, however. First, both the Destruction of Humanity myth and Jer 51:38–39 highlight the lively character of the supreme deity's agent: Sakhmet revels in the carnage she causes, stating that exercising "power over humanity is pleasing to her heart," while the leonine Babylonians roar and caterwaul as if spoiling for fight. Second, both Jer 51:38–39 and the Destruction of Humanity myth acknowledge the positive effects of alcohol,

---

was interpolated in the Masoretic Text from Jer 51:23 or 28, where these words appear in parallel.

22. The relationship between Jer 51:38–39 and Jer 51:40 also requires clarification. At first glance, verse 40 appears to continue the oracle begun in verse 38, even though it follows the concluding phrase "Oracle of Yahweh" in verse 39. The lion-like Babylonians are now likened to sheep and goats led to the slaughter: "I will bring them down like lambs to slaughter, like rams and he-goats" (אורידם כברים לטבוח כאילים עם עתודים). Comparison with Jer 51:57, however, suggests that verse 40 is a later addition to the preceding verses. The gloss on Jer 51:38–39 in Jer 51:57 does not refer to verse 40 at all, even though it assiduously copies the other details of Babylon's punishment from verse 39. The absence of this material from Jer 51:57, in turn, suggests that verse 40 was added to verses 38–39 after the composition of Jer 51:57 in order to furnish a more gruesome demise for the Babylonians than mere alcohol poisoning.

unlike the "cup of wrath" episode, which focuses solely on the negative effects of inebriation (e.g., loss of motor control and critical thinking). The consumption of beer gladdens Sakhmet/Hathor's heart (line 90), while Yahweh's draft quells the Babylonians' anger and renders them happy—before ultimately killing them. These uniquely shared motifs suggest that resemblance between the Destruction of Humanity myth and Jer 51:38–39 is not the result of a later redactor mining the Hebrew Bible for prophetic motifs.

Chronological Issues

Relative chronology also complicates the comparison of Jer 51:38–39 and the Destruction of Humanity myth. The only surviving version of the Destruction of Humanity myth dates to the fourteenth century BCE, almost seven centuries before the earliest texts preserved in the book of Jeremiah.[23] Later allusions to the Destruction of Humanity myth from the Ptolemaic period (323–30 BCE), however, suggest that this story continued to be known and transmitted until the 1st century BCE, long after the period of Judahite-Egyptian contact in the Saite period.[24] The ritual calendar from the Ptolemaic temple of Mut at Karnak makes several allusions to the Destruction of Humanity myth.[25] The most explicit

---

23. For the date of the myth see Hornung, *Der ägyptische Mythos*, 80; and Anthony J. Spalinger, "The Destruction of Mankind: A Transitional Literary Text," *SAK* 28 (2000): 282.

24. Caution is necessary at this point. The Destruction of Humanity myth shares several features with a second myth known as the myth of the Departed Goddess, which proved extremely popular in the Ptolemaic period. In both myths, Re seeks to pacify a violent leonine goddess by means of alcohol. His motivation for doing so, however, differs between the two myths. In the destruction myth, Re subdues Hathor/Sakhmet in order to save humanity from total annihilation. In the departure myth, by contrast, Re must pacify a violent goddess before enticing her to return to Egypt. Due to the similarities between the two myths, references to drinking and pacification alone are insufficient to identify allusions to the Destruction of Humanity myth in later Egyptian texts. Instead, it is better to focus on unique aspects of the destruction myth, such as the rebellion against the sun god and the use of blood-colored beer to appease the wrath of the goddess. For more on the differences between the two myths see Hermann Junker, *Der Auszug der Hathor-Tefnut aus Nubien* (Berlin: Königl. Akademie der Wissenschaft, 1911), 16–19; Germond, *Sekhmet et la protection du monde*, 131–48.

25. As Spalinger, Betsy M. Bryan, and John Coleman Darnell point out, the goddesses Hathor, Sakhmet, and Mut shared several features, including their role as the eye of the sun god, and were often identified in Egyptian literature and religious traditions (Spalinger, "Religious Calendar Year," 166; Betsy M.

reference appears in line 34: "Beer with *djdj* [dye] is made abundant for her on these occasion(s) of the Valley Feast—it being more excellent than blood, being the works of the beer goddess—in order to gladden her heart in her anger" (*bꜥḥ.tw n.s ḏsr m djdj m tr nn n ḥꜣb jn.t tn.tj r try m kꜣ.wt mnqt r snꜥꜥ jb.s n qn.t.s*).²⁶ As in the Destruction of Humanity myth, the Karnak liturgy alludes to the use of blood-colored beer to quell the wrath of the angry goddess and connects the myth with a ritual celebration.²⁷ Additional references to the myth appear in lines 17, 24, 25, 35, 39, 41, and 42 of the Karnak Calendar and include allusions to the rebellion of humanity, the violent rage of the goddess, and the area of *jꜣmw*.²⁸

Allusions to the Destruction of Humanity myth also appear in several texts from the Ptolemaic temple at Edfu. A wall inscription located in the first hypostyle hall and dated to the reign of Ptolemy VIII, Euergetes II (182–116 BCE) describes a ritual performed for Hathor: "Offering wine mixed with *djdj* [dye] to the Libyan, who dwells in the West" (*ḥnk jrp ꜣbḥ.tj m djdj n tmḥjt ḥr jb jmn.t*). The text then goes on to identify the Libyan as "Hathor, mistress of *jꜣmw*, eye of Re in the midst of Edfu, the lady, the beautiful cow of the west, to whom the intoxicating drink is offered in order to pacify her heart with the blood of her father's enemy" (*ḥwt-ḥrw nb.t jꜣmw jr.t rꜥ ḥr jb bḥdt ḥnw.t jḥ.t jmn.t nfr.t ḥnk.tj n.s tḥ r sḥtp jb.s ḥr wtr.w nw sbj n jtj.s*).²⁹ As Kurth notes, these passages exhibit five parallels with the Destruction of Humanity myth. In both texts:

Bryan, "Hatshepsut and Cultic Revelries in the New Kingdom," in *Creativity and Innovation in the Reign of Hatshepsut*, ed. José M. Galán, Betsy M. Bryan, and Peter F. Dorman, SAOC 68 [Chicago: The Oriental Institute of the University of Chicago, 2014], 100; John Coleman Darnell, "The Apotropaic Goddess in the Eye," *SAK* 24 [1997]: 1997, 45n67). As a result, Mut took on the role of Hathor/Sakhmet in the version of the Destruction of Humanity myth associated with the Karnak temple. See also Hoenes, *Untersuchungen zu Wesen und Kult*, 175–79, and Richard Jasnow and Mark Smith, "'As for Those Who Have Called Me Evil, Mut will Call Them Evil': Orgiastic Cultic Behaviour and Its Critics in Ancient Egypt," *Enchoria* 32 (2010/2011): 18.

26. Spalinger, "Religious Calendar Year," 176.

27. See Siegfried Schott, *Das schöne Fest vom Wüstentale: Festbräuche einer Totenstadt*, Abhandlungen der Geistes- und Sozialwissenschaftlichen Klasse 11 (Wiesbaden: Franz Steiner, 1953), 771–75, for an overview of the "Feast of the Beautiful Valley" and 840–41 for the connection between Hathor and this festival.

28. Spalinger, "Religious Calendar Year," 167, 170–72, 176, 178–79.

29. Dieter Kurth, "Ein Mythos des Neuen Reiches in einer ptolemäischen Ritualszene," in *L'Égyptologie en 1979: Axes prioritaires de recherches*, Colloques internationaux du Centre national de la recherche scientifique 595.1 (Paris: Éditions de Centre national de la recherche scientifique, 1982), 129–132, 129. For the text of this inscription see Émile Chassinat and Maxence de Rochemonteix,

(1) someone offers an intoxicating beverage tinted with *djdj*-dye to Hathor (2) in order to pacify her rage; (3) the color of this beverage resembles human blood; (4) the goddess is associated with the area of *jꜣmw*; and (5) the goddess acts violently against her father's enemies.[30]

The Ptolemaic references to the Destruction of Humanity myth indicate that this story continued to be known and transmitted in Egypt until the 1st century BCE, long after the period of Egyptian-Judahite contact in the Saite period. At the same time, the longevity of the myth complicates any attempt to reconstruct the process of transmission from Egypt to Judah: the Destruction of Humanity myth remained in circulation for at least fourteen hundred years and could have entered Judah at any time during this period. We can narrow down this date range, however, by establishing a plausible date for the composition of Jer 51:38–39.

The Date of Jeremiah 51:38–39

Dating Jer 51:38–39 proves difficult since these verses do not contain any historical references, despite their otherwise rich imagery. But we can establish a date for this oracle on the basis of other criteria. Jeremiah 51:38–39, and the oracles against Babylon more generally, presuppose Babylonian domination of Judah, and as such, most likely originated after the Babylonian annexation of Judah in 604 BCE. At the same time, it is unlikely that Jer 51:38–39 and the literary core of the oracles significantly postdate the fall of Babylon in 539 BCE. It would be strange, after all, for a Judahite writer to compose an oracle against Babylon once the Babylonians ceased to be politically relevant. These preliminary observations suggest that many of the oracles against Babylon originated sometime between 604 BCE and 539 BCE, a long period of time to be sure, but one in which many Judahites lived under Saite rule.

This conclusion receives support from other quarters. While many of the oracles against Babylon envision a violent end for the Mesopo-

---

Le temple d'Edfou: Tome troisième (Cairo: Institut français d'archéologie orientale, 1928), 253, lines 2–8.

30. Kurth, "Ein Mythos des Neuen Reiches," 130. Along these lines, a fourth-century BCE healing statue from Naples may contain a third post-Saite allusion to the Destruction of Humanity myth when it refers to Sakhmet as "Sakhmet the Great, the [eye] of Re, mistress of heaven, mistress of all the gods, who subdues the rebels" (*sḫmt ꜣ.t [jr.t] rꜥ nb(.t) p.t ḥnw.t nṯr.w nb.w wꜥf sbj.w*). For this statue, see Lázló Kákosy, *Egyptian Healing Statues in Three Museums in Italy: Turin, Florence, Naples* (Turin: Ministero per i beni e le attività culturali, Soprintendenza al Museo delle antichità egizie, 1999), 134.

tamian superpower and its capital on the lower Euphrates, in reality the Persian king Cyrus entered Babylon in peace. He did not need to conquer the city.[31] This discrepancy suggests that the literary core of Jer 50–51 predates the fall of Babylon, since a later author would not compose an incorrect oracle.[32] Furthermore, none of the oracles within Jer 50 and 51 mention Cyrus or the Achaemenids as the author of Babylon's destruction, but instead attribute Babylon's downfall to groups or individuals other than Cyrus. Jeremiah 50:3, 9, 41–42, and 51:48 variously identify Babylon's conquerors as "a nation from the north" (גוי מצפון), "a company of great nations from the land of the north" (קהל גוים גדלים מארץ צפון), "a people... from the north" (עם ... מצפון), and "destroyers ... out of the north" (השודדים ... מצפון), while Jer 51:11 credits "the kings of the Medes" (מלכי מדי) with Babylon's destruction. And in the extended description of Babylon's downfall in Jer 51:27–28, "Urartu, Mannea, and Scythia" (אררט מני ואשכנז) team up with "the kings of the Medes" (מלכי מדי) to conquer the city. The reference to the Medes in this passage and Jer 51:11, in turn, suggests that these verses predate Cyrus's conquest of Media in 550 BCE.[33] Similarly, the reference to multiple rulers in Jer 51:46 may allude to the power struggle that occurred between Nebuchadnezzar's death in 562 BCE and Nabonidus's ascension in 555 BCE and suggests an even earlier date for some of the oracles within Jer 50–51.[34]

Although Jer 51:38–39 most likely dates sometime between 604 and 539 BCE, it is possible that this passage reflects an earlier borrowing of the Destruction of Humanity myth. There is, however, very little concrete evidence for an earlier adaptation of the myth. Egyptian figurines from Judah attest to interest in leonine goddesses like Hathor and Sakhmet during the tenth to the eighth centuries BCE.[35] But the simple presence of figurines depicting Sakhmet and related goddesses in Judah does not necessarily imply that Judahites adopted the Destruction of Humanity myth at this time. Judahites may have imported these figurines for aesthetic rather than religious reasons, and without evidence regarding the Judahite reception of these objects, it is precarious to

---

31. Briant, *From Cyrus to Alexander*, 41; Reimer, "Jeremiah before the Exile?," 216; McKane, *Commentary on Jeremiah 26–52*, 1250.

32. Schmid, "Prognosis and Postgnosis in Biblical Prophecy," 112–13.

33. Briant, *From Cyrus to Alexander*, 31; Reimer, "Jeremiah before the Exile?," 216.

34. Smelik, "Function of Jeremiah 50 and 51," 96.

35. Christian Herrmann, *Ägyptische Amulette aus Palästina/Israel: Mit einem Ausblick auf ihre Rezeption durch das Alte Testament*, OBO 138 (Göttingen: Vandenhoeck & Ruprecht, 1994), 146–48.

posit the adoption of Egyptian mythological material during the tenth to the eighth centuries BCE.[36] In the absence of other evidence, therefore, I would date the adaptation of the Destruction of Humanity myth to the Saite period.[37]

6.3. HISTORICAL BACKGROUND OF THE MYTH'S ADAPTATION

Jeremiah 51:38–39 represents a radical departure from the anti-Egyptian texts analyzed in the preceding chapters: instead of celebrating Babylonian victories over Egypt or casting Nebuchadnezzar as a potential liberator, it adapts an Egyptian myth in order to condemn Babylonian aggression. Its creator must have had access to Egyptian cultural material and an axe to grind against Babylon. In the remainder of this chapter, I will argue that the Judahites living in the eastern Nile Delta had both the means and motive to create Jer 51:38–39 and are, therefore, the most likely composers of this text. They may have seen or participated in festivals in honor of Hathor, Sakhmet, or Mut and have become acquainted with a version of the Destruction of Humanity myth as part of these rites. They were also adversely affected by Nebuchadnezzar's repeated invasions of Egypt.

Both the Book of the Heavenly Cow and the festal calendar from the Mut temple at Karnak connect the Destruction of Humanity myth to religious festivals. The Book of the Heavenly Cow associates the myth with the New Year, while the Karnak Calendar links it to the "Beautiful Feast of the Valley."[38] Unfortunately, it is unclear how these particular

---

36. Christopher B. Hays has argued that these figurines attest to the worship of Mut in eighth-century BCE Judah and that Isa 28:1–22 satirizes several aspects of her cult (Christopher B. Hays, "The Covenant with Mut: A New Interpretation of Isaiah 28:1–22," *VT* 60 [2010]: 212–40; Christopher B. Hays, "The Egyptian Goddess Mut in Iron Age Palestine: Further Data from Amulets and Onomastics," *JNES* [2012]: 299–314; Christopher B. Hays, *A Covenant with Death: Death in the Iron Age II and Its Rhetorical Uses in Proto-Isaiah* [Grand Rapids, MI: Eerdmans, 2015], 288–314). According to his interpretation, the references to drunkenness in verses 3 and 7 allude to the bacchanalia celebrated in honor of Mut. If he is correct, then it is possible that Judahites learned a version of the Destruction of Humanity myth in the eighth century BCE as part of these rites since—in the Ptolemaic period, at least—they served to commemorate the Destruction of Humanity myth.

37. Schipper, "Egypt and the Kingdom of Judah," 200–226; Schipper, "Egyptian Imperialism after the New Kingdom," 268–90; Schipper, "Egypt and Israel," 30–47; Ben-Dor Evian, "Past and Future of 'Biblical Egyptology,'" 3–5.

38. The Cairo Calendar—a chronological list of religious celebrations

6. Lions Gone Wild

festivals would have been celebrated, but, as Betsy Bryan notes, celebrations in honor of Hathor, Sakhmet, and related goddesses were often raucous, nocturnal affairs, where participants consumed copious amounts of alcohol in order to achieve a beatific vision of the deity.[39] The most important part of the festivals occurred when participants awoke the following day, proving that the goddess had returned to her benevolent form and humanity had been saved.[40]

The boisterous character of these festivals means that they would be highly visible to Judahites living in Egypt, who, as the later Elephantine papyri suggest, had Egyptian neighbors and family members and were already curious about Egyptian religious practices. The Judahite man Anani counted the Egyptians Ḥor and Pamet as his neighbors (B3 7:7–8; B3 12:30), while the Egyptian Ḥarrudj lived next door to the Judahite woman Mibtaḥiah according to B2 7:15.[41] Judahites at Elephantine also intermarried with the local Egyptian community. Mibtaḥiah, for example, married the Egyptian builder Esḥor (B2 6), while Ananiah married the Egyptian freedwoman Tapmet (B3 12:1–2).[42] Mixed Egyptian-Hebrew names like Ananiah son of Psamtik (ענניה בר פסמשך) (D9 10) and Eswere daughter of Gemariah (אסורי ברת גמריה) (B5 5:13) hint at further cases of intermarriage since individuals in the ancient Near East often received a name in their mother's native language.[43] These close civic

---

dated to either the Nineteenth or Twentieth Dynasty—also associates a festival in honor of Sakhmet with the New Year. The relevant section of the calendar describes this festival as "the festival of Sakhmet, which Re made for her when he pacified her" (ḥꜣb sḫmt jr sj n.s rꜥ ḥft shtp.n.f st), alluding to the use of alcohol to quell the rage of the goddess. For the text of the Cairo Calendar see Abd el-Mohsen Bakir, *The Cairo Calendar No. 86637* (Cairo: Antiquities Department of Egypt, 1966), 11; for its dating, see Bakir, *Cairo Calendar*, 6; René van Walsem, "Month Names at Deir el-Medîna," in *Gleanings from Deir el-Medîna*, ed. R. J. Demarée and Jac. J. Janssen, *Eg. Uitg.* 1 (Leiden: NINO, 1982), 217.

39. Bryan, "Hatshepsut and Cultic Revelries," 115, 123; see also Mark De-Pauw and Mark Smith, "Visions of Ecstasy: Cultic Revelry before the Goddess Ai / Nehemanit," in *Res severa verum gaudium: Festschrift für Karl-Theodor Zauzich zum 65. Geburtstag am 8. Juni 2004*, ed. Friedhelm Hoffmann and Heinz-Josef Thissen, Studia Demotica 6 (Leuven: Peeters, 2004), 86.

40. Bryan, "Hatshepsut and Cultic Revelries," 115.

41. See also Cornelius von Pilgrim, "Tempel des Yahu und 'Straße des Königs'—Ein Konflikt in der späten Perserzeit auf Elephantine," in *Egypt—Temple of the Whole World: Studies in Honour of Jan Assmann*, ed. Sibylle Meyer, NBS 47 (Leiden: Brill, 2003), 308.

42. Van der Toorn, *Becoming Diaspora Jews*, 55.

43. Bezalel Porten, "Egyptian Names in Aramaic Texts," in *Acts of the Seventh International Conference of Demotic Studies, Copenhagen, 23–27 August 1999*, ed. Kim Ryholt (Copenhagen: University of Copenhagen, 2002), 300–301.

and familial contacts led some Judahites to adopt aspects of Egyptian religious practice. In D7 21:3, for example, the Judahite man Giddel blesses his superior, Micaiah, to both Yahweh and Khnum, an Egyptian deity whose temple stood in Elephantine. And B2 8:5 mentions that Mibtaḥiah swore an oath by the Egyptian goddess Sati as part of a legal procedure.[44]

Based on this evidence, I argue that the Judahites living in the eastern Nile Delta witnessed or took part in rituals for Hathor, Sakhmet, or Mut and became acquainted with the Destruction of Humanity myth through this ritual modality. These individuals—who came primarily from the non-elite sector of society as I argued in chapter 3—also had good reason to condemn Babylon: Nebuchadnezzar's attack on Judah in 586 BCE had driven them from their homes and claimed the lives of friends and family members, and his campaigns against Egypt threatened their well-being.[45] Indeed, life in the Egyptian diaspora may have led them to reevaluate the relative danger posed by Egypt and Babylon. Although they had suffered under Saite rule and may once have seen Nebuchadnezzar as a potential liberator, they now lived in Egypt. By adapting an Egyptian myth, they both denounced Babylon and signaled a closer affiliation with their new home.[46]

---

44. As Annalisa Azzoni points out, individuals usually swore by a personal deity at Elephantine rather than one stipulated by the court (Annalisa Azzoni, *The Private Lives of Women in Persian Egypt* [Winona Lake, IN: Eisenbrauns, 2013], 116). Thus, Mibtaḥiah most likely considered Sati her personal goddess.

45. For these campaigns see chapter 2 as well as Edward Lipiński, "The Egypto-Babylonian War of the Winter 601–600 B.C.," *AION* 32 (1972): 235–41; Basílico and Lupo, "Final Stage and Abandonment of Tell el-Ghaba, North Sinai," 135–44; Abd el-Maksoud and Valbelle, "Une stèle de l'an 7 d'Apriès," 12; Jansen-Winkeln, "Die Siegesstele des Amasis," 132–53.

46. It is also possible that Judahite scribes adapted the Destruction of Humanity myth in Judah before the fall of Jerusalem in 586 BCE. During the Saite period, some scribes received training in hieratic in order to record the collection of taxes and the distribution of rations using the Egyptian system of accounting (Schipper, "Egypt and the Kingdom of Judah," 211; Lemaire and Vernus, "Le ostraca paleo-hébreux de Qadesh Barnéa," 345; Cohen and Bernick-Greenberg, *Excavations at Kadesh Barnea*, 247). There is also some circumstantial evidence that they learned and copied literary texts (Schipper, "Egypt and the Kingdom of Judah," 211; Schipper, "Egypt and Israel," 39–40; Bernd U. Schipper, "Die Lehre des Amenemope und Prov. 22,17–24,22: Eine Neubestimmung des literarischen Verhältnisses," *ZAW* 117 [2005]: 53–72, 232–48). If so, then Judahite scribes working on behalf of the Saite administration could have learned a version of the Destruction of Humanity myth and adapted it to express their animosity toward the Babylonians. These individuals, after all, were part of the Egyptian bureaucracy and stood to lose a lot from a change in administrative

6.4. CONCLUSION

In this chapter, I have argued that non-elite Judahites living in the eastern Nile Delta adapted the Egyptian Destruction of Humanity myth in Jer 51:38–39 in order to critique Babylon. Although the Babylonians once carried out Yahweh's judgment on the Nations/Egypt—just as Hathor/Sakhmet executed Re's judgment on humanity—they had overstepped their bounds by threatening the Judahite diaspora in Egypt and needed to be reined in. Like Re in the Destruction of Humanity myth, Yahweh uses alcohol to quell the violent rage of his erstwhile agents. Ultimately, Jer 51:38–39 reevaluates the relative dangers posed by Egypt and Babylon: for the Judahites living in Egypt, Nebuchadnezzar was no longer a liberator, but a threat to the safety they enjoyed.

---

structure. But it is unclear whether the Destruction of Humanity myth formed part of the Saite scribal curricula, and so I find this scenario less plausible.

7.
Conclusion

7.1. SUMMARY OF PREVIOUS CHAPTERS

During the late seventh and early sixth centuries BCE, the Saite pharaohs ruled Judah as a vassal state. As part of this arrangement, certain members of the Judahite elite—the Pashḥurs of the world—participated in the Egyptian administration of Judah serving as messengers and scribes. Non-elite Judahites were not so lucky. They fought in the Egyptian army in Mesopotamia, Egypt, and the Levant, produced food for the mercenaries that the Saite pharaohs stationed in Judah, and paid taxes to the Egyptian crown. They also formed an important component of the Judahite diaspora communities in Egypt that emerged after the fall of Jerusalem. As I have argued throughout this study, the book of Jeremiah reflects the experiences of non-elite Judahites during this tumultuous period, and recognition of this dynamic changes how we read and interpret Jeremiah in three ways. It helps explain the antipathy toward Egypt found throughout the book of Jeremiah; it provides a historical anchor for redactional approaches to dating the text; and it forces us to reevaluate the work's overwhelming support for Babylon.

Many of the references to Egypt in the book of Jeremiah denounce the injustices of the Saite period and wish for liberation from Saite oppression. Jeremiah 2:14–19, for example, condemns Judahite collaborators for valuing material rewards more than their compatriots' lives. Judging from the reference to Assyria, this passage most likely dates sometime between the advent of Saite control over Judah in 620 BCE and the final fall of the Assyrian Empire in 609 BCE. The earliest form of Jer 25:15–29 expresses the hope that the Babylonian victory at Carchemish portends the end of Saite control over Judah, while Jer 46:2–12 celebrates the Egyptian defeat at Carchemish. The following oracle in Jer 46:14–24 gleefully predicts a Babylonian victory over Nekau II at Migdol and Memphis—contrary to the course of history—and, therefore, dates shortly before the first Babylonian invasion of Egypt in 601 BCE. And finally, the two short oracles found in Jer 46:25–26 applaud either the second or third Babylonian invasion of Egypt.

Other texts are less hostile toward Egypt. In part, this is due to the presence of Judahite diaspora communities living along the Nile in the years after 586 BCE. The oracle in Jer 43:8–13 originated in Daphnae and dates shortly before Nebuchadnezzar II's second invasion of Egypt in 582 BCE. This text may have served to warn the Judahite community at Daphnae of the impending attack. Jeremiah 44, by contrast, reflects contact between Judah and the Judahite diaspora community in Upper Egypt around the time of the Egyptian civil war of 570 BCE or the third Babylonian invasion of Egypt in 568 BCE, nearly three decades before the reference to the Elephantine community found in Second Isaiah. Jeremiah 51:38–39 originated in the Egyptian diaspora during the exilic period and adapts the Egyptian Destruction of Humanity myth to criticize Babylon. Although the Babylonians once served as Yahweh's agent—freeing Judah from Egyptian control in 604 BCE—they have overstepped their bounds by destroying Jerusalem and threatening the diaspora communities in the eastern Nile Delta and need to be subdued. To do so, Yahweh plies the Babylonians with intoxicating beverages, much like Re uses beer to subdue the leonine goddess Sakhmet and to avert the destruction of humanity in the Egyptian myth.

7.2. OPPORTUNITIES FOR FURTHER RESEARCH

The results of this study suggest several possibilities for further research, including the identification of other Saite-period texts outside of the book of Jeremiah and the analysis of intercultural contacts between Judahites and Aegean populations during the Saite period. In this section, I will briefly sketch some possible approaches to these topics.

Given the extent of Egyptian-Judahite interaction during the Saite period, other biblical texts are likely to reflect the experiences of Judahites living under Saite rule. Potential candidates include Ezekiel's oracles against Egypt in chapters 29–32, the Table of Nations in Gen 10, and the Exodus itinerary in the Pentateuch. The oracles against Egypt in Ezekiel contain detailed historical information regarding the use of foreign mercenaries in the Egyptian army (Ezek 30:5) as well as references to various Egyptian and Babylonian military campaigns (Ezek 29:17–20; 30:20–26). They also condemn Egyptian military aid

7. Conclusion

as worthless—a claim borne out by Saite pharaohs' repeated refusal to honor their vassal treaties. The Table of Nations, on the other hand, lists several Aegean populations, such as Lydians (לודים) and Cretans (כפתרים), as Egypt's offspring (Gen 10:13–14), and this fictive genealogy could reflect the Saite pharaohs' reliance on Carian and Ionian mercenaries from Lydia (Herodotus, *Hist.* 2.152). Finally, the Exodus itinerary includes two delta cities that rose to prominence in the Saite period and may have hosted Judahite diaspora communities: Migdol and Daphnae (alias Baal-zephon in Exodus[1]).[2] More work is needed, but these texts may reflect the experiences of Judahites living under Saite rule.

The results of this study also open up new avenues for the study of cultural contact between Judahites and other Near Eastern and Aegean populations. The Saite pharaohs, after all, hired, conscripted, and coerced a wide variety of ethnic groups to fight on their behalf. The biblical text alone mentions Cushites, Lydians, Libyans, and Cyrenians fighting under the Egyptian banner (Jer 46:9; Ezek 27:10; 30:5); extra-biblical evidence adds Judahites, Phoenicians, and Greeks. As shown in chapters 2 and 3, the multicultural nature of the Egyptian army facilitated cultural contact between Judahites and various Aegean groups. Ceramic evidence indicates that Ionian mercenaries were stationed at the Egyptian fortress of Meṣad Ḥashavyahu, while the Arad ostraca mention two different groups of Aegean soldiers—Kittim and Carians—that were temporarily garrisoned at the fortress of Arad.[3] A combination of archaeological and textual evidence even suggests that Judahite and Aegean soldiers fought side-by-side at the battle of Carchemish on behalf of Nekau II: archaeologists recovered a Greek shield and greave from the ruins of the city, and Berossus (cited in Josephus's *Ag. Ap.* 1.137) mentions that Nebuchadnezzar II captured Judahite prisoners of war

---

1. Baal-zephon seems to be an alternative name for Daphnae derived from the religious practices of its Phoenician inhabitants. A sixth- or fifth-century BCE Phoenician letter from Saqqara (*KAI* 50) invokes "Baal Zephon" (בעל צפן) alongside of "all the gods of Daphnae" (כל אל תחפנחס).

2. The seemingly Egyptian toponym פי החירת in the Exodus itinerary may also reflect the geography of the Nile Delta during the Saite period. Recently, I have argued that פי החירת is actually a native Hebrew phrase meaning "at the entrance of the camps" (Wilson-Wright, "Camping along the Ways of Horus," 261–64). If this argument proves correct, then פי החירת could refer to the military camps (Στρατόπεδα) that Psamtik I established at the mouth of the Pelusiac branch of the Nile near Daphnae and Migdol to house the Ionian and Carian mercenaries serving in his army according to Herodotus (*Hist.* 2.154) and Diodorus Siculus (*Bib. hist.* 1.67.1).

3. Fantalkin, "Meẓad Ḥashavyahu," 103; Aharoni, *Arad Inscriptions*, 12, 37.

following the battle.[4] Contact between Judahites and Aegean groups was not necessarily limited to military contexts, however. Excavators in the city of David recovered a late seventh- or early sixth-century ostracon bearing Greek letters.[5] According to Alon de Groot and Hannah Bernick-Greenberg, both the fabric of the sherd and the style of chiseling indicate that the ostracon was produced in Jerusalem itself.[6] This object thus attest to the presence of Greek-speaking individuals in Jerusalem, perhaps as part of a trading venture.

The book of Jeremiah itself may even reflect the fruits of Greek-Judahite cultural contact in the Saite period. According to Jer 51:59–64, Jeremiah wrote "all the misfortune that would befall Babylon in a single scroll—all of these words written against Babylon" (את כל הרעה אשר תבוא אל בבל אל ספר אחד כל הדברים האלה הכתבים אל בבל, verse 60) and then entrusted it to the quartermaster Seraiah with a peculiar set of instructions:[7]

Jeremiah 51:61–64

[61] [...] When you come to Babylon, you will see and read all of these words. [62] And you will say, "O Yahweh, you yourself threatened to destroy this place so that no one dwells in it—from man to beast—indeed it shall be ruined forever." [63] And when you finish reading this scroll, tie a stone around it and throw it into the midst of the Euphrates [64] and say, "Thus shall Babylon sink and rise no more because of the misfortune I am bringing against it." [...]

---

4. Woolley, *The Town Defenses*, 79, 125, pl. 24, 25a; *BNJ* 680; Barclay, *Flavius Josephus: Against Apion*, 83.

5. Alon De Groot and Hannah Bernick-Greenberg, *Area E: Stratigraphy and Architecture: Text*, vol. VIIA of *Excavations at the City of David 1978–1985 Directed by Yigal Shiloh*, QEDEM 53 (Jerusalem: Institute of Archaeology, the Hebrew University of Jerusalem, 2012), 168. Excavators originally identified the script of this ostracon as Ancient South Arabian, but Benjamin Sass cogently argues that the ostracon records an early form of the Greek alphabet (Benjamin Sass, "Arabs and Greeks in Late First Temple Jerusalem," *PEQ* 122 [1990]: 59–61). Paula Perlman (personal communication) agrees with Sass's re-identification and has suggested that some of the other ostraca from the city of David excavations thought to contain Ancient South Arabian letters might also record Greek.

6. De Groot and Bernick-Greenberg, *Area E: Stratigraphy and Architecture: Text*, 168.

7. The placement of this episode immediately after the oracles against Babylon in Jer 50:1–51:58 as well as the phrase "all these words that are written concerning Babylon" (כל הדברים האלה הכתבים אל בבל) in verse 60 suggest that the scroll was thought to contain the text of Jer 50:1–51:58—or at least part of it.

7. Conclusion

[...]⁶¹ כבאך בבל וראית וקראת את כל הדברים האלה ⁶²ואמרת יהוה אתה דברת אל המקום הזה להכריתו לבלתי היות בו יושב למאדם ועד בהמה כי שממות עולם תהיה ⁶³והיה ככלתך לקרא את הספר הזה תקשר עליו אבן והשלכתו אל תוך פרת ⁶⁴ואמרת ככה תשקע בבל ולא תקום מפני הרעה אשר אנכי מביא עליה [...]

As W. Sherwood Fox noted already in 1914, Jeremiah's instructions to Seraiah share many formal characteristics with the ritual actions used to "activate" Greek curse tablets, a group of ritual texts found across the Mediterranean world from the sixth century BCE to the fourth century CE.[8] Such texts were usually written on lead tablets and contained maledictions directed at an individual or small group.[9] Like Jeremiah's scroll, they were ritually "activated" by reading their contents aloud and depositing them in a body of water or subterranean place.[10] Several curse tablets even liken the fate of their intended victim to the fate of the tablet itself—e.g., "just as this lead is useless, so may those who have been written here be useless" (καὶ ὡς οὗτος ὁ μόλυβδος ἄχρηστος ὣς ἄχρηστα εἶναι τῶν ἐνταῦθα γεγραμμένων; DTA 106, cf. DTA 105, 107)—much like Jeremiah links Babylon's fate to the fate of Seraiah's scroll.[11] Taken together, these similarities suggest that the author of Jer 51:59–64 had knowledge of Greek curse tablets, which they could have acquired as a result of Greek-Judahite contact during the Saite period as outlined above.[12] It is still possible, however, that this passage stems from a later time, especially given the later contact between Judeans and Greeks during the Hellenistic period and the longevity of the Greek curse tablet tradition.

7.3. CONCLUDING THOUGHTS

Judah was under Egyptian control for approximately twenty-six years during the Saite period and as a result, the average Judahite suffered. While certain members of the Judahite elite participated in the Egyptian

---

8. William Sherwood Fox, "Old Testament Parallels to Tabellae Defixionum," *The American Journal of Semitic Languages and Literatures* 30 (1914): 112–13, 123.

9. John G. Gager, ed., *Curse Tablets and Binding Spells from the Ancient World* (Oxford: Oxford University Press, 1992), 3.

10. Gager, *Curse Tablets*, 18–21.

11. Gager, *Curse Tablets*, 4; Richard Wuensch, *Inscriptiones Graecae III, Appendix: Defixionum Tabellae* (Berlin: Georg Reimer, 1897), 27–28.

12. The imagery of Jer 46:20 may also reflect contact between Judahites and Greeks during the Saite period. Daniel E. Gerschenson argues that the characterization of Egypt as a heifer attacked by a gadfly in this verse alludes to the myth of Io's Flight to Egypt (Daniel E. Gerschenson, "A Greek Myth in Jeremiah," *ZAW* 108 [1996]: 192–200).

administration of the Levant and received material rewards for their troubles, non-elite Judahites fought and died in support of the pharaohs' strategic goals, fed the foreign mercenaries stationed in Judah, and paid taxes that funded the Egyptian war-machine. They also formed a large component of the Judahite diaspora in Egypt. Several texts in the book of Jeremiah—ranging from the historical overview in 2:14–19 to the oracles against Egypt in chapter 46—offer a window into the experiences of everyday Judahites during this time. They express antipathy toward Egypt, hope in the possibility of liberation by Babylon, tension between Judahite collaborators and Judahite soldiers, and disillusionment with Babylon among the Judahites living in Egypt. In short, they help us understand what life was like during this turbulent period.

Bibliography

Abd el-Maksoud, Mohamed, and Dominique Valbelle. "Une stèle de l'an 7 d'Apriès découverte sur le site de Tell Défenneh." *REg* 64 (2013): 1–13.

Abd el-Maksoud, Mohamed et al. "The Excavations of 2009 at Tell Dafana." Pages 130–34 in *Tell Dafana Reconsidered: The Archaeology of an Egyptian Frontier Town*. Edited by François Leclère and Jeffrey Spencer. London: The British Museum, 2014.

Adiego, Ignacio J. *The Carian Language*. HdO 86. Leiden: Brill, 2007.

Aggoula, Basile. "Remarques sur l'inventaire des inscriptions de Palmyre, Fasc XI et XII." *Sem* 29 (1979): 109–17.

Agut-Labordère, Damien. "Plus que des mercenaires!: L'intégration des hommes de guerre grecs au service de la monarchie saïte." *PALLAS* 89 (2012): 293–306.

———. "The Saite Period: The Emergence of a Mediterranean Power." Pages 965–1027 in *Ancient Egyptian Administration*. Edited by Jaun Carlos Moreno García. HdO 104. Leiden: Brill, 2013.

Aharoni, Yohanan. *The Arad Inscriptions*. Jerusalem: The Israel Exploration Society, 1981.

Aḥituv, Shmuel. *Echoes from the Past: Hebrew and Cognate Inscriptions from the Biblical Period*. Jerusalem: Carta, 2008.

———. "Pashhur." *IEJ* 20 (1970): 95–96.

Albertz, Rainer. *Die Exilszeit: 6. Jahrhundert v. Chr.* BE 7. Stuttgart: Kohlhammer, 2001.

Allen, Leslie C. *Jeremiah: A Commentary*. OTL. Louisville: Westminster John Knox, 2008.

Allen, Spencer L. "An Examination of Northwest Semitic Divine Names and the *Bet*-locative." *JESOT* 2 (2013): 61–82.

———. *The Splintered Divine: A Study of Ištar, Baal, and Yahweh Divine Names and Divine Multiplicity in the Ancient Near East*. SANER 5. Berlin: De Gruyter, 2015.

Alt, Albrecht. "Psammetich II. in Palästina und in Elephantine." *ZAW* 30 (1910): 288–97.

Asher-Greve, Julia M., and Joan Goodnick Westenholz. *Goddesses in Context: On Divine Powers, Roles, Relationships and Gender in Mesopotamian Textual and Visual Sources*. OBO 259. Freiburg: Academic Press, 2013.

Asheri, David, Alan Lloyd, and Aldo Corcella. *A Commentary on Herodotus Books I–IV*. Edited by Oswyn Murray and Alfonso Moreno. Translated by Barbara Graziosi, Matteo Rossetti, Carlotta Dus, and Vanessa Cazzato. Oxford: Oxford University Press, 2007.

Avigad, Nahman. *Hebrew Bullae from the Time of Jeremiah: Remnants of a Burnt Archive*. Translated by R. Grafman. Jerusalem: Israel Exploration Society, 1986.

Azzoni, Annalisa. *The Private Lives of Women in Persian Egypt*. Winona Lake, IN: Eisenbrauns, 2013.

Baden, Joel S. *The Composition of the Pentateuch: Renewing the Documentary Hypothesis*. ABRL. New Haven: Yale University Press, 2012.

Bakir, Abd el-Mohsen. *The Cairo Calendar No. 86637*. Cairo: Antiquities Department of Egypt, 1966.

Barclay, John M. G., ed. *Flavius Josephus: Against Apion*. Flavius Josephus Translation and Commentary 10. Leiden: Brill, 2007.

Barkay, Gabriel. *Ketef Hinnom: A Treasure Facing Jerusalem's Walls*. Jerusalem: The Israel Museum, 1986.

———. "The Tomb of Pharaoh's Daughter: A Reconsideration" [Hebrew]. Pages 127–55 in *City of David Studies of Ancient Jerusalem: Proceedings of the Sixth Conference*. Edited by Eyal Miron. Jerusalem: Megalim, 2005.

Barstad, Hans M. "Jeremiah the Historian: The Book of Jeremiah as a Source for the History of the Near East in the Time of Nebuchadnezzar." Pages 87–98 in *Studies on the Text and Versions of the Hebrew Bible in Honour of Robert Gordon*. Edited by Geoffrey Khan and Diana Lipton. Leiden: Brill, 2011.

Basílico, Susana, and Silvia Lupo. "The Final Stage and Abandonment of Tell el-Ghaba, North Sinai: A Site on the Egyptian Eastern Border." Pages 135–44 in *Proceedings of the Ninth International Congress of Egyptologists*. Edited by Jean-Claude Goyon and Christine Cardin. OLA 150. Leuven: Peeters, 2007.

Beaulieu, Paul-Alain. *The Pantheon of Uruk during the Neo-Babylonian Period*. CM 25. Leiden: Brill, 2003.

Begg, Christopher. *Josephus' Story of the Later Monarchy (AJ 9,1–10,185)*. BETL 145. Leuven: Leuven University Press, 2000.

Bell, Lanny David. "A Collection of Egyptian Bronzes." Pages 397–420 in *Ashkelon 3: The Seventh Century B.C.* Edited by Lawrence E. Stager, Daniel M. Master, and J. David Schloen. Winona Lake, IN: Eisenbrauns, 2011.

Ben-Dor Evian, Shirly. "Egypt and the Levant in the Iron Age I–IIA: The Ceramic Evidence." *TA* 38 (2011): 94–119.

———. "The Past and Future of 'Biblical Egyptology.'" *Journal of Ancient Egyptian Interconnections* 18 (2018): 1–11.

Bernard, André, and Olivier Masson. "Les inscriptions grecques d'Abou-Simbel." *REG* 70 (1957): 1–46.

Beyer, Francis. *Ägyptische Namen und Wörter im Alten Testament*. ÄAT 93. Münster: Zaphon, 2019.

Biberstein-Kazimirski, Albert de. *Dictionnarie arabe-français*. 2 Vols. Paris: Maison-neuve, 1860.
Biddle, Mark E. *A Redaction History of Jeremiah 2:1–4:2*. AThANT 77. Zurich: Theologischer Verlag, 1990.
Bienkowski, Piotr. "Edom during the Iron II Period." Pages 782–94 in *The Oxford Handbook of the Archaeology of the Levant c. 8000–332 BCE*. Edited by Margreet L. Steiner and Ann E. Killebrew. Oxford: Oxford University Press, 2014.
Bietak, Manfred. "Comments on the 'Exodus.'" Pages 163–71 in *Egypt, Israel, and Sinai: Archaeological and Historical Relationships in the Biblical Period*. Edited by Anson F. Rainey. New York: Syracuse University Press, 1987.
———. *Tell el-Dab'a II*. Vienna: Österreichischen Akademie der Wissenschaft Wien, 1975.
Blenkinsopp, Joseph. *Isaiah 1–39*. AB 19. Yale: Yale University Press, 2000.
Blöbaum, Anke Ilona. *"Denn ich bin ein König, der die Maat liebt": Herrscherlegitimation im spätzeitlichen Ägypten: Eine vergleichende Untersuchung der Phraseologie in den offiziellen Königsinschriften vom Beginn der 25. Dynastie bis zum Ende der makedonischen Herrschaft*. Aegyptiaca Monasteriensia 4. Aachen: Shaker Verlag, 2006.
Boeser, Pieter A. A. *Die Denkmäler der saïtischen, griechisch-römischen, und koptischen Zeit*. Leiden: Brill, 1915.
Braun, T. F. R. G. "The Greeks in the Near East." Pages 1–31 in *The Expansion of the Greek World: Eighth to Sixth Centuries BC*, vol. 3,3 of *The Cambridge Ancient History*. Edited by John Boardman and Nicholas Geoffrey Lemprière Hammond. 2nd ed. Cambridge: Cambridge University Press, 1982.
Briant, Pierre. "The Achaemenid Empire." Pages 105–28 in *War and Society in the Ancient and Medieval Worlds: Asia, The Mediterranean, Europe, and Mesoamerica*. Edited by Kurt Raaflaub and Nathan Rosenstein. Cambridge: Harvard University Press, 1999.
———. *From Cyrus to Alexander: A History of the Persian Empire*. Translated by Peter T. Daniels. Winona Lake, IN: Eisenbrauns, 2002.
Brueggemann, Walter. *A Commentary on Jeremiah: Exile and Homecoming*. Grand Rapids, MI: Eerdmans, 1998.
Bryan, Betsy M. "Hatshepsut and Cultic Revelries in the New Kingdom." Pages 93–123 in *Creativity and Innovation in the Reign of Hatshepsut*. Edited by José M. Galán, Betsy M. Bryan, and Peter F. Dorman. SAOC 68. Chicago: The Oriental Institute of the University of Chicago, 2014.
Buhl, Marie-Louise. *The Late Egyptian Anthropoid Stone Sarcophagi*. Copenhagen: Nationalmuseet, 1959.
Bunnens, Guy. "Phoenicia in the Late Iron Age: Tenth Century BCE to the Assyrian and Babylonian Periods." Pages 57–73 in *The Oxford Handbook of the Phoenician and Punic Mediterranean*. Edited by Brian R. Doak and Carolina López-Ruiz. Oxford: Oxford University Press, 2019.
Butts, Aaron Michael. "Reduplicated Nominal Patterns in Semitic." *JAOS* 131 (2011): 83–108.

Calabro, David. "The Hieratic Scribal Tradition in Preexilic Judah." Pages 77–85 in *Evolving Egypt: Innovation, Appropriation, and Reinterpretation in Ancient Egypt*. Edited by Kerry Muhlstein and John Gee. Oxford: Archaeopress, 2012.

———. "Personal Names with Egyptian Elements in Preexilic Hebrew Inscriptions." Pages 95–118 in *These Are the Names*. Edited by Aaron Demsky. Studies in Jewish Onomastics 5. Ramat-Gan: Bar-Ilan University Press, 2011.

Carroll, Robert P. *Jeremiah: A Commentary*. OTL. Philadelphia: Westminster Press, 1986.

Carter, Charles E. *The Emergence of Yehud in the Persian Period: Social and Demographic Study*. JSOTSup 294. Sheffield: Sheffield Academic Press, 1999.

Cassimatis, Hélène. "Des Chypriotes chez les pharaons." *Les cahiers du centre d'études chypriotes* 1 (1984): 33–38.

Chassinat, Émile. "Textes provenant du Sérapéum de Memphis." *RT* 22 (1900): 163–80.

———. "Un interprète égyptien pour les pays chananéens." *BIFAO* 1 (1900): 98–100.

Chassinat, Émile, and Maxence de Rochemonteix. *Le temple d'Edfou: Tome troisième*. Cairo: Institut français d'archéologie orientale, 1928.

Chaveau, Michel. "Le saut dans le temps d'un document historique: Des Ptolémées aux Saïtes." Pages 39–45 in *La XXVIe dynastie, continuités et ruptures: Actes du colloque international organisé les 26 et 27 novembre 2004 à l'Université Charles-de-Gaulles, Lille 3: Promenade saïte avec Jean Yoyotte*. Edited by Didier Devauchelle. Paris: Cybele, 2011.

Chevereau, Pierre-Marie. *Prosopographie des cadres militaires égyptiens de la Basse Époque: Carrières militaires et carrières sacerdotales en Égypte du XIe au IIe siècle avant J.-C.* Paris: Antony, 1985.

Ciancaglini, Claudia A. *Iranian Loanwords in Syriac*. Beiträge zur Iranistik 28. Wiesbaden: Dr. Ludwig Reichert, 2008.

Cody, Aelred. "When Is the Chosen People Called a *Gôy*?" *VT* 14 (1964): 1–6.

Cogan, Mordechai. *1 Kings*. AB 10. New York: Doubleday, 2000.

Cohen, Rudolph, and Hannah Bernick-Greenberg. *Excavations at Kadesh Barnea (Tell El-Qudereit) 1976–1982*. IAA Reports 34.1–2. Jerusalem: IAA, 2007.

Cornhill, Carl H. *Das Buch* Jeremia. Leipzig: Tauchnitz, 1905.

Couroyer, Bernard. "Menues trouvailles à Jérusalem." *RB* 77 (1970): 248–52.

Cross, Frank Moore. "Inscriptions in Phoenician and Other Scripts." Pages 333–72 in *Ashkelon 1: Introduction and Overview (1985–2006)*. Edited by Lawrence E. Stager, J. David Schloen, and Daniel M. Master. Winona Lake, IN: Eisenbrauns, 2008.

Da Riva, Rocío. *The Inscriptions of Nebuchadnezzar at Brisa (Wadi esh-Sharbin, Lebanon): A Historical and Philological Study*. AfOB 32. Wien: Institut für Orientalisk der Universität Wien, 2012.

Daressy, M. Georges. "Une trouvaille des bronzes à Mit Rahineh." *ASAE* 3 (1902): 139–50.

Darnell, John Coleman. "The Apotropaic Goddess in the Eye." *SAK* 24 (1997): 35–48.

Daviau, P. M. Michèle. "In the Shadow of a Giant: Egyptian Influence in Transjordan during the Iron Age." Pages 234–73 in *Walls of the Prince. Egyptian Interactions with Southwest Asia in Antiquity: Essays in Honour of John S. Holladay, Jr.*. Edited by Timothy P. Harrison, Edward B. Banning, and Stanley Klassen. Leiden: Brill, 2015.

De Groot, Alon, and Hannah Bernick-Greenberg. *Area E: Stratigraphy and Architecture: Text*. Vol. VIIA of *Excavations at the City of David 1978–1985 Directed by Yigal Shiloh*. QEDEM 53. Jerusalem: Institute of Archaeology, the Hebrew University of Jerusalem, 2012.

Delcor, Mathias. "Le culte de la 'reine du ciel' selon Jer 7,18; 44,17–19.25 et ses survivances: Aspects de la religion populaire féminine aux alentours de l'Exil de Juda et dans les communautés juives d'Égypte." Pages 101–22 in *Von Kanaan bis Kerala: Festschrift für Prof. Mag. Dr. Dr. J. P. M. van der Ploeg O. P. zur Vollendung des siebzigsten Lebensjahres am 4. Juli 1979*. Edited by Wilhelmus C. Delsman. AOAT 211. Neukirchen-Vluyn: Neukirchener, 1982.

DePauw, Mark, and Mark Smith. "Visions of Ecstasy: Cultic Revelry before the Goddess Ai / Nehemanit." Pages 67–93 in *Res severa verum gaudium: Festschrift für Karl-Theodor Zauzich zum 65. Geburtstag am 8. Juni 2004*. Edited by Friedhelm Hoffmann and Heinz-Josef Thissen. Studia Demotica 6. Leuven: Peeters, 2004.

Dewrell, Heath D. "Depictions of Egypt in the Book of Hosea and Their Implications for Dating the Book." *VT* 71 (2021): 503–30.

Diakonoff, Igor Mikhailovich. "The Near East on the Eve of Achaemenian Rule (Jeremiah 25)." Pages 223–30 in *Variatio Delectat. Iran und der Westen: Gedenkschrift für Peter Calmeyer*. Edited by Reinhard Dittman et al. AOAT 272. Münster: Ugarit-Verlag, 2000.

Diodorus Siculus. *The Library of History*, vol. 1: *Books 1–2.34*. Translated by C. H. Oldfather. LCL. Cambridge: Harvard University Press, 1933.

Donner, Herbert, and Wolfgang Röllig. *Kanaanäische und aramäische Inschriften*. 2nd ed. Wiesbaden: Harrassowitz, 1966–1969.

Drewnowska-Rymarz, Olga. *Mesopotamian Goddess Nanāja*. Warsaw: Agade, 2008.

Driver, G. R. "Linguistic and Textual Problems: Jeremiah." *JQR* 28 (1937): 97–129.

Edel, Elmar. "Amasis und Nebukadrezar II." *GöMisz* 29 (1978): 13–20.

Eilers, Wilhelm. "Kleinasiatisches." *ZDMG* (1940): 189–233.

Elgavish, David. "Extradition of Fugitives in International Relations in the Ancient Near East." Pages 33–57 in *The Jerusalem 2002 Conference*. Edited by Hillel Gamoran. *Jewish Law Association Studies* 14. Binghampton, NY: Global Academic Publishing, 2004.

Ellenbogen, Maximilian. *Foreign Words in the Old Testament*. London: Luzac, 1962.

Ellis, Teresa Ann. "Jeremiah 44: What if 'the Queen of Heaven' Is Yhwh?" *JSOT* 33 (2009): 465–88.

Emerton, John Adney. "Lice or a Veil in Song of Songs 1:7?" Pages 127–40 in *Understanding Poets and Prophets: Essays in Honour of George Wishart Anderson*. Edited by A. Graeme Auld. JSOTSup 152. Sheffield: JSOT Press, 1993.

Eph'al, Israel. "Nebuchadnezzar the Warrior: Remarks on His Military Achievements." *IEJ* 53 (2003): 178–91.

Fantalkin, Alexander. "Coarse Kitchen and Household Pottery as an Indicator for Egyptian Presence in the Southern Levant: A Diachronic Perspective." Pages 233–41 in *Ceramics, Cuisine and Culture: The Archaeology and Science of Kitchen Pottery in the Ancient Mediterranean World*. Edited by Michela Spataro and Alexandra Villing. Oxford: Oxbow Books, 2015.

———. "Identity in the Making: Greeks in the Eastern Mediterranean during the Iron Age." Pages 199–208 in *Naukratis: Greek Diversity in Egypt*. Edited by Alexandra Villing and Udo Schlotzhauer. The British Museum Research Publication 162. London: The British Museum, 2006.

———. "Meẓad Ḥashavyahu: Its Material Culture and Historical Background." *TA* 28 (2001): 3–165.

———. "Why Did Nebuchadnezzar Destroy Ashkelon in Kislev 604 BCE?" Pages 87–111 in *The Fire Signals of Lachish: Studies in the Archaeology and History of Israel in the Late Bronze Age, Iron Age, and Persian Period in Honor of David Ussishkin*. Edited by Israel Finkelstein and Nadav Na'aman. Winona Lake, IN: Eisenbrauns, 2011.

Fantalkin, Alexander, and Ephraim Lytle. "Alcaeus and Antimenidas: Reassessing the Evidence for Greek Mercenaries in the Neo-Babylonian Army." *Klio* 98 (2016): 90–117.

Fischer, Georg. "Jer 25 und die Fremdvölkersprüche: Unterschiede zwischen hebräischem und griechischem Text." *Bib.* 72 (1991): 474–99.

———. *Jeremia 1–25*. HThKAT. Freiburg: Herder, 2005.

———. *Jeremia 26–52*. HThKAT. Freiburg: Herder, 2005.

Fox, William Sherwood. "Old Testament Parallels to Tabellae Defixionum." *The American Journal of Semitic Languages and Literatures* 30 (1914): 111–24.

Freedy, Kenneth S., and Donald B. Redford. "The Dates in Ezekiel in Relation to Biblical, Babylonian, and Egyptian Sources." *JAOS* (1970): 462–85.

Freytag, Georg Wilhelm Friedrich. *Lexicon Arabico-Latinum*. 4 vols. Halle: Schwetscke, 1830–1837.

Fuchs, Gisela. "Das Symbol des Bechers in Ugarit und Israel: Vom 'Becher der Fülle' zum 'Zornesbecher.'" Pages 65–84 in *Verbindungslinien: Festschrift für Werner. H. Schmidt zum 65. Geburtstag*. Edited by Axel Graupner, Holger Delkurt, and Alexander B. Ernst. Neukirchen-Vluyn: Neukirchener, 2000.

Gager, John G., ed. *Curse Tablets and Binding Spells from the Ancient World*. Oxford: Oxford University Press, 1992.

Galvin, Garret. *Egypt as a Place of Refuge*. FAT 2/51. Tübingen: Mohr Siebeck, 2011.

Garfinkel, Yosef. "MLṢ HKRSYM in Phoenician Inscriptions from Cyprus, the QRSY in Arad, HKRSYM in Egypt, and BNY QYRS in the Bible." *JNES* 47 (1988): 27–34.

Gauthier, M. Henri. "Un monument nouveau du roi Psamtik II." *ASAE* 34 (1934): 129–34.
Gelb, Ignace J. et al., eds. *The Assyrian Dictionary of the Oriental Institute of the University of Chicago*, 21 vols. Chicago: The Oriental Institute, 1956–2010.
Germond, Philippe. *Sekhmet et la protection du monde*. Aegyptiaca Helvetica 9. Geneva: Éditions de Belles-Lettres, 1981.
Gerschenson, Daniel E. "A Greek Myth in Jeremiah." *ZAW* 108 (1996): 192–200.
Gesenius' Hebrew Grammar. Edited by Emil Kautzsch. Translated by Arthur E. Cowley. 2nd ed. Oxford: Oxford University Press, 1910.
Gesundheit, Shimon. "The Question of LXX Jeremiah as a Tool for Literary-Critical Analysis." *VT* 62 (2012): 29–57.
Gitin, Seymour. "Neo-Assyrian and Egyptian Hegemony over Ekron in the Seventh Century BCE: A Response to Lawrence E. Stager." *ErIsr* 27 (2003): 55*–61*.
———. "The Philistines in the Prophetic Texts: An Archaeological Perspective." Pages 273–90 in *Hesed Ve-Emet: Studies in Honor of Ernest S. Frerichs*. Edited by Jodi Magness and Seymour Gitin. BJS 320. Atlanta: Scholars Press, 1998.
Glanz, Oliver. *Understanding Participant-Reference Shifts in the Book of Jeremiah: A Study of Exegetical Method and Its Consequences for the Interpretation of Referential Incoherence*. SSN 60. Leiden: Brill, 2013.
Görg, Manfred. "Der Spiegeldienst der Frauen (Ex 38,8)." *BN* 23 (1984): 9–13.
———. "Namen und Titel in 1 Kön 11,19f." *BN* 26 (1987): 22–26.
Gorris, Elynn, and Yasmina Wicks. "The Last Centuries of Elam: The Neo-Elamite Period." Pages 249–72 in *The Elamite World*. Edited by Javier Álvarez-Mon, Gian Pitero Basello, and Yasmina Wicks. London: Routledge, 2018.
Goyon, Jean-Claude. *Le ritual du sḥtp Sḫmt au changement de cycle annuel: D'après les architraves du temple d'Edfou et textes parallèles, du Nouvel Empire à l'époque ptolémaïque et romaine*. Cairo: Institut français d'archéologie orientale, 2006.
Grabbe, Lester L. "'The Lying Pen of the Scribes'? Jeremiah and History," in *Essays on Ancient Israel and Its Near Eastern Context: A Tribute to Nadav Na'aman*. Edited by Yaira Amit et al., 189–204. Winona Lake, IN: Eisenbrauns, 2006.
Grayson, A. Kirk. *Assyrian and Babylonian Chronicles: Texts from Cuneiform Sources*. Winona Lake, IN: Eisenbrauns, 2000.
Greenberg, Gillian. *Translation Technique in the Peshitta to Jeremiah*. MPIL 13. Leiden: Brill, 2002.
Grelot, Pierre. *Documents araméens d'Égypte*. LAPO 5. Paris: Cerf, 1972.
Haider, Peter W. "Epigraphische Quellen zur Integration von Griechen in die ägyptische Gesellschaft der Saïtenzeit." Pages 197–215 in *Naukratis: Die Beziehungen zu Ostgriechenland, Ägypten und Zypern in archaischer Zeit. Akten der Table Ronde in Mainz, 25.–27. November 1999*. Edited by Ursula Höckman and Detlev Kreikenbom. Möhnesee: Bibliopolis, 2001.
Hays, Christopher B. *A Covenant with Death: Death in the Iron Age II and Its Rhetorical Uses in Proto-Isaiah*. Grand Rapids, MI: Eerdmans, 2015.

———. "The Covenant with Mut: A New Interpretation of Isaiah 28:1–22." *VT* 60 (2010): 212–40.

———. "The Egyptian Goddess Mut in Iron Age Palestine: Further Data from Amulets and Onomastics." *JNES* (2012): 299–314.

Hayward, Robert. *The Targum of Jeremiah: Translated, with Critical Introduction, Apparatus, and Notes*. The Aramaic Bible 12. Wilmington, DE: Michael Glazier, 1987.

Henkelman, Wouter F. M. "Cyrus the Persian and Darius the Elamite: A Case of Mistaken Identity." Pages 577–617 in *Herodot und das Persische Weltreich: Akten des 3. Internationalen Kolloquiums zum Thema "Vorderasien im Spannungsfeld klassischer und altorientalischer Überlieferungen," Innsbruck, 24.–28. November 2008*. Edited by Robert Rollinger, Brigitte Truschnegg, and Reinhold Bichler. Wiesbaden: Harrassowitz, 2011.

Herodotus. *The Persian Wars*, vol. 1: *Books 1–2*. Translated by Alfred Denis Godley. LCL. Cambridge: Harvard University Press, 1920.

———. *The Persian Wars*, vol. 2: *Books 3–4*. Translated by A. D. Godley. LCL. Cambridge: Harvard University Press, 1921.

———. *The Persian Wars*, vol. 3: *Books 5–7*. Translated by A. D. Godley. LCL. Cambridge: Harvard University Press, 1992.

Herrmann, Christian. *Ägyptische Amulette aus Palästina/Israel: Mit einem Ausblick auf ihre Rezeption durch das Alte Testament*. OBO 138. Göttingen: Vandenhoeck & Ruprecht, 1994.

———. "Egyptian Amulets." Pages 359–96 in *Ashkelon 3: The Seventh Century B.C.* Edited by Lawrence E. Stager, Daniel M. Master, and J. David Schloen. Winona Lake, IN: Eisenbrauns, 2011.

Herrmann, Siegfried. "Lud, Luditer." *BHH* 2:1108.

Hillers, Delbert R. *Covenant: The History of a Biblical Idea*. Baltimore: Johns Hopkins University Press, 1969.

———. "Notes on Palmyrene Aramaic Texts." *Aram* 7 (1995): 73–88.

Hillers, Delbert R., and Eleonora Cussini. *Palmyrene Aramaic Texts*. Baltimore: Johns Hopkins University Press, 1996.

Hoenes, Sigrid-Eike. *Untersuchungen zu Wesen und Kult der Göttin Sachmet*. Bonn: Rudolf Habelt, 1976.

Hoffmeier, James K. *Ancient Israel in Sinai: The Evidence for the Authenticity of the Wilderness Tradition*. Oxford: Oxford University Press, 2005.

———. "A New Insight on Pharaoh Apries from Herodotus, Diodorus and Jeremiah 46:17." *JSSEA* 11 (1981): 165–70.

Holladay, John S., Jr. "Judeans (and Phoenicians) in Egypt in the Late Seventh to Sixth Centuries B.C." Pages 405–37 in *Egypt, Israel, and the Ancient Mediterranean World: Studies in Honor of Donald B. Redford*. Edited by Gary N. Knoppers and Antoine Hirsch. PAe 20. Leiden: Brill, 2004.

Holladay, William L. *Jeremiah 1: A Commentary on the Book of the Prophet Jeremiah, Chapters 1–25*. Hermeneia. Philadelphia: Fortress Press, 1989.

———. *Jeremiah 2: A Commentary on the Book of the Prophet Jeremiah, Chapters 26–52*. Hermeneia. Philadelphia: Fortress Press, 1989.

Holm, Tawny L. "Nanay and Her Lover: An Aramaic Sacred Marriage Text from Egypt." *JNES* 76 (2017): 1–37.
Homès-Fredericq, Denyse. "Late Bronze and Iron Age Evidence from Lehun in Moab." Pages 187–202 in *Early Edom and Moab: The Beginning of the Iron Age in Southern Jordan*. Edited by Piotr Bienkowski. SAM 7. Sheffield: Sheffield Academic Press, 1992.
Hornkohl, Aaron D. *Ancient Hebrew Periodization and the Language of the Book of Jeremiah: The Case for a Sixth-Century Date of Composition*. SSLL 74. Leiden: Brill, 2014.
Hornung, Erik. *Der ägyptische Mythos von der Himmelskuh: Eine Ätiologie des Unvollkommenen*. OBO 46. 2nd ed. Freiburg: Academic Press, 1997.
Hussein, Hesham M., and Sayed Abd el-Aleem. "Tell el-Kedwa (Qedua): Saite Fortresses on Egypt's Eastern Frontier. The 2007 Season of SCA Fieldwork." Paper presented at the MSA/EES Delta Survey Workshop 2013, 22–23 March, Cairo.
———. "The Way(s) of Horus in the Saite Period: Tell el-Kedwa and its Key Location Guarding Egypt's Northeastern Frontier." *JAEI* 7 (2015): 1–13.
Huwyler, Beat. *Jeremia und die Völker: Untersuchungen zu den Völkersprüchen in Jeremia 46–49*. FAT 20. Tübingen: Mohr Siebeck, 1997.
Iacovou, Maria. "Cyprus during the Iron Age through the Persian Period: From the 11th Century BC to the Abolition of the City-Kingdoms (c. 300 BC)." Pages 795–824 in *The Oxford Handbook of the Archaeology of the Levant c. 8000–332 BCE*. Edited by Margreet L. Steiner and Ann E. Killebrew. Oxford: Oxford University Press, 2014.
———. "Historically Elusive and Internally Fragile Island Polities: The Intricacies of Cyprus's Political Geography in the Iron Age." *BASOR* 370 (2013): 15–47.
Ivantchik, Askold. "Cimmerians." *EBR* 5:323–24.
James, T. G. H. "Egypt: The Twenty-Fifth and Twenty-Sixth Dynasties." Pages 677–747 in *The Assyrian and Babylonian Empires and other States of the Near East: From the Eighth to the Sixth Centuries BC*. Vol. 3,2 of *The Cambridge Ancient History*. Edited by John Boardman et al. Cambridge: Cambridge University Press, 1991.
Jansen, H. Ludin. *The Coptic Story of Cambyses' Invasion of Egypt: A Critical Analysis of Its Literary Form and Its Historical Purpose*. Oslo: Dybwad, 1950.
Jansen-Winkeln, Karl. "Die Siegesstele des Amasis." *ZÄS* 141 (2014): 132–53.
Janzen, J. Gerald. *Studies in the Text of Jeremiah*. Cambridge: Harvard University, 1973.
Jasnow, Richard, and Mark Smith. "'As for Those Who Have Called Me Evil, Mut will Call Them Evil': Orgiastic Cultic Behaviour and Its Critics in Ancient Egypt." *Enchoria* 32 (2010/2011): 9–53.
Jastrow, Marcus. *Dictionary of the Targumim, the Talmud Babli and Yerushalmi, and the Midrashic Literature*. Peabody, MA: Hendrickson, 2006.
Jeffreys, David. "The Survey of Memphis, Capital of Ancient Egypt: Recent Developments." *Archaeology International* 11 (2008): 41–44.

Jeon, Jaeyoung. "Egyptian Gola in Prophetic and Pentateuchal Traditions: A Socio-Historical Perspective." *JAEI* 18 (2018): 12–23.

Joisten-Pruschke, Anke. *Das religiöse Leben der Juden von Elephantine in der Achämenidenzeit*. Wiesbaden: Harrassowitz, 2008.

Jones, Michael. "The Temple of Apis in Memphis." *JEA* 76 (1990): 141–47.

Josephus, Flavius. *Jewish Antiquities*. Vol. 4: *Books 9–11*. Translated by Ralph Marcus. LCL. Cambridge: Harvard University Press, 1937.

Jost, Renate. *Frauen, Männer und die Himmelskönigin: Exegetische Studien*. Gütersloh: Gütersloher, 1995.

———. "Kuchen für die Himmelskönigin in Jer 17,17f. und der Jer 44, 15–25." Pages 238–53 in *Essen und Trinken in der Bibel: Ein literarische Festmahl für Rainer Kessler zum 65. Geburtstag*. Edited by Michaela Geiger, Christl M. Maier, and Uta Schmidt. Gütersloh: Gütersloher, 2009.

Joüon, Paul, and Takamitsu Muraoka. *A Grammar of Biblical Hebrew*. SubBi 27. 2nd ed. Rome: Pontifical Biblical Institute, 2007.

Junker, Hermann. *Der Auszug der Hathor-Tefnut aus Nubien*. Berlin: Königl. Akademie der Wissenschaft, 1911.

Kahn, Dan'el. "Judean Auxiliaries in Egypt's Wars Against Kush." *JAOS* 127 (2007): 507–16.

———. "Nebuchadnezzar and Egypt: An Update on the Egyptian Monuments." *HeBAI* 7 (2018): 65–78.

———. "Some Remarks on the Foreign Policy of Psammetichus II in the Levant (595–589)." *JEH* 1 (2008): 139–57.

———. "Why Did Necho II Kill Josiah?" Pages 511–28 in *There and Back Again—the Crossroads II: Proceedings of an International Conference Held in Prague, September 15–18, 2014*. Edited by Jana Mynářová, Pavel Onderka, and Peter Pavúk. Prague: Charles University in Prague, 2015.

Kahn, Dan'el, and Oded Tammuz. "Egypt Is Difficult to Enter: Invading Egypt—A Game Plan (Seventh–Fourth Centuries BCE)." *JSSEA* 35 (2008): 37–66.

Kákosy, Lázló. *Egyptian Healing Statues in Three Museums in Italy: Turin, Florence, Naples*. Turin: Ministero per i beni e le attività culturali, Soprintendenza al Museo delle antichità egizie, 1999.

Kamil, Jill. "Ancient Memphis: Archaeologists Revive Interest in a Famous Egyptian Site." *Archaeology* 38 (1985): 25–31.

Kammerzell, Frank. *Studien zu Sprache und Geschichte der Karer in Ägypten*. GOF 4.27. Wiesbaden: Harrassowitz, 1993.

Kaplan, Philip. "Cross-Cultural Contacts among Mercenary Communities in Saite and Persian Egypt." *MHR* 18 (2003): 1–31.

Katzenstein, H. Jacob. "Gaza in the Neo-Babylonian Period (626–539 BCE)." *Transeuphratène* 7 (1994): 35–49.

———. *The History of Tyre: From the Beginning of the Second Millennium BCE until the Fall of the Neo-Babylonian Empire*. Beer-Sheva: Ben-Gurion University of the Negev Press, 1997.

Kaufman, Stephen A. et al. *The Comprehensive Aramaic Lexicon* (http://cal.huc.edu).

Keel, Othmar. "Seals and Seal Impressions." Pages 341–58 in *Ashkelon 3: The Seventh Century B.C.* Edited by Lawrence E. Stager, Daniel M. Master, and J. David Schloen. Winona Lake, IN: Eisenbrauns, 2011.
Kenyon, Kathleen M. *Excavations at Jericho II: The Tombs Excavated in 1955–1956.* London: British School of Archaeology in Jerusalem, 1965.
Kratz, Reinhard G. *The Prophets of Israel.* Translated by Anselm C. Hagedorn and Nathan MacDonald. CrStHB 2. Winona Lake, IN: Eisenbrauns, 2015.
Kurth, Dieter. "Ein Mythos des Neuen Reiches in einer ptolemäischen Ritualszene." Pages 129–32 in *L'Égyptologie en 1979: Axes prioritaires de recherches*, Colloques internationaux du Centre national de la recherche scientifique 595.1. Paris: Éditions de Centre national de la recherche scientifique, 1982.
Labow, Dagmar, ed. *Flavius Josephus: Contra Apionem.* Vol. 1: *Einleitung, Text, Textkritischer Apparat, Übersetzung und Kommentar.* BWANT 167. Stuttgart: Kohlhammer, 2005.
Lambdin, Thomas O. "Egyptian Loanwords in the Old Testament." *JAOS* 73 (1953): 145–55.
Lane, William Edward. *An Arabic-English Lexicon*, 8 Vols. (Vols. 6–8 ed. Stanley Lane-Poole). London: Williams and Norgate, 1863–1893.
Langdon, Stephen. *Die neubabylonischen Königsinschriften.* Translated by Rudolf Zehnpfund. Leipzig: J. C. Hinrichs, 1912.
Leahy, Anthony. "The Earliest Dated Monument of Amasis and the End of the Reign of Apries." *JEA* 74 (1988): 183–99.
Leclère, François. "Introduction to the Objects from Tell Dafana." Pages 41–50 in *Tell Dafana Reconsidered: The Archaeology of an Egyptian Frontier Town.* Edited by François Leclère and Jeffrey Spencer. London: The British Museum, 2014.
———. *Les villes de Basse Égypte au Ier millénnaire av. J. C.: Analyse archéologique et historique de la topographie urbaine.* BdE 144. Cairo: Institut français d'archéologie orientale, 2008.
———. "Tell Dafana: Identity, Exploration and Monuments." Pages 1–40 in *Tell Dafana Reconsidered: The Archaeology of an Egyptian Frontier Town.* Edited by François Leclère and Jeffrey Spencer. London: The British Museum, 2014.
Lemaire, André. "Les inscriptions de Khirbet el-Qôm et l'ashérah de YHWH," *RB* (1977): 595–608.
———. "Notes d'épigraphie nord-ouest sémitique." *Semitica* 30 (1980): 17–32.
Lemaire, André, and Pascal Vernus. "Le ostraca paleo-hébreux de Qadesh Barnéa." *Orientalia* 49 (1980): 341–45.
Leuchter, Mark. *The Polemics of Exile in Jeremiah 26–45.* Cambridge: Cambridge University Press, 2008.
Levin, Christoph. *Die Verheißung des neuen Bundes in ihrem theologiegeschichtlichen Zusammenhang ausgelegt.* FRLANT 137. Göttingen: Vandenhoeck & Ruprecht, 1985.
Levy, Jacob. *Wörterbuch über die Talmudim und Midraschim.* Edited by Lazarus Goldschmidt. 4 Vols. 2nd ed. Berlin: Harz, 1924.
Lipiński, Edward. "The Egypto-Babylonian War of the Winter 601–600 B.C." *AION* 32 (1972): 235–41.

———. *On the Skirts of Canaan in the Iron Age: Historical and Topographical Researches.* OLA 153. Leuven: Peeters, 2006.

Lipschits, Oded. *The Fall and Rise of Jerusalem: Judah and Babylonian Rule.* Winona Lake, IN: Eisenbrauns, 2005.

Liwak, Rüdiger. *Der Prophet und die Geschichte: Eine literar-historische Untersuchung zum Jeremiabuch.* BWANT; Stuttgart, Kohlhammer, 1987.

Lloyd, Alan B. *Herodotus Book II: Commentary 99–182.* EPRO 43/3. Leiden: Brill, 1988.

Lopes, Maria Helena Trinidade. "The Apries Palace Project." *EA* 42 (2013): 36–37.

———. *Mênfis: O rosto de Apriés.* Lisbon: Tinta-da-Chian, 2010.

Lundbom, Jack R. *Jeremiah 1–20: A New Translation with Introduction and Commentary.* AB 21A. New Haven: Yale University Press, 1999.

———. *Jeremiah 21–36: A New Translation with Introduction and Commentary.* AB 21B. New Haven: Yale University Press, 2004.

———. *Jeremiah 37–52: A New Translation with Introduction and Commentary.* AB 21C. New Haven: Yale University Press, 2004.

Lupo, Silvia. "The Argentine Archaeological Mission at Tell el-Ghaba: A Third Intermediate-Early Saite Period Site on the Ancient Egyptian Eastern Border. Remarks and Main Results." *TdE* 7 (2016): 89–110.

———. *Tell el-Ghaba III: A Third Intermediate-Early Saite Period Site in the Egyptian Eastern Border. Excavations 1995–1999 and 2010 in Areas I, II, VI and VIII.* BARIS 2756. Oxford: Archaeopress, 2015.

Machinist, Peter. "Assyria and Its Image in First Isaiah." *JAOS* 103 (1983): 719–37.

MacKenzie, Duncan. *Excavations at Ain Shems (Beth-Shemesh).* Palestine Exploration Fund Annual 2. Manchester: Palestine Exploration Fund, 1912.

Maier, Aren M. "The Relations between Egypt and the Southern Levant during the Late Iron Age: The Material Evidence from Egypt." *Ägypten und Levant* 12 (2003): 235–46.

Maier, Christl M. *Jeremiah als Lehrer der Tora: Soziale Gebote des Deuteronomiums in Fortschreibungen des Jeremiabuches.* FRLANT. Göttingen: Vandenhoeck & Ruprecht, 2002.

———. "The Nature of Deutero-Jeremianic Texts." Pages 103–23 in *Jeremiah's Scriptures: Production, Reception, Interaction and Transformation.* Edited by Hindy Najman and Konrad Schmid. Leiden: Brill, 2016.

Maier, Michael P. *Ägypten—Israels Herkunft und Geschick: Studie über einen theopolitischen Zentralbegriff im hebräischen Jeremiabuch.* ÖBS 21. Frankfurt: Peter Lang, 2002.

Mankowski, Paul V. *Akkadian Loanwords in Biblical Hebrew.* HSS 47. Winona Lake, IN: Eisenbrauns, 2000.

Mariette, Auguste. *Œuvres diverses*, Bibliothèque égyptologique 18, Paris: Ernest Leroux, 1904.

Masson, Olivier, and Jean Yoyotte. "Une inscription ionienne mentionnant Psammétique Ier." *Epigraphica Anatolica* 11 (1988): 171–79.

Mazar, Eilat, and Reut Livyatan Ben-Arie. "Hebrew and Non-Indicative Bullae." Pages 299–362 in *Area G*, vol. 1 of *The Summit of the City of David Excavations 2005–2008, Final Reports*. Edited by Eilat Mazar. Jerusalem: Shoham, 2015.

McCarter, P. Kyle. "Aspects of the Religion of the Israelite Monarchy: Biblical and Epigraphic Data." Pages 137–55 in *Ancient Israelite Religion: Essays in Honor of Frank Moore Cross*. Edited by Patrick D. Miller, Paul D. Hanson, and S. Dean McBride. Philadelphia: Fortress Press, 1987.

McCown, Chester Charlton. *Archaeological and Historical Results*, vol. 1 of *Tell en-Naṣbeh: Excavated under the Direction of the Late William Frederic Badè*. Berkeley: The Palestine Institute of Pacific School of Religion, 1947.

McKane, William. *A Critical and Exegetical Commentary on Jeremiah*, vol. 1: *Commentary on Jeremiah 1–25*. ICC. Edinburgh: T&T Clark International, 1986.

———. *A Critical and Exegetical Commentary on Jeremiah*, vol. 2: *Commentary on Jeremiah 26–52*. ICC. Edinburgh: T&T Clark International, 1986.

———. "Poison, Trial by Ordeal and the Cup of Wrath." *VT* 30 (1980): 474–92.

———. "Worship of the Queen of Heaven (Jer 44)." Pages 318–24 in *Wer ist wie du, Herr, unter den Göttern: Studien zur Theologie und Religionsgeschichte Israels: Für Otto Kaiser zum 70. Geburtstag*. Edited by Ingo Kottsieper. Göttingen: Vandenhoeck & Ruprecht, 1994.

Miller, J. Maxwell, and John H. Hayes. *A History of Ancient Israel and Judah*. 2nd ed. Louisville: Westminster John Knox, 2006.

Muchiki, Yoshiyuki. *Egyptian Proper Names and Loanwords in Northwest Semitic*. SBLDS 173. Atlanta: Scholars Press, 1999.

Mumford, Gregory D. "Egypto-Levantine Relations During the Iron Age to the Early Persian Periods (Dynasties Late 20 to 26)." Pages 141–204 in *Egyptian Stories: A British Egyptological Tribute to Alan B. Lloyd on the Occasion of His Retirement*. Edited by Thomas Schneider and Kasia Maria Szpakowska. Münster: Ugarit-Verlag, 2007.

———. "International Relations between Egypt, Sinai and Syria-Palestine in the Late Bronze Age to Early Persian Period (Dynasties 18–26: c. 1550–525 BC)." PhD thesis, University of Toronto, 1998.

Muraoka, Takamitsu. *A Greek-English Lexicon of the Septuagint*. Leuven: Peeters, 2009.

Muscarella, Oscar White. "Parasols in the Ancient Near East." *Notes in the History of Art* 18 (1999): 1–7.

Na'aman, Nadav. "An Assyrian Residence at Ramat Raḥel?" *TA* 28 (2001): 260–80.

———. "The Kingdom of Judah under Josiah." *TA* 18 (1991): 3–71.

———. "Nebuchadnezzar's Campaign in Year 603 B.C.E." *BN* (1992): 41–44.

———. "The Shihor of Egypt and Shur That Is before Egypt." *TA* 7 (1980): 95–109.

Naveh, Joseph. "More Hebrew Inscriptions from Meṣad Ḥashavyahu." *IEJ* 12 (1962): 27–32.

Niditch, Susan. *The Symbolic Vision in Biblical Tradition*. HSM 30. Chico: Scholars Press, 1983.

Niemeier, Wolf-Dietrich. "Archaic Greeks in the Orient: Textual and Archaeological Evidence." *BASOR* 322 (2001): 11–32.

———. "Greek Mercenaries at Tell Kabri and Other Sites in the Levant." *TA* 29 (2002): 328–31.

Nissinen, Martti. *Ancient Prophecy: Near Eastern, Biblical, and Greek Perspectives*. Oxford: Oxford University Press, 2018.

Noonan, Benjamin J. *Non-Semitic Loanwords in the Hebrew Bible: A Lexicon of Language Contact*. LSAWS 14. Winona Lake, IN: Eisenbrauns, 2019.

Noth, Martin. *Könige I, 1–16*. BKAT 9/1. Neukirchen-Vluyn: Neukirchener, 1983.

Olyan, Saul M. "Some Observations Concerning the Identity of the Queen of Heaven." *UF* 19 (1987): 161–74.

Oren, Eliezer D. "Ethnicity and Regional Archaeology: The Western Negev under Assyrian Rule." Pages 102–5 in *Biblical Archaeology Today (1990): Proceedings of the Second International Conference on Biblical Archaeology*. Edited by Avraham Biran and J. Aviram. Jerusalem: Israel Exploration Society, 1993.

———. "Migdol: A New Fortress on the Edge of the Eastern Nile Delta." *BASOR* 256 (1984): 7–44.

Ossing, Jürgen. "Zum Lautwechsel *i* ↔ ʿ unter Einfluss von *ḫ*." *SAK* 8 (1980): 217–25.

Pallotino, Massimo. "Vaso egiziano inscritto proveniente dal villaggio preistorico di Coppa Nevigata." *Atti dell'Accademia Nazionale dei Lincei, Classe di Scienze morali, storiche e filosofiche* 6 (1952): 580–90.

Parrot, André. *Mission archéologique de Mari*. 4 parts. Paris: Geuthner, 1956–1986.

Parry, Donald W., and Elisha Qimron. *The Great Isaiah Scroll (1QIsa^a): A New Edition*. DJD 32. Leiden: Brill, 1999.

Pat-El, Na'ama. "The Morphosyntax of Nominal Antecedents in Semitic and an Innovation in Arabic." Pages 28–47 in *Proceedings of the Oslo-Austin Workshop in Semitic Linguistics*. Edited by Lutz Edzard and John Huehnergard. Wiesbaden: Harrassowitz, 2014.

Payne-Smith, Robert. *Thesaurus Syriacus*. 3 Vols. Oxford: Clarendon 1878–1901.

Pelletier, André. *Lettre d'Aristée à Philocrate: Introduction, texte critique, traduction et notes, index complet des mots grecs*. Sources Chrétiennes 89. Paris: Les Éditions du Cerf, 1962.

Perdu, Olivier. "Saites and Persians (664–332)." Pages 141–58 in *A Companion to Ancient Egypt*. Edited by Alan B. Lloyd. 2 vols. Malden, MA: Wiley-Blackwell, 2010.

Perignotti, Sergio. *I Greci nell'Egitto della XXVI dinastia*. PBE 4. Bologna: La Mandragora, 1999.

Petrie, W. M. Flinders. *Tanis: Nebesheh (Am) and Defenneh (Tahpanhes)*. Memoir of the Egypt Exploration Fund 4. London: Trübner & Co., 1888.

Petrie, W. M. Flinders, and Ernest McKay. *Heliopolis, Kafr Ammar and Shurafa*. London: School of Archaeology in Egypt, 1915.

Petrie, W. M. Flinders, and J. H. Walker. *The Palace of Apries (Memphis II)*. London: School of Archaeology in Egypt, 1909.

Peust, Carsten. *Egyptian Phonology: An Introduction to the Phonology of a Dead Language*. Monographien zur ägyptischen Sprache 2. Göttingen: Peust & Gutschmidt, 1999.

Pilgrim, Cornelius von. "Tempel des Yahu und 'Straße des Königs'—Ein Konflikt in der späten Perserzeit auf Elephantine." Pages 303–17 in *Egypt— Temple of the Whole World: Studies in Honour of Jan Assmann*. Edited by Sibylle Meyer. NBS 47. Leiden: Brill, 2003.

Pohlmann, Karl-Friedrich. *Studien zum Jeremiabuch: Ein Beitrag zur Frage nach der Entstehung des Jeremiabuches*. FRLANT 118. Göttingen: Vandenhoeck & Ruprecht, 1978.

Pope, Marvin H. *Song of Songs*. AB 7C. Yale: Yale University Press, 1995.

Porten, Bezalel. *Archives from Elephantine: The Life of an Ancient Jewish Military Colony*. Berkeley: University of California Press, 1968.

———. "Egyptian Names in Aramaic Texts." Pages 283–327 in *Acts of the Seventh International Conference of Demotic Studies, Copenhagen, 23–27 August 1999*. Edited by Kim Ryholt. Copenhagen: University of Copenhagen, 2002.

———. "The Identity of King Adon." *BA* 44 (1981): 36–52.

———. "Settlement of the Jews at Elephantine and the Arameans at Syene." Pages 451–70 in *Judah and the Judeans in the Neo-Babylonian Period*. Edited by Oded Lipschits and Joseph Blenkinsopp. Winona Lake, IN: Eisenbrauns, 2003.

Porten, Bezalel, and Ada Yardeni. *Textbook of Aramaic Documents from Egypt*. 4 vols. Jerusalem: Hebrew University Press, 1986–1999.

Press, Michael D. "Faience and Alabaster Vessels." Pages 321–430 in *Ashkelon 3: The Seventh Century B.C.* Edited by Lawrence E. Stager, Daniel M. Master, and J. David Schloen. Winona Lake, IN: Eisenbrauns, 2011.

Qimron, Elisha. *The Hebrew of the Dead Sea Scrolls*. HSS 29. Atlanta: Scholars Press, 1986.

Rabin, Chaim, Shemaryahu Talmon, and Emanuel Tov, eds. *The Book of Jeremiah*. The Hebrew University Bible. Jerusalem: Magnes Press, 1997.

Rast, Walter E. "Cakes for the Queen of Heaven." Pages 167–80 in *Scripture in History and Theology: Essays in Honor of J. Coert Rylaarsdam*. Edited by Arthur L. Merrill and Thomas W. Overholt. Pittsburgh: Pickwick Press, 1977.

Reich, Nathaniel. *Papyri juristischen Inhalts in hieratischer und demotischer Schrift aus dem British Museum*. Vienna: A. Hölder, 1914.

Reimer, David. "Jeremiah before the Exile?" Pages 207–24 in *In Search of Preexilic Israel: Proceedings of the Oxford Old Testament Seminar*. Edited by John Day (London: T&T Clark, 2004).

Reyes, Andres T. *Archaic Cyprus: A Study of the Textual and Archaeological Evidence*. Oxford: Clarendon, 1994.

Roberts, J. J. M. *First Isaiah*. Hermeneia. Minneapolis: Fortress Press, 2015.

———. "Isaiah's Egyptian and Nubian Oracles." Pages 201–9 in *Israel's Prophets and Israel's Past: Essays on the Relationship of Prophetic texts and Israelite History in Honor of John H. Hayes*. Edited by Bard E. Kelle and Megan Bishop Moore. LHBOTS 446. New York: T&T Clark, 2006.

Rohrmoser, Angela. *Götter, Tempel und Kult der Judäo-Aramäer von Elephantine: Archäologische und schriftliche Zeugnisse aus dem perserzeitlichen Ägypten.* AOAT 396. Münster: Ugarit-Verlag, 2014.

Rudolph, Wilhelm. *Jeremia.* Handbuch zum Alten Testament 12, 3rd ed. Tübingen: Mohr Siebeck, 1968.

Saleh, Abdel-Aziz. *Excavations at Heliopolis: Ancient Egyptian Ounû.* 2 vols. Cairo: Cairo University Faculty of Archaeology, 1981–1983.

Sass, Benjamin. "Arabs and Greeks in Late First Temple Jerusalem." *PEQ* 122 (1990): 59–61.

Sauneron, Serge, and Jean Yoyotte. "La campagne nubienne de Psammétique II et sa signification historique." *BIFAO* 50 (1952): 157–207.

———. "Sur la politique palestinienne des rois saïtes." *VT* 2 (1952): 131–36.

Schipper, Bernd U. "Die Lehre des Amenemope und Prov. 22,17–24,22: Eine Neubestimmung des literarischen Verhältnisses." *ZAW* 117 (2005): 53–72, 232–48.

———. "Egypt and Israel: The Ways of Cultural Contacts in the Late Bronze Age and Iron Age (20th–26th Dynasty)." *Journal of Ancient Egyptian Interconnections* 4 (2012): 30–47.

———. "Egypt and the Kingdom of Judah under Josiah and Jehoiakim." *TA* 37 (2010): 200–226.

———. "Egyptian Imperialism after the New Kingdom: The 26th Dynasty and the Southern Levant." Pages 268–90 in *Egypt, Canaan, and Israel: History, Imperialism and Ideology: Proceedings of a Conference at the University of Haifa, 3–7 May 2009.* Edited by Shay Bar, Dan'el Kahn, and Judith J. Shirley. Leiden: Brill, 2011.

———. *Israel und Ägypten in der Königszeit: Die kulturellen Kontakte von Salomo bis zum Fall Jerusalems.* OBO 170. Göttingen: Vandenhoeck & Ruprecht, 1999.

Schmid, Konrad. "The Book of Jeremiah." Pages 431–50 in *T&T Clark Handbook of the Old Testament: An Introduction to the Literature, Religion and History of the Old Testament.* Edited by Jan Christian Gertz, Angelika Berlejung, Konrad Schmid, and Markus Witte. Translated by Jennifer Adams-Maßmann. London: T&T Clark, 2012.

———. "How to Date the Book of Jeremiah: Combining and Modifying Linguistic- and Profile-based Approaches." *VT* 68 (2018): 444–62.

———. "Prognosis and Postgnosis in Biblical Prophecy." *SJOT* 31 (2018): 106–20.

Schmidt, Werner H. *Das Buch Jeremia: Kapitel 1–20.* ATD 20. Göttingen: Vandenhoeck & Ruprecht, 2008.

———. *Das Buch Jeremia: Kapitel 21–52.* ATD 21. Göttingen: Vandenhoeck & Ruprecht, 2013.

Schmitz, Philip C. "The Phoenician Contingent in the Campaign of Psammetichus II against Kush." *JEH* 3 (2010): 321–37.

Schneider, Thomas. "Jeremia in Memphis: Eine Neusituierung von Jeremia 46,13–24." Pages 79–97 in *Prophetie und Psalmen: Festschrift für Klaus Seybold zum 65. Geburtstag.* Edited by Beat Huwyler, Hans-Peter Mathys, and Beat Weber. AOAT 280. Münster: Ugarit-Verlag, 2001.

Schott, Siegfried. *Das schöne Fest vom Wüstentale: Festbräuche einer Totenstadt.* Abhandlungen der Geistes- und Sozialwissenschaftlichen Klasse 11. Wiesbaden: Franz Steiner, 1953.
Seidl, Theodor. *Der Becher in der Hand des Herrn: Studie zu den prophetischen "Taumelbecher"-Texten.* ATSAT 70. St. Ottilien: EOS, 2001.
Sharp, Carolyn J. *Prophecy and Ideology in Jeremiah: Struggles for Authority in the Deutero-Jeremianic Prose.* London: T&T Clark, 2003.
———. "'Take Another Scroll and Write': A Study of the LXX and MT of Jeremiah's Oracles against Egypt and Babylon." *VT* 47 (1997): 487–516.
Smelik, Klass A. D. "The Function of Jeremiah 50 and 51 in the Book of Jeremiah." Pages 87–98 in *Reading the Book of Jeremiah: A Search for Coherence.* Edited by Martin Kessler. Winona Lake, IN: Eisenbrauns, 2004.
Sokoloff, Michael. *A Dictionary of Jewish Babylonian Aramaic of the Talmudic and Geonic Periods.* Ramat Gan: Bar Ilan University Press, 2002.
Spalinger, Anthony J. "The Destruction of Mankind: A Transitional Literary Text." *SAK* 28 (2000): 257–82.
———. "Egypt and Babylon: A Survey (620 B.C.–550 B.C.)." *SAK* (1977): 221–44.
———. "A Religious Calendar Year in the Mut Temple at Karnak." *REg* 44 (1993): 161–84.
Spencer, Jeffrey. "Catalogue of Egyptian Pottery, Transport Amphorae and Ostraca from Tell Dafana in the British Museum." Pages 99–117 in *Tell Dafana Reconsidered: The Archaeology of an Egyptian Frontier Town.* Edited by François Leclère and Jeffrey Spencer. London: The British Museum, 2014.
———. "Egyptian Pottery and Imported Transport Amphorae from Tell Dafana: Types and Distribution." Pages 90–98 in *Tell Dafana Reconsidered: The Archaeology of an Egyptian Frontier Town.* Edited by François Leclère and Jeffrey Spencer. London: The British Museum, 2014.
Stager, Lawrence E. "Ashkelon and the Archaeology of Destruction: Kislev 604 BCE." *ErIsr* 25 (1996): 61*–74*.
Stager, Lawrence E. et al. "Stratigraphic Overview." Pages 215–326 in *Ashkelon 1: Introduction and Overview (1985–2006).* Edited by Lawrence E. Stager, J. David Schloen, and Daniel M. Master. Winona Lake, IN: Eisenbrauns, 2008.
Steindorff, Georg. "The Statuette of an Egyptian Commissioner in Syria." *JEA* (1939): 30–33.
Steiner, Margreet L. "Moab during the Iron II Period." Pages 770–81 in *The Oxford Handbook of the Archaeology of the Levant c. 8000–332 BCE.* Edited by Margreet L. Steiner and Ann E. Killebrew. Oxford: Oxford University Press, 2014.
Steiner, Richard C. "The Aramaic Text in Demotic Script." Pages 309–27 in *Canonical Compositions from the Biblical World*, vol. 1 of *The Context of Scripture.* Edited by William W. Hallo. Leiden: Brill, 1997.
———. *Disembodied Souls: The Nefesh in Israel and Kindred Spirits in the Ancient Near East, with an Appendix on the Katumuwa Inscription.* ANEM 11. Atlanta: SBL Press, 2015.

———. "The Two Sons of Neriah and the Two Editions of Jeremiah in the Light of Two Atbash Code-Words for Babylon." *VT* 46 (1996): 74–84.

Sternberg, Heike. "Sachmet." *LÄ* 5:323–33.

Stipp, Hermann-Josef. "The Concept of the Empty Land in Jeremiah 37–44." Pages 103–54 in *The Concept of Exile in Ancient Israel and Its Historical Contexts*. Edited by Ehud Ben Zvi and Christopher Levin. BZAW 404. Berlin: De Gruyter, 2010.

———. *Das masoretische und alexandrinische Sondergut des Jeremiabuches: Textgeschichtlicher Rang, Eigenarten, Triebkräfte*. OBO 136. Göttingen: Vandenhoeck & Ruprecht, 1994.

———. "Formulaic Language and the Formation of the Book of Jeremiah." Pages 145–65 in *Jeremiah's Scriptures: Production, Reception, Interaction, and Transformation*. Edited by Hindy Najman and Konrad Schmid. JSJSup 173. Leiden: Brill, 2017.

———. "Jeremiah 24: Deportees, Remainees, Returnees, and the Diaspora." Pages 163–79 in *Centres and Peripheries in the Early Second Temple Period*. Edited by Christoph Levin and Ehud Ben Zvi. Tübingen: Mohr Siebeck, 2016.

———. *Jeremia 25–52*. HAT I/12,2. Tübingen: Mohr Siebeck, 2019.

———. "Legenden der Jeremia-Exegese (II): Die Verschleppung Jeremias nach Ägypten." *VT* 64 (2014): 654–63.

———. *Studien zum Jeremiabuch: Text und Redaktion*. FAT 96. Tübingen: Mohr Siebeck, 2015.

Strawn, Brent A. *What Is Stronger than a Lion? Leonine Image and Metaphor in the Hebrew Bible and Ancient Near East*. OBO 212. Freiburg: Academic Press, 2005.

Streck, Michael P., and Nathan Wasserman. "More Light on Nanāya." *ZA* 102 (2012): 183–201.

Tallquist, Knut. *Akkadische Götterepitheta: Nach den Stämmen ihrer Anfangswörter alphabetisch geordnet*. SO 1. Helsinki: Societas Orientalis Fennica, 1938.

Talshir, Zipora. "The Three Deaths of Josiah and the Strata of Biblical Historiography (2 Kings XXIII 29–30; 2 Chronicles XXXV 20–5; 1 Esdras I 23–31)." *VT* 46 (1996): 213–36.

Theis, Christoffer. "Sollte Re sich schämen? Eine subliminale Bedeutung des Namens חפרע in Jeremia 44,30." *UF* 42 (2010): 677–91.

Thiel, Winfried. *Die deuteronomistische Redaktion von Jeremia 26–45: Mit einer Gesamtbeurteilung der deuteronomistischen Redaktion des Buches Jeremia*. WMANT 52. Neukirchen-Vluyn: Neukirchener Verlag, 1981.

Thissen, Heinz-Josef. *Die Lehre des Anchscheschonqi (P. BM 10508)*. PTA 32. Bonn: Habelt, 1984.

Toorn, Karel van der. "Anat-Yahu, Some Other Deities, and the Jews of Elephantine." *Numen* 39 (1992): 80–101.

———. *Becoming Diaspora Jews: Behind the Story of Elephantine*. ABRL. New Haven: Yale University Press, 2019.

———. *Papyrus Amherst 63*. AOAT 448. Münster: Ugarit-Verlag, 2018.

Tov, Emanuel. "The Literary History of the Book of Jeremiah in Light of Its Textual History." Pages 211–37 in *Empirical Models for Biblical Criticism*. Edited by Jeffrey Tigay. Philadelphia: University of Pennsylvania Press, 1985.
———. *Textual Criticism of the Hebrew Bible*. 3rd rev. ed. Minneapolis: Fortress Press, 2012.
Trimm, Charlie. *Fighting for the King and the Gods: A Survey of Warfare in the Ancient Near East*. RBS 88. Atlanta: SBL Press, 2017.
Tufnell, Olga. *Lachish III (Tell ed-Duweir): The Iron Age*. The Wellcome-Marston Archaeological Research Expedition to the Near East 3. London: Oxford University Press, 1953.
Tur-Sinai, Naftali Herz. *Die Heilige Schrift*. Frankfurt: J. Kaufmann, 1937.
Unger, Eckhard. *Babylon: Die heilige Stadt nach der Beschreibung der Babylonier*. 2nd ed. Berlin: de Gruyter, 1970.
Ussishkin, David. *The Village of Silwan: The Necropolis from the Period of the Judean Kingdom*. Jerusalem: Israel Exploration Society, 1993.
Villiers, Gerda de. "Where Did She Come from and Where Did She Go? (the *Queen of Heaven* in Jeremiah 7 and 44)." *OTE* 15 (2002): 620–27.
Vittmann, Günter. *Ägypten und die Fremden im ersten vorchristlichen Jahrtausend*. Mainz: Philipp von Zabern, 2003.
———. *Der demotische Papyrus Rylands 9*. 2 vols. ÄAT 38. Wiesbaden: Harrassowitz, 1998.
———. "Kursivhieratische und frühdemotische Miszellen." *Enchoria* 25 (1999): 111–27.
Vriezen, Karel J. H. "Cakes and Figurines: Related Women's Cultic Offerings in Ancient Israel?" Pages 251–63 in *On Reading Prophetic Texts: Gender-Specific and Related Studies in Memory of Fokkelien van Dijk-Hemmes*. Edited by Bob Becking and Meindert Dijkstra. Leiden: Brill, 1996.
Walsem, René van. "Month Names at Deir el-Medîna." Pages 215–44 in *Gleanings from Deir el-Medîna*. Edited by Robert Johannes Demarée and Jacobus Johannes Janssen. *Eg. Uitg.* 1. Leiden: NINO, 1982.
Waltke, Bruce K., and M. O'Connor. *An Introduction to Biblical Hebrew Syntax*. Winona Lake, IN: Eisenbrauns, 1990.
Ward, William A. "The Egyptian Objects." Pages 83–87 in *The Pottery of Tyre*. Edited by Patricia M. Bikai. Warminster: Aris and Phillips, 1978.
Weinberg, Joel. "Gedaliah, the Son of Ahikam in Mizpah: His Status and Role, Supporters and Opponents." *ZAW* 119 (2007): 356–68.
Wenning, Robert. "Griechische Söldner in Palästina." Pages 257–68 in *Naukratis: Die Beziehungen zu Ostgriechenland, Ägypten und Zypern in archaischer Zeit. Akten der Table Ronde in Mainz, 25.–27. November 1999*. Edited by Ursula Höckman and Detlev Kreikenbom. Möhnesee: Bibliopolis, 2001.
Westenholz, Joan Goodnick. "Trading the Symbols of the Goddess Nanaya." Pages 167–98 in *Religions and Trade: Religious Formation, Transformation and Cross-Cultural Exchange between East and West*. Edited by Peter Wick and Volker Rabens. Dynamics in the History of Religions 5. Leiden: Brill, 2014.
Wilson-Wright, Aren M. "Camping along the Ways of Horus: A Central Semitic Etymology for *pî ha-ḥîrot*." *ZAW* 129 (2017): 261–64.

Wimmer, Stefan. *Palästinisches Hieratisch*. ÄAT 75. Wiesbaden: Harrassowitz, 2008.
Wiseman, Donald John. *Chronicles of Chaldaean Kings (626–556 B.C.)*. London: Trustees of the British Museum, 1956.
Woolley, C. Leonard. *The Town Defenses*, vol. 2 of *Carchemish: Report on the Excavations at Djerabis on Behalf of the British Museum*. London: Trustees of the British Museum, 1921.
Wright, Benjamin G. *The Letter of Aristeas: 'Aristeas to Philocrates' or 'On the Translation of the Law of the Jews.'* CEJL 9. Berlin: De Gruyters, 2015.
Wuensch, Richard. *Inscriptiones Graecae III, Appendix: Defixionum Tabellae*. Berlin: Georg Reimer, 1897.
Yaron, Reuven. "Who Is Who in Elephantine?" *Iura* 15 (1964): 167–72.
Yassine, Khair. *Tell el Mazar I: Cemetery A*. Amman: University of Jordan Press, 1984.
Yeivin, Shmuel. "A Hieratic Ostracon from Tel Arad." *IEJ* 16 (1966): 153–59.
Younker, Randall W. "Ammon during the Iron II Period." Pages 757–69 in *The Oxford Handbook of the Archaeology of the Levant c. 8000–332 BCE*. Edited by Margreet L. Steiner and Ann E. Killebrew. Oxford: Oxford University Press, 2014.
Zadok, Ran. "On Anatolians, Greeks, and Egyptians in 'Chaldean' and Achaemenid Babylonia." *TA* 32 (2005): 76–106.
Zawadski, Stefan. "Nebuchadnezzar and Tyre in the Light of New Texts from the Ebabbar Archive in Sippar." *ErIsr* 27 (2003): 276*–81*.
Zecchi, Marco. "A Note on Two Egyptian Seal Impressions from Karkemish." *Orientalia* 83 (2014): 202–7.
Ziegler, Joseph. *Ieremias, Baruch, Threni, Epistula Ieremiae*. Septuaginta 15. Göttingen: Vandenhoeck & Ruprecht, 1957.

Ancient Sources Index

Hebrew Bible

Genesis
10   49
10:13–14   173
28:14 LXX   81
31:21   64
32:7   16
36:37   64

Exodus
4:27   16
12:38   76
26:24   152
27:11   82

Numbers
6:24–26   44

Deuteronomy
19:6   158

Joshua
8:18   121
8:26   121
9:11   16
13:3   70

1 Samuel
2:3   102
23:28   16
30:24   152

2 Samuel
1:20   70
12:31   118
19:16   16

1 Kings
11:5   145
11:19–20   101
11:33   145
15:13   145
18:16   16
20:27   16

2 Kings
8:8   16
8:9   16
9:18   16
12:18   132
16:10   16
23   16, 103
23:4   145
23:6   145
23:7   145
23:13   145
23:29   104
23:29–30   13, 15–16
23:30   17
23:30–34   17
23:31   18
23:33   16–17, 46, 104

2 Kings *(cont.)*
23:33–34   17
23:34   19, 104
23:35   46, 104
23:36   18
24:1   21, 24
24:6   25
24:7   25
24:8   25
24:10–16   25
24:12   60
24:14–16   60
25:7   60
25:11–12   50, 59

Isaiah
5:29   65
7:18   67–68
7:20   64
11:7   152
11:11   51
11:14   152
19:23–25   67–68
21:2   87
23:3   70
28:1–22   166
31:3   152
49:12   56
51:17   73, 160
51:20   157

Isaiah *(cont.)*
51:22   73, 160
52:4   67–68
52:8   152

Jeremiah
1:13   81
1:14   81
1:15   81, 122
2:14–19   6, 63–71, 79, 114, 171, 176
2:15   160
2:16   1, 4, 52, 99
2:18   64
2:19   64
3:12   81
3:18   81
4:6   81
4:7   65, 160
4:29   69
5:9   75
5:29   75
6:1   81
6:22   81
7:16–20   142, 145–46
7:18   134, 148
7:28   75
9:10   76
9:25   78
10:22   81
13:20   81
15:12   81
16:15   81
19–25   88
20:1–6   40
23:8   81
24:1–10   53
24:5   53
24:8   50, 52–53
25:1–14   8, 83, 160
25:9   81–82
25:9–12   159
25:11   82
25:12   82
25:15–16   88
25:15–26   84, 160
25:15–29   6, 63, 71–90, 114, 126, 153, 156, 171

Jeremiah *(cont.)*
25:27–29   83–84
25:30   160
26:15 LXX   3
26:20–23   41
26:20–24   45
26:22   28
27   90
27:1–11   83
29:2   60
29:25   102
31:8   81
31:35   105
32:21   64
32:26   81
36:22   43
37–43   127
37:1–10   28
37:1–43:7   132
37:5   1, 27
37:7   27
37:11   27
38   90
38:1   38, 40
38:2   90
38:4–5   45
38:14–24   45
40:8   42
41:17   116
42–43   127–29
42:1–43:7   1, 116, 127–29
42:12   55
42:15–17   132
42:16   126
42:17   128, 132–33
43   58
43:2–3   116
43:5–7   50, 53–56
43:5–12   60
43:6   116
43:7   4
43:8   4
43:8–13   2, 6, 115–29, 156, 172
43:9   4
43:9–10   118
43:9–12   54
43:9–13   52

Jeremiah *(cont.)*
44   138, 172
44:1   4, 50–52, 58–59, 99, 131–32, 138
44:1–28   51
44:2–14   138
44:7–8   130
44:12   132
44:13   146
44:14   147
44:15   51, 100–101, 133, 138
44:16   133
44:16–19   6–7, 130–31, 134, 138–39, 141
44:17–19   134
44:19   133, 148–49
44:20   134, 138
44:21–23   135, 138
44:24–25   6–7, 130–31, 135, 137–38, 141
44:25   135–36
44:26–27   138
44:26–29   137
44:27   131
44:28   138–39, 146
44:29   138
44:29–30   139
44:30   2, 104, 113, 137–39
46   176
46:2   93, 104
46:2–12   19–20, 171
46:2–26   6, 63, 90–114, 126, 156
46:3–12   6, 63, 93–97, 114
46:6   81
46:9   49, 173
46:10   81
46:12   152
46:13–26   2
46:14   4, 52
46:14–24   6, 63, 98–108, 114, 172
46:15   102
46:15–16   112
46:16   101–2

Ancient Sources Index

Jeremiah *(cont.)*
46:17 103–5
46:18 104
46:19 4
46:20 81, 105, 175
46:21 106–7
46:22 107
46:24 81, 107
46:25 1
46:25–26 63, 110–14, 172
46:26 98–108
47:1 24
47:2 81
48:13 146
49:12 73, 160
49:22 78
50–51 165
50:1–51:58 174
50:3 81, 165
50:9 81, 165
50:17 156, 160
50:41 81
50:41–42 165
51:7 73–74, 88, 156, 160
51:11 165
51:20–23 156, 159
51:23 161
51:24 159
51:27–28 165
51:28 161
51:38–39 7, 151–69
51:40 161
51:41–44 152
51:44 112
51:46 165
51:48 165
51:57 152, 157, 160–61
51:59–64 174–75
51:60 174
51:61–64 174

Ezekiel
17:15 27, 41
17:17 28

Ezekiel *(cont.)*
23:31–34 73, 160
27:10 173
29:1–17 28
29:15 110
29:16 113
29:17 32
29:17–20 172
29:18–19 28, 31–33
30:5 49, 77, 172–73
30:5 LXX 95
30:20–25 28
30:20–26 172
31:15 157
32:1–16 28–29

Hosea
7:11 67–68
9:3 67–68
9:6 67–68
11:5 67–68
11:11 67–68
12:2 67–68

Amos
2:6–8 71
3:12 65
8:13 157

Jonah
4:8 157

Micah
4:13 64
7:12 64

Nahum
2:12–13 65
2:14 101–2
3:8 112
3:9 95
3:14 118

Habakkuk
2:16 73, 160

Zechariah
9:10 64
10:10–11 67–68

Psalms
11:6 73, 160
51:4 102
72:8 64
75:9 73, 160

Ruth
1:8 137
3:3 64
3:4 64

Lamentations
2:8 152
4:17 29
4:21 73, 77
5:6 67

Esther
1:14 87

Daniel
10:4 64
11:17 132

Ezra
6:22 67

Nehemiah
13:3 76

1 Chronicles
13:5 70

2 Chronicles
35 103
35:20 104
35:20–27 15–16, 18
36 103
36:4 19, 104

Ancient Near Eastern Texts

Abu Simbel graffiti	36, 39	Elephantine papyri *(cont.)*	
Adon letter	22–23, 42	TAD A4 10:6	56
Amasis Stela	2, 4, 30–32	TAD B2 6	167
Anatolia inscription	106	TAD B2 7:15	167
Apis temple artifacts	101	TAD B2 8:5	145, 168
Apis Temple Stela	46	TAD B3 7:7–8	167
Apries Stela	99, 125	TAD B3 12:1–2	167
Arad ostraca	41, 173	TAD B3 12:30	167
1	48	TAD B5 5:13	167
18	48	TAD B7 2:7	145
34	41	TAD C3A 15:127–28	145
54	38	TAD D7 21:3	144–45, 168
88	18	TAD D9 10	167
Aroer Ostracon	38	Greek curse tablets	
Babylonian Chronicle	19, 21–26, 55, 93	DTA 105	175
		DTA 106	175
Bar-rākib Inscription		DTA 107	175
KAI 216	18	Heliopolis Stela	26
Berossus		Hermopolis papyri	142, 144
Babyloniaca	19–20, 36, 49, 70, 173	Hermopolis Papyrus 1	
		TAD A2 1:1	142
Buhen inscriptions	39	Istanbul Prism	25
Burnt Bullae Archive		Kadesh Barnea inscriptions	41
88	42	Kadesh Barnea Ostracon	
151	38	5	41
152	38	Karnak Calendar	163, 166
Cairo Calendar	166–67	Khirbet el-Qôm tomb inscriptions	42
Carian inscriptions	39	Lachish letters	41
Carthage inscriptions		3	28, 50, 52, 55, 59
KAI 81:1	111	Meṣad Ḥashavyahu Ostracon	47
city of David bullae	38	Mit Rahina inscriptions	39
city of David ostracon	174	Papyrus Amherst 63	142, 144
Coppa Nevigata inscription	36–37	II:11	143
cuneiform tablets		Pediese Statue inscription	42
BM 33041	2, 31–32, 95	Petition of Pediese	
Daphnae Stela	29	Papyrus Rylands 9	26
Edfu temple inscription	163	RIMA	
Egyptian papyri		2:195–96	160
BM 10113	31	SAA	
Elephantine papyri	144, 167	02 005 r iv 6'	143
TAD A2 1:1	143–44	Sais Stela	26
TAD A3 3	51	Saqqara Letter	
TAD A3 3:1–4	57	*KAI* 50	173
TAD A4 7:1	147	Silwan Monolith	43
TAD A4 7:13–14	56	Tell Dafana Stela	4
TAD A4 8:1	147	Wadi Brisa Inscription	33–34, 46–47, 89–90
TAD A4 8:12–13	56		

Ancient Sources Index

Dead Sea Scrolls

1Q
   Isaᵃ 49:12   56, 147

Ancient Jewish Writers

Josephus
  Against Apion
    1.135   20
    1.135–41   19
    1.136–37   36
    1.137   49, 70, 173
    1.138   19–20

Josephus *(cont.)*
  Jewish Antiquities
    10.85   25
    10.88–89   24–25
    10.110   27
    10.182   4, 29

Greco-Roman Literature

Diodorus Siculus   31, 103
  Bibliotheca historica
    1.46   124
    1.66   10
    1.67.1   59, 173
    1.68.1   27, 46
    1.68.2–5 30
Herodotus   31, 103
  Historiae
    1.76   58
    2.30   57, 119
    2.152   10, 173
    2.153   101
    2.154   59, 173
    2.157   11
    2.159   22, 24, 129

Herodotus *(cont.)*
  Historiae (cont.)
    2.161   27, 46
    2.161–63 30
    2.168   107
    2.169   30
    2.181   95
    2.182   46
    3.8   78–79
    6.6   58
Letter of Aristeas 14, 56–57
    1.13   13, 36, 50
Strabo
  Geographica
    17.1.27–28 124

Author Index

Abd el-Maksoud, Mohamed, 4, 29, 99, 126, 168
Adiego, Ignacio J., 39, 49
Aggoula, Basile, 118
Agut-Labordère, Damien, 10, 39, 106
Aharoni, Yohanan, 18, 37–38, 41, 48, 173
Aḥituv, Shmuel, 28, 38, 47
Albertz, Rainer, 56, 127
Allen, Leslie C., 71, 74, 80, 95, 97, 106, 116, 118, 121–22, 140, 144, 146, 148, 156
Allen, Spencer L., 111
Alt, Albrecht, 14
Asher-Greve, Julia M., 143
Asheri, David, 28, 31
Avigad, Nahman, 38, 42
Azzoni, Annalisa, 168

Baden, Joel S., 133
Bakir, Abd el-Mohsen, 167
Barclay, John M. G., 20, 36, 50, 174
Barkay, Gabriel, 43–44
Barstad, Hans M., 2–3
Basílico, Susana, 29, 168
Beaulieu, Paul-Alain, 143
Begg, Christopher, 24, 27, 29, 103
Bell, Lanny David, 10
Ben-Dor Evian, Shirly, 3, 42, 66, 166
Bernard, André, 36, 39
Bernick-Greenberg, Hannah, 37, 41, 168, 174
Beyer, Francis, 51, 124

Biberstein-Kazimirski, Albert de, 120
Biddle, Mark E., 65, 68–69
Bienkowski, Piotr, 85
Bietak, Manfred, 70
Blenkinsopp, Joseph, 87
Blöbaum, Anke Ilona, 4, 31–32
Boeser, Pieter A. A., 39
Braun, T. F. R. G. (Thomas), 48
Briant, Pierre, 57–58, 165
Brueggemann, Walter, 2
Bryan, Betsy M., 162–63, 167
Buhl, Marie-Louise, 39
Bunnens, Guy, 78
Butts, Aaron Michael, 105

Calabro, David, 38, 41–42
Carroll, Robert P., 51, 65, 67, 70, 74–75, 83, 97, 100–101, 104–5, 121, 146, 148, 152, 156–57
Carter, Charles E., 55
Cassimatis, Hélène, 49
Chassinat, Émile, 42, 46, 163
Chaveau, Michel, 11–12
Chevereau, Pierre-Marie, 37
Ciancaglini, Claudia A., 121
Cody, Aelred, 75
Cogan, Mordechai, 66
Cohen, Rudolph, 37, 41, 168
Corcella, Aldo, 28, 31
Cornhill, Carl H., 104
Couroyer, Bernard, 44
Cross, Frank Moore, 10
Cussini, Eleonora, 118

Author Index

Da Riva, Rocío, 34, 46, 90
Daressy, M. Georges, 39
Darnell, John Coleman, 162–63
Daviau, P. M. Michèle, 85
De Groot, Alon, 174
Delcor, Mathias, 144, 149
DePauw, Mark, 167
Dewrell, Heath D., 68
Diakonoff, Igor Mikhailovich, 73, 77, 79, 86
Drewnowska-Rymarz, Olga, 143
Driver, G. R., 74, 157

Edel, Elmar, 95
Eilers, Wilhelm, 49
Elgavish, David, 42
Ellenbogen, Maximilian, 43
Ellis, Teresa Ann, 136, 142
Emerton, John Adney, 122
Eph'al, Israel, 25–26, 30, 33–34

Fantalkin, Alexander, 12–13, 21–23, 36, 47–48, 173
Finkel, I., 22
Fischer, Georg, 8, 73, 75, 77, 79, 81, 83, 93, 103, 105
Fox, William Sherwood, 175
Freedy, Kenneth S., 26–28, 32
Freytag, Georg Wilhelm Friedrich, 120
Fuchs, Gisela, 73, 160

Gager, John G., 175
Galvin, Garret, 1, 3, 100, 104
Garfinkel, Yosef, 48
Gauthier, M. Henri, 26
Germond, Philippe, 158, 162
Gerschenson, Daniel E., 175
Gesundheit, Shimon, 8, 159
Gitin, Seymour, 10, 22
Glanz, Oliver, 65
Görg, Manfred, 40, 101
Gorris, Elynn, 78, 89
Goyon, Jean-Claude, 158
Grabbe, Lester L., 2, 32, 97, 99
Grayson, A. Kirk, 15, 19, 21, 26, 55, 89, 93, 109, 129
Greenberg, Gillian, 103, 148
Grelot, Pierre, 145

Haider, Peter W., 10, 39
Hayes, John H., 12, 127
Hays, Christopher B., 166
Hayward, Robert, 121
Henkelman, Wouter F. M., 80
Herrmann, Christian, 10–11, 165
Herrmann, Siegfried, 49
Hillers, Delbert R., 118
Hoenes, Sigrid-Eike, 153, 157–58, 163
Hoffmeier, James K., 70, 103–4
Holladay, John S., Jr., 58–59, 115
Holladay, William L., 52–53, 65–67, 70, 73–75, 77, 94, 97, 100–101, 104–5, 117, 120–21, 123–25, 129, 139, 146, 149, 152, 156–57
Holm, Tawny L., 143
Homès-Fredericq, Denyse, 85
Hornkohl, Aaron D., 112
Hornung, Erik, 153, 162
Huwyler, Beat, 2, 74–79, 81, 86–87, 94–97, 100–101, 104–5

Iacovou, Maria, 27, 48, 77–78
Ivantchik, Askold, 79

James, T. G. H., 27
Jansen, H. Ludin, 118, 124
Jansen-Winkeln, Karl, 4, 31–32, 168
Janzen, J. Gerald, 7, 43, 52, 64, 75, 79, 82, 94, 104–5, 111, 113, 117–18, 122, 125, 135–36, 160
Jasnow, Richard, 163
Jastrow, Marcus, 118
Jeffreys, David, 100
Jeon, Jaeyoung, 53, 145
Joisten-Pruschke, Anke, 144
Jones, Michael, 101
Jost, Renate, 142, 148
Junker, Hermann, 162

Kahn, Dan'el, 11, 14–17, 24–27, 33, 50, 71, 100, 113, 123
Kákosy, László, 164
Kamil, Jill, 100
Kammerzell, Frank, 39
Kaplan, Philip, 10, 39, 56, 59
Katzenstein, H. Jacob, 28
Keel, Othmar, 11
Kenyon, Kathleen M., 44

Kratz, Reinhard G., 123
Kurth, Dieter, 163–64

Labow, Dagmar, 20
Lambdin, Thomas O., 43
Lane, William Edward, 120
Langdon, Stephen, 32
Leahy, Anthony, 31, 140
Leclère, François, 67, 100–101, 106, 119–20, 124
Lemaire, André, 38, 41–42, 168
Leuchter, Mark, 129
Levin, Christoph, 65, 68–69
Levy, Jacob, 118–19
Liddell, Henry George, 59
Lipiński, Edward, 21–22, 98, 168
Lipschits, Oded, 22, 56
Livyatan Ben-Arie, Reut, 38
Liwak, Rüdiger, 66, 70
Lloyd, Alan B., 9, 28, 31
Lopes, Maria Helena Trinidade, 100, 106
Lundbom, Jack R., 70, 73, 82–83, 94, 96–97, 100, 102, 105–6, 116–18, 121, 123, 140, 148, 156
Lupo, Silvia, 29, 168
Lytle, Ephraim, 21

Machinist, Peter, 65, 160
MacKenzie, Duncan, 44
Maier, Aren M., 58, 115
Maier, Christl M., 53, 133, 145
Maier, Michael P., 71, 74–75, 77, 101, 105
Mankowski, Paul V., 144
Mariette, Auguste, 46
Masson, Olivier, 36, 39, 106
Mazar, Eilat, 38
McCarter, P. Kyle, 111
McCown, Chester Charlton, 44
McKane, William, 2, 52, 64, 66–67, 70–71, 73–75, 77, 79, 82, 86–87, 94, 100–101, 105, 130–31, 134, 136–37, 148, 152, 156–58, 160, 165
McKay, Ernest, 124
Miller, J. Maxwell, 12, 127
Muchiki, Yoshiyuki, 43, 51, 124
Mumford, Gregory D., 9, 44
Muscarella, Oscar White, 122

Na'aman, Nadav, 12, 16–17, 22, 47, 70
Naveh, Joseph, 48
Niditch, Susan, 53
Niemeier, Wolf-Dietrich, 20, 36
Nissinen, Martti, 123
Noonan, Benjamin J., 43, 120
Noth, Martin, 66

O'Connor, Michael Patrick, 76, 79
Olyan, Saul M., 142
Oren, Eliezer D., 11, 57–59, 70, 99, 120
Ossing, Jürgen, 43

Pallotino, Massimo, 37
Parrot, André, 148
Parry, Donald W., 56
Pat-El, Na'ama, 106
Payne-Smith, Robert, 118, 120, 158
Pelletier, André, 13–14, 36, 50, 57
Perdu, Olivier, 9–10
Perignotti, Sergio, 37, 39
Perlman, Paula, 174
Petrie, W. M. Flinders, 99–100, 106, 119–20, 124
Peust, Carsten, 104
Pilgrim, Cornelius von, 167
Pohlmann, Karl-Friedrich, 51, 55, 117, 123, 127–28, 134, 146
Pope, Marvin H., 148
Porten, Bezalel, 23, 28, 56, 143–44, 167
Press, Michael D., 11

Qimron, Elisha, 56, 136

Rast, Walter E., 148
Redford, Donald B., 26–28, 32
Reich, Nathaniel, 31
Reimer, David, 2, 32, 99, 165
Reyes, Andres T., 27
Roberts, J. J. M., 68, 87
Rochemonteix, Maxence, marquis de, 163
Rohrmoser, Angela, 57
Rudolph, Wilhelm, 101

Saleh, Abdel-Aziz, 124
Sass, Benjamin, 174

Author Index

Sauneron, Serge, 14
Schipper, Bernd U., 3–4, 10–12, 18, 26, 28, 40–43, 57, 66, 86, 166, 168
Schmid, Konrad, 8, 32, 53, 69, 99, 165
Schmidt, Werner H., 52–53, 64, 74–75, 79, 86–87, 93, 97, 100–101, 105, 116, 118, 121–22, 139–40, 148, 156
Schmitz, Philip C., 36, 48
Schneider, Thomas, 100–101, 103–7
Schott, Siegfried, 163
Scott, Robert, 59
Seidl, Theodor, 73, 160
Sharp, Carolyn J., 73, 93–96, 98, 100, 103, 105, 107, 111, 127
Smelik, Klass A. D., 2, 74, 156, 165
Smith, Mark, 163, 167
Sokoloff, Michael, 118
Spalinger, Anthony J., 26, 158, 162–63
Spencer, Jeffrey, 115–16
Stager, Lawrence E., 22, 95
Steindorff, Georg, 42
Steiner, Margreet L., 85
Steiner, Richard C., 28, 136, 143
Sternberg, Heike, 153, 157–58
Stipp, Hermann-Josef, 51, 53–56, 74, 77–79, 81–84, 86, 89, 93–95, 97–98, 100, 103–5, 107, 109–10, 116–17, 125, 127–30, 134, 138, 157
Strawn, Brent A., 65, 160
Streck, Michael P., 143

Tallquist, Knut, 142–43
Talshir, Zipora, 16
Tammuz, Oded, 24, 33, 100
Theis, Christoffer, 104
Thiel, Winfried, 130, 133, 135, 139–40, 146–47
Thissen, Heinz-Josef, 118
Toorn, Karel van der, 56–57, 143–46, 167

Tov, Emanuel, 7–8, 80, 102
Trimm, Charlie, 55
Tufnell, Olga, 44
Tur-Sinai, Naftali Herz, 122

Unger, Eckhard, 25
Ussishkin, David, 43

Valbelle, Dominique, 4, 29, 99, 126, 168
Vernus, Pascal, 41, 168
Villiers, Gerda de, 142
Vittmann, Günter, 23, 26, 39, 48–49
Vriezen, Karel J. H., 148

Walker, J. H., 99–100, 106
Walsem, René van, 167
Waltke, Bruce K., 76, 79
Ward, William A., 40
Wasserman, Nathan, 143
Weinberg, Joel, 127
Wenning, Robert, 12, 36
Westenholz, Joan Goodnick, 143
Wicks, Yasmina, 78, 89
Wilson-Wright, Aren M., 59, 173
Wimmer, Stefan, 41
Wiseman, Donald John, 15, 17, 19, 21–22, 24, 26, 55, 89, 93, 109, 129
Woolley, C. Leonard, 20–21, 174
Wright, Benjamin G., 14, 36, 50, 57
Wuensch, Richard, 175

Yaron, Reuven, 144
Yassine, Khair, 85
Yeivin, Shmuel, 41
Younker, Randall W., 85
Yoyotte, Jean, 14, 106

Zadok, Ran, 22, 49
Zawadski, Stefan, 33
Zecchi, Marco, 21, 98

Subject Index

Abu Salima, Tell, 10
  location, 11
Aegean groups. *See* cultural contacts: between Judahites and Aegean groups
Aegean mercenaries, 48–49
'Ajjul, Tell el-, 10
  location, 11
alcohol
  in Cairo Calendar, 167
  used for punishment, 73, 153, 160
  used to appease wrath, 157–58, 161–62
  See also beer
Amasis II, 30–32, 139–40
Ammon, 85
  location, 80
Amun (deity), 111–13
Amun-Re (deity), 124, 126
anti-Saite oracles, Jer 2:14–19
  dating, 66–69, 171
  interpretation, 70–71
  translation and content, 64–66
anti-Saite oracles, Jer 25:15–29
  dating, 85–87, 171
  interpretation, 87–90
  list of nations, 72–75, 79–80, 83–86, 89
  textual and redactional criticism, 73–85
  translation and content, 71–73
anti-Saite oracles, Jer 46:2–26
  dating, 90–91, 97, 109, 112–13, 171–72

anti-Saite oracles, Jer 46:2–26 *(cont.)*
  interpretation, 93–98, 110
  reconstruction of earliest form, 96–97, 108
  textual and redactional criticism, 98–108, 110–14
  translation and content, 90–93
Apis bull, 100–101, 106–9
Apries, 27–32, 103–4, 139–40
Arad, 18, 36–37, 173
  location, 11
Arameans. *See* cultural contacts: between Judahites and Arameans
Ashdod, 11
Ashkelon, 10, 21–23
  location, 11, 13, 15
Assurbanipal, 10
Assyrian campaigns, against Egypt, 9–10, 14
atbaš ciphers
  for Babylon, 82
  for Elam, 79–80, 85
auxiliaries. *See* mercenaries and auxiliaries

Baal-zephon, 173
Babylon
  atbaš cipher for, 82
  dating of references to, 171–72
  fall of, 164–66
  location, 15, 80
  rationale for punishment of, 158–59

Babylonian campaigns
  against Egypt, 23–26, 29–33
  locations in Egypt, 30, 33
  against northern territories, 14–19
  See also Egypto-Babylonian conflict
Babylonian diaspora, 55, 60
Babylonians. See cultural contacts: between Judahites and Babylonians
battle of Carchemish, 19–21, 55, 63, 86, 97, 173
beer
  in Destruction of Humanity myth, 153–55, 162
  in Karnak Calendar, 163
  used by Re, 172
  See also alcohol
Book of the Heavenly Cow, 166
Buz, location, 80

Cambyses Romance, 118
campaigns against Egypt. See Assyrian campaigns; Babylonian campaigns
Carchemish
  battle of, 19–21, 55, 63, 86, 97, 173
  location, 15
  objects recovered from, 20–21, 173
Carian mercenaries, 10, 39, 48–49, 58–59, 173
ciphers. See atbaš ciphers
city-states
  Philistine, 21–23
  Phoenician, 46, 78
conscription, Judahites subjected to, 6, 50, 63, 90
contacts, cultural. See cultural contacts
corvée labor, 47–49
Cretans, 49
cultural contacts
  among Judahite communities, 115–16, 129–30, 141, 146–47
  between Judahites and Aegean groups, 172–74
  between Judahites and Arameans, 144–45
  between Judahites and Babylonians, 128–29

cultural contacts *(cont.)*
  between Judahites and Egyptians, 167–68
  between Judahites and Greeks, 174–75
"cup of wine" motif, 73–76, 88
"cup of wrath" oracle. See anti-Saite oracles, Jer 25:15–29
curse tablets, 175
Cushites, 173
Cypriote mercenaries, 48–49
Cyprus, location, 80
Cyrenians, 173

Dafana, Tell, 4
Daphnae, 4, 50–52, 58–59, 173
  casemate structures at, 119–21
  community at, 115–16, 126–27
  location, 13, 30, 33
  royal palace at, 118
  urban geography of, 126
Dedan, location, 80
Departed Goddess myth, 162
Destruction of Humanity myth
  adaptation of, 172
  allusions to, 162–64
  content and translation, 153–55
  dating of adaptation, 164–66
  historical background of adaption, 165–69
  vs. oracles against Babylon, 155–58, 161–62
Deuteronomistic History, 145
diaspora communities, 147. See also Babylonian diaspora; Egyptian diaspora texts; Judahite diaspora in Egypt, evidence for
diaspora texts. See Egyptian diaspora texts
diplomatic service, 41–42

Edom, 85
  location, 80
Egypt
  campaigns against. See Assyrian campaigns; Babylonian campaigns
  civil war (570/568 BCE), 30–31
  control over Judah, 35–61

Egypt *(cont.)*
  dating of references to, 171–72
  influence on Levantine coast, 11
  location, 80
  strategic interests, 12
  victories at Migdol and Gaza, 24–25
  See also oracles against Egypt; Patros, land of
Egyptian diaspora texts, Jer 43:8–13
  context, 115–16
  dating, 125–26, 128–29, 172
  interpretation, 126–27
  reconstruction of earliest form, 124–25
  text and translation, 117
  textual and redactional criticism, 118–24
Egyptian diaspora texts, Jer 44:16–19, 24–25
  context, 130–31
  dating, 139–40, 172
  interpretation, 141–47
  text and translation, 141
  textual and redactional criticism, 131–39
Egyptian personal names, adopted by members of Judahite elite, 38–40
Egyptian scribal practices, training in, 40–41. *See also* hieratic scribal activity
Egyptians. *See* cultural contacts: between Judahites and Egyptians
Egypto-Babylonian conflict (610–601 BCE), key sites, 15
Egyptomania, 1
Ekron, 10, 21–23
  location, 15
Elam
  atbaš cipher for, 79–80, 85
  location, 80
Elephantine, 56–57, 167–68
elite and non-elite Judahites. *See* Judahite elite, members of; Judahite non-elite, members of
Euphrates River, 64
Exodus itinerary, 59, 173

Far'ah, Tell el-, 10, 11
festivals, religious, 166–67
forced labor. *See* corvée labor
fortresses, 36. *See also* Arad; Kadesh Barnea; Meṣad Ḥashavyahu; Migdol; Shiḥor

garrisons, Judahite, 37, 49, 56–57, 59
Gaza, 21
  location, 13, 15, 30
Ghaba, Tell el-, 29
  location, 33
Greek curse tablets, 175
Greek mercenaries, 36, 39
Greeks, fighting under Egyptian banner, 173. *See also* cultural contacts: between Judahites and Greeks

Hamath, location, 15
Haror, Tell, 10
Harran, 14–15
  location, 15
Hathor (deity), 153–57, 162–64. *See also* Destruction of Humanity myth
Heavenly Cow, Book of the, 166
Heliopolis, 123–24
  location, 13, 30
Herr, Tell el-, 57
Hesi, Tell el-, 10
  location, 11
hieratic scribal activity, in Judah, 37, 41, 168. *See also* Egyptian scribal practices
Hisn, Kom el-, 31

Ilahun, 59
Instructions of Chasheshonqy, 118
Io's Flight to Egypt myth, 175
Ionian mercenaries, 10, 13, 36, 58–59, 173

Jehoahaz (king), 17–18
Jehoiachin (king), 25
Jehoiakim (king), 17–18, 21, 24, 45
Jeremiah (book), textual history, 7–8. *See also* anti-Saite oracles; Egyptian diaspora texts

Jeremiah (prophet), flight to Egypt, 116
Jerusalem, location, 13
Josiah (king), 14–18, 66
Judah, kingdom of
  Egyptian control over, 12–14
  switching allegiance between Egypt and Babylon, 44–45
  See also Saite period in Judah
Judahite diaspora in Egypt, evidence for
  book of Jeremiah, 50–56
  Elephantine papyri, 56–57
  material culture, 58
  specific sites, 50–51
  summary, 58–60, 176
Judahite elite, members of
  access to Egyptian goods and services, 43–45
  Egyptian control over Judah and, 35, 60–61
  experience during Saite period, 37–45
  sympathizing with non-elite Judahites, 45
  working as messengers and diplomats, 41–42
Judahite garrisons, 37, 49, 56–57, 59
Judahite non-elite, members of
  Egyptian control over Judah and, 60–61
  experience during Saite period, 35, 37, 45–50
  punitive tribute imposed on, 45–46
  subjected to conscription, 49–50
  subjected to corvée labor, 47–49
Judahite soldiers, 49–50, 59
Judahites
  in Babylon, 147
  in Upper Egypt, 144–47, 172–73
  See also cultural contacts; Judahite elite, members of; Judahite non-elite, members of

Kadesh Barnea, 36–37
  location, 11
Kafr Ammar, 58
Ketef Hinnom, grave goods from burial caves at, 44

Kimuḫu, 15, 19
King's Highway, location, 11
Kittim, 48

leonine imagery, 153, 156, 160–61. See also Hathor; Sakhmet
Libyans, 173
"lions gone wild" motif, 152–53. See also alcohol; beer; leonine imagery
Lydians, 49, 173

Marea, 31
Mari, 148
material rewards, for members of Judahite elite, 43–45
Media, location, 80
Megiddo, location, 13, 15
Memphis, 4, 50–52, 59, 99–100
  location, 13, 15, 30
mercenaries and auxiliaries
  in Egypt's service, 36
  employed by Saite pharaos, 47–48
  See also Aegean mercenaries; Carian mercenaries; Cypriote mercenaries; Greek mercenaries; Ionian mercenaries; Phoenician mercenaries
Meṣad Ḥashavyahu, 13, 23, 36–37, 47, 173
  location, 11, 15
Migdol, 50–52, 57–59, 99–100, 173
  location, 15, 30, 33
military encounters. See Assyrian campaigns; Babylonian campaigns
Moab, 85
  location, 80
Momemphis, 30–31
Mut (deity), 162–63, 166
myth of the Departed Goddess, 162
myth of the Destruction of Humanity. See Destruction of Humanity myth

Nabonidus, 34, 165
Nabopolassar, 15
Nebuchadnezzar II
  ascension to throne, 93

Nebuchadnezzar II *(cont.)*
  Egyptian campaigns, 29–33
  Levantine campaigns, 19–23, 33–34
  siege of Jerusalem, 27–29
  See also Babylonian campaigns: against Egypt
Nebuzaradan, 50, 59
Necho. *See* Nekau II
Nekau I, 10
Nekau II
  alternative names for, 103–4
  imposing punitive tribute on Judah, 45–46
  northern campaigns, 14–19

onomastics, 38–40
oracles against Egypt, in Ezekiel, 172–73. *See also* anti-Saite oracles

Pashḥur (name), popularity in Saite Judah, 38–40
Pashḥur son of Immer, 40, 44–45
Pashḥur son of Malkiah, 40, 44–45, 60
Patros, land of, 50–51, 133
Pediese son of Opay, 42
personal names. *See* Egyptian personal names
Philistia, location, 80
Philistine city-states, 21–23
Phoenician city-states, 46, 78
Phoenician mercenaries, 36, 173
Pithom, 58–59
Psamtik I, 10–14, 50
Psamtik II, 26–27
punishment, metaphor for. *See* "lions gone wild" motif

Qedua, Tell el-, 57
Queen of Heaven (deity)
  cakes baked for, 148
  identity of, 142–44
  worship and cult of, 130, 134, 144–46, 148
"Queen of Heaven" source, 138–39, 141, 147. *See also* Egyptian diaspora texts, Jer 44:16–19, 24–25
Quramati, 15, 19

Re (deity), 153–55, 162. *See also* Destruction of Humanity myth
religious festivals, 166–67
rewards, material, for members of Judahite elite, 43–45
routes. *See* trade routes
Ruqeish, Tell er-, 10
  location, 11

Sais, location, 13, 30
Saite period in Judah
  as background to book of Jeremiah, 1
  664–620 BCE, 9–12
  620–610 BCE, 12–14
  610–605 BCE, 14–19
  605–601 BCE, 19–23
  601–598 BCE, 23–26
  598–586 BCE, 26–29
  586–568 BCE, 29–34
  See also anti-Saite oracles
Sakhmet (deity), 153, 155–58, 162–64, 167. *See also* Destruction of Humanity myth
Saqqara, 58
scribal practices. *See* Egyptian scribal practices; hieratic scribal activity
Seraʿ, Tell, 10
  location, 11
Sheshach, 82
Shiḥor, 33, 70
Sidon, location, 13, 15, 80
soldiers, Judahite, 49–50, 59
Syenians, land of the, 56

Table of Nations, 49, 173
Taharqo, 10
Tahpanhes. *See* Daphnae
Tanutamani, 10
Tebilla, Tell, 58–59
Tema, location, 80
Thebes, location, 30
Tiglath-pileser III, 18
Timnah, 22
trade routes, linking Egypt with the Arabian Peninsula and the Aegean, 12–13
Tyre
  location, 13, 15, 80
  vase fragment from, 40

Subject Index

Upper Egypt. *See* Patros, land of

Via Maris, location, 33

Ways of Horus, 58–59

Yavneh-Yam, 13

Zedekiah (king), 45

Στρατόπεδα, 58–59, 173

חפרע (Jer 44:30), 104, 109
כון "cakes," 144
להעצבה (Jer 44:19 MT), 148–49
מלבן (Jer 43:9), 118–20
מלט (Jer 43:9), 120–21
נהר, 64
ערב "mixed people," 76–77
פוט "Cyrene," 95
פי החירת, 59, 173
שפרור (Jer 43:10), 121–22

www.ingramcontent.com/pod-product-compliance
Lightning Source LLC
Chambersburg PA
CBHW021706230426
43668CB00008B/742